Changing America's Tax System:
A Guide to the Debate

About the Authors

The American Institute of Certified Public Accountants (AICPA) is the premier national professional organization for CPAs, with more than 328,000 members in public practice, industry, government, and education.

Martin A. Sullivan has a B.A. in Economics from Harvard University and a Ph.D. in Economics from Northwestern. He has served as an economist for the Office of Tax Analysis of the U.S. Treasury Department and for the staff of the Joint Committee on Taxation of the U.S. Congress. He is now an economic consultant and an Adjunct Scholar at the American Enterprise Institute.

Changing America's Tax System: A Guide to the Debate

By
The American Institute of Certified Public Accountants
and
Martin A. Sullivan, Ph.D.

John Wiley & Sons, Inc.
New York • Chichester • Brisbane • Toronto • Singapore

Notice to Readers

This book is based on the AICPA tax practice study *Flat Taxes and Consumption Taxes: A Guide to the Debate*. Such studies are designed as educational and reference material for the members of the Tax Division and others interested in the subject. They do not establish policy positions, standards, or preferred practices.

Acknowledgments

The AICPA Tax Division acknowledges the efforts of the Consumption Taxation Task Force and the Tax Policy and Planning Committee in the preparation of this publication.

Consumption Taxation Task Force
Byrle M. Abbin, Chair
Gary Cesnik
Edmund Outslay
Lawrence Zommick
Phillip Tatarowicz

Tax Policy and Planning Committee (1994–95)
Steven J. Leifer, Chair
Victor E. Barton
Lorence L. Bravenec
Stanley E. Heyman
Brent H. Hill
James A. Moore
James E. Power
William L. Raby
Judyth A. Swingen
Donna M. Zerbo

Tax Executive Committee (1994–95)
Deborah Walker, Chair
Harvey L. Coustan
Ira Bergman
Rick G. Betts
Robert L. Holman
William F. Huber
David A. Lifson
Lorin D. Luchs
C. Ellen MacNeil
Michael E. Mares
Dan L. Mendelson
Eileen J. O'Connor
Robert M. Pielech
Jay Starkman
Samuel P. Starr

AICPA Tax Division Staff
Gerald W. Padwe, Vice President-Tax
Edward S. Karl, Director
Carol B. Ferguson, Technical Manager

Special acknowledgment is given to Byrle Abbin, Chair, Consumption Taxation Task Force, for his effort and dedication to this project.

Contents

Foreword

Muriel F. Siebert

There is a great debate consuming the minds of the American people—and that debate is none other than the one about taxes—current taxes, revolutionary taxes, flat taxes, consumption taxes. The discussion has been raging in Congress, in the media, and in America's public and private arenas. But what exactly do all these proposals, projections, potential results, and scenarios mean to the American citizen—and who, in fact, *is* this American citizen? The variables are extensive and complex: a diversity of proposals, with many nuances and varieties—and a diversity of American citizens, with all of our nuances and varieties. Clearly, there is a maze of possible combinations to be explored.

We don't yet know which of the proposals—or which parts of them—may come into existence; nor do we know exactly how that would affect us. But what we do know is that if fundamental tax reform does become a reality, then this reality will have definite real-life effects and consequences—some good, some bad—on all of us.

In current discussions and publications regarding the proposed reforms, proponents and opponents often project results and ramifications that reflect their own opinions. It is not easy to separate fact from opinion, nor to determine the effect of any or all of the conceivable scenarios on our own lives. How, then, can we come to a reasonable conclusion about the effect of these changes on our future? And consequently, how can we make a difference in the political process which will determine that future?

What we need is an objective presentation of the various tax proposals in discussion, a presentation which states the facts as they are, impartially, and without subjective input, thus allowing us to digest the information and make up our own minds about the consequences.

Changing America's Tax System: A Guide to the Debate does precisely that. Authored by the American Institute of Certified Public Accountants and Martin A. Sullivan, Ph.D., this book combines the professional tax and accounting expertise of the AICPA with the economic insight of Dr. Sullivan. It is a clear and direct discussion of the various proposals being debated. Not only does this book review and analyze the competing proposals, it also provides Americans with examples of the possible consequences of each proposal on our finances, and how these consequences would vary depending on our economic situations.

This information is essential—to professionals, advisors, business owners, and the individual taxpayer—to gain an unbiased understanding of the issues, to derive a personal assessment of the issues, and to determine exactly how our personal situation, as well as the situation of other Americans, will be changed. The last item is most important: because once that determination is made, Americans will, as we always have, participate in the political system by making our voices heard... at the ballot box.

Preface

The United States faces concerns about productivity and competitiveness, lack of consistency with major trading partners and a bewilderment with the complexity of the current tax system. All of these factors contribute to an increasing interest in numerous proposals to drastically change the federal tax system.

For years, there have been concerns that foreign competitors may get the upper hand in the international marketplace because their value-added taxes are rebated to their exporters at the border whereas U.S. exporters get no relief from income tax. Economists and tax policy experts have expressed concerns about various aspects of the U.S. tax system—its inefficiency, its complexity, its excessive intrusion into activities of businesses and individuals. As a result, a number of consumption tax alternatives have been floated—such as the Business Transfer Tax (by Senator Roth in 1985) and a cash flow consumption tax (by the Treasury Department in 1977)-—but none gained political support substantial enough to consider enactment a serious possibility.

All of that has now changed. Recently a number of proposals with serious political backing have been presented. Tax reform is an issue in the 1996 Presidential campaign—and in the Congress.

The purpose of this book is to educate and enlighten CPAs, executives, financial and tax officers of corporate and business America, members of Congress and their staffs, and other interested parties with regard to how these different approaches operate. There are analyses of "big picture" aspects as well as ease of compliance and administrability of the various proposals. In addition, we explore the overall effect of each proposal on industrial sectors, both those which emphasize export and those which rely more on importation, and on the general economic effect on savings. Chapters 2 through 5 provide a description of the four major types of consumption taxes. Chapters 6 through 8 review the major economic policy issues surrounding the proposed new tax. Chapter 9 introduces, in general terms, the issues that are likely to be of concern to businesses under any new consumption taxes. Chapters 10 and 11 describe the two leading proposals now under consideration by policy makers in Washington. Chapters 12 and 13 provide detailed estimates of the impact of these proposals on business and individual tax liability. Chapter 14 through 17 examine the special problems that consumption taxation poses for housing, financial institutions, state and local governments, charitable organizations, and financial statements.

We examine and identify the "winners" and "losers" in business sectors under various proposals, as well as compare the impact on individuals at various income levels. The analysis of business is not limited to just corporations; it includes personal-service businesses that will become subject for the first time to a second level of tax even though they operate in unincorporated form.

Of the major proposals, only the Nunn-Domenici USA Tax has a fairly comprehensive plan expressed in statutory text together with detailed explanatory narration. Commentators already have noted "missing pieces" and challenged certain inconsistencies in it. For the others, proposed statutory language is either very terse or nonexistent, the framework of this analysis being based on sponsors' press releases, media interviews, and other published statements. As a result, significant gaps exist and an ultimate analysis is not yet possible. Thus the intent of this publication is to add to common understanding of the proposals' operation, their advantages, and the deficiencies through an objective analysis. Moreover, the analysis was made on the basis on sponsors' statements that their proposals are intended to replace the present Federal income tax system.

There is no intention at this time to express preference for any of the alternatives or to make an AICPA policy statement as to whether any of these alternatives would be preferable to our current income tax system.

Executive Summary

Americans want fundamental tax reform and, more than ever before, the U.S. Congress is inclined to grant their wish. Many proposals now before Congress would entirely eliminate the $700 billion in annual revenue from the individual and corporate income tax.

To replace this lost revenue, a variety of new tax systems have been proposed. These new taxes come in all shapes and sizes, but they have one common characteristic. They are taxes on *consumption* and, as such, have the potential to improve America's international competitiveness—primarily by increasing private savings. In addition, because entirely new systems are being devised, there is tremendous opportunity for simplification.

No matter how simple the new system, however, the transition to it involves enormously complex political, economic, and technical issues. It is true that most industrialized countries have adopted consumption taxes. But these taxes, for the most part, just served as replacements for poorly functioning excise taxes. No major industrialized country has ever repealed its personal or corporate income taxes.

And nothing in U.S. history can serve as precedent. Such sweeping legislation as the Reagan tax cuts of 1981 and the income tax reforms of 1986 pale in significance compared with the proposals now being floated.

Clearly, as this nation moves closer to fundamental tax reform, it moves deeper into uncharted territory. This publication is designed to help all interested Americans begin to understand how consumption taxes will affect their economy, their businesses, and their own personal finances.

The Major Alternatives

There are many types of consumption taxes, but four are critical to understanding the current debate:

1. *Retail Sales Tax*—levied by most states
2. *Value-Added Tax*—levied by every major industrialized country, except the United States and Australia

3. *Flat Tax*—proposed by House Majority Leader Dick Armey
4. *Unlimited Savings Allowance (USA) Tax*—proposed by Senator Sam Nunn and Senator Pete Domenici

Retail Sales Tax

A federal retail sales tax at first appears to be an attractive alternative to current law because individuals would no longer file tax returns. A heavy burden would, however, be placed on retailers and tax administrators, particularly if legislators provide exemptions for favored businesses and products.

Even without special exceptions, there are substantial problems, including evasion by small retailers that do not report sales and by business owners that purchase items for personal use. These problems would be particularly severe if a federal retail sales tax had rates in excess of 20 percent—which would be required to replace revenues loss from the repeal of the income tax.

A retail sales tax also faces the large political hurdles of being a highly visible regressive tax and of encroaching on the states' sales taxes. While a federal retail sales tax might be administratively feasible as a supplement to the current income tax, it does not seem likely that such a tax would be a good replacement for the current system.

Value-Added Tax

Value added is the difference between the value of a business's sales and its purchases from other businesses. A value-added tax (VAT) is a tax on businesses that is collected as goods move through different stages of production. Most value-added taxes in place throughout the world are *credit-invoice* value-added taxes. These taxes require firms to keep a detailed record of each sale and purchase. In the United States, there is currently little interest in a credit-invoice value-added tax.

One alternative to the credit-invoice method of implementing a VAT is known as the *subtraction* method. The subtraction method is widely considered to be simpler than the credit-invoice method because such taxes may be implemented without new recordkeeping requirements and may instead use existing books and records. The two leading alternatives now being considered for the United States, the Flat Tax and the USA Tax, are variants of a subtraction-method VAT.

The Flat Tax

The Flat Tax has two components: a business tax and the individual tax. The 17 percent *business* tax is imposed on all businesses, not just corporations. The business tax base is business receipts reduced by (1) wages and (2) purchases from other businesses. Under this new tax, the entire cost of new plant and equipment may be deducted in the first year, and overseas subsidiaries of U.S. businesses are exempt from tax. These advantages to businesses are offset by the loss of deductions for interest payments and for fringe benefits.

Under the *individual* Flat Tax, a 17 percent tax is imposed on wages and pension distributions. Interest, dividends, and capital gains are exempt. Large personal and dependency exemptions would remove tens of millions of taxpayers from the tax rolls. Under proposed Armey legislation, a family of four would be subject to tax only for wages in excess of $31,000.

Except as described above, the Flat Tax has no other deductions or credits. Most notably, there are no deductions for home mortgage interest, charitable contributions, state income taxes, and property taxes.

It is important to recognize that with a 17 percent rate, a Flat Tax that replaces current income taxes would likely be a large revenue loser. Some economists have argued that a Flat Tax rate of at least 23 percent would be required to avoid revenue losses.

The USA Tax

Like the Flat Tax, the USA Tax has a business tax and an individual tax. The USA *business* tax has a rate of 11 percent and is imposed on *all* businesses. Also, like the Flat Tax, the entire cost of new plant and equipment may be deducted in the first year and overseas subsidiaries of U.S. businesses are exempt from tax. There are three key differences between the USA and Flat business taxes. Under the USA business tax, (1) the deduction for wages is replaced with a payroll tax credit in the amount of 7.65 percent of most wages, (2) exports are exempt from tax, and (3) an 11 percent duty is imposed on imports.

The USA *individual* tax has graduated rates up to 40 percent. For a family of four the 40 percent rate could apply to incomes as low as $41,000. Unlike the Flat Tax, there are deductions for charitable contributions and for mortgage interest. There is also a new deduction for income that is saved. In addition, individuals get a 7.65 percent tax credit on most wages.

The Big Policy Issues

Impact on Saving and Economic Growth

There is no dispute that saving is critical to economic growth. Saving provides the funding for capital formation that gives U.S. workers the tools to be more productive and competitive. There is also no dispute that the U.S. rate of saving is low whether compared with other countries or with past U.S. rates. The replacement of the current U.S. tax system with a consumption tax would increase the after-tax return to capital and would eliminate the bias inherent in the current tax against capital formation.

There is dispute, however, as to how much such tax changes can increase private saving. Even under the most optimistic set of assumptions, it is unlikely that a switch from an income tax to a consumption tax can increase the rate of U.S. saving to a level comparable to that of its major trading partners.

Nevertheless, even modest changes in the rate of saving can have a positive impact on economic growth over the long term. Thus, although there is a high degree of uncertainty, legislation that would replace the current income tax with a consumption tax has significant upside potential from the standpoint of promoting U.S. competitiveness.

Balance of Trade

Most consumption tax systems exempt exports and impose tax on imports. (The Flat Tax is an important exception to this rule.) Although these "border tax adjustments" are often perceived as beneficial to a nation's balance of trade, there is broad agreement among economists that these adjustments are unlikely to have any significant impact on trade. Consumption taxes can, however, improve the trade balance to the extent they are able to increase domestic saving.

Redistribution

Consumption taxes are widely perceived as placing an undue burden on the poor and elderly. Any politically realistic consumption tax will likely be supplemented by features to alleviate the burden on low-income households.

Most of the states with retail sales taxes and other countries with value-added taxes exempt necessities such as food, clothing, and health care from the tax base, with the intent of reducing the tax burden on the poor. The exemption of necessities, however, is not particularly effective in mitigating the regressivity of consumption taxes.

Some form of tax credit or standard deduction will likely play an important role in alleviating the regressivity of any new consumption tax enacted into law.

Simplification

The proposed new consumption taxes have tremendous potential for simplification. This is particularly true because under the proposals some of the more complex areas of current law—namely the tax treatment of pensions, of international income, and of corporate acquisitions—become obsolete.

New tax systems, however, may entail new compliance requirements that add complexity. For example, the USA Tax must have complicated rules to determine "new" saving that is eligible for deductions, and under the Flat Tax, businesses must be able to differentiate between business expenses (which are deductible) and fringe benefits (which are not deductible).

In addition, much of the complexity of the current tax code is attributable to dozens of targeted tax benefits. Proposed tax laws often appear simpler than existing taxes because existing law has been subject to successive legislative amendments that add complexity. It is highly probable that any new consumption tax would accrete substantial complexity (at the outset as well as in subsequent legislation) as Congress found it necessary to provide tax relief for a variety of taxpayers. Finally, there will be costs to government and taxpayers of transitioning from one system to another.

Transition

Without special transition rules, the replacement of an income tax with a consumption tax would haphazardly subject many individuals and businesses to large tax penalties. In the absence of transition relief, saving and investment done prior to enactment would have to pay significantly higher tax than under prior law. (In contrast, new saving and investment would be tax-free.) These retroactive tax increases would unfairly burden not only elderly individuals who are no longer saving, but also mature businesses that are no longer investing. In addition, without adequate transition relief, tax reform proposals could have a large and significant impact on the financial statements of many firms.

Transition relief is expensive both in terms of lost revenue and in terms of administrative and compliance costs.

Inflation

A consumption tax is unlikely to have any sustained impact on the rate of inflation. There may, however, be a onetime impact on the overall price level if the Federal Reserve responds to the tax change with an expansion of the money supply.

The Impacts on Different Types of Businesses

Corporate Businesses

In general, under both the Flat Tax and the USA Tax, labor-intensive firms—such as those in the construction, service, and transportation sectors—bear a greater share of the total corporate tax burden than they would under the current corporate income tax. Capital-intensive industries—like those in the communications and public utilities sectors—are likely to pay less taxes.

The exclusion of exports from gross receipts provides large tax benefits to those firms that export. For a typical manufacturing exporter, the exclusion of exports available under the USA Tax can easily cut a business's tax liability in half. In contrast, the Flat Tax does not exempt exports.

Noncorporate Businesses

Both the USA proposal and the Flat Tax impose new tax burdens on noncorporate businesses. For a typical small business, the USA Tax imposes a greater business tax burden than the Flat Tax.

One way of assessing the impact on noncorporate business is to compare the combined individual and business tax burdens before and after the imposition of a new consumption tax. The combined burden for the owners of unincorporated businesses under the Flat Tax appears to be less than under current law. In contrast, the total tax burden under the USA Tax appears to be greater than current law, particularly for high-income owners of unincorporated businesses whose compensation would be subject to a combined business and individual tax rate in excess of 50 percent.

The Impact on Individuals

Relative to current law, the USA Tax generally provides tax relief to low- and high-income taxpayers, and a modest tax increase to middle-income taxpayers.

The Flat Tax appears to provide tax relief to nearly all individual taxpayers (except those low-income households receiving refunds under current law from the earned income tax credit). This tax relief is particularly large for high-income taxpayers because interest, dividends, and capital gains are exempt from tax.

Some Important Details

Housing

In most other countries with consumption taxes, new housing is subject to tax and existing housing is exempt. Under both the USA Tax and the Flat Tax, new residential construction is subject to business tax.

Under the individual Flat Tax, the elimination of the deduction for mortgage interest (along with the loss of deductions for property taxes) adversely affects homeowners. Under the individual USA Tax, which allows deductions for mortgage interest, housing continues to enjoy its tax-favored status.

Banking, Insurance, and Other Financial Service Providers

Because it is difficult to identify and value services provided by financial institutions, no other country with a consumption tax has been able to properly tax financial services. Any rules that can be devised to include financial services in a new U.S. consumption tax are likely to be extremely complex and—if not carefully formulated—could significantly impact the competitive balance among various financial service providers.

State and Local Governments

State and local governments could suffer financial hardship if their taxes are not deductible against federal tax—as is the case under both the Flat Tax and the USA Tax. In addition, a new federal consumption tax might encroach on the states' ability to levy their own sales taxes. Repeal of the federal income tax will surely complicate administration of state income taxes.

Charitable Organizations

Under some tax reform proposals, donors to charitable organizations lose the benefit of deductions for contributions, and the charitable organizations themselves are liable for tax on their activities.

Estate and Gift Taxation

It is an open question whether estate and gift taxes would be retained or repealed under any tax reform proposal enacted into law. The Armey Flat Tax repeals estate and gift taxes. The USA Tax retains the current estate and gift tax structure. (The USA Tax also amends current law by replacing tax-free stepup basis with carryover basis at death.)

Conclusion

As much as lawmakers may want to satisfy the public's desire to eliminate the income tax and replace it with a simple tax, there are no easy solutions.

There are unresolved questions concerning the impact of these tax changes on saving, productivity, trade, interest rates, and inflation. There is debate about the compliance and administrative costs of these new proposals and about the amount of revenue they raise. There are a host of unresolved technical issues—transition relief, banking and financial products, and housing.

Finally, there are numerous political issues that have not even yet begun to sort themselves out because so few taxpayers understand the impacts of the proposed new taxes. There is, of course, the age-old issue of rich versus poor. And, if that were not enough, politicians must still address concerns surrounding redistribution of the tax burden from the young to the elderly, from low-tax to high-tax states, from capital-intensive to labor-intensive industries, from exporters to importers, and from corporate to noncorporate businesses.

The Current Debate

Summary

- Members of Congress have expressed considerable interest in repealing both the individual and corporate income taxes and replacing them with consumption taxes. No major industrialized nation has ever repealed its income tax.

- There are four basic types of consumption taxes:
  1. Retail sales tax
  2. Credit-invoice value-added tax
  3. Subtraction-method value-added tax
  4. Individual consumption tax

- Compared to income taxes, consumption taxes provide greater incentives for saving. However, because saving is concentrated in high-income households, consumption taxes can impose a relatively larger burden on low-income households.

- Although the term *flat tax* generally means a tax with a single rate, in the current debate the term refers to a single-rate value-added tax collected in part from business and in part from individuals. In its proposed form, the Flat Tax would eliminate most tax preferences and thereby significantly reduce complexity.

- Although there are substantial opportunities for simplification, it is reasonable to expect that any consumption tax enacted into law will include numerous exceptions and special rules. Thus, it is unlikely any new consumption tax will be as simple as proponents insist.

Farewell, Income Tax?

The United States is in the early stages of a major debate about a fundamental restructuring of its tax system. The magnitude of change contemplated is unprecedented. Under numerous proposals currently being considered, *all* federal income taxes—accounting for over $700 billion in revenue in 1995[1]—would be repealed. Some proposals also provide substantial relief from payroll taxes, which provide nearly $500 billion in revenue.[2] These would be replaced by taxes on consumption. It is true that most industrialized countries have adopted consumption taxes. However, these taxes largely served as replacements for unwieldy systems of excise taxes.[3] No major industrialized country has ever repealed its individual and corporation income taxes.

Many current proposals for restructuring the U.S. tax system are as sweeping in concept as they are in terms of revenue. There are at least four components to the current debate:

1. *Competitiveness.* The proposed changes intend to increase competitiveness of domestic businesses through increased capital formation and, in the case of some proposals, by improving the terms of international trade.

2. *Tax simplification.* The proposed changes aim to eliminate the complexity of the current system.

3. *Tax reform.* The proposed changes would repeal most of the special tax breaks in current law.

4. *Redistribution.* The proposed changes may significantly redistribute the burden of taxation. In particular, compared to income taxes, consumption taxes are considered to be more burdensome on low-income households.

If enacted, the proposed changes would make the *Tax Reform Act of 1986* look like an insignificant piece of legislation. Given the enormous difficulties in achieving passage of that legislation, longtime observers of the process are skeptical. Yet few are willing to write off the possibility of enactment of a consumption tax. Leaders of both major political parties have voiced support and introduced legislation to radically restructure the U.S. tax system. Fundamental reform is now on the front burner, and the 1996 election is likely to turn up the heat.

This is a remarkable turn of events given the poor prospects for passage of any type of consumption tax until just recently. Consumption taxes have gone from political obscurity to political celebrity in less than a decade. The nadir of consumption tax popularity was immediately after the 1980 defeat of former Ways and Means Committee Chairman Al Ullman, who had proposed

---

[1]The Office of Management and Budget estimates that in fiscal year 1995 the federal government will receive $151 billion in revenue from the corporation income tax, $589 billion from the individual income taxes, and $484 billion in revenue from payroll taxes. See U.S. Executive Office of the President (1995), p. 23. One of the two leading consumption tax proposals would include substantial tax credits for most payroll taxes—collecting total receipts from new taxes to more than $1 trillion annually.

[2]The Armey Flat Tax proposal explicitly repeals the estate and gift tax.

[3]"The defects of the cascade turnover taxes (see Chapter 2 discussion) were the driving force behind EEC adoption of the value-added tax. The multiple taxation of products, relatively favorable taxation of concentrated enterprises, and uncertain border tax adjustments combined to create an intolerable situation in the common market." Carlson (1980), p. 71.

a value-added tax (VAT) prior to his failed reelection bid. There were some proposals for consumption taxes during the 1980s, but none with any prospect of passage or even serious consideration by Congress. Significant congressional interest in consumption taxation did not rekindle until the early 1990s as Congress became increasingly concerned about U.S. competitiveness. This interest gained further momentum with the 1994 elections, and the concept of consumption taxation now enjoys the support of many congressional leaders.

Prior to recent developments, the proponents of consumption taxation were mainly business leaders concerned about capital formation and economists concerned about deficit reduction. Their efforts went largely unnoticed except by a few tax professionals. Now there is interest among the general public, and press coverage of the issue is widespread. There is particular interest in the proposed Flat Tax. Proponents claim that the Flat Tax is so simple that businesses and individuals would have only to file postcard-sized returns. This has great appeal to a general public frustrated with the complexity of the current system.

One key development in the politics of consumption taxation is the appearance of an emerging consensus among certain political groups about the use of consumption tax revenues. In the past, consumption taxes have been proposed to increase government spending, to reduce the deficit, and even to *reduce* income and payroll taxes. In all of these cases, the current tax system would largely remain intact. Furthermore, proposed consumption taxes usually had rates in the single digits. Most of the current support for consumption taxation is conditioned upon use of revenues for *elimination* of individual and corporate taxation.[4] Replacement consumption taxes could easily have tax rates that exceed 20 percent.[5]

Recognizing the difference between an *add-on* consumption tax and a *replacement* consumption tax is critical for ascertaining the economics as well as the administration of the tax. Only a replacement consumption tax has the potential to increase private saving.[6] Only a replacement consumption tax has the potential to significantly reduce complexity. Unlike many other recent studies of consumption taxation, this publication will focus attention almost exclusively on consumption taxation as a *replacement* for the current system of income taxation.[7]

---

[4]The rapidity of this change in sentiment about the nature of consumption taxes for the United States is evident by comparing the tone of the current debate to that of several relatively recent studies. The working assumption of these studies is that any new consumption tax would be an add-on, rather than a substitute, to the current system. See, for example, U.S. Department of Treasury (1984), McLure (1987), Congressional Budget Office (1992), U.S. General Accounting Office (1993), and Metcalf (1995).

[5]According to the Congressional Budget Office (1995), it is estimated that the individual income tax and corporate income tax would generate $772 billion and $172 billion in fiscal year 2000. Also according to the CBO, a broad-based 5 percent VAT would generate $198 billion in fiscal year 2000. Therefore, a broad-based VAT would have to have a rate of approximately 25 percent to replace revenue lost from repeal of the individual and corporate income taxes.

[6]The impact of consumption taxes on saving is discussed in Chapter 6.

[7]In order to emphasize the context of this study, the term *replacement consumption tax* will be frequently used.

Consumption Tax Alternatives

Comparison to Income Taxes

The most important difference between an income tax and a consumption tax is that a consumption tax eliminates the tax burden on income from saving and investment.[8] Under a consumption tax, income that is saved is not taxed. By providing greater rewards for saving than an income tax, replacement consumption taxes have the potential to increase private saving. Most economists believe that the lack of saving lies at the core of the current shortcomings in the U.S. economy. If saving does indeed respond positively to increases in its after-tax return, a replacement consumption tax could increase private saving. Increasing saving would likely increase domestic capital formation, which in turn boosts the productivity of U.S. workers, boosts real wages, and increases the rate of economic growth.

Saving, however, is something that the wealthy do more of than the poor. Therefore, consumption taxes generally place greater overall burden on low-income households than do income taxes. This potential to shift tax burden to low-income households is the major objection to consumption tax, but savings differences are not the only reason. A proportional, rather than progressive, rate structure is another major factor.

Finally, consumption taxes often are implemented in such a manner that imports are subject to tax while exports are exempt. Most economists believe that such "border tax adjustments" do not have any significant impact on international trade. Nevertheless, consumption taxes may still have impacts on international trade, particularly if they can be used to improve economic performance by increasing saving.[9]

Different Types of Consumption Taxes

There are four major types of consumption taxes that are relevant to the current debate:

1. Retail sales tax

2. Credit-invoice value-added tax

3. Subtraction-method value-added tax

4. Individual consumption tax[10]

A retail sales tax is a tax on final sales by retail businesses to consumers. Imposed by almost all of the states, it is a tax familiar to most Americans. A value-added tax is a tax on the value added of all businesses—the difference

---

[8]A VAT can be based on income or consumption (Break 1985), but income-based VATs are not currently under consideration.

[9]The impact of consumption taxes on trade is the subject of discussion in Chapter 7.

[10]The terms *personal consumption tax* and *expenditures tax* are also often used to describe an individual consumption tax.

between a business's *gross receipts* from the provision of goods and services less *costs* of goods and services acquired from other businesses. There are two major types of value-added taxes under consideration: the credit-invoice method VAT, used by most U.S. trading partners, and the subtraction-method VAT, currently the favorite of consumption tax advocates in the United States. (The Flat Tax is a type of subtraction-method VAT.)[11] An individual consumption tax is a tax on each individual's annual consumption, measured as the difference between that individual's annual income and annual saving.

Comparison of Types of Consumption Taxes

The major argument in favor of adopting any consumption tax is its potentially favorable impact on U.S. competitiveness. The major political obstacle is its potential to be regressive. These potential impacts are largely similar for each of the four major types of consumption taxes. Choosing among them is *not* a matter of economics.

There are, however, several important differences among these types of consumption taxes. Each imposes different compliance costs—not only in terms of total cost but also in terms of the distribution of these costs across taxpayer groups. Each of these taxes also imposes different administrative costs on government. Some of these taxes would certainly face vigorous opposition from the states while others probably would not. Some of these taxes would be vigorously opposed by our trading partners while others likely would not. The taxes also differ in how they are perceived by the public—some appear as highly visible separately stated regressive taxes on consumers, while others are considered "hidden" taxes imposed on business.

One other difference is their degree of *flexibility*. Different types of consumption taxes vary in their ability to provide preferential treatment to certain types of products and to certain classes of taxpayers. As a matter of pure tax policy the broadest consumption tax base would be preferable. Special exceptions reduce the economic efficiency of a consumption tax.[12] However, no matter how desirable from an economic or administrative perspective, political reality makes it unlikely. Providing special exceptions to broad-based consumption taxes is common to all consumption taxes currently in existence. And this has been the American way of implementing tax policy. As a matter of political acceptability, a tax that is better able to accommodate special-interest provisions ultimately may prove to be more salable.[13]

---

[11]The terms *personal consumption tax* and *expenditures tax* are also often used to describe an individual consumption tax.

[12]Narrowing the tax base reduces efficiency for at least three reasons. First, exceptions cause consumers to distort their consumption and businesses to alter their production in order to avoid tax. Second, rates of tax will have to be increased to make up for revenue losses due to special exceptions. Third, a broad consumption tax base in general would be easier to administer.

[13]On the other hand, some would prefer to make special-interest provisions as difficult as possible to accommodate. This is a somewhat naive strategy given that Congress's desire to compromise and accommodate has rarely been constrained by concerns about complexity or economic efficiency. And taxpayers are less inclined to complain about complexity when that complexity is accompanied by tax relief.

Simplification and Broadening the Tax Base

As noted, it is not just the *adoption* of a consumption tax, but the *replacement* of income taxes with a consumption tax that lies at the center of the current debate on restructuring the U.S. tax system. As enormous as this change would be, the scope of the current debate is even broader. The public interest in the Flat Tax is indicative of the breadth of issues now on the table.

Like other consumption tax proposals, the Flat Tax would eliminate the individual and corporate income taxes and would replace them with a broad-based consumption tax collected from both business and individuals. But the Flat Tax proposal does not stop there. It entirely revamps the rate structure. It replaces the progressive rates of current law with a *single tax rate* for both business and for individuals. It is a radical base-broadening *tax reform*, eliminating numerous credits, exclusions, and deductions, intended to achieve a wide variety of social and political objectives. It is also, in its current form, massive *simplification*. Any one of these changes on its own would be an extraordinary legislative event.[14, 15]

There is little doubt that current tax law is often incomprehensible to most taxpayers and that there is tremendous interest in simplification. What is less clear is how well consumption tax alternatives in practice would fare in terms of administration and compliance costs. Although a move from consumption taxation generally has the *potential* to reduce complexity, it is an open question whether significant simplification can actually be realized.[16]

Complexity Inherent in the Income Tax

Some of the complexity under current law is unique to the income tax, and a switch to a pure consumption tax would eliminate this complexity.[17] This is particularly true for business taxation and the taxation of income from saving and investment. For example, depreciation and amortization provisions ordinarily would be replaced with expensing.[18] There would, therefore, no longer be disputes over capitalizing business development costs because all business costs are immediately deductible. Costs of inventories would be deducted at the time costs were incurred. The corporate income tax and the

---

[14]Much confusion arises because the more general, generic term *flat tax* is used interchangeably with the specific Flat Tax proposals offered by Majority Leader Armey and others. Although it has a nice ring to it, the term *flat tax* is not the best description of the proposals now bearing that label. First of all, the term is not precisely applied because there would actually be a second, zero tax bracket for low-income households who are allowed large personal exemptions. At the same time, the term is overly broad. In the context of taxation, *flat* is an adjective that is usually applied to rates. Flat tax rates can be applied to a consumption or an income base. Furthermore, a tax system with a single rate of tax need not be simpler than a system with multiple rates.

[15]Thus, there are lowercase *f* flat taxes and capital *F* Flat Taxes. In this publication, most references will be to the specific proposals like those offered by Majority Leader Armey and will therefore be capitalized.

[16]See AICPA (1990).

[17]This is the basic theme of U.S. Treasury (1977) and Bradford (1980).

[18]Although every major proposal has included a provision for expensing, it is not inherent to a value-added tax.

corporate alternative minimum tax would be eliminated. The notoriously complex rules surrounding corporate distributions, liquidations, and reorganizations would become almost entirely obsolete. And because most consumption taxes are "territorial"—that is, tax is imposed only on activity within its borders—all foreign-source income would be exempt from U.S. tax, eliminating the need for foreign-tax-credit and for antideferral rules.[19] Furthermore, under a consumption tax, most income generated by personal saving would effectively be exempt from tax.[20] As a result, a replacement consumption tax eliminates the need for the complicated rules associated with preferential treatment of types of saving by individuals. For example, complex rules concerning pensions, IRAs, tax-exempt bonds, annuities, and life insurance could be eliminated because all saving would receive tax-favored treatment.[21]

Complexity Shared by Income and Consumption Taxes

Nevertheless, many of the issues that are the source of complexity under the current income tax will remain equally complex after the switch to consumption taxation. For example, the age-old problem of distinguishing between business expenses and expenditures on personal consumption does not disappear. Business meals, home office deductions, and education expenses are just three areas of contention that will remain in any realignment from income to consumption taxation.

Complexity Due to Special Provisions

Then there is the complexity in current law that is due to special tax breaks and limitations on those breaks. It is often remarked that consumption taxes appear simpler than income taxes because they are idealized proposals untainted by legislative compromise. If history is any guide, consumption tax proposals will accrete complexity as they move through the legislative process and as subsequent Congresses amend the initial legislation.[22] A great deal of complexity under current law is a byproduct of a political system that endeavors to compromise rather than simplify—and of a system that wishes to use the tax code to achieve a wide variety of social and economic objectives that have little to do with raising revenue.

Many consumption tax proposals, especially those of the Flat Tax variety, include significant base broadening. For example, under the Armey proposal, the exclusion of employer-provided benefits from the tax base and the deductibility of home mortgage interest, charitable contributions, and state and local taxes would be eliminated. Clearly, if in addition to transforming

---

[19]Complex source rules, however, would still be an issue as they are under the income tax system.

[20]As shall be explained in greater detail in Chapter 6, the exclusion of saving from the consumption tax base is the equivalent of exempting investment income from tax.

[21]As shall be explained in greater detail below, consumption taxes provide relief for investment in capital either by exempting investment income from tax or by allowing deductions for investment. Senators Nunn and Domemici have proposed allowing deductions for new investment in municipal bonds *and* retaining the exemption of interest from these bonds.

[22]The higher the rates the more likely this is to occur.

the income tax base into a consumption tax base, Congress also undertook broadening the tax base, much additional simplification would result.[23] It is not so clear, however, why such tax reform will be more successful under the umbrella of consumption taxation than under that of income taxation. Special-interest groups would surely mount massive lobbying efforts to proposed curtailment of benefits. While the political dynamics surrounding tax law changes may be different now than in the past, it seems unlikely the system is immune from the influence of special interests.

Complexity Unique to Consumption Taxes

In the move from an income to a consumption tax, simplicity is not entirely a one-way street. It is likely that some new complexities will arise as the imposition of consumption taxes introduces new administrative and compliance issues not present under the income tax. For example, a credit-invoice value-added tax would, in many respects, increase recordkeeping requirements of businesses. Under the credit-invoice method, business would be required to retain records of all invoices in order to earn tax credits. At a minimum, under a subtraction-method VAT, taxpayers would be required to revise their accounting procedures so as to include a set of books using alternative capital recovery methods and to differentiate nondeductible internal costs from deductible external costs. An individual consumption tax would require taxpayers and tax authorities to maintain previously unrequired records of changes in their total savings balances and net indebtedness.

Complexity During Transition

Finally, there is the enormous issue of transition. In order to avoid penalizing taxpayers caught between the old income tax and any new consumption tax, complex transition rules are likely to be included into any new tax plan. For businesses, there are likely to be special rules for cost recovery of previously acquired (but not fully depreciated) capital. For individuals, some sort of provision for basis recovery on existing assets would likely be included (so that only gains, and not the entire proceeds on the sale of existing capital, would be subject to tax). The general public, tax departments of businesses, and tax advisors would have to be educated as to the working of this new system. IRS employees would play a major role in this process, but they also would have to be educated. Finally, the IRS would have to devise new tax forms, instructions, audit procedures, and regulations.

This discussion of complexity has presupposed that any new consumption tax would be used to replace the income tax. If instead the consumption tax was an add-on tax—that is, consumption tax revenues were used for deficit reduction, or government-provided universal health coverage, or were only sufficient to reduce (and not eliminate) income taxes—the imposition of this second tax system on top of the current one would result in a vast increase in the complexity of the U.S. tax system.

---

[23]However, this is not always the case. For example, the Armey Flat Tax would eliminate the deductibility of employer-provided health insurance. Separating the costs of this insurance from other costs could impose a new compliance burden on taxpayers.

2

A Retail Sales Tax

Summary

- A national retail sales tax might be an attractive revenue source because it is relatively uncomplicated and familiar to most Americans.

- Some issues that are particularly problematic for a federal retail sales tax are:
  1. Potential for widespread evasion by small retailers
  2. Potential for widespread evasion by business purchasers of items for personal use
  3. Objections by states to sharing a major revenue source

- The validity of these issues increases with the tax rate. While it does not seem likely that a retail sales tax is a good replacement for income taxes, it might be viable as a supplement to existing taxes.

In weighing consumption tax options, it seems reasonable to start with the familiar. Most Americans encounter retail sales taxes every day. They are levied by forty-five states and by numerous local jurisdictions. Americans seem to have accepted the current level of state sales taxes, and they do not seem to bear them the same hostility that they have for income taxes.[1] Although retail sales taxes are highly visible in that they are stated separately from purchase prices, most consumers face no compliance burden. Retail businesses file sales tax returns and make sales tax payments to state and local authorities.[2]

From the perspective of promoting economic efficiency, a retail sales tax should tax all consumption equally in order not to distort consumer choices and to keep tax rates low. Only *final* sales by businesses—that is, sales by

---

[1]See Break (1985).

[2]The objections raised by the states to a federal retail sales tax are discussed in Chapter 16.

businesses *to consumers*—should be subject to tax. The taxation of sales by businesses *to other businesses* would result in overtaxation of consumption because final sales would bear not only retail sales tax but also the costs of whatever taxes are paid on inputs used to produce, market, or distribute consumer products. This overtaxation of certain products was a major factor contributing to the adoption of European and Canadian value-added taxes.

Because retail sales taxes are imposed on final sales within the taxing jurisdiction, they are, in effect, exempt from tax goods produced within and sold outside that jurisdiction. Similarly, the tax would also be imposed on goods produced outside and consumed inside the jurisdiction. Thus, a federal retail sales tax would exempt exports and impose a tax on imports. This feature, shared with many consumption taxes, is particularly attractive to domestic businesses competing in the international market place.[3]

In practice, states' retail sales taxes fall short of the ideal of taxing all consumption once. On one hand, states exempt many final goods and services. This results in undertaxation of some sectors. On the other hand, states tax many intermediate goods. This results in overtaxation of some sectors.

Statutory Exemptions

In practice, state governments exempt many types of goods and services from sales tax for a variety of reasons. Some products are exempted from taxation because they are considered necessities—such as food, clothing, and housing. Because necessities are generally a larger fraction of income for the poor than for the wealthy, such exemption confers tax relief that is proportionately greater for low-income households. (However, as shall be discussed in detail later, granting such relief still leaves the poor bearing a greater relative burden than the wealthy.) Some services, like many types of financial services, are exempt because of the great difficulty in identifying the amount of such services.[4] Some services, like those provided by governments (federal, state, and local) and charitable organizations, are exempt because it is difficult to place a dollar amount on these services—and because it is good politics. Finally, other goods are exempt because they are considered "merit" goods that deserve public support—such as goods and services provided by charities. It is also quite common for state sales taxes to provide broad exemptions for services.

For whatever reason exemptions are granted, they generally increase the administrative burdens of tax authorities and compliance burdens of taxpayers, in addition to impeding economic efficiency. It is widely acknowledged that the administrative costs of a retail sales tax would be greatly

---

[3]Thus, retail sales taxes operate under the *destination* principle. When exports are included in the tax base and imports are not taxed, a consumption tax is said to operate under the origin principle. It would be possible to structure a retail sales tax to operate under the origin principle, but in practice, retail sales taxes and value-added taxes utilize the destination, not the source, principle. As shall be discussed in greater detail in Chapter 7, economists believe consumption taxes should operate under the destination principle so that consumer choice between imports and domestically produced goods is not distorted.

[4]See Chapter 14 for a discussion of the difficulties in taxing financial services.

reduced if no exemptions or special rates were allowed.[5] Much time and debate are involved in identifying exactly which items should be exempt from taxation. Once these items have been identified, retail businesses must distinguish taxable from nontaxable sales. In the case of service providers, invoices to customers must allocate total charges between taxable products and nontaxable provision of services.

This complexity is not inherent in the structure of the tax, but the result of political considerations. It seems highly unrealistic to assume that enactment of a consumption tax would not include tax relief for certain sectors. Political considerations will likely complicate the administration of any retail sales tax.[6] All states with sales taxes—as well as almost every country with a retail sales tax or value-added tax—provide numerous instances of preferential treatment.[7] There is nothing in the history of the federal tax legislative process to suggest that a federal consumption tax would be untainted by special-interest provisions. Proponents of various consumption tax plans with no special tax relief will face a heavy burden in explaining how their proposals can maintain their conceptual simplicity in the face of myriad political forces.

Taxation of Intermediate Goods

Even if all exemptions for politically favored consumer products were somehow eliminated, the problem of separating taxable sales to consumers from nontaxable sales to businesses would remain. State governments generally use two methods—both imperfect—to help separate retail sales from nonretail sales. The first is to grant "exemption certificates" to business taxpayers. The second is to impose sales tax on some types of products irrespective of whether sales are retail. Because of the bluntness of each of these tools, retail sales taxes overtax final sales of some products at the same time they undertax sales of other products.

When intermediate goods are taxed, the purchase price of the final product embodies not only the tax on the final sale, but also the tax on inputs to the final product. For example, if a state sales tax of 5 percent is imposed on delivery services, and sales taxes also apply to the purchase of gasoline and computers that account for 20 percent of the cost of delivery services, the total state-imposed sales tax on delivery services is 6 percent. This phenomenon is referred to as tax *cascading*. Cascading can result in higher tax burdens on products that happen to use more intermediate goods subject to tax. It can also result in unfair competition within industries if firms provide their own intermediate inputs and their competitors must purchase intermediate inputs in taxable transactions.

---

[5]See, for example, U.S. Treasury (1984), Cnossen (1989), and U.S. General Accounting Office (1980).

[6]This is the working hypothesis made by McLure (1987), former Deputy Assistant Secretary of the Treasury for Tax Policy, in his study of value-added taxation. The major reason for his preference for a credit-invoice value-added tax over a subtraction method value-added tax is its superior ability to accommodate the political compromises that he considers inevitable.

[7]One notable exception is the broad-based single-rate VAT introduced by New Zealand in 1986. The only significant exemption is rental payments for residential housing.

In its 1984 study of consumption taxes, the Treasury Department reported that approximately 20 percent of state sales taxes were collected on intermediate goods. This occurs because certain products, such as gasoline, tools, and office equipment, are sometimes taxed regardless of whether they are used by business or by consumers. It is not clear whether cascading is an inherent problem of retail sales taxes. As discussed below, a thorough sorting out of business and nonbusiness uses of certain types of property would at a minimum add complexity and might greatly increase compliance costs. State governments probably consider these nonretail taxes a relatively painless method of raising revenue.

As shall be explained further below, cascading is not an issue under a value-added tax (under either the credit-invoice or subtraction methods). For example, under the credit-invoice method, any taxes paid on intermediate sales between businesses would be rebated to the business making sales to consumers. In the example used in the prior paragraph, the taxes on gasoline (collected by the gas station) and on computers (collected by the computer dealer) would be rebated to the company providing delivery services to consumers.

It is also important to note that the tax treatment of exports may be problematic when a sales tax system includes some nonretail sales. Unlike a value-added tax, a retail sales tax has no mechanism for rebating nonretail taxes on exports. Even if rebates are attempted, they usually can only be implemented with a rough estimate as to the amounts of tax paid at intermediate levels. If the burden of proof is placed on exporters to demonstrate the payment of tax at intermediate levels, it is likely—given the difficulty exporters would have identifying and documenting taxes paid by all their suppliers (and at prior levels of production)—that the rebates will be less than the taxes paid, resulting in a penalty on exports. On the other hand, governments predisposed to promoting their exports may be generous in their estimates of intermediate-level taxes in order to use rebates as a mechanism for export subsidies.

Cascading has been recognized as a problem by foreign governments that have relied heavily on sales taxes. Moreover, the problem of cascading taxes—particularly in the context of international trade—is often cited as a major reason for adoption of value-added taxes throughout the world.

Evasion by Business Purchasers

Under a retail sales tax, it may be possible for businesses—especially closely held businesses—to claim exemption on items that are used wholly for personal consumption. States usually grant businesses "exemption certificates" that allow them to make purchases without payments of sales tax. There is, however, little to prevent bearers of exemption certificates from purchasing items and then using them for personal consumption.

Beyond checking the validity of the exemption certificate, it is not reasonable to expect sellers to aid much in enforcement. In order to determine whether items should be taxable or tax-exempt, sellers would have to know the use to which items would be put. Sellers of goods and services cannot read buyers' minds to know the intended use of purchased items. And of course, sellers do not want to lose a sale, much less the goodwill of a customer, by challenging purchasers.

Unless special precautions are taken, a retail sales tax places little burden of proof on business purchasers. The only way business purchases can be audited is if the seller retains records of business purchases, including the business purchasers' taxpayer identification numbers. Even with such exhaustive recordkeeping, the threat of audit in most cases would not be significant, given the small amount of tax any single taxpayer could evade with purchases from a single retailer. These issues exist now and mechanisms are in place to control tax avoidance, but attempts at evasion may increase at higher levels of tax.

There may be a greater threat of audit in the case of big-ticket items— such as automobiles and personal computers—that have extensive business and personal use. In these cases, it does not seem inappropriate to require recordkeeping of taxpayer identification numbers by sellers. Still, detection of evasion would require audit of both sellers and purchasers. One alternative possibility is for the government to consider rebates instead of exemptions for large-ticket items (such as rebates payable upon receipt of valid invoices to tax authorities). Rebates, however, would entail substantial administrative costs.

The problem of distinguishing business items from personal-use items is hardly restricted to retail sales taxation or to consumption taxes in general. Under the income tax, small business owners have similar incentives to claim business deductions for items of personal use. (In fact, the higher the marginal rate of income tax, the greater the incentive for evasion.) Under the income tax, however, the business must stand ready to defend all deductions claimed, and even a valid business deduction improperly documented can be disallowed. Under a credit-invoice VAT, businesses may attempt to claim credits on items purchased for personal use. Similarly, under a personal consumption tax or a subtraction method VAT, closely held businesses may attempt to deduct as business expenses the cost of items purchased for personal consumption. Thus, evasion through overstatement of business expenses is a significant concern under almost any tax.

There is, however, a critical difference in detecting evasion under a retail sales tax versus other consumption taxes: Evasion by retail sales tax purchasers would require cross-checking and the auditing of multiple taxpayers. Under other types of taxation, evasion can be detected by audit of the purchaser. Given the difficulty even in the best of circumstances of distinguishing business- from personal-use items, the problem of evasion by business purchasers under a retail sales tax cannot be easily dismissed.

Evasion at the Retail Level

Perhaps the most cited difficulty with enactment of a federal retail sales tax is the likely lack of compliance by retailers. The tax rate of a federal sales tax that would be necessary to replace income tax revenue would almost certainly exceed 20 percent.[8] Most tax administrators believe that 10 or 12

---

[8]See Chapter 9, Table 9.8.

percent of gross receipts is the maximum burden that may be reasonably placed on a sector comprised of numerous small businesses.[9] Because tax is imposed only at the point of final sale, weaknesses in collections at that point would be particularly harmful to compliance compared to an income tax or value-added tax in which the compliance burden is spread more evenly across businesses and, in the case of the individual income tax, on tens of millions of individual taxpayers. Compliance by small business is already an issue under both the federal income tax and state sales taxes. In fact, under a VAT, many commentators argue that significant exemptions—or subsidies—should be granted to small businesses because of the high compliance costs. This would not be possible under a retail sales tax without a substantial loss of revenue.

Real-world experience seems to support the comments of tax administrators that there is an upper limit on the rate of retail sales tax. While most countries with value-added taxes have standard rates of 15 or 20 percent, retail sales tax rates are usually less than 5 percent. Among developed economies other than the United States, only Iceland and South Africa now have retail sales tax rates in excess of 10 percent.[10] Given this evidence, and given the existence of current state sales taxes, there seems to be little room for an additional federal sales tax that would not result in significant compliance problems for both state and federal tax collectors. Nevertheless, the retail sales tax cannot be ignored as an option as an add-on tax. As concluded by one prominent commentator when asked about the viability of retail sales tax for the United States: "The answer to the question is simple. Provided the retail sales tax rates are low and not too different between (especially neighboring) countries, the retail sales tax is a good alternative to the VAT."[11]

---

[9]See McLure (1987), p. 107, Tait (1993), p. 18, and Tanzi (1994), pp. 48–52.

[10]Tait (1988), p. 18.

[11]Tanzi (1994), p. 51.

Appendix to Chapter 2

Reasons Why Evasion Is a Larger Problem Under a Retail Sales Tax Than a Value-Added Tax

Understandably, many politicians—as well as the general public—are more comfortable with the notion of replacing the income tax with a sales tax than a value-added tax. However, of the two alternatives, many tax experts only consider value-added taxation viable. The purpose of this appendix is to summarize why a retail sales tax is not held in high esteem by tax administrators.

There are several reasons why enforcement is a problem at the retail level under any kind of tax:

- It is not usually possible to cross-check retailer sales with the records of purchasers because taxable sales by retailers are made to consumers.

- The retail sector has a relatively large proportion of small businesses. Evasion by small business is more likely than by large business because audits are much less likely and the relative costs of compliance higher.

- The life expectancy of a small retail business is short. Collections from a discontinued business can be difficult and costly.

A retail sales tax imposes its entire compliance burden on the sector from which collections are most troublesome.[12] The retail sector must remit far greater amounts of revenue under a sales tax than under a VAT or an income tax. In addition, a retail sales tax imposes the unique compliance burden of requiring a separation of receipts between taxable sales to consumers and nontaxable sales to other businesses.

---

[12]Although there is more total revenue at risk under a retail sales tax, it is interesting to note that *on the margin* the *incentives* for retailers to evade tax are no more than they would be under a value-added tax with an equal rate. (Furthermore, marginal incentives are likely to be larger under an income tax, assuming the rate of income tax is greater than the rate of consumption tax.) Assuming the national sales tax rate was 25 percent, one dollar of unreported retail sales reduces tax revenue by 25 cents. One dollar of unreported retail sales would also reduce revenue by 25 cents under a 25 percent VAT. (A small business owner in the top bracket can reduce income taxes by 40 cents on each dollar.) Taxpayers' marginal incentives, however, may not be all that matters in determining the amount of tax evasion. For example, the dependency of the retail sales tax on small business would mean greater noncompliance under a retail sales tax. In addition, if retailers can totally avoid being identified as taxpayers or if collection is difficult (for example, in the case of firms going out of business), the rewards for sales tax evasion can be greater under a retail sales tax than under a VAT (or an income tax).

The Credit-Invoice Method VAT

Summary

- Almost every industrialized country has a credit-invoice value-added tax. The credit-invoice VAT, however, is not among the proposals currently receiving the most attention in the United States.

- A credit-invoice VAT imposes new compliance costs on business by requiring both seller and buyer to keep detailed records of each transaction. Compliance costs increase substantially as the number of tax rates and the number of exemptions increase.

- This recordkeeping improves compliance thorough cross-checking of taxes (paid by sellers) with credits (claimed by buyers). It also eliminates the need for retailers to distinguish sales to business from sales to consumers.

- Relief from the VAT is provided through exemption and through zero-rating. In general, zero-rating provides more satisfactory results than simple exemption from tax.

Currently in the United States there is tremendous interest in consumption taxes, but there is little interest in *the* consumption tax most widely used in other countries. The credit-invoice method VAT is the method most popular with foreign governments for implementing a consumption tax. Nevertheless, the credit invoice method is not receiving any significant consideration on Capitol Hill.

Most of what has been written about consumption taxes—particularly concerning administration and compliance issues—has focused on the credit-invoice method. And while there are important differences between current U.S. proposals for consumption taxes (non-credit invoice) and foreign VATs (credit invoice) in place, there are a sufficiently large number of similarities that the United States can benefit greatly by taking into account the experience of other countries.

Finally, the credit-invoice method cannot be written off as an option for the United States. It seems fair to say that until just a few years ago, the credit-invoice method VAT was among the most—if not the most—viable consumption tax options under consideration in the United States. The prospect for a credit-invoice method VAT could rise again if concerns about compliance become greater, or if Congress decides that it must provide exemptions to governments, nonprofit institutions, and certain businesses. It is interesting to note that the Canadian government proposed a subtraction method VAT in the mid-1980s but ultimately adopted a credit-invoice method in 1991.[1]

The Concept of "Value Added"

For each business *value added* is the contribution of its labor and its capital to national output. It may be measured using either of two methods: the *subtraction* method or the *addition* method (Table 3.1). Under the subtraction method, value added is measured as the difference between the firm's sales and the firm's purchases from other businesses. Under the addition method, value added is calculated as the sum of a firm's payments to its workers and return to owners (and lenders) of the firm for the use of their invested capital.

Table 3.1   Calculation of Value Added by Subtraction and by Addition

Income Statement	
Sales	$100
Less Payments to Other Businesses	$40
Less Wages	$50
Equals Profit	$10
A. Value Added by Subtraction	
Sales	$100
Less: Payments to Other Businesses	$40
Equals value added	$60
B. Value Added by Addition	
Wages	$50
Plus Profit	$10
Equals Value Added	$60

---

[1]Substantial revisions to the Canadian value-added tax are now under consideration. Canada retained its income tax system.

In this example, value added equals $60 when measured as the difference between business receipts and payments to other businesses (the subtraction method). Value added also equals $60 when measured by addition of wages and profits (the addition method). It is important to note that financial flows (i.e., the payment and receipt of investment income as well as any increase or decrease in investment balances) between businesses are not included in the calculation. Most notably, interest income is not included in gross receipts and interest payments are not deductible.

The addition method is rarely applied in other countries nor has it been included in any proposals for federal taxation in the United States.[2] The subtraction method is currently used in Japan, and this method is now receiving the most consideration in the United States. In concept, the credit-invoice method is more closely related to the subtraction method.

The Equivalence of Final Sale Price to Total Value Added

In a modern economy, the process by which most consumer products are brought to market involves a long chain of production and distribution comprising many businesses. In this chain each business purchases goods and services from other businesses. These purchases from other businesses serve as inputs to the goods and services provided by that business to its own customers. At the end of the chain are retailers who make sales to household consumers. Table 3.2 provides an example showing how the sum of value added equals the retail price of the goods sold to the final consumer. At each link in the production-distribution chain the business adds value to its purchased inputs.

Table 3.2   The Value Added Chain

Business Chain	Sales	Purchases	Value Added
Link # 1: Farmer	20	0	20
Link # 2: Miller	50	20	30
Link # 3: Baker	100	50	50
Sum			100

- *Link #1.* In this simple example, the farmer uses his own land and seed and purchases no inputs from other businesses. He sells his wheat for 20 cents. This 20 cents is the farmer's value added.
- *Link #2.* The miller purchases the wheat from the farmer for 20 cents. The wheat is then ground into flour and sold to the baker for 50 cents. The difference between the 50-cent sale and the 20 cents of cost is the miller's value added.

---

[2]The addition method is used by the state of Michigan. The Michigan Single Business Tax is generally considered to be very complex. The addition method has also been considered for use in determining value added of financial institutions, which is difficult to measure under more conventional methods of calculating VAT liability.

- *Link #3.* The baker purchases the flour from the miller for 50 cents. The flour is then used to bake bread and sold to consumers for one dollar. The difference between the one-dollar sale and the 50 cents of cost is the baker's value added.

The example shows that the total value added at each stage of the production process equals the final sales price.

By not specifying how the cost of "purchases" would be measured, the above example abstracts from the important issue of capital cost recovery. All proposals for credit-invoice VATs, as well as most credit-invoice VATs currently in force throughout the world, allow a benefit for the entire cost of capital expenditures in the year of purchase (i.e., to be "expensed"), instead of allowing a benefit of the cost over the life of the asset. As shown in the Appendix to this chapter, in order to make a value-added tax a consumption tax, it is essential to allow the expensing of capital purchases.[3]

The Credit-Invoice Method

The Basic Mechanics of the Credit-Invoice Method

Under the credit-invoice method, tax is imposed on each firm's gross receipts. In addition, tax credits are available to the extent each business can show that its suppliers paid tax on their sales to that business. The amount of creditable taxes appears on the invoice provided by suppliers to the business. For example, in Table 3.2, the miller had $50 of sales and $20 of purchases from the farmer. If the rate of tax is 10 percent, the miller pays $5 of tax on gross receipts and also receives $2 of credit. The $2 of credit corresponds to the tax paid by the farmer, and this $2 is reported on the invoice provided by the farmer to the miller. Table 3.3 summarizes the basic operation of a credit-invoice method VAT as it would apply to the example shown in Table 3.2.

Table 3.3   The Operation of a 10 Percent Credit-Invoice VAT Compared to a 10 Percent Retail Sales Tax

Business Chain	Sales	Gross VAT	Credits	Net VAT	Retail Tax
Link # 1: Farmer	20	2	0	2	0
Link # 2: Miller	50	5	2	3	0
Link # 3: Baker	100	10	5	5	10
Total		17	7	10	10

The table also shows that, because total value added equals the retail sales prices, a comprehensive value-added tax imposes the same total burden as a comprehensive retail sales tax (with the same tax rate).

---

[3]If, instead of expensing, capital purchases were amortized using depreciation schedules reflecting their true decline in value, the tax would be equivalent to an income tax.

Comparison to a Retail Sales Tax

Because a retail sales tax and a credit-invoice VAT (with the same rate) generally impose the same amount of tax on the same tax base (i.e., total final sales), economists believe that the taxes will have largely the same impacts on saving, international trade, and the distribution of income. To economists, the differences between a retail sales tax and a credit-invoice VAT are primarily matters of administration and compliance.

In order to better understand the credit-invoice method, it is useful to divide the calculation of tax liability into two parts: (1) the calculation of gross VAT and (2) the calculation of credit.

The calculation of *gross* VAT is largely similar to a retail sales tax. Both taxes apply the rate of tax to gross taxable sales. Because both taxes are, usually, separately stated at the cash register, they are both highly visible to consumers.[4] Both taxes routinely exempt exports. To the extent there are exemptions or special rates for certain types of products, taxpayers must differentiate between sales of exempt and nonexempt products under both taxes.

There are, however, some important differences between the calculation of gross VAT and a retail sales tax. In one respect a retail sales tax is simpler than the calculation of gross VAT: A retail sales tax applies only to *retail* business while a VAT applies to *all* business. On the other hand, a retail tax is more complicated than gross VAT because under a VAT, it is not necessary to make a distinction between sales to business or sales to consumers. Under a VAT, all sales by businesses are taxable. If the purchaser is a business, the tax will be creditable. Thus, one of the most vexing administrative problems of a retail sales tax is absent under a VAT.

The most important distinguishing feature of the credit-invoice method is the second part of the VAT calculation—the calculation of credits. There are no tax credits under a retail sales tax. Under the credit-invoice method, gross liabilities of businesses are substantially reduced by credits. It is noteworthy that businesses earn credits only for taxes paid *by other businesses*. The credits are only allowed if the taxpayer has a verifiable record of taxes paid by the seller. This unique *interdependence* of tax liability is important for at least two reasons.

The first reason is administration and compliance. All transactions between businesses are subject to tax and both buyer and seller must keep records of tax liability associated with that transaction. If the buyer does not maintain a detailed record of the date of purchase, the type of product, the identification of the seller, and the amount of tax paid by the seller for each transaction, the VAT credit can be denied for that transaction (see Box 3.1). Not surprisingly, tax authorities like this feature of the VAT. All credit claims by purchasers can be cross-checked with the records of sellers.[5] On the

---

[4]The separate statement of tax is a feature of all retail sales taxes and many VATs. It would be possible, with some minor adjustments, to impose both taxes without this feature.

[5]Under a VAT, final sales to consumers cannot be cross-checked because only sellers maintain records. So, in the case of final sales, credit-invoice VATs have the same type of enforcement problems as retail sales taxes. Because consumers do not maintain detailed records of their spending, underreported sales cannot be cross-checked against the records of purchasers.

other hand, the credit-invoice VAT places an enormous new compliance burden on businesses that is not present under a retail sales tax or an income tax.

Box 3.1   Invoice Information Retained by Buyers and Sellers for Each Transaction Under a Credit-Invoice VAT[6]

- Name and address of person issuing invoice
- VAT registration number
- Serial number of the invoice
- Date and issue of the invoice
- Date of supply of goods or services
- A description of goods and services
- Amount charged, excluding VAT
- Rate of tax
- Name and address of customer

The second reason why interdependence of tax liability is important is its unusual effect on tax exemption. Under an income tax or almost any other type of consumption tax, exemption only affects the exempted taxpayer, and exemptions generally reduce overall tax receipts. However, under the credit-invoice method of calculating VAT, the impacts of exemption can extend far beyond the exempted party, and tax exemption can even have the unintended side effect of *increasing* taxation. This is explained more fully in the following section.

Exemption from a Credit-Invoice Value-Added Tax

One of the more tedious aspects of learning about value-added taxation is understanding how tax relief may be implemented. In practice, value-added taxes usually have numerous special rates and exemptions. There are two basic methods of providing tax relief under a VAT: *exemption* and *zero-rating*. Understanding the impact of exemption and zero-rating is critical to understanding the impacts of a credit-invoice VAT on those sectors and products frequently provided VAT relief, such as food, housing, medical care, small business (including farmers), exports, used goods, state and local governments, financial intermediaries, and charitable organizations. In addition, the differences between exemption and zero-rating also serve to highlight some important differences between the credit-invoice and subtraction methods of calculating VAT.

Exemption of a business under a credit-invoice VAT removes tax liability and the availability of credit, leaving the business in a zero-tax position. This is not, however, the end of the story. It is still possible for an exempt

---

[6]Tait (1988), pp. 279–280.

business to face a significant burden from a VAT. Overall burden may increase because business customers of an exempt business will be unable to receive tax credits on purchases from the exempt business. In a competitive market, the exempt business that gives its customers invoices without credits will have to reduce its prices or lose sales.

While exemption can increase burden, it can also reduce burden or leave it unchanged from what it would be without exemption. Whether exemption from a credit-invoice VAT increases, reduces, or does not affect burden depends on where in the production-distribution chain exemption is granted:

1. If a business at the *beginning* of the production chain is exempt, no tax is paid by the exempt business, but an additional amount of tax is paid by the next business in the chain that exactly offsets this. In this case, total VAT liability is the *same* as in the case without exemptions.

2. If an *intermediate* business is exempt from tax, the business making purchases from that exempt business is not able to credit any taxes paid by business earlier in the chain. Thus, the purchaser from an exempt business pays as much tax as if no tax were previously paid. In this case, total VAT liability is *greater* than the case without exemptions.

3. If a retailer making *final* sales is exempt from tax, all taxes on value added prior to purchases by the retailer are properly paid and the value added by the retailer is exempt from tax. In this case, total VAT liability is *less* than the case without exemptions.

These three points are illustrated in Table 3.4. While exemption is seemingly the most straightforward way of relieving administrative burden, its impact on the tax burdens associated with different products can be markedly uneven. As a rough rule of thumb, however, it can be noted that *businesses that provide goods and services to other businesses will generally be hurt by exemption, while businesses that provide goods and services to consumers will generally benefit from exemption.*

In general, the degree of overtaxation associated with any product will be greater, the closer the exempted business is to the retail level. Thus, exemption of millions of small farmers, with relatively small purchases from other businesses,[7] is unlikely to result in significant overtaxation of food and might well be justified by the significant reduction in compliance and administrative costs.

It should also be noted that under credit-invoice VATs, many businesses would be due refunds because a significant portion of their sales is not subject to tax.

---

[7]Furthermore, to help alleviate any overtaxation when farmers are exempt, farm implements, seed, and fertilizer can be exempt from tax.

Table 3.4   The Effects of Exemption at Various Stages of Production Under a Credit-Invoice Method

	No Exemptions	Exempt Farmer	Exempt Miller	Exempt Baker
Farmer				
Gross VAT	2	—	2	2
Credits	0	—	0	0
Net VAT	2	—	2	2
Miller				
Gross VAT	5	5	—	5
Credits	2	0	—	2
Net VAT	3	5	—	3
Baker				
Gross VAT	10	10	10	—
Credits	5	5	0	—
Net VAT	5	5	10	—
Total VAT	10	10	12	5

Zero-Rating as an Alternative to Exemptions

The large and uneven economic distortions that can result from exemptions has led to the use of zero-rating as an alternative to exemption. When the sales of a business are zero-rated, the business must still become part of the VAT system and file annual returns. However, the business's compliance burden is not so much an issue because zero-rated taxpayers receive refunds. (In fact, under most VAT systems where exemptions are allowed, many businesses opt to remain zero-rated taxpayers.) A zero-rated business pays no gross VAT but is eligible for credits. Besides being good for the zero-rated firm, the economic impacts are much more even than under a system of exemptions. Any zero-rating before the retail stage does not impact total liability of a final product. And zero-rating at the retail stage results in complete exemption of a product. These points are illustrated in Table 3.5.

Table 3.5   The Effects of Zero-Rating at Various Stages of Production Under a Credit-Invoice Method

	No Zero-Rating	Zero-Rated Farmer	Zero-Rated Miller	Zero-Rated Baker
Farmer				
Gross VAT	2	0	2	2
Credits	0	0	0	0
Net VAT	2	0	2	2
Miller				
Gross VAT	5	5	0	5
Credits	2	0	−2	2
Net VAT	3	5	−2	3
Baker				
Gross VAT	10	10	10	0
Credits	5	5	0	5
Net VAT	5	5	10	−5
Total VAT	10	10	10	0

Conclusion

Despite widespread acceptance throughout the rest of the industrialized world, perceived high compliance costs and the perceived similarity to sales taxation have kept the credit-invoice method from playing a prominent part in the current consumption tax debate in the United States. Instead a somewhat similar alternative—the subtraction method VAT—lies at the core of almost all current consumption tax proposals. This is the topic of the next chapter.

Appendix to Chapter 3

How to Make a VAT a Consumption Tax

One of the most prominent features of a consumption tax imposed on businesses is the immediate writeoff of the full price of capital purchases. (Under a credit-invoice VAT, the equivalent of expensing is achieved by allowing a tax credit for the full price of capital purchases.) Expensing does more than just simplify the tax and enhance its political appeal; it is *the* feature of a value-added tax that makes it a consumption tax. The example in Table 3A.1 illustrates why.

In this example, it is assumed that the economy is composed of two industries—a consumer-goods industry and a capital-goods industry. Value added is most often calculated by allowing deductions for the entire purchase price of new capital (i.e., expensing). In this case, total value added in the economy equals total consumption of 100. If, however, value added is calculated by allowing depreciation instead of expensing, then total value in the economy equals total income of 105. Thus, a value-added tax with depreciation (instead of expensing) would not be a consumption tax but an income tax.

Table 3.A1   Expensing Makes a VAT a Consumption Tax

	Consumer-Goods Industry	Capital-Goods Industry	Total Economy
INCOME STATEMENTS:			
(1) Sales	100	25	125
(2) Purchased capital	25	0	25
(3) Depreciation	20		20
(4) Wages	70	20	90
(5) Profits	10	5	15
VALUE ADDED —TWO METHODS:			
Value added (depreciation method) Sales (1) *minus* Depreciation (3)	80	25	105
Value added (expensing method) Sales (1) *minus* Purchases (2)	75	25	**100**
ECONOMIC STATISTICS:			
Total Income *Equals* Wages *Plus* Profit			105
Consumption *Equals* Total Income *Less* Net Investment *Equals* Consumption			**100**

The Subtraction-Method VAT

Summary

- The subtraction-method VAT is the general type of consumption tax now receiving the most attention on Capitol Hill.

- No country except Japan (using a 3 percent rate) has any experience implementing a subtraction-method VAT.

- A subtraction-method VAT is likely to be simpler to administer than a credit-invoice VAT.

- Besides being somewhat simpler, a subtraction-method VAT may be more politically viable than a credit-invoice VAT. A subtraction-method VAT has an appearance similar to that of the corporation tax while a credit-invoice VAT more closely resembles a sales tax.

Although its proponents may not like to admit it, the subtraction-method VAT has a great deal in common with the credit-invoice VAT. The tax base is calculated as the difference between business receipts and purchases from other businesses. So, like the credit-invoice method, the starting point in calculating tax liability is gross business receipts. Instead of credits, however, the subtraction method uses deductions to modify the tax on gross receipts to a value-added tax. Given the same tax rate, the subtraction and credit-invoice methods collect the same amount of tax from taxpayers. This is illustrated in Table 4.1.

**Table 4.1   Comparison of the Subtraction Method and the Credit-Invoice
Method**

10 % Subtraction-Method VAT		10% Credit-Invoice VAT	
Link #1: Farmer			
Sales	20	Sales	20
Purchased Inputs	0	Gross Tax	2
Value-added	20	Invoice Credits	0
VAT	2	VAT	2
Link # 2: Miller			
Sales	50	Sales	50
Purchased Inputs	20	Gross Tax	5
Value-added	30	Invoice Credits	2
VAT	3	VAT	3
Link #3: Baker			
Sales	100	Sales	100
Purchased Inputs	50	Gross Tax	10
Value-added	50	Invoice Credits	5
VAT	5	VAT	5
Total VAT	10		10

Gross receipts do not include financial income or other proceeds from sale of financial assets. Nor do they include export sales. There are deductions only for inputs purchased from other businesses. *There are no deductions for wages paid to one's own employees or for interest payments. On the other hand, capital expenditures are written off when purchased, and business inputs are deducted when purchased even if they only accumulate in inventory.* A simple comparison of the corporate income tax and the subtraction-method VAT is presented in Table 4.2.

There are no significant differences in the economic impacts between a subtraction-method and credit-invoice-method VAT. Like the retail sales tax, both are taxes on consumption (assuming immediate deductions for capital expenditures). Both equally have the ability to increase capital formation and improve competitiveness. Both potentially have the same impacts on the distribution of the tax burden. There are, however, three important differences between the credit-invoice method and the subtraction method: (1) differences in compliance and administrative costs, (2) different degrees of flexibility, and (3) differences in the perceived similarity to a retail sales tax.

Table 4.2   Comparison of Corporate Income Tax and a Subtraction-Method VAT

	Income Tax	VAT
Business Receipts—Domestic	90	90
Business Receipts—Exports	10	—
Interest Income	5	—
Total Gross Receipts	105	90
Business Purchases (Other than capital)	35	35
Wages	45	—
Interest Expense	10	—
Depreciation	10	—
Capital Spending	—	15
Total Deductions	*100*	*50*
Tax Base	5	40

Administration and Compliance

The basic difference between the credit-invoice method and the subtraction-method VAT is that tax liability under the subtraction-method tax paid by purchasers may be calculated without reference to taxes paid by sellers. Generally, proponents argue that this greatly reduces the compliance burden in two ways. First, businesses selling products do not have to provide tax information on invoices to business customers or retain records of these invoices. Secondly, businesses buying products do not have to retain special tax records of each purchase in order to claim credits.

Under the subtraction method, businesses can use annual accounting flows similar to those used under current financial and tax accounting rules to calculate tax liability. Businesses would not be required to keep detailed records of each transaction. It is important to note, however, that current accounting records would have to be supplemented to determine the subtraction method liability. For example, cost categories such as cost of goods sold and advertising would have to be divided between (nondeductible) internal costs and (deductible) purchases from other businesses. In addition, the subtraction-method VAT permits deduction of the full purchase price of capital when acquired. Similarly, inventory items (such as supplies, repair parts, and other items usually capitalized under an income tax) are deducted when purchased, not when removed from inventory.

Despite these adjustments, it seems likely that a subtraction-method VAT entails lower compliance costs for business taxpayers than a credit-invoice VAT. This simplification, however, comes at the cost of increased potential for evasion and less flexibility.

Under a subtraction-method VAT compliance is likely to be lower than under a credit-invoice VAT because it is more difficult for tax collectors to cross-check business tax returns under the subtraction method. Duplicate records of invoices held by sellers and *business* purchasers make it much easier to identify unreported sales under a credit-invoice VAT. Tax evasion by retailers not reporting sales to *consumers*, however, is still a problem under the subtraction method as it is under the credit-invoice method and the income tax.[1]

Flexibility

Many commentators have pointed out that a credit-invoice VAT is much better able to accommodate tax relief for particular products and particular business sectors than the subtraction method.[2] This lack of flexibility is considered by some to be an advantage of the subtraction-method VAT because an absence of preferential treatment would reduce complexity and improve economic efficiency. On the other hand, this inflexibility is seen as a disadvantage by those who believe some types of special relief are desirable or inevitable, and without the ability to accommodate certain sectors of the economy (e.g., farmers, health care providers, state and local governments, charitable and cultural organizations) a value-added tax should not or could not be enacted. This point deserves serious attention because it is important in determining how the tax will be administered and in determining the political dynamics surrounding its passage (as well as postenactment modifications).

Like a retail sales tax and credit-invoice VAT, preferential treatment of products (e.g., food, exports) under a subtraction-method VAT is effected by identifying those products at the *retail* level and excluding them from the tax base. As noted above, preferential treatment adds significant administrative and compliance costs but no more so for the subtraction-method VAT than a retail sales tax or a credit-invoice VAT. Therefore, a subtraction-method VAT can be effectively administered at multiple rates as long as preferential rates are imposed at the retail level.[3]

The critical difference between the subtraction and credit-invoice methods is preferential treatment before the retail level. A credit-invoice VAT is particularly well-suited to provide preferential treatment for nonretail sales

---

[1]If VAT rates are lower than current income tax rates, the incentives to underreport sales would be less.

[2]See, for example, Congressional Budget Office (1992), McLure (1987), and U.S. Treasury (1984).

[3]If preferential rates were provided at the retail level, a subtraction-method VAT would face the problem—similar to that encountered under a retail sales tax—of distinguishing retail from nonretail sales. However, the items likely to receive preferential treatment under a VAT—off-premise consumption of food, clothing, public transportation, and medical care—are much easier to identify as retail sales than those at issue under a retail sales tax—such as tools, personal computers, and automobiles.

(e.g., small farmers). As shown in Table 3.5 in the previous chapter, the sales of the zero-rated taxpayer escape tax and even generate rebates for that taxpayer, but the overall taxation of the final product is unchanged. As a result, the credit-invoice VAT does distort consumer choice, and therefore ultimately is not likely to bestow any particularly large benefits on the zero-rated business.

Unlike the case of zero-rating under a credit-invoice VAT, preferential treatment of nonretail sales under a subtraction method VAT results in uneven taxation of final products. If nonretail sales are exempt (or subject to preferential rates),[4] there is no tax on the seller's value added. However, unlike a subtraction-method VAT, the lost revenue is not made up further along the production chain. Thus, exemption at the intermediate level *does* provide relief for the final product. This is illustrated in the first column (Example #1) of Table 4.3 where the intermediate producer—the miller—is exempt from the system.

Table 4.3   The Distortionary Effects of Exemption of Intermediary Sales Under the Subtraction Method

	Example #1: Final Product Fully Taxable	Example #2 Final Product Exempt from Tax
Farmer—TAXABLE		
Receipts	20	20
Purchases	0	0
Value-Added	20	20
VAT	**2**	**2**
Miller—EXEMPT		
Receipts	50	50
Purchases	20	20
Value-Added	30	30
VAT	**0**	**0**
Baker—TAXABLE		
Receipts	100	0
Purchases	50	50
Value-Added	50	−50
VAT (or Refund)	**5**	**(5)**
Total Value-Added Tax (or Refund)	**7**	**(3)**
Note: VAT Using Credit-Invoice Method	10	0

[4]Zero-rating is not an alternative under a subtraction-method VAT (unless it is significantly modified to be similar to a credit-invoice VAT).

However, if there is preferential treatment of nonretail sales under a subtraction-method VAT *and* final sales are excluded (e.g., exports, food), the preferentially treated final sales do better than being exempt or zero-rated. Their tax is not only eliminated, but they get a subsidy because they, in effect, are being granted a rebate for taxes not paid at prior levels. This is illustrated in the second column (Example #2) of Table 4.3.

There are three responses to the problem of exemption of intermediate product sales under a subtraction-method VAT. One is to not allow preferential rates or exemption of products before the retail level. (This seems to be the response favored by most proponents of subtraction-method VATs.) It is important to note that such a restriction does not hinder implementation of policies intending to promote trade (e.g., exemption of exports) and policies intending to provide relief for low-income households (i.e., exemption of food and medical care). Such a restriction, however, would be an impediment to providing relief for small business and small farmers who often face a disproportionate compliance burden and are at the same time politically influential.

The second response to the problem is to disallow deductions for business purchases on which no tax was paid. This would require sellers reporting to buyers that tax was paid and the buyer and seller keeping records of all transactions. The administration of such a system would be much different from that of a credit-invoice VAT.

Finally, the problem—particularly if not of a large magnitude—can simply be ignored: Allow deductions even though there have been exemptions prior to the retail level.

Perceived Similarity to a Retail Sales Tax

Economists are often indifferent in their choice of consumption taxes because different types of consumption taxes are widely believed to have similar economic impacts. Politicians, on the other hand, are acutely sensitive to the differences between consumption taxes. This is because the public has a very different perception about the various types of consumption taxes, and politicians realize that it is the *public* perception of consumption taxes that will drive the political debate.

There are *two* notions of a subtraction-method VAT that make it more attractive to the general public than a credit-invoice VAT. The first is its dissimilarity in appearance to a sales tax. The second is its similarity in appearance to a corporate income tax.

Retail sales taxes are widely perceived as regressive taxes. From the point of view of the final consumer, a retail sales tax and a credit-invoice VAT are indistinguishable. Both types of tax are collected at the cash register and are stated separately from the retail prices.

If a subtraction-method VAT is not stated separately (as under all recent proposals), it does not have the appearance of a sales tax. Moreover, the subtraction-method VAT imposes significant tax liabilities on large businesses as does the corporate income tax. This similarity in appearance to the corporate income tax should not be discounted. Many current proposals would use the revenues from a subtraction-method VAT to replace the corporate income tax. Much of the current public affinity for the corporate income tax and the corporate alternative minimum tax is due to the perceived unfairness of large corporations not paying tax. Given the history of the corporate income tax and the corporate alternative minimum tax, it is likely there would be a significant public outcry if large corporations paid no tax.[5]

It is not only the public's perceptions that matters in the choice between the credit-invoice and subtraction methods. State governments may be more willing to accept a "hidden" subtraction-method VAT that does not visibly compete with its retail sale tax base than a credit-invoice VAT that does. The perceptions of foreign governments also matter. However, in this case, it is preferable for the tax to be considered a sales tax. Under the General Agreements on Tariffs and Trade (GATT), "indirect taxes" (like sales taxes) may be rebated at the border, but "direct" taxes (like the individual and corporate income taxes) may not.[6] This is an area of strong controversy and debate.

---

[5]Even though almost all economists believe the burden of a consumption tax falls on consumption, and many economists believe the burden of the corporate income tax is borne by capital, replacement of the corporate income tax with a subtraction-method VAT might be politically acceptable. It probably is more palatable than the replacement of the corporate income tax with a retail sales tax—even though economists consider both proposals are economically equivalent.

[6]The impact of consumption taxes on international trade is discussed in greater detail in Chapter 8.

5

The Individual Consumption Tax

Summary

- Unlike other types of consumption taxes that are collected from businesses, an individual consumption tax is collected from individuals. Households would file annual returns as they now do for the income tax.

- To its proponents, the major advantage of an individual consumption tax compared to other consumption taxes is that the inherent regressivity of the consumption tax base may be offset with a progressive rate structure.

- Under the tax, consumption is calculated by subtracting net savings from total income. This deduction for net savings presents numerous practical difficulties, particularly during the transition from an income to a consumption tax.

- The major disadvantage of an individual consumption tax compared to other consumption taxes is its complexity.

Retail sales taxes and value-added taxes are consumption taxes collected from businesses. In contrast, an individual consumption tax[1] is imposed solely on individuals. Under an individual consumption tax, individuals would file annual returns as is done under current individual income tax rules. The defining difference between the current income tax and an individual consumption tax is that the new tax would allow an unlimited deduction for net annual additions to saving. In order to arrive at net additions to saving, additions to savings must be reduced by dissaving in the form of additional borrowing.

---

[1]The individual consumption tax is also referred to as the *personal consumption tax* or the *expenditures tax*. Sometimes the individual consumption tax that is part of the Nunn-Domenici proposal is called the *Savings Exempt Income Tax* (SEIT) or the *Unlimited Saving Allowance* tax (USA tax).

The basic calculation of an individual consumption tax is illustrated with the following simple example in Table 5.1:

Table 5.1   Calculation of the Individual Consumption Tax

Income		**$100**
Plus		
New Loan for Automobile Purchase	$15	
Reduction in Mortgage Principal	($10)	
Net New Debt		**$5**
Less		
Beginning-of-Year Bank Balance	$40	
End-of-Year Bank Balance	($50)	
Increase in Saving		**($10)**
***Equals* Consumption Tax Base**		**$95**

In this example, a family has $100 of wage and interest income. Because it has taken out a new car loan of $15 and paid off $10 of mortgage principal, its net new debt is $5. This is $5 over and above income available for consumption. On the other hand, the family was also able to increase its bank balance by $10. This is $10 of income not used for consumption. Thus, after adding and subtracting from loan and savings balances, this family has $95 available for consumption.

Many commentators have noted that an individual consumption tax is probably the most complex of all types of consumption taxes.[2] Despite this additional complexity, some still consider individual consumption taxes an attractive option because of their unique ability to address issues of regressivity. Because the tax is levied on households and not businesses, there can be a progressive rate structure. Retail sales taxes and value-added taxes (levied on businesses) can only alleviate regressivity through adjustments to the tax *base* and/or with administratively complex refundable credits. As shall be discussed in greater detail in Chapter 8, preferential treatment of necessities is administratively complex and economically inefficient. Moreover, such adjustments to the tax base are not particularly effective in achieving distributional objectives. An individual consumption tax, on the other hand, can achieve almost any desired distribution of after-tax income solely through adjustments to the tax *rate*.

Thus, at first glance, it appears an individual consumption tax is the best of both worlds. There need not be a tradeoff between economic efficiency and equity. An individual consumption tax has all of the economic benefits of a consumption tax base. At the same time, the tax can be made to be just as progressive as the current income tax. The individual consumption tax has not, however, received even a small fraction of the attention that is given to other consumption taxes.

---

[2]See, for example, Graetz (1979), Kuttner (1987), and Toder (1995).

Except for brief temporary appearances in India and Sri Lanka, tax authorities around the world have had no experience with an individual consumption tax. The Treasury Department proposed an individual consumption tax in 1942 to help fund wartime spending and reduce consumption, but the proposal got nowhere in Congress. The Treasury Department again brought attention to the idea with a major study of tax reform in 1977, but again the plan was just presented as an option—and did not receive serious consideration by Congress. More recently, however, the individual consumption tax has received significant attention as one (along with a subtraction-method VAT imposed on business) of the two major components of the legislation (S. 722) proposed by Senators Nunn and Domenici in April 1995. Until the introduction of this legislation, there had been no serious congressional consideration of an individual consumption tax.[3]

The problem with an individual consumption tax is the difficulty in finding a workable method of calculating the deduction for new saving—the deduction that lies at the heart of an individual consumption tax. In order to better understand the issues involved, it is useful to differentiate "old saving" (that is, the individual net wealth at the time of enactment of the tax) from "new saving" (additions to net wealth after enactment). It is likely that the two would be treated differently under any individual consumption tax.

New Saving

New saving would be treated like deductible contributions to an individual retirement account (IRA) that had no limitations on the amount of deductions or the timing of withdrawals. Taxpayers would deduct all income saved, including net additions to bank, mutual fund, and brokerage accounts; all purchases of stocks, bonds, and other financial instruments; and all investments in partnerships and proprietorships. When funds were withdrawn from such investments—whether in the form of income or reduction of principal, the entire amount of the proceeds would be subject to tax.[4]

Conversely, proceeds from new loans or other forms of indebtedness would be included in the tax base, while payments of both interest and principal would be deducted.

The computation of the deduction for new saving would require knowledge of the annual change in the outstanding balance of each taxpayer's investments and indebtedness. Under an individual consumption tax, the custodian of each investment and indebtedness account would have to report these amounts to taxpayers once a year as they now report interest earned and paid.

---

[3]Chapter 11 provides more detail of the Nunn-Domenici proposal.

[4]With regard to taxing the entire proceeds from investment, tax professionals can think in terms of the entire amount being gain. Tax basis is zero because the entire value of the initial investment is written off when the investment is made.

Old Saving

Saving accumulated before the enactment is more problematic than new saving for two reasons. The first is a matter of compliance. The second is a matter of fairness.

Once an individual consumption tax comes into effect, all additions to saving would be deductible and all withdrawals would be taxable. Shifting funds from one investment to another (e.g., depositing a dividend in a bank account) has no tax consequences because receipts (dissaving) are exactly offset by saving. A large revenue loss could result, however, if somehow existing wealth was undetected by tax authorities, and then these funds were deducted when invested in new forms. This could occur if prior to enactment individuals drew down their saving and held it in cash. The investment of this cash subsequent to the enactment date would result in deductions despite lack of additional new saving. In order to prevent this, it has been noted that it may be necessary to require taxpayers to declare (subject to certain de minimis rules) their outstanding cash balances at the outset. It is not clear how such a requirement would be enforced.[5]

The other important transition issue is primarily a matter of policy. Under the standard operating rules of an individual consumption tax, all proceeds from saving are included in gross receipts and subject to tax. The taxation of the entire proceeds, however—and not just capital gains, dividends, interest, and other capital income—results in large tax penalties in the case of existing saving. Thus, the standard operating rules of the tax would result in harsh treatment of old saving, and many would consider such tax treatment a retroactive tax increase. This burden would fall primarily on the elderly who draw down their saving during retirement.[6]

In order not to impose a double burden on the elderly (and others drawing down saving to consume), special transition relief is required. One method of providing this relief would be to treat existing saving like new saving and allow the balance of existing saving to be deducted at the time of enactment.[7] Then, under the regular rules of the individual consumption tax, all proceeds can be included when the assets are sold or the account is closed out. There are, however, several potential objections to this type of transition relief. First, given the enormous amount of individual wealth outstanding in the United States, this deduction for all existing basis would result in an enormous revenue loss (and an increase in tax rates to pay for the loss). Secondly, a significant portion of old saving received favorable treatment under the income tax (IRAs, pensions, life insurance, annuities, and tax-exempt bonds). Having never been subject to tax (or having received substantial tax relief), this saving would not be subject to "double taxation" upon enactment of an individual consumption tax. Third, given that two

---

[5]Perhaps U.S. citizens could be required to exchange their green money for red money.

[6]It is important to recognize that the burdensome taxation of old saving under an individual consumption tax with transition relief is exactly equivalent to what would be experienced under a retail sales tax or a value-added tax.

[7]This deduction of basis is equivalent to selling the asset at the time of enactment and paying income tax on any gain, and then reinvesting and deducting the entire proceeds.

major objectives of implementing a consumption tax are to increase saving and to simplify taxation, some propose moving to a new system cold turkey, (i.e., without transition relief) because tax relief for old saving does nothing to increase incentives for new saving and such rules are extremely complex.[8] Finally, some question whether the "retroactive" tax burden imposed on old saving is truly "unfair."[9] They conclude that it is entirely appropriate to impose an additional tax burden on the elderly given the transfer of wealth being exacted by the Social Security system from the current work force to current retirees.[10] This last view—if it ever gets serious attention in the political arena—will undoubtedly be met with fierce opposition from those savers that would have their after-tax income subject to tax a second time under the consumption tax.

Tax Rates Under an Individual Consumption Tax

Although particular proposals must be evaluated with a full array of details, two general observations can be made about tax rates that might prevail under a *replacement* consumption tax. In general, because total consumption is less than income, it can be expected that a consumption tax will have higher rates than an income tax. (If, however, significant base broadening occurs, this need not be the case.) Second, because upper-income families consume proportionately less of their income than lower-income families, it is generally necessary for a consumption tax to have more steeply graduated rates than under current law in order to achieve the same degree of progressivity as current law.

Overview of the Four Major Types of Consumption Taxes

This and the prior three chapters have attempted to provide some operational details of different types of consumption taxes. Table 5.2 provides a summary comparison of some of the major features of these taxes. Columns (A) and (B) of this table highlight some practical issues already discussed. Administrative issues and public perceptions of these taxes vary dramatically. Columns (C) through (F) summarize the economywide effects of these taxes. *Despite their considerable operational differences, these taxes in their basic forms do not have fundamentally different effects on growth, trade, inflation, and the distribution of income.* These economic issues are explored in more detail in Chapters 6 through 8.

Each of the four major types of consumption taxes (like any tax) has its weaknesses. From Table 5.2, the following conclusions may be drawn:

---

[8]This is the position taken by Sam Gibbons, ranking minority member of the House Ways and Means Committee. See Gibbons (1994).

[9]See Graetz (1977).

[10]See Makin (1987).

- Because regressivity is a major problem with consumption taxes, the ability to implement a progressive rate structure could make the *individual consumption tax* a highly attractive option. An individual consumption tax, however, loses much of its luster because of its complexity—particularly with regard to computing a deduction for saving.

- A *retail sales tax* is generally perceived as regressive and may not be enforceable at rates necessary to make it a replacement tax. Nevertheless, the perceived simplicity of a retail sales tax is attractive to voters.

- Many of the enforcement problems prevalent under a retail sales tax disappear under a *credit-invoice VAT*. Like a retail sales tax, however, a credit-invoice VAT is highly visible and perceived as regressive by the public. Moreover, it imposes substantial new compliance burdens on businesses. Even the credit-invoice VAT's advantages over other VATs—its ability to effectively provide product and business exemption—is often perceived as a weakness by those who would prefer a consumption tax not have any special tax breaks.

- From the standpoint of political viability, the *subtraction-method VAT* appears to pose the least difficulty. Administrative and compliance costs seem relatively low. Except for the individual consumption tax, it is no better or worse than most other consumption taxes with regard to growth or income distribution. Moreover, because it is promoted as a tax on business, the public may have some trouble recognizing its regressivity (no matter how much economists may insist this is the case).[11]

After reviewing some major economic issues in Chapters 6 through 8, the remainder of this study—Chapters 9 through 17—is devoted to describing how actual proposals might impact business. One major finding is that a replacement subtraction-method VAT would radically shift the tax burden from individuals to businesses. Furthermore, within the business sector, it radically shifts the burden from capital- to labor-intensive industries.

The Flat Tax modifies the basic structure of a subtraction-method VAT by removing the wage component of value added from the business tax base and instead imposes a wage tax on individuals. In so doing, the Flat Tax distributes the tax burden between businesses and individuals and across businesses in a manner that much more closely resembles current law. (To be sure, there are still major differences, but these differences in tax payments are far less than those that would be experienced under a plain vanilla subtraction VAT.) Given that a consumption tax with a less radical alteration in tax collections is likely to have more political viability, the Flat Tax may be viewed as a political refinement of the subtraction-method VAT.

---

[11]See Chapter 9.

Table 5.2 Summary Comparison of Major Types of Consumption Tax

Replacement Tax	(A) Complexity	(B) Perception	(C) Probable Effect on Growth	(D) Probable Effect on Inflation	(E) Probable Effect on Trade	(F) Impact on Income Distribution
(1) Retail Sales Tax	Enforcement Problems at High Rates	Like State Sales Taxes	Promotes Growth (to Extent Saving Increases)	One-time Increase in Price Level (if Fed Goes Along)	May Improve Trade Balance (if Saving Increases)	Regressive
(2) Credit-Invoice VAT	High Compliance Costs (Particularly with Multiple Rates)	Like State Sales Taxes	Promotes Growth (to Extent Saving Increases)	One-time Increase in Price Level (if Fed Goes Along)	May Improve Trade Balance (if Saving Increases)	Regressive
(3) Subtraction VAT	Most Information From Existing Books	Like Corporate Income Tax	Promotes Growth (to Extent Saving Increases)	One-time Increase in Price Level (if Fed Goes Along)	May Improve Trade Balance (if Saving Increases)	Regressive
(4) Individual Consumption Tax	Problems with Deduction for Saving	Like Individual Income Tax	Promotes Growth (to Extent Saving Increases)	Tax on Individuals Less Likely to Increase Prices	May Improve Trade Balance (if Saving Increases)	Depends on Rate Structure

The Effect of Consumption Taxes on Saving, Inflation, and the Business Cycle

Summary

- Proponents of consumption taxation argue:
  1. Saving is critical to long-term economic growth.
  2. The current U.S. saving rate is low compared to the rate of U.S. saving in the past and compared with rates of saving in other countries.
  3. The replacement of an income tax with a consumption tax would increase the after-tax rate of return on saving (by eliminating the bias against saving inherent in the income tax).
  4. An increase in the after-tax rate of return on saving will increase private saving.

- There is broad agreement among economists about all of these points except the last one: Economists dispute the magnitude of the response of private saving to a replacement consumption tax. Given the uncertainty of economic analysis, it is unlikely any consensus about the general impact of taxes on saving will emerge in the foreseeable future.

- A replacement consumption tax is unlikely to have much impact on the business cycle.

- A consumption tax may have a onetime impact on the price level if the Federal Reserve increases the money supply.

Capital formation is a critical ingredient of economic growth, but the money has to come from somewhere. The vast majority of funds necessary to purchase new equipment, new plant, new roads, and new technology come from saving. Without increases in saving, any increase in one type of investment (e.g., new machinery) must be at the expense of other types of investment (e.g., technology). With more capital, workers have more tools that enable them to be more productive. Productivity growth leads to higher wages and a higher standard of living.

The financial markets channel funds to purchasers of capital who need the funds. Although there is a tendency to focus on personal savings by individuals—primarily in the form of pensions and accounts with financial intermediaries—significant funding for capital spending in the United States comes from other businesses (i.e., retained earnings), state governments (that generate budget surpluses), and foreign individuals and businesses investing in the United States.

It is important to note that saving can also be negative as well as positive. When consumption exceeds income, there is a drain on funds available for capital investment. Therefore, from the standpoint of capital formation, reducing indebtedness by individuals is just as important as increasing savings by individuals. Of course, the biggest culprit of them all when it comes to dissaving is the deficit-prone Federal government. It is often remarked that the surest method of increasing national saving is to reduce the federal budget deficit.

There is substantial disagreement among economists about the impact of a replacement consumption tax on saving and economic growth. Some claim the impact is dramatically large. Others argue it is imperceptibly small. Unfortunately, this difference of opinion is unlikely to be resolved any time soon. Decision makers in both the private and public sectors will have to evaluate consumption taxes with this uncertainty.

The Low Level of U.S. Saving

Since peaking in 1978 at 8.1 percent of total Gross Domestic Product, the annual rate of saving in the United States has rarely exceeded 4 percent. As shown in Table 6.1, net saving by individuals, by businesses, and by governments have all declined.

Table 6.1   Components of National Saving as a Percentage of GDP

Average over Period:	Net Personal Saving	Net Business Saving	Net Govt. Saving	Total National Saving
1950-59	4.7	2.8	−0.1	7.4
1960-69	4.7	3.6	−0.1	8.1
1970-79	5.5	2.6	−1.0	7.2
1980-89	4.8	1.6	−2.5	3.9
1990-92	3.5	1.6	−3.5	1.7

Source: Joint Committee on Taxation (1995).

Not only is the U.S. rate of savings low by historical standards but, as shown in Chart 6.1, it is also extremely low in comparison to other major industrialized countries.

Chart 6.1   National Savings as Percentage of GDP, 1989

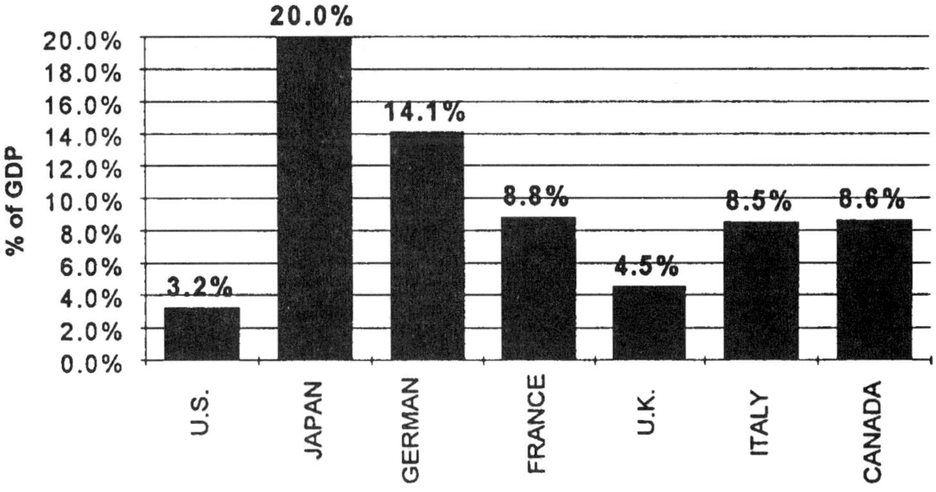

Source: U.S. Congress, Joint Committee on Taxation (1995).

The Impact of Taxes on the Rate of Return

Two fundamental observations can be made about the impact of taxes on saving. The first is that an income tax penalizes saving: The more an individual saves, the greater his or her lifetime tax burden. This is illustrated in the example in Table 6.2.

In this simple example, two individuals live only two periods ("working years" and "retirement"), and they start out with the same initial wealth (from wages or inheritance) of $100. The "spender" consumes all of his wealth during his working years. The "saver" invests and does not consume anything until retirement. Proponents of tax change argue that despite the same initial opportunities and the same lifetime wealth (measured as the present value of lifetime consumption), the burden of taxation is greater for the saver.

The second fundamental observation about taxes and saving is that a consumption tax neither rewards nor penalizes saving. The burden of taxation is the same irrespective of an individual's savings behavior. The example in Table 6.3 shows the tax burden of the saver and spender under a consumption tax.

Table 6.2   Comparing the Income Tax Burden of a Spender and a Saver

Assumptions:

Pre-tax Return	8.0%	
Tax Rate	30.0%	
After Tax Return	5.6%	

A. "spender"

	Present Value	Period 1	Period 2
Income		$100.00	$ 0.00
Saving		$ 0.00	$ 0.00
Consumption	$70.00	$ 70.00	$ 0.00
Taxes	$30.00	$ 30.00	$ 0.00

B. "saver"

	Present value	Period 1	Period 2
Income		$100.00	$ 5.60
Saving		$ 70.00	($73.92)
Consumption	$70.00	$ 0.00	$73.92
Taxes	$31.59	$ 30.00	$ 1.68[1]

Table 6.3   Comparing the Consumption Tax Burden of a Spender and a Saver

Assumptions:

Pre-tax Return	8.0%	
Tax Rate	30.0%	

A. "spender"

	Present Value	Period 1	Period 2
Income		$100.00	$ 0.00
Saving		$ 0.00	$ 0.00
Consumption	$70.00	$ 70.00	$ 0.00
Taxes	$30.00	$ 30.00	$ 0.00

B. "saver"

	Present value	Period 1	Period 2
Income		$100.00	$ 8.00
Saving		$100.00	($108.00)
Consumption	$70.00	$ 0.00	$ 75.60
Taxes	$30.00	$ 30.00	$ 32.40[2]

---

[1]$1.68 tax at 6 percent rate of return has a present value of $1.59.

[2]Present value.

The present value of an individual's lifetime tax burden is unaffected by the amount of saving under a consumption tax. Thus, *a consumption tax does not—by itself—provide any incentive to increase savings. The benefit to saving is the removal of the income tax from saving income.*

Evidence of the Responsiveness of Savings to Tax Changes

Calculations like the ones presented above are often used to illustrate the detrimental impact of income taxation on after-tax return to saving. There is, however, substantial uncertainty about whether this change in the after-tax *return* to saving will affect the *amount* of saving. Moreover, it is not even clear for a given change in the rate of return what direction the change in amount may be.

It is natural to expect that an increase in the returns to saving will increase saving: With greater rewards for saving, individuals will do more of it. The opposite, however, may also be true. This may be understood by considering the case of a "target saver." A target saver would be an individual who saves to achieve a certain dollar amount of future consumption (e.g., tuition for a child's college education). An increase in the after-tax rate of *return* on saving would reduce the amount of savings necessary to achieve the desired amount of saving.[3] Another example of target saving that *declines* with increases in rate of return is the funding of defined benefit pension plans: When interest rates increase, employers can more easily meet their pension obligations and therefore reduce their funding of pension plans.

Empirical research by economists does little to clear up the ambiguity as to the effects of a consumption tax on saving. (In fact, given the importance of the responsiveness of savings to changes in the after-tax rate of interest, there have been remarkably few studies that attempt direct empirical estimates. This is because of the significant practical difficulties in formulating meaningful statistical tests.) Many economists believe that saving is not responsive to the rate of interest or that statistical tests are not conclusive.[4] Others believe that saving is responsive to the return on savings.[5]

The work of Michael Boskin, former Chairman of the President's Council of Economic Advisors, is frequently cited by proponents of consumption taxes as evidence of the responsiveness of savings to changes in taxation. His estimates of responsiveness of saving are at the upper end of empirical estimates. At the other end of the spectrum, many economists believe that changes in the after-tax return to saving has little or no effect on saving. In order to ascertain the order of magnitude of the possible effects of a consumption tax, Boskin's work can be used as a point of reference as a reasonable upper-range empirical estimate of the responsiveness of saving to taxes. A reasonable lower-range estimate is no effect at all.

---

[3]For example, suppose the parents of a newborn wish to provide $100,000 of college tuition to their child on the child's eighteenth birthday. If the rate of interest is 8 percent and the parents' tax bracket is 30 percent, they would have to save $3,182 annually to accumulate $100,000 in eighteen years. If their savings is exempt from tax, they only need to save $2,472 annually in order to achieve their objective.

[4]See, for example, Boskin (1978).

[5]See, for example, von Furstenberg (1981).

Boskin's best estimate is that for a 1 percent increase in the after-tax return to saving there will be a 0.4 percent increase in the amount of saving. Thus, with the elimination of an income tax with a rate of 40 percent,[6] there would be an increase in *personal* saving of approximately 25 percent.[7] Using the data shown in Table 6.1, it can be seen that using this estimate a replacement consumption tax would have increased personal saving from 4.8 percent to approximately 6.0 percent during the 1980s and from 3.5 percent to 4.3 percent during the 1990–1992 period.[8]

If, on the other hand, the elasticity of saving is close to zero—as maintained by many economists—tax changes will have little impact on saving.

The Impact of Saving on Growth

Given the magnitude of these estimates, it is unlikely that any change in taxation can fundamentally solve the problem of low saving in the United States. Assuming the upper-bound estimates of responsiveness are correct, a replacement consumption tax would result in a significant increase in saving, but such an increase would only partially offset the large recent declines in the personal saving rate in the United States. For example, assuming an elasticity of saving of 0.4, a replacement consumption tax that became fully effective in 1990 would do little more than restore the rate of personal saving to that which prevailed during the 1980s. From an international perspective, these changes also seem small. The most optimistic estimate of increases in the saving rate resulting from a replacement consumption tax still results in a rate of U.S. saving far below that of most trading partners.

If upper-range estimates are correct, savings would increase by approximately one percent of GDP (in 1995)—about $70 billion. An increase of $70 billion in savings sustained over a period of years can result in a substantial increase in the nation's productive capacity. In ten years, for example, this

---

[6]Although there are many instances in which the marginal rate of tax on saving exceeds 40 percent (e.g., dividends received by individuals subject to both individual and corporate tax, and capital gains due to inflation that are subject to tax), the vast majority of private saving in the economy is taxed at rates below 40 percent (e.g., saving by those not in the top marginal bracket, pension saving, life insurance, annuities, and IRAs).

[7]The elimination of a 40 percent tax raises the after-tax rate of return by 67 percent. (For example, if the before-tax rate of return is 10 percent, the after-tax would increase from 6 to 10 percent.) The elasticity of 0.4 is multiplied by 67 percent to arrive at an estimate of 26.7 percent increase in private saving.

[8]There is a class of theoretical models, known as *life-cycle models*, which predict extremely high responses of saving to changes in the interest rate. (Savings elasticity in the order of magnitude of 1.0 or 2.0 are common in these models.) These models in general have wide acceptance as theoretical constructs in the economics profession, but there have been no compelling explanations of why the high responsiveness of saving to changes in the interest rate predicted by these models is not observed in the economy. For arguments for and against the usefulness of the life-cycle models of savings see Starrett (1988) and Summers (1988).

would result in a *net* increase in the capital stock of $700 billion. If that capital had a rate of return of 10 percent, that would be a $70 billion permanent increase in the economy, an increase of approximately 1 percent.[9]

Impact on the Business Cycle and Inflation

Business Cycle Effects

Up to this point this chapter has focused on long-term *supply-side* effects of a replacement consumption tax. Although widely discredited since its heyday of influence in the 1960s, the predicted impact of a consumption tax by *demand-side* or *Keynesian* economists still deserves consideration (if only because it has so long dominated the textbooks and press reports). In a nutshell, Keynesian economics says if there is significant unemployment and less than full capacity utilization, the economy can be expanded because increases in government deficits can help spur private and public spending.

This type of reasoning has lead to some concerns that a tax on consumption could be a significant drag on the economy that could lead to recession. There are many good arguments to discredit this claim, but perhaps the best in this case is that most consumption taxes under consideration would be offset by reductions in income taxes. Because there would be no change in the deficit, the impact on overall demand would be small.[10]

Inflationary Effects

Because it is widely believed that the burden of consumption taxes will result in higher prices, there are concerns that a consumption tax will be

---

[9]This calculation is provided to give an understanding of a reasonable *order of magnitude* in the potential change in the economy that results from an increase in saving. Economists alternatively might use models employed in a branch of economics known as *growth theory*. In this framework, one might observe that the return to capital (in the form of corporate profits, interest, and some reasonable portion of proprietorship income) accounts for about 20 percent of GDP (i.e., about $1.5 trillion), and the current size of the business capital stock producing that GDP is about $10 trillion. $700 billion of saving could increase that capital stock by about 7 percent. If income from capital also increased by 7 percent, this would be an increase in national income of about $150 billion (or about 2 percent of GDP).

There are two reasons to expect this measurement might be biased upward. First, it is common to assume that capital is subject to diminishing returns, i.e., the additional $700 billion in capital is unlikely to be as profitable as the initial $7 trillion. Second, measured capital does not take into account intangibles (such as patents, trademarks, goodwill, etc.). To the extent profits may be attributable to these factors, increases in tangible capital might not be accompanied by rates of return that include returns to both tangible and intangible capital. (Although, it is often argued that capital formation spurs technological innovation.)

[10]The case can be made that placing a heavier tax burden on consumption and a lesser burden on saving will dampen overall demand (macroeconomists refer to this as the theory of the *balanced-budget multiplier*), but these impacts—to the extent they exist at all—are likely to be small and temporary. Any reductions in overall demand due to reduced consumption are likely to be offset by increases in spending on plant and equipment.

accompanied by an increase in the rate of inflation.[11] If consumption taxes imposed on businesses are passed forward in higher prices, the effect on the price level will depend on the rate of tax and the comprehensiveness of the tax base. If the rate of tax is 15 percent, and the tax applies to 80 percent of the goods and services in the economy, the increase in the price level that accompanies the imposition of the tax could be 12 percentage points.

Because changes in the price level are ultimately controlled by monetary policy, any increase in the price level from a consumption tax would have to be accommodated by the Federal Reserve (i.e., a 12 percent increase in the price level would have to be accompanied by an increase in the money supply of approximately 12 percent). Because the Federal Reserve's actions are not under the direct control of Congress or the President, it is difficult to know how the Federal Reserve policy would react to the imposition of a large consumption tax.

It is also important to stress that any changes in the price level due to the imposition of a new consumption tax (or an increase in the rate of an existing tax) are likely to be onetime changes in the price *level* and not permanent increases in the *rate* of inflation.

Conclusion

In terms of its impact on saving, there is substantial uncertainty surrounding the enactment of a replacement consumption tax. "Definitive" statements about a consumption tax's impact on saving and economic growth should be accepted warily. One thing that does seem clear is that even under the most optimistic assumptions, it seems unlikely that a replacement consumption tax can increase U.S. saving to a level comparable with that of its major trading partners.

Potentially the impact on long-term economic growth can be significant. If saving is not responsive to tax changes, however, the impacts on growth will be small. In summary, with regard to economic growth, a replacement consumption tax is unlikely to do any harm but does have significant upside potential. Most conclude its impact on inflation will be a short-term initial increase only.

---

[11]The choices faced by business will be (1) raise prices, (2) absorb costs, or (3) reduce wages (because there is no income tax).

7

Consumption Taxes and International Trade

Summary

- Most consumption taxes operate under the destination principle (that is, they tax domestic consumption not domestic production).

- In order to effect the destination principle, value-added taxes rebate tax on exports and impose import duties. These are known as border tax adjustments.

- Border tax adjustments are necessary to maintain a level international playing field between domestic and foreign producers.

- Consumption taxes that replace income taxes may improve the trade balance if they can increase national saving.

A major issue in consumption taxation is whether or not tax should be levied on domestic *production*—in which case exports would be taxed and imports would be exempt—or on domestic *sales*—in which case exports would be exempt and imports would be taxed. The difference may have important implications for international trade.

Taxes on production are said to follow the *origin principle*. Taxes on sales are said to follow the *destination principle*. From an economic perspective, the destination principle is superior to the origin principle because it is less likely to distort consumers' choices between domestic and imported goods. In practice, most consumption taxes are imposed only on domestic sales.[1] In addition, most consumption tax proposals—with the notable exception of the Flat Tax—are imposed on domestic sales. Income taxes, on the other hand, are typically imposed on domestic production.[2]

Throughout this publication it has been emphasized that it is important when evaluating a consumption tax to distinguish the case of an add-on consumption tax from a replacement consumption tax. This is particularly true in evaluating international issues. As shall be discussed in greater detail below, most economists believe that consumption taxes levied on the destination principle are neutral with regard to international trade. Therefore, an *add-on* consumption tax operating under the destination principle does *not* have any major effect on the trade balance. In contrast, many economists believe that income taxes, levied on the origin principle, can be detrimental to international trade. Therefore, it is only when a consumption tax *replaces* an income tax that there may be a benefit to international trade.

This chapter provides a more detailed discussion of the arguments for and against these assertions.

Border Tax Adjustments

It is easy to apply the destination principle under some consumption taxes. For a retail sales tax and a personal consumption tax, the taxation of purely domestic sales follows naturally from the mechanical application of the tax.[3] For value-added taxes, however, a concerted effort must be made. In order for value-added taxes to apply to only domestic sales, there must be special rules for both domestic production sold abroad (i.e., exports) and foreign production sold domestically (i.e., imports). These special rules are called *border tax adjustments*. To relieve exports of tax, firms exclude receipts from exports sales from the tax base. To tax imports, duties are imposed at the

---

[1]Under the General Agreement on Tariffs and Trade (GATT), rebates are allowed for exports and taxation of imports are allowed in the case of indirect taxes. Indirect taxes are taxes imposed on products, such as retail sales taxes and VATs using the credit-invoice method tax. Border tax adjustments are not allowed in the case of direct taxes. Direct taxes are imposed on wages and profits. Even if border tax adjustments on direct taxes were allowed under GATT, it is not at all clear how they would be implemented. Generally, one would expect the amount of corporation tax associated with the final sales price of any product to be positively related to the capital intensity of its production. However, beyond this generalization, there is no clear guidance as to how much corporate tax should be attributed to a product. Any method of allocating a firm's corporate tax to its exports would be arbitrary. Taxation of imports would even be more problematic. Arbitrary assignments of tax would have to be estimated from the amount of tax paid by domestic firms computing similar products. Given that profitability varies considerably from year-to-year, border tax adjustments on imports would have to be recalibrated frequently. Such changes, however, could never be frequent enough because import taxes are imposed on transactions, but profit taxes of firms selling comparable products are not computed—even on a preliminary basis—until several months after the end of the taxable year.

[2]The United States provides some partial relief from its income tax for certain types of exports.

[3]A retail sales tax achieves the destination principle by taxing only domestic retail sales. A personal consumption tax taxes only domestic consumers, so imported goods are subject to tax and exported goods are excluded.

border. Without border tax adjustments, value-added taxes would be levied on domestic production.

International competition for sales into *domestic* markets is preserved by use of border tax adjustments on *imports*. With these adjustments, goods produced abroad and domestically are both subject to the same tax. For example, under a 10 percent VAT, all domestic goods and services are taxed at a 10 percent rate and imports are subject to a 10 percent duty at the border. Even though border tax adjustments on imports to some may have the appearance of a tariff, there is no discrimination against imports or favoritism to domestic producers because the sales of both importers and domestic producers are subject to the same tax.

International competition in *overseas* markets is preserved by border tax adjustments on *exports*. With these adjustments, exported goods are exempt from tax as are the goods of their foreign competitors selling in foreign markets. For example, if the United States levied a 10 percent destination-principle VAT, exports to Canada would be exempt from U.S. tax as would goods produced and sold in Canada. Sometimes this preferential treatment of exports vis-à-vis goods sold in domestic markets is likened to an export subsidy, but as can be seen by the above example, they are necessary to maintain a level playing field between overseas markets.

In conclusion, border tax adjustments in and of themselves appear not to have any significant impacts on trade. On the contrary, economists argue that border tax adjustments are necessary to maintain a level international playing field for traded goods. Yet, there are still many reasons to believe consumption taxes may have a positive impact on the trade balance *if consumption tax revenues are used to reduce income taxes or to reduce the federal budget deficit.*

Trade Balance and Saving

To the extent that a consumption tax increases saving, there may be a positive impact on the trade balance. This is because there is a linkage between domestic saving and the value of the dollar, and—in turn—between the value of the dollar and the trade balance. If domestic saving increases, there is generally less need for foreign capital to finance domestic investment. Reduced capital inflows into the United States mean that foreign investors have less need for U.S. currency. A reduction in this demand for dollars causes its price to drop (just as a reduction in the demand for apples causes the price of apples to drop).

This decline in value—or depreciation—of the dollar is beneficial to U.S. trade. A depreciation of the dollar means that foreigners wishing to purchase U.S. goods (in dollars) will find these goods less expensive in their currency. This decline in price will stimulate increased exports. Similarly, a depreciation of the dollar means that consumers in the United States will have to pay more in U.S. dollars for foreign goods (whose prices are denominated in foreign currency). This increase in price means reduced imports. Both increased exports and reduced imports improve the trade balance.

The chain of causation from increased saving to an improved trade balance is summarized in Figure 7.1.

Figure 7.1 The link between savings and trade

```
Increased (private or public) Saving →
Reduced Capital Inflows →
Reduced Demand for Dollar →
Decline in Value of Dollar →
Lower Export/Higher Import Prices →
Increased Exports/Reduced Imports →
```

Increased Saving by Reduced Federal Budget Deficits

Deficits by the federal government are a form of negative saving. For the reasons outlined above, there is broad agreement among economists that the increase in national saving that would result from reduction in the federal budget deficit would reduce the trade deficit. (This is often referred to as the *twin deficits* problem.) Despite strong sentiment for deficit reduction, however, use of a consumption tax for deficit reduction is not currently receiving any notable attention by Congress. In the current political climate, it seems much more likely that deficit reduction will be achieved through reductions in federal spending.

Increased Saving By Reducing the Income Tax

Nearly all economists state that income taxes are inefficient taxes because they penalize individuals for saving. Corporate taxes are particularly inefficient because they add an *additional* layer of income taxation to the income from certain types of capital (i.e., equity financed) of certain businesses (i.e., corporations). Thus, not only is there a bias against capital formation, there is additional discrimination across different types of capital. Given the absence of these problems under a consumption tax, it should not be surprising that replacement of the income tax with a consumption tax can improve overall U.S. economic performance and the U.S. trade balance in particular.

If the burden of income taxation takes the form of a reduced after-tax return on investment (i.e., the burden of the income tax is on capital), removal of the tax will increase the after-tax return to saving.[4] To the extent

---

[4]Even if repeal of the income tax does not increase the return to saving, there can still be a positive impact on the trade balance. Instead of reducing profits, the burden of income taxes might be passed forward in the form of higher prices. Under this alternative scenario, reducing income taxes can reduce prices. A replacement consumption tax would cause an offsetting price increase. In the context of trade, however, the impact on prices is not offsetting because a border-adjustable tax (i.e., a consumption tax) would replace a tax without border adjustments (i.e., the corporate income tax). Thus, if the burden of income taxes is passed forward in higher prices, a replacement consumption tax can reduce prices on exports. Although there is no definitive answer to the question of the incidence of business income taxes, this discussion shows that a positive effect on trade is possible whether the burden of income taxes is borne by consumers or is borne by business.

that saving responds positively[5] to the increase in the after-tax return on investment, the increase in domestic personal saving could positively impact the trade balance. The chain of causation is similar to that which would result from a reduced federal budget deficit (illustrated in Figure 7.1): Increased domestic saving reduces the need for inflows of foreign capital, reducing the demand for dollars, and causing a depreciation. This depreciation, in turn, reduces the price of U.S. exports and increases the price of U.S. imports.

Exchange Rate Adjustments

Up to this point, this chapter has ignored the impact of trade flows on exchange rates. Exchange rate adjustments can be particularly important in evaluating origin-based taxes—like the Armey Flat Tax—or any other taxes that might impact trade. Economists believe that when exchange rates are flexible (as they have been generally since 1971) even consumption taxes without border tax adjustments will not distort international trade. This is because exchange rates will adjust in a manner that will have the same impact as border tax adjustments.[6]

The basic argument is best understood with an example. Suppose that a 10 percent value-added tax is imposed *without* border tax adjustments (i.e., like the Flat Tax). In this case, most economists assume the domestic price level would increase by 10 percent. Without border tax adjustments, export prices would also increase by 10 percent, and import prices would remain at their before-tax levels. In this case, exports would be at a competitive disadvantage and imports would be at a competitive advantage. These changes, however, would reduce the demand for the dollar and, as a result, cause the dollar to depreciate. Economists believe that equilibrium in foreign exchange markets could be restored only when the dollar depreciated by 10 percent. This decline in the exchange rate would obliterate any impact of the VAT on trade. As a result of the depreciation of the currency, imports are 10 percent more expensive—just as if there were border tax adjustments imposed on imports. Similarly, as a result of the depreciation, there is a 10 percent reduction in the price of exports that exactly offsets the 10 percent increase in price due to the lack of border tax adjustments.

This view is widely held by economists.[7] It follows from the basic tenet of international finance that exchange rates adjust to restore equilibrium to international markets. In equilibrium, a country's trade deficit is equal to net foreign investment, that is,

Imports *minus* Exports *equals* Net Capital Inflows

---

[5]This is the primary topic of discussion in Chapter 6.

[6]If indeed it is true that in a world of freely floating exchange rates there is no difference between an origin-principle and destination-principle value-added tax, a strong case can be made for preference for an origin-principle tax because border tax adjustments involve considerable administrative and compliance costs.

[7]See, for example, U.S. Congress, Joint Committee on Taxation (1991).

Given this identity, and assuming that net capital inflows are unaffected by the imposition of a consumption tax, there is no clear-cut reason to disagree with economic reasoning. It is likely that any positive impact of a consumption tax on trade will be offset by exchange rate movements in order that equality in the above equation is maintained.[8]

Therefore, as long as net capital flows are unaffected, exchange rate movements can eliminate any detrimental impact of an origin-based tax on trade. Moreover, because capital inflows are likely to be reduced under a replacement consumption tax (as discussed in the previous section), it is still possible for a replacement origin-principle consumption tax—like the Flat Tax—to positively impact the trade deficit despite the absence of border tax adjustments. Thus, even in the context of a non-border-adjustable VAT, the central issue is again the impact of a replacement consumption tax on saving.

Conclusion

Economists generally agree that (1) it is unlikely for border tax adjustments *per se* to have any significant impact on the trade balance *and* (2) it is unlikely that a lack of border tax adjustments will have any significant impact on the *overall* trade balance once exchange rates have adjusted (although they may have some important differential impacts across industries). In either case, a consumption tax is likely to improve the trade balance only by causing a dollar depreciation that would follow from any increase in domestic saving. A consumption tax might increase *private* saving if it is a replacement tax that increases the after-tax return to saving. A consumption tax can increase *public* saving by using revenues to reduce the federal budget deficit.

---

[8]The above reasoning does not say anything about the differential impact of these changes across industries. For example, suppose that the burden of the corporate tax is on consumers because the tax results in higher prices, and assume the tax is repealed and replaced with a consumption tax. The repeal of the corporate income tax will not result in a uniform reduction in prices. It will generally reduce prices more in high-profit and capital-intensive sectors of the economy. Any offsetting exchange rate adjustment will uniformly impact the price of all products. In the end, there may be no change in overall exports, but it may be the case that capital-intensive firms' exports increased while other firms' exports decreased.

8

Consumption Taxes and Income Distribution

Summary

- Consumption taxes are widely perceived as placing undue burdens on the poor. There are two reasons for this perception: (1) Consumption as a percentage of annual income is greater for low-income households than high-income households, and (2) consumption taxes generally do not have progressive rates.

- Many economists believe that consumption taxes appear more regressive than they really are. This is because there are systematic biases in the standard measures of "rich" and "poor."

- Nevertheless, any politically realistic consumption tax will likely be supplemented with features to alleviate the burden on low-income households.

- The exemption of necessities is not a particularly effective method of reducing regressivity of consumption taxes.

- Some form of tax credit for low-income households likely will play an important role in alleviating the regressivity of any consumption tax enacted into law.

On average, low-income households consume a larger proportion of their income than do high-income households. For this reason, consumption taxes are widely considered regressive.[1] This is particularly true if the consumption tax is levied—as is often the case—at a single, flat rate.

---

[1]If tax as a percentage of income is greater for low-income households than high-income households, the tax system is considered *regressive*. Conversely, if tax as a percentage of income is lower for low-income households than high-income households, the tax system is considered *progressive*. If tax as a percentage of income is the same for all taxpayers, the system is considered *proportional*.

Regressivity is the Achilles' heel of consumption taxation. No matter how effective any consumption tax might be in increasing saving, improving the trade balance, and reducing complexity, such a tax might never become law solely because it is regressive. In order to be politically viable, the basic structure of any consumption tax may have to be substantially modified or supplemented in order to eliminate its inherent regressivity. Moreover, if a consumption tax replaces the current income tax, the new tax likely must go beyond avoiding regressivity. In order to gain acceptance, it may have to be as progressive as current law.[2] Methods of alleviating regressivity are among the most important issues in the design of consumption taxation systems, and a variety of options are available. All of these mechanisms, however, greatly increase administrative and compliance costs.

It is also important to recognize that despite the widespread perception of regressivity by the general public, there have been a variety of challenges to this traditional view:

1. Government transfer programs that favor the poor should be taken into account when evaluating regressivity. The benefits provided by these programs may substantially offset any burden imposed by a consumption tax on a large portion of low-income families.

2. The economic growth that could result from the imposition of a consumption tax could make everybody better off, so the focus on *relative* burden may be misplaced.

3. It is possible that the corporate income tax is not borne by capital but by consumers, in which case the current tax system may not be as progressive as is commonly believed. In that case, a switch to consumption taxation may not alter the distribution of the tax burden by as much as is commonly perceived.

4. Economic well-being is usually measured by reference to annual income instead of lifetime income. Most economists believe that use of annual income as a measure of well-being makes consumption taxes appear more regressive than they really are. Some economists even argue that a consumption tax is fairer than an income tax.[3]

Although these arguments are well understood by the experts, to date they have not entered the mainstream political debate. It is also unclear if they ever will; one impediment is that they are unfamiliar or relatively difficult to understand.[4]

In any case, it is likely that methods of alleviating regressivity—not the larger question of whether consumption taxes are actually regressive—will take center stage in the consumption tax debate.[5]

---

[2]Richard Gephardt, the Minority Leader of the House of Representatives, has recently proposed an income tax with a progressive rate structure and few deductions or exclusions. The top bracket is 39 percent and is applicable to all forms of income including capital gains.

[3]This argument is often made by David Bradford, a former Treasury Department Deputy Assistant Secretary (Tax Policy). See, for example, Bradford (1986).

[4]The Appendix to this chapter provides more explanation of these arguments.

Methods of Alleviating Regressivity

There are three general methods of reducing the regressivity of consumption taxes. The first is to provide tax exemptions and/or low tax rates for low-income households and to increase tax rates with the level of income. This type of progressive rate structure can be implemented only under a personal consumption tax.[6] The second method is to provide tax exemptions or tax reductions for the products consumed in greater proportions by low-income households. Tax relief for food and other necessities is practical only under a retail sales tax or a value-added tax. The third method is to provide tax credits or direct payments to households to compensate them for their disproportionate burden. These payments may be implemented under any type of consumption tax, but are less costly to administer if they piggyback on a personal income or personal consumption tax already in place.

Progressive Rates

As noted, a progressive rate structure is practical only under a personal consumption tax. If it can be implemented, almost any degree of progressivity can be achieved. For example, large personal exemptions could keep tens of millions of households free of tax. Rates could be slightly or steeply progressive. As discussed in Chapter 5, however, there is considerable uncertainty about the practicality and popularity of a personal consumption tax. Calculating the net savings deduction under a personal consumption tax would entail substantial administrative and compliance burdens, making it the most complex of all major types of consumption taxes. A personal consumption tax has never been enacted into law in any modern developed economy.[7]

Exemption of Necessities

In practice, the method most often used to alleviate regressivity of consumption taxes is the exemption of products considered necessities. Most value-added taxes in other countries as well as most retail sales taxes implemented by the states provide tax relief for food, health care, housing, and other necessities. As indicated in Table 8.1, these items generally represent a larger fraction of income for low-income households than high-income households.

---

[5]No matter how meritorious these new methods might be, change will be difficult. To the extent these changes are not well understood, many will be suspicious of technical changes with such large political ramifications. Opponents of consumption taxation are likely to claim that "the books are being cooked" or that "the rules are being changed in the middle of the game." As the debate in consumption taxation develops, it will be interesting to see whether proponents of consumption taxation will accept the traditional view of regressivity and fight their battle on those terms or whether they will try to redefine the terms of the debate.

[6]Someday it may be technologically feasible to produce nontransferable identification cards electronically encoded with each consumer's tax rate. These cards would be presented at the cash register so that retail sales tax and VAT burdens may be adjusted according to each individual's circumstances. Still, substantial enforcement and administrative problems would exist under such a system.

[7]See Chapter 11 for a discussion of the Nunn-Domenici proposal, which includes—along with a subtraction-method VAT—a personal consumption tax.

Table 8.1   Expenditures on Necessities as a Percentage of Total Consumption

Income Group	Food at Home	Shelter	Health Care	Total
Lowest Fifth	17.1%	29.9%	12.2%	59.2%
Highest Fifth	11.0%	27.5%	11.2%	49.6%

Source: Vasquez (1987), p. 321.

Although tax relief for these items reduces regressivity, a consumption tax with preferences for certain types of consumption greatly increases administrative and compliance costs.[8] Preferences also take their toll in terms of economic efficiency. When certain consumption items receive preferential treatment, consumers are likely to rearrange their consumption patterns to avoid tax.[9] Distortions result throughout the economy as consumption shifts toward items receiving preferential treatment. Furthermore, given the necessity of achieving certain revenue targets, any exception provided for certain items results in higher taxation for other items. These higher rates of tax further distort consumption and reduce the economic benefits of consumption taxation.

Perhaps the most disappointing aspect of this type of tax relief is its failure to substantially reduce the regressivity of the tax. Although, as a percentage of income, the benefit of exempting food helps the poor, a substantial portion of the revenue cost of preferential treatment for food provides benefit to upper-income households as well. Most studies show that tax relief for necessities does somewhat alleviate regressivity, but not by much. The result of one of these studies is shown in Table 8.2. The table shows that under a broad-based 10 percent value-added tax, the lowest-income group would pay tax equal to 14 percent of income while the wealthiest families would pay consumption tax equal to 1.6 percent of income. If the tax base is narrowed to zero-rate (i.e., to remove tax on) home-prepared food, medicine, and utilities, the lowest-income group would pay tax equal to 9.3 percent of income while the tax on the highest-income group would remain almost unchanged at 1.5 percent of income.

Furthermore, in order to make up for the revenue loss by zero-rating necessities, the overall tax rate must be increased. In this case, the 10 percent rate must be increased from 10 to 13.7 percent. As a result, the net absolute impact on the poor as a result of zero-rating of necessities is small. Under a narrow-based tax, the lowest-income groups would pay tax equal to 12.8 percent of income compared to the 14 percent they would pay under a broad-based VAT that generated the same amount of revenue.

---

[8]Among the more famous examples was whether or not "Head and Shoulders" dandruff shampoo would receive preferential treatment under the French value-added tax as a health product. Another administrative nightmare was determining which food items would be subject to California's "snack tax."

[9]For example, at a donut shop in Virginia, some patrons were observed eating donuts in their cars in the parking lot rather than at the counter. This inefficient (and messy) behavior is the result of preferential treatment given under the Virginia sales tax to carryout food.

Table 8.2   Effective Tax Rates Across Income Groups of a Broad-Based VAT and of a VAT Excluding Necessities

Proposal	Adjusted Gross Income ($ thousands)							
	0–10	10–15	15–20	20–30	30–50	50–100	100–200	+200
(1) 10% Broad-Based VAT	14.0%	9.1%	7.5%	6.3%	5.1%	4.0%	3.1%	1.6%
(2) 10% VAT excluding Food, Medicine, and Utilities	9.3%	6.3%	5.3%	4.5%	3.8%	3.1%	2.6%	1.5%
(3) 13.7% VAT excluding Food, Medicine, and Utilities [equal revenue to (1)]	12.8%	8.6%	7.2%	6.2%	5.2%	4.2%	3.6%	2.1%

Source: Brashares, Spreyer, and Carlson (1988), p. 171.

Tax Credits and Transfer Payments

Another method of alleviating the regressivity of a consumption tax is to increase the availability of tax credits or transfer payments to low-income households. This type of relief from a consumption tax could take a variety of forms.

Expansion of the EITC

The earned income tax credit primarily provides refundable income tax credits to low-income working families who have children.[10] The credit was significantly expanded as part of the Omnibus Reconciliation Act of 1993. The advantage of further expanding the EITC to offset the regressivity of a consumption tax is that the administrative structure is already in place and, because it is refundable, the credit can provide benefits to families who do not pay income tax. The major shortcoming of the credit as it is currently structured is that it does not help the poor who are not working or who do not have children. There are also substantial problems for the EITC of fraudulent claims.[11]

---

[10]Under changes instituted as part of the Omnibus Reconciliation Act of 1993, some limited relief is available to working families without children.

[11]See, for example, Steuerle (1995).

Payroll Tax Credit

Allowing consumption taxes to be credited against payroll taxes is another method of alleviating regressivity. (This is a feature of the Nunn-Domenici proposal.) Currently, payroll taxes are imposed in equal amounts on employers and employees. Each pays a tax of 7.65 percent on the first $61,200 (1995 level) of wages and 1.45 on all wages above that amount. Given this rate structure, and the absence of standard deductions and personal exemptions, the payroll tax is a highly regressive tax. A payroll tax credit would be somewhat broader than the EITC because it applies to all workers regardless of family status. Moreover, the credit can provide relief without refunds for many low-income working families because the payroll tax applies to every dollar of wages while the income tax only applies after personal exemptions and deductions. If the credit is not refundable, it can avoid encountering some of the fraud problems that plague the EITC. However, a payroll tax credit does not help the poor who are unemployed. The payroll tax credit also would not alleviate the burden on certain low-income retirees who depend on small amounts of dividend and interest income.

New Broad-Based Refundable Tax Credit

An alternative to a payroll tax credit or an expansion of the EITC would be to implement a new refundable credit (or, equivalently, undertake a significant restructure of the EITC such that it applied to all low-income individuals regardless of family or employment status). Ideally, such a credit would be equal or proportional to the burden of the consumption tax on low-income households. If successful, such a program would greatly expand the administrative and compliance costs because millions of low-income households who now do not file tax returns would be required to file.

There may be a problem of insufficient participation. State experience with programs designed to provide relief from sales taxes has not generally been successful in inducing low-income individuals to file tax returns to obtain refunds.[12] Compared to a state credit, the filing rate for a national tax credit might be improved by greater public awareness (e.g., because of television) and by a larger amount of credit that might be available from a tax with a rate high enough to replace the revenues lost by the current income tax. On the other hand, there could be a problem of too much participation—that is, fraud—as there has been for the EITC.

Transfer Payments

Yet another method of alleviating the regressivity of a consumption tax would be to work entirely outside of the tax system by increasing government transfer payments to low-income households. It is important, though, to note that some government transfer payments would likely increase automatically with the imposition of a business consumption tax. This is because many existing programs automatically index their benefits for inflation. If a

---

[12]There have been some successes at the state level. See, Kuttner (1987) for discussion of New Mexico's experience with a refundable tax credit.

household receives all of its income in the form of indexed transfer payments, the household will be fully insulated from the effects of the tax (e.g., a 10 percent rise in the price level due to a 10 percent VAT will be matched by a 10 percent increase in government support). Examples of indexed transfer payments include Social Security and federal employee retirement benefits.

However, many transfer payments are not indexed for inflation, and many low-income taxpayers bearing the burden of a consumption tax may not be receiving any significant assistance from the government. Examples of transfer payments not indexed for inflation are unemployment benefits and AFDC benefits.

Upon imposition of a consumption tax, the federal government could mandate increases in nonindexed transfers to offset the impact of the tax. In addition, the government might use the revenues from a consumption tax to expand eligibility for existing programs or to fund entirely new programs. While such benefits would not be captured in standard distributional tables that only record the impacts of taxation, they would in fact offset the burden of a consumption tax.

Appendix to Chapter 8

Why Consumption Taxes May Not Be Regressive

This chapter explored the center stage of the political debate about income distribution and income taxes: how consumption taxes may be made less regressive. This Appendix examines the somewhat more academic arguments as to why consumption taxes might not be as regressive as they first appear. Although these arguments have not yet received attention in the political arena—even proponents of consumption taxes do not frequently espouse them—this is unlikely to remain the case if consumption taxes undergo thorough consideration.

A Broader View of Government Redistribution

The tax system has a major impact on the distribution of income, but so do a wide variety of government programs. Social Security, Medicare, Medicaid, Food Stamps, and Aid to Families with Dependent Children (AFDC) are just some of the federal government's spending programs that collectively amount to a massive redistribution of wealth across income groups and across generations. Some argue that it is misleading and arbitrary to focus attention on the distributional effects of the tax system without looking at the uses of government revenues as well. For example, in analyses of the "fairness" of the tax system it is common practice to include refundable earned income tax credits (Internal Revenue Code Section 32) in the distributional analysis, but AFDC payments (not in the Code)—though in many ways functionally equivalent—are not included. Certainly one's views about the appropriateness of a heavy tax burden on the poor should take into account the use of those revenues. A greater tax burden on low-income households may be more tolerable if those revenues are used to provide food, medical care, and education to the poor. Nevertheless, the notion of including both taxes *and transfers* in distributional analyses has received remarkably little attention.

Economic Growth

Changes in tax law simultaneously may affect the overall *amount* of national income as well as its *distribution*. In its official distributional analyses, the federal government generally holds economic growth constant. (The main reason for this is that there is a great deal of dispute and uncertainty about the impact of taxes on the overall economy.) Thus, government distribution analyses assume tax policy is a zero-sum game.

Despite the difficulties with precise quantification, most economists acknowledge that a replacement consumption tax will increase economic growth—particularly in the long run. Many would consider it particularly misleading to assume economic growth will be unaffected in a distributional analysis of a replacement consumption tax. Even if the *relative* burden of some income groups increases, it may be possible for all income groups to be better off if all incomes rise sufficiently.

Incidence

It is critical to recognize that the burden or "incidence" of a tax is not always on those writing checks to the government. For example, there is much dispute about whether the burden of the corporate income tax is borne by shareholders of corporations. To some degree the burden may be shared by the owners of all businesses (because rates of return are driven lower), by business customers (because prices rise), or by employees (because wages fall) as a result of the tax.

In the case of consumption taxes, the general consensus among economists is that the tax is passed forward to consumers in the form of higher prices. There is one important caveat, however. If the Federal Reserve does not "accommodate" the introduction of a consumption tax with an increase in the money supply, it is unlikely prices can rise.[13] In this case, economists believe the burden of the tax would be passed backward to employees in the form of lower wages. If this were to occur, consumption taxes would still be regressive because wages account for a larger percentage of income among low-income households than high-income households. Still, there is an important difference between a consumption tax that increases prices and a consumption tax that would reduce wages: The nonworking poor who did not receive government support indexed to inflation would bear a considerably lower diminished burden under a consumption tax that resulted in lower wages. Thus, there must always be much uncertainty about how the burden would be shared among low-income households because it depends so much on the actions of an independent Federal Reserve.

It is also important to note that the substantial uncertainty about the incidence of the corporate income tax can have a large impact on the consumption tax debate. Almost all major consumption tax proposals call for elimination of the corporate income tax. If the burden of this tax is perceived to be on capital, it is a progressive tax. This is the current view of the Treasury Department.[14] On the other hand, some commentators believe the burden of the corporation is passed along—at least partially—to the consumer in

---

[13]One of the less controversial propositions of macroeconomics is that changes in the money supply are highly correlated with changes in the price level.

[14]See, for example, Toder (1995).

the form of higher prices. The more the corporate income tax is considered progressive, the more difficult it will be for new consumption tax proposals to maintain distributional neutrality to current law.[15]

Redefining Regressivity

Perhaps the notion that is most damaging to the idea that consumption taxes are regressive is recognition that fairness should not be evaluated by comparing taxes paid as a percentage of annual income. The problem with using annual income as a measure of economic well-being is that many households with low annual incomes are not really poor. Many individuals with significant wealth earn relatively little current income. Sometimes this is due to transitions in and out of the workforce (e.g., career switching, child rearing, temporary layoffs). In other cases, relatively well-off individuals may earn low incomes because they have not yet entered the workforce (e.g., graduate students) or they have retired. Trying to alleviate the burden of these individuals should not receive the same priority as families with similar incomes and no wealth, but this type of distinction is not often made in distribution analyses.

It is sometimes advocated that annual consumption rather than annual income is a better measure of economic well-being. Some argue that each individual should be taxed on consumption rather than on income because income is what one "puts into" the economy while consumption is what one "takes out." The more accepted argument is that wealth or lifetime income are better measures of economic well-being than annual income, and consumption is a good proxy for measuring wealth or lifetime income.[16] Although there is some dissent, the notion that lifetime income is a better approximation of economic well-being has wide acceptance by economists. The major issue is not so much with the concept but with the practical application of the concept. It is much more difficult to measure lifetime income than annual income.

Despite considerable uncertainty about the details, there is little doubt that any movement away from annual income and toward lifetime income as a measure of economic well-being will make consumption taxes appear considerably less regressive.

---

[15]Uncertainty about the incidence of the corporate income tax has caused congressional analysts to simply exclude the tax from its distributional analysis. For a review of issues surrounding official distribution analysis, see Sullivan (1995).

[16]Most economists accept the notion that—in general—changes in consumption are highly correlated with changes in wealth or lifetime income. On the other hand, annual income varies considerably from year to year and is not as closely related to wealth.

The Impact of Consumption Taxes on Business: Some Basics

Summary

- In order to assess the impact of a replacement consumption tax, businesses should take into account:
  - Tax liability under a consumption tax (over several years)
  - Potential changes in the economy
  - Potential elimination of current tax preferences
  - Transition provisions
  - Changing impacts over the business cycle
  - The impact on financial statements

- The corporate income tax is a tax on a small slice of business income: Only income from equity-financed capital in corporate form is subject to tax. In contrast, a value-added tax is a tax on income from both debt and equity—and it taxes the capital income generated by partnerships, Subchapter S corporations, and sole proprietorships as well as corporations.

- More importantly, a value-added tax is also a tax on all wages paid by business to employees. For most businesses, total wages and benefits are many times larger than total interest, dividends, and retained earnings.

- Most value-added taxes provide substantial relief for firms that export and for firms with large new investment in plant and equipment.

- Nevertheless, on net, the value-added tax base is many times larger than the income tax base for most firms. Whether or not a business has a lower tax liability under a replacement VAT depends on whether rates can be sufficiently reduced to offset the increased tax burden due to base broadening.

For economists it is all very simple. Businesses should not be greatly concerned about their tax liability under a consumption tax. Once the economy has fully adjusted to the imposition of a consumption tax, there will be no burden on business. In response to a consumption tax, prices will rise and the burden will be passed forward to customers in higher prices. There is no adverse effect on after-tax profits.

Businesses, however, are not so sure. The abstractions of economists—the "market forces" that make pricing adjustments—are the everyday reality faced by business. Businesses cannot take for granted that consumption taxes can be automatically passed forward in the form of higher prices without any adverse impact on their sales or market share. Therefore, businesses want to know (1) whether they pay more or less tax under a consumption tax than an income tax and (2) the relative burden of each consumption tax. Politicians, in turn, also wish to determine these impacts in order to ascertain political support and opposition to various plans.

It is inevitable that current consumption tax proposals will be revised and many new consumption proposals will introduced. At this stage in the process, it is probably more important for businesses to grasp concepts rather than details about how consumption taxes can affect businesses. Unfortunately, the instincts of experts schooled in income taxation are not particularly helpful under the proposed new regimes. This chapter tries to help readers become familiar with the new issues that businesses may confront under a consumption tax.

The analysis is divided into five parts. Part A focuses on the impact of tax changes on tax liability—that is, the actual amount of taxes paid. Part B focuses on the impact of changes in the economy that might result from imposition of a replacement consumption tax. Part C discusses the impact of the elimination of tax preferences. Part D examines certain issues that arise in the transition from an income to a consumption tax. And Part E looks at how consumption taxes and income taxes differ in their treatment of business over the business cycle and over the firm's own life cycle.

Direct Impacts on Business Tax Liability

Retail Sales Tax

Under a national sales tax, only retail businesses collect taxes. Therefore, if all income taxes were repealed, businesses without retail sales would entirely escape tax liability (along with approximately 130 million individual tax filers). Retailers would bear the bulk of the burden in terms of compliance costs as well as actual liability.

Individual Consumption Tax

Under an individual consumption tax, only individuals pay tax. If all income taxes are repealed, businesses would be entirely exempt from tax. Moreover, there would be no direct impact on prices because businesses would not have any tax burden to pass on to consumers in the form of higher prices.

Value-Added Taxes

Unlike gross receipts (the base of the sales tax) or profits (the base of business income taxes), value added is not a concept that is routinely encountered by tax professionals in the United States. Nor is the concept of value added included on financial statements. Therefore, the impact of a replacement value-added tax on a business's tax liability usually cannot be easily determined. The income tax base and a value-added tax base are vastly different. The major differences are summarized in Table 9.1. (Question marks indicate that not all major consumption taxes have that particular feature.)

Table 9.1   Comparison of a VAT to an Income Tax

Major Advantages of a VAT

1. Expensing of Capital Purchases
2. Exemption of Exports from Taxable Receipts (?)
3. Foreign Subsidiaries Exempt from Tax
4. Lower Rate (?)
5. Payroll Tax Credit (?)

Major Disadvantages of a VAT

1. Interest Not Deductible
2. Wages Not Deductible (?)
3. Fringe Benefits Not Deductible
4. Import Duty (?)
5. Noncorporate Business Subject to Business Tax
6. Local Taxes Not Deductible (?)
7. Tax Credits and Other Tax Benefits Repealed (?)

With all of these major changes—some major benefits, some major drawbacks—it is nearly impossible to know which businesses would be hurt and which would benefit by a switch to a value-added tax without detailed analysis.

To begin the comparison of business tax liability under income and value-added taxes, this section examines a purely domestic firm, that is, a firm with no overseas operations and no international transactions. For the moment also, the all-important issue of tax rates will be put aside in order to focus on differences between income and consumption tax bases.

The Nondeductibility of Interest and Wages

Unlike the income tax, a value-added tax does not include any deductions for wages or for interest expenses. As illustrated in Table 9.2, these changes from current law unambiguously broaden the business tax base.

Table 9.2   Example of the Impact of Nondeductibility of Wages and Interest on the Tax Base

Income Tax			Subtraction VAT		
Sales		100	Sales		100
Purchases	50		Purchases	50	
Depreciation	15		Depreciation	15	
Wages	25				
Interest	3				
Total Costs		93	Total Costs		65
Profit		7	Value-Added[1]		35

For many leveraged firms, the loss of interest deductions could be a major setback.[2] In general, however, the loss of deduction for wages and fringe benefits will have a much larger impact. The significance of the loss of the deduction for wages and fringe benefits can hardly be overemphasized. Even for the most capital-intensive firms, wages are usually many times larger than total profits. In the example, the value-added tax base is five times larger than the income tax base. This broadening of the tax base is primarily attributable to the nondeductibility of wages. As shall be seen in Chapter 12, when actual data for the U.S. economy are examined, changes in the tax base of this order of magnitude are not uncommon. In fact, for most firms they are likely to be larger.

The Temporary and Permanent Benefits of Expensing

The previous example neglected one important benefit that is common to all current VAT proposals: In lieu of deductions for capital recovery, businesses will be allowed to expense capital purchases. Expensing provides a significant benefit from newly purchased capital. The acceleration of capital recovery to the first year provides a tax benefit that is (under reasonable conditions) approximately equivalent to tax exemption for all income generated by the capital being expensed.

In the context of the income tax, expensing provides enormous benefits. Newly purchased capital is effectively exempt from the tax. Moreover, if newly purchased capital is financed with debt, the combination of the deduction for interest and newly purchased capital can easily generate more

---

[1]In this example, value-added is calculated using the income method, that is, capital costs are recovered over time rather than expensed. All current proposals for a value-added tax allow expensing so that the tax is a consumption tax. (See the Appendix to Chapter 3 for further discussion of why expensing makes a value-added tax a consumption tax.) Expensing is discussed in the subsection that immediately follows.

[2]In 1992, for example, corporations had taxable income of approximately $570 billion and interest deductions of approximately $597 billion. See *Statistics of Income Bulletin*, Fall (1994), p. 181. Thus, for the corporate sector as a whole, loss of the interest deduction would approximately double the tax base.

deductions than income. In this case, effective tax rates on new capital are driven below zero, that is, the purchase of new capital is not only exempt from tax, it generates deductions that may be used to shelter other income.

In the context of the value-added tax, however, the benefit of expensing—while significant—is not so dominant. As under the income tax, expensing effectively exempts the income from new capital. For highly leveraged firms, however, interest deductibility provided near total exemption from the income tax. For these firms, the loss of interest deductibility by itself may entirely offset any benefit from expensing. Nevertheless, the loss of deductions for wages is far more important. Because income from capital is a relatively small component of total value added for most firms, the favorable impact of expensing on a firm's tax liability in almost all cases will be more than completely offset by the inclusion of labor costs in the tax base.

Permanent Effects Although usually small compared to wage costs, the impact of expensing is still important. In order to better understand them, it is useful to distinguish permanent effects from temporary effects. Over the long term, the benefit of expensing amounts to the replacement of a depreciation deduction by a deduction for new capital purchases. On average, it can be expected that a deduction for expensing will be somewhat larger than a deduction for depreciation. For example, if a firm grows at a rate of 5 percent annually and writes off its capital over ten years (using the straight-line method), it will have an expensing deduction approximately 33 percent larger than its depreciation deduction. For the economy as a whole, the National Income and Product Accounts published by the Commerce Department indicate new capital expenditures are approximately 45 percent larger than economic depreciation.[3] Changes of this order of magnitude are illustrated in Table 9.3

Table 9.3   Example of the Impact of Expensing on the VAT Base

Subtraction VAT (income method)			Subtraction VAT (consumption method)		
Sales		100	Sales		100
Purchases	50		Purchases	50	
Depreciation	15		Expensing	20	
Total Costs		65	Total Costs		70
Value Added[4]		35	Value-Added[5]		30

---

[3]Economic Report of the President (1995).

[4]In this example, value added is calculated using the income method; that is, capital costs are recovered over time rather than expensed. All current proposals for a value-added tax allow expensing so that the tax is a consumption tax. (See the Appendix to Chapter 3 for further discussion of why expensing makes a value-added tax a consumption tax.)

[5]In this example, value added is calculated using the consumption method, that is, capital costs are expensed.

Temporary Impacts A larger impact of a switch from depreciation to expensing occurs in the short term while taxpayers are able to deduct depreciation of existing capital in addition to expensing new capital purchases. (There is some issue as to whether these transition deductions should be allowed or modified, but almost all proposals currently under consideration provide such relief.) Over time, of course, these effects become increasingly less important.

Because of these types of timing issues, commonly employed snap-shot cash flow analyses of changes in tax liability due to a replacement VAT can be misleading—particularly for capital-intensive firms. Consider the stylized example in Table 9.4, where a highly capital-intensive business that is not growing has 100 each of income, capital purchases, and depreciation (straight-line over 10 years) annually.

Table 9.4   Example of Differences in VAT Liability During and After Transition

	Current Law	VAT Year 1	VAT Year 5	VAT Year 10
Sales	100	100	100	100
Less				
Purchases	(80)	(80)	(80)	(80)
Depreciation	(10)	(9)	(5)	0
Expensing	0	(10)	(10)	(10)
Interest	(5)	0	0	0
Tax Base	5	1	5	10

Under the current income tax, this business can deduct depreciation and interest expense. Under a subtraction-method VAT, the business can expense new capital purchases and—during the transition—depreciation on capital in place prior to the effective date of the new consumption tax. At the beginning of the transition period, the loss of interest deductions is offset by the ability to expense combined with deductibility of transition depreciation. This advantage dissipates over time as older capital is discarded. In this example, by year 10, depreciation allowances for existing capital are no longer available and—on a cash flow basis—the taxpayer has a larger tax base than under the income tax.

Impact of a Replacement VAT on International Business

There are three major impacts of a value-added tax on international business: (1) the exclusion of exports from the tax base, (2) the taxation of imports, and (3) the exemption of foreign subsidiaries and branches of U.S. businesses from U.S. tax. As noted in Chapter 7, the exclusion of exports and the taxation of imports—the so-called *border tax adjustments*—are necessary to effect the destination principle. Under the destination principle, final goods and services are taxed where they are consumed, not where they are produced. With one very notable exception—the Armey Flat Tax—almost all consumption taxes are administered in a manner consistent with the destination principle.

Exports The exclusion of exports from taxable gross receipts can have enormous impacts on some firms' tax liability. This is illustrated in the example in Table 9.5.

Table 9.5   Examples of the Importance of Exports on VAT Liability

	Export-Intensity		
	No Exports	Average	Above Average
A. Corporate Income Tax			
Domestic Receipts	1000	950	600
Exports	0	50	400
Total Receipts	1000	1000	1000
Less			
Purchases	(500)	(500)	(500)
Wages	(300)	(300)	(300)
Depreciation	(100)	(100)	(100)
	(900)	(900)	(900)
Taxable Income	100	100	100
Corp. Tax @35%	35	35	35
B. Value-Added Tax			
Domestic Receipts	1000	950	600
Less			
Purchases	(500)	(500)	(500)
Depreciation	(50)	(50)	(50)
Expensing	(100)	(100)	(100)
	(650)	(650)	(650)
Value-Added	350	300	-50
VAT @20%	70	60	-10

Imports Import duties imposed under consumption taxes unambiguously increase business tax liabilities. Obviously, greater reliance on imports results in greater tax, as illustrated in the example in Table 9.6.

Table 9.6   Example of the Importance of Imports on VAT Liability

	Import-Intensity		
	No Imports	Average	Above Average
A. Corporate Income Tax			
Receipts	1000	1000	1000
Purchases			
Domestic	(500)	(450)	(300)
Imports	0	(50)	(200)
Less			
Wages	(300)	(300)	(300)
Depreciation	(100)	(100)	(100)
	(900)	(900)	(900)
Taxable Income	100	100	100
Corp. Tax @35%	35	35	35
B. Value-Added Tax			
Receipts	1000	1000	1000
Less			
Purchases			
Domestic	(500)	(450)	(300)
Imports	(0)	(50)	(200)
Depreciation	(50)	(50)	(50)
Expensing	(100)	(100)	(100)
	(650)	(650)	(650)
Value-Added	350	350	350
Plus Imports	0	50	200
VAT Base	350	400	550
VAT @20%	70	80	110

It is important to stress here that the burden of an import duty need not be direct. For example, clothing manufactured abroad may result in higher costs for clothing retailers even when retailers purchase their products from wholesalers who do the importing. It is also important not to examine the impacts of the import tax in isolation. Import prices indeed may rise, but it is also possible (as claimed by economists) that the cost of domestically produced goods is likely to rise commensurately. If this is the case, importers should expect increases in costs, but they should not feel singled out—or necessarily expect any advantages of switching to domestic suppliers.

Exemption of Foreign Subsidiaries All consumption tax proposals exempt foreign subsidiaries and branches of U.S. businesses from tax. (This is known as a *territorial* tax system.) Under the current system, U.S. businesses are subject to tax on their worldwide income. However, it is standard practice among nations to give host countries primary tax jurisdiction over multinationals operating outside their home country. The United States grants U.S. multinational corporations a tax credit for taxes paid. U.S. firms can incur U.S. tax liability on their foreign-source income only if the average tax rate on foreign-source income is below the U.S. rate. Although there are numerous exceptions, the vast majority of foreign-source income is subject to relatively little U.S. tax.[6]

For most firms, the change in tax liability resulting from a switch from the current system (taxation of worldwide income with foreign tax credits) to a territorial system will not result in enormous changes in tax liability. However, tax compliance and international tax planning will be vastly simplified. (This is true, of course, only with regard to U.S. federal income tax. Businesses still have to contend with numerous issues that result from income taxes imposed by state as well as foreign governments.)

There are at least three areas where tax considerations will be changed dramatically under a territorial system:

First, there are location decisions. Under current U.S. tax law, it is highly advantageous for U.S. multinational corporations to "average" income from a high-tax jurisdiction (like Germany) with income from a low-tax jurisdiction (like Ireland). Thus, under the current system, a U.S. multinational corporation with an existing facility in Germany can reap substantial benefits by opening a second facility in Ireland. Conversely, a U.S. multinational with a single facility in Ireland will not necessarily bear the full burden of high German tax rates if a second facility is opened in Germany. Real-world fact patterns are more complex, but the net result is that current tax considerations in location decisions must take into account the interaction of new taxes on the existing web of U.S. liabilities. Under a territorial system, the net tax burden of locating in a jurisdiction will depend only on the tax rate in that jurisdiction.

On net, one would expect a switch in the composition of investment away from high-tax countries to low-tax countries. Currently, the effective tax rate on investment in low-tax countries is somewhere between the foreign tax rate and U.S. tax rate. Under a territorial system, the effective rate of tax would be the foreign rate. This would encourage investment in low-tax countries. Currently, the effective tax rate in high-tax countries is somewhere between the high foreign tax rate and the U.S. tax rate. Under a territorial system, the rate of tax would be the high foreign rate. This would discourage investment in high-tax countries.

---

[6]Obviously, the whole system of U.S. tax treaties—based on U.S. *worldwide* corporate and individual *income* taxation—would have to be thoroughly reexamined if the U.S. system were replaced with a *territorial, consumption* tax.

Second, there is the issue of repatriation. Under current U.S. law, profits of overseas subsidiaries are taxable only when subsidiaries pay dividends to their U.S. parent or when subsidiaries become subject to any of a number of complex antideferral rules. Under a replacement VAT, antideferral rules would be eliminated. Moreover, the timing of repatriation of profits would not be an issue because this would no longer be a taxable event.

Finally, for both U.S. multinational corporations operating abroad and foreign multinationals operating in the United States, transfer pricing would no longer be an issue for federal tax purposes. This follows not from the tax being territorial, but is the result of border tax adjustments.[7] When a foreign multinational imports from a related corporation, U.S. tax must be paid on the import price, but reducing the import price only commensurately increases U.S. tax (by reducing deductions for purchased inputs). So the total tax on a foreign multinational is unaffected by how prices are set by related parties. Similarly, there is no advantage to manipulating export prices because gross receipts are entirely exempt from tax in any case. The example in Table 9.7 shows the tax liability of a dealer importing television sets from a related manufacturer at $125 and $150. In both cases, total U.S. tax liability is the same.

Table 9.7   Example of the Irrelevance of Transfer Prices for a Border-Adjustable VAT

A. High Transfer Price		B. Low Transfer Price	
Gross Receipts	200	Gross Receipts	200
Cost of Imports	(150)	Cost of Imports	(125)
Value-Added	50	Value-Added	75
VAT @10%	5	VAT @10%	7.5
Import Duty @10%	15	Import Duty @10%	12.5
Total U.S. Tax	20	Total U.S. Tax	20

Impact of a Replacement VAT on Noncorporate Business

Under a replacement VAT, all businesses—including Subchapter S corporations, partnerships, sole proprietorships as well as other passthrough entities—would be subject to tax. If VAT revenues were used solely to replace the corporate income tax, the new tax would undoubtedly represent a major new burden for noncorporate businesses—particularly service businesses with few inputs other than labor.

---

[7]Because there are no border tax adjustments under the Armey Flat Tax, there would still be incentive to manipulate transfer prices. However, the nature of these incentives may be different than under the prevailing 35 percent corporate income tax. Because of the low rate of tax under the Armey plan (17 percent, after a transition period), there would generally be an incentive (except in the case of transactions with related companies operating in tax havens with accumulated net operating losses) to set transfer prices of exports high and transfer prices of imports low.

Most consumption tax proposals, however, usually include individual and payroll tax relief as well. In these cases, it is not always clear whether a replacement consumption tax will hurt noncorporate business. Under many reasonable scenarios, it is possible for owners of noncorporate business to be better off under a replacement consumption tax. For example, in a system that repealed the current individual and corporate income tax system and replaced it with a 25 percent VAT (and assuming no changes in payroll taxes), a sole proprietorship with $1 million of wage and profits paid to its owner would incur $250,000 of tax liability (and no individual tax) under the VAT but would pay well over $300,000 of individual income tax under current law.

The treatment of noncorporate businesses highlights the importance of looking at changes to the taxation of individual as well as businesses per se. The impact of the total (i.e., both entity and individual) tax impact on noncorporate businesses will be examined more closely in the following chapters after the details of both the individual and business tax components of new consumption tax proposals have been discussed.

Tax Rates

It is easy to get lost in technicalities and forget about the important, but simple, details. Obviously, the rate of consumption tax is critical. What rate is reasonable to expect? There are several possible answers, and they are all over the lot.

Early press reports about the Nunn-Domenici Tax indicated the rate of tax for the plan's business subtraction-method VAT could be as low as 9 percent. Its rate on introduction was 11 percent. (The Nunn-Domenici plan also includes an individual consumption tax with rates as high as 40 percent.[8])

The Armey Flat Tax has a rate of 17 percent (after a transition period with a rate of 19 percent). The Armey legislation, however, also includes substantial controls on government spending. So the tax provisions by themselves are not revenue neutral. The Department of the Treasury has estimated that a revenue-neutral rate for the Armey plan would be approximately 24 percent.

As indicated earlier, a broad-based VAT would have required a rate of 25 percent to make up revenues for repealing both the individual and corporate income tax. If payroll taxes were also repealed, the rate would have to be about 33 percent. If preferential treatment were granted, rates could even be higher.

In summary, legislation introduced to date has used rates far below the current 35percent corporate rate. However, as seen from Table 9.8, anything is possible.[9] The table shows that replacing revenues lost due to the repeal of the individual income tax would require imposition of a VAT with a rate of 19.5 percent. Replacing the corporate income tax would add 4.2 percent to the VAT rate. And replacing the payroll taxes would add 15.6 percent to the VAT rate. To *totally* replace the current tax system would require a consumption tax rate in excess of 40 percent. This does not include higher rates that might be required to account for any permanent or transitional relief.

---

[8]The rate as high as 40 percent starts at $24,000 or less.

[9]Data are from Congressional Budget Office (1995), pp. 332 and 393.

**Table 9.8   Tax Rates Required to Raise Revenue
Sufficient to Replace Current U.S. Taxes**

	Year 2000 ($Billions) Revenue	Replacement VAT Rate	Cumulative Increase in VAT Rate
5% Broad-Based VAT	$198.3	5.0%	–
Individual Income Tax	$772	19.5%	19.5%
Corporate Income Tax	$167	4.2%	23.7%
Business Payroll Tax	$309	7.8%	31.5%
Individual Payroll Tax	$309	7.8%	39.3%
Estate and Gift Tax	$ 20	0.5%	39.8%
Excise Taxes	$ 59	1.5%	41.3%

Indirect Impact on Business Through Economic Changes

Can Economic Benefits Be Realized?

The most-cited reason for enacting a replacement consumption tax is its overall positive impact on economic growth. The underlying economic reasoning is basically this: The replacement of an income tax with a consumption tax increases the after-tax return to saving and removes the penalty income taxes impose on saving. To the extent this increase in after-tax returns increases saving, it is likely that interest rates will drop and domestic capital formation will increase. Increases in domestic capital formation means that workers will have more capital to work with and be more productive. In the long run, this means a higher standard of living and a larger economy. The potential economic changes that might result from a replacement consumption tax are listed in Table 9.9.

**Table 9.9   Summary of Potential Macroeconomic Effects
of a Replacement Consumption Tax**

- Increased Saving
- Reduced Consumer Spending
- Reduced (before tax) Interest Rates
- Increased Capital Formation
- Increased Overall Long-Term Growth
- Higher Prices (short term)

Despite the widespread acceptance in political circles of the need for tax change, the reasoning is hardly iron-clad. First, the numerous tax incentives for saving and investment already in the current income tax code leave some question as to whether the switch from the current system (which many economists characterize as a "hybrid income-consumption tax") to a pure consumption tax will really have that large an impact on the overall cost of new capital. Second, increased domestic saving may just be used to fund overseas investment that would have little impact on domestic capital formation and growth. Third, interest rates may be more influenced by the flow of international capital than domestic savings so interest rates may not be significantly impacted by changes in domestic saving.

These potential shortcomings in the economic reasoning in favor of consumption taxes are overshadowed by the central question of whether these changes in the after-tax return induced by saving have any impact on saving at all. This was discussed in some detail in Chapter 6. After decades of analysis and debate, it seems fair to say that no consensus has emerged in the economics profession as to the impact of a replacement consumption tax on saving. If there is a large impact on saving, then it is likely that interest rates will drop, domestic capital formation will increase, and productivity, wages, and the size of the overall economy will all increase. If there is no significant impact on saving, there will be little impact on saving, interest rates, productivity, wages, and economic growth.

Uncertainty for Business Planners

The problem for business planning is that either scenario is possible. Predictions are precarious because they depend on empirical economic analyses that are subject to dispute. Models used by economists are simply not reliable. Moreover, there is often a remarkable consistency between an economist's political views and the results of his or her economic analysis.[10] Despite the conviction of many economists as to the impact of a consumption tax, it seems fair to say economic modeling has not sufficiently advanced to predict results with any degree of certainty, and that the analysis using existing models is inconclusive.[11]

It will be important for businesses to sort through ideologically charged debate in order to ascertain the most likely economic impacts of a consumption tax. Businesses cannot rule out the possibility that, as a result of enactment of a replacement consumption tax, overall business conditions might sufficiently improve so as to offset any negative effects of increased tax liability. Business also cannot rule out that there will not be any perceptible effects of macroeconomic conditions as a result of the changes.

This is particularly difficult for businesses operating in sectors sensitive to changes in the macroeconomy. For example, financial service businesses may be more concerned about the impact of a consumption tax on their products than on direct tax liability. Firms that specialize in lending may be

---

[10]For example, it is quite common for economists of liberal persuasion to argue that saving and investment are unresponsive to changes in taxes while at the same time quite common for conservative economists to believe that saving and investment are responsive to tax changes.

[11]The United States has had extensive experience with the investment tax credit since its original enactment in 1962 until its repeal in 1986. Although there have been hundreds of studies of the impact of the investment tax credit, there is no consensus in the economics profession about the impact of the credit on investment.

concerned about the new level playing field for debt and equity financing. Retailers may be concerned about declines in consumption and the higher cost of imports. Construction firms and manufacturers of consumer durables may benefit from lower pretax rates of interest.

Impact from Loss of Tax-Advantaged Treatment

Although the Tax Reform Act of 1986 reduced or eliminated numerous special-interest provisions, many remain. Their annual dollar value totals in the hundreds of billions.[12] Their elimination would have a large impact on certain businesses—either directly on tax liability or indirectly through the impact on customers and suppliers.

Most consumption tax proposals currently under consideration eliminate numerous special tax benefits (known as *tax expenditures*) available under existing law. To many businesses, preferential treatment under current law can provide significant benefits, and each business's overall appraisal of a new consumption tax may be dependent on whether preferential treatment is maintained under the new system. To help sort out some of these issues, it is useful to divide current tax expenditures into two categories.

Obsolete Tax Expenditures

First, there are those tax rules that provide treatment that is considered preferential under an income tax but would become standard under a consumption tax. For example, interest on most municipal bonds is exempt from tax under current law, and this is considered a major tax benefit. Under a consumption tax, all interest income would be exempt (or provide tax treatment that is largely equivalent to exemption). Thus, under a consumption tax municipal bond interest would continue to be tax-free but this would no longer be considered a tax benefit. This type of tax expenditure can be called an *obsolete tax expenditure*. A list of tax expenditures whose status would no longer be special is provided in Table 9.10. Most of these tax benefits are made obsolete by the elimination of tax on income from capital under a consumption tax. Some tax expenditures relating to international taxation, however, would no longer be tax benefit items because under a standard consumption tax exports are exempt from tax and because all foreign-source income would be exempt from tax.

Prior beneficiaries of tax expenditures made obsolete by a consumption tax may be hurt by the change even though they receive the same tax benefits under the new tax. This would happen because *relative* advantages have been eliminated by a consumption tax. For example, under current law, many products offered by life insurance companies provide unique tax advantages not available from products provided by banks and other financial firms. Elimination of these special provisions can impact businesses by eliminating competitive advantages.

---

[12]See, for example, United States Senate, Committee on the Budget (1992).

Table 9.10   Obsolete Tax Expenditures: Examples of Current Tax Preferences Eliminated Because They (or Their Equivalent) Are Automatically Provided Under a Consumption Tax

1. Exclusion of Employer Pension Contribution and Earnings
2. Stepup Basis on Capital Gains at Death
3. Accelerated Depreciation
4. Deferral of Capital Gains on Home Sales
5. Exclusion of Interest on State and Local Debt
6. Exclusion of Interest on Life Insurance Saving
7. Preferential Treatment of Capital Gains
8. Exception from the Passive Loss Rules for $25,000 of Rental Loss
9. Net Exclusion of Individual Retirement Account Contributions
10. Exclusion of Capital Gains on Home Sales for Persons Over the Age of 55
11. Possessions Tax Credit
12. Expensing of R&D
13. ESOP Benefits
14. Deferral of Unrepatriated Foreign Source Income
15. Expensing for Certain Small Investments
16. Exclusion of Income of Foreign Sales Corporations
17. Favorable Source Rules for Exported Goods
18. Deferral of Interest on Savings Bonds
19. Deferral of Income on Installment Sales
20. Exclusion of Income Earned Abroad by U.S. Citizens
21. Expensing of Multiperiod Timber Growing Costs
22. Deferral of Gains from Sales of Broadcasting Facilities to Minority-Owned Business
23. Special Rules for Allocation of Research Expenditures
24. Expensing of Exploration and Development Costs

It is still possible to restore these items to situations of relative tax advantage by providing them with even greater benefits than they receive under current law. It seems likely that there will be political pressures to retain preferential treatment for certain types of investments under a consumption tax. For example, under the consumption tax proposed by Senators Nunn and Domenici, interest on municipal bonds would remain tax exempt even though the purchase price of these bonds is deductible. Retaining this preferential treatment may solve some political difficulties, but it leaves the new consumption tax with the same economic distortions and administrative costs as current law.

Consumption Tax Expenditures

Second, there are tax benefits that could still be considered tax benefits after a switch to a consumption tax. For example, tax credits for research expenditures are equally viable under a consumption tax and an income tax. These types of tax expenditures can be called *consumption tax expenditures*, and they are listed in Table 9.11.

While obsolete tax expenditures are in effect automatically repealed by a replacement consumption tax, there is no mechanical linkage between a replacement consumption tax and repeal of consumption tax expenditures. For example, with regard to the research credit, all of the policy reasons for enactment of the credit remain intact under a consumption tax. Current rules for the research credit could remain largely unchanged. The only difference is that the credit would be used to reduce consumption rather than income taxes.[13]

In general, it will probably be more difficult for Congress to eliminate consumption tax expenditures than those made obsolete by replacement of income tax with a consumption tax. These tax provisions would not be eliminated out of logical necessity, but in the spirit of tax reform. As noted in Chapter 1, except for the political dynamics, there is no particular reason to link the switch from an income tax to a consumption tax with elimination of these preferences. Nevertheless, most consumption tax proposals call for the elimination of most tax preferences. (At one extreme, the Armey Flat Tax proposal repeals all special-interest provisions.)

In all cases, businesses will want to carefully peruse these lists in order to determine which tax expenditures are of importance to their own tax liabilities as well as those of their customers, suppliers, and employees.

Transition Treatment

Although they often sound like nothing more than nebulous technicalities, the tax rules that govern the transition from an income tax to a new consumption tax can be of critical importance to some businesses.

In the context of income tax legislation, "transition relief" has often been a euphemism for exceptions that postpone or otherwise mitigate adverse tax changes. These rules have served more to lubricate the political process rather than to address inconsistencies in the tax law. In contrast, special rules during a transition from an income tax to a consumption tax often are necessary to prevent retroactive tax *increases* on existing business operations. In many cases, the absence of special transition rules can result in businesses being haphazardly subject to tax penalties. These tax burdens serve no policy or political objective (except by dumb luck). In many cases, the incongruities between an income and consumption tax result in double taxation of income from business operations set in motion long before enactment.

---

[13]Because of differences in the tax base, there would be a difference in the utilization of tax credits. Because almost all firms, including startups, are taxable under a VAT, most firms would be able to use their credits immediately and would make little use of carryforward provisions.

**Table 9.11   Consumption Tax Expenditures: Current Tax
Preferences that Could Survive the Transition
from Consumption to Income Tax**

1. Exclusion of Employer Contributions for Medical Insurance Premiums and Medical Care
2. Deductibility of Mortgage Interest on Owner-Occupied Homes
3. Deductibility of State and Local Taxes
4. Deductibility of Charitable Contributions
5. Exclusion of Social Security Benefits for Retired Workers
6. Earned Income Credit
7. Credit for Child and Dependent Care Expenses
8. Low-Income Housing Credit
9. Exclusion of Benefits for Armed Forces Personnel
10. Exclusion of Employer Provided Parking
11. Exclusion of Veterans Disability Compensation
12. Exclusion of Social Security Disability Benefits
13. Additional Deduction for the Elderly
14. Percentage Depletion
15. R&E Credit
16. Alternative Fuel Production Credit
17. Exclusion of Scholarship and Fellowship Income
18. Exclusion of Employer Provided Child Care
19. Exclusion of Public Assistance Benefits
20. Exclusion of Employee Meals and Lodging
21. Parental Personal Exemption for Students Age 19 and Over
22. Exclusion of Railroad Retirement System Benefits
23. Targeted Jobs Credit
24. Exemption of Credit Union Income
25. Empowerment Zones
26. Exclusion of Parsonages Allowances
27. Special Rules for Allocation of Research Expenditures
28. Deductibility of Casualty Losses
29. Credit for Disable Access Expenditures
30. Exclusion from Income of Conservation Subsidies Provided by Public Utilities
31. Exclusion of Employer Premiums on Accident and Disability Insurance
32. Small Life Insurance Company Deduction
33. Exclusion of Military Disability Pensions
34. Special Blue Cross/Blue Shield Deduction
35. Tax Incentives for Preservation of Historic Structures

Table 9.11   Consumption Tax Expenditures: Current Tax Preferences that Could Survive the Transition from Consumption to Income Tax (continued)

36. Cancellation of Indebtedness

37. Tax Exemption for Certain Insurance Companies

38. Exclusion of Special Benefits for Disabled Coal Miners

39. Exclusion of Employer Provided Educational Assistance

40. Investment Credit for Rehabilitation of Structures

41. Exclusion of Veterans Pensions

42. Expending of Certain Agricultural Outlays

43. Exclusion of GI Bill Benefits

44. New Technology Credit

45. Tax Credit for Elderly and Disabled

46. Special Rules for Mining Reclamation Reserves

47. Tax Credit and Deduction for Clean-Burning Fuels

There is no doubt that transition relief makes a replacement consumption tax more complex. During the transition, taxpayers may have to keep records to comply with rules relating to both the old and new tax regimes. Therefore, even if the new tax system will ultimately be more simple than current law, during the transition it may be more complicated. Most consumption tax proposals have at least *some* transition relief. The major impediment to more complete transition relief is the steep revenue cost. To pay for transition provisions, most tax plans that include them must have higher tax rates during the transition period. Because of the added complexity and revenue cost, at least one prominent Member of Congress[14] has advocated a cold-turkey approach, that is, no transition relief for the switch from an income tax to a consumption tax.

Depreciation

The importance of transition depreciation deductions has already been noted in Chapter 3. If businesses are not allowed deductions for depreciation allowances outstanding on the date of enactment of a replacement consumption tax, these existing assets will bear a tax penalty (i.e., bear a greater burden of tax than under existing law).[15] This burden seems particularly harsh when contrasted with the treatment of newly purchased capital which—due to availability of expensing—would be effectively exempt from tax. Without transition rules allowing depreciation of existing assets, a business making

---

[14]Senior Democrat on the Ways and Means Committee, Sam Gibbons of Florida.

[15]Closely related to this issue is the treatment of the sale of partially depreciated plant and equipment after enactment. Without special transition rules, the full sale proceeds will enter the tax base of the seller.

an investment in an asset shortly before the effective date will face a sharp increase in tax while those making the same investment shortly after enactment will be effectively tax exempt.

Because of the inherent difficulties of switching to an entirely new system, it is likely that many months or even years might transpire between the time of enactment (or the time when the likelihood of enactment seems certain) and the effective date of a new replacement consumption tax. In this case, the stiff penalty on preenactment investment that results from the absence of transition relief could cause a severe slowdown in business investment. This slowdown would likely be followed by a rapid burst of investment once the favorable tax rules of the new regime became effective.

Amortization of Existing Inventories

Most consumption tax proposals would allow items put into inventory and similar capitalized items to be deducted when purchased instead of when used. Thus, unlike an income tax, a consumption tax allows deductions for additions to inventory. However, also unlike an income tax, reductions to inventory are not deductible unless special transition rules are put into effect In order to not penalize businesses, the balance of inventories and other capital items existing on the date of enactment should be deductible when balances drop below the date-of-enactment level. Otherwise, businesses will be denied deductions for legitimate costs.

Carryover of Net Operating Losses and Tax Credits

The availability of net operating losses can be an important source of value for a firm that expects to be profitable in the future. If net operating losses could not be used under a new business tax, there could be a substantial reduction in a firm's value. Similarly, the inability to utilize unused business tax credits against a new business consumption tax could represent a substantial reduction in value for a business. On financial statements, unused operating losses and tax credits are shown as prepaid tax assets. Their elimination would require a writeoff of that asset.[16] The most prominent business credits under existing law are the alternative minimum tax credit, the foreign tax credit, the credit for research expenditures, the alternative fuels credit, and the targeted jobs tax credit.[17]

Accrual-To Cash-Method Accounting

Many consumption tax proposals purport to place all businesses on the cash method of accounting. Special transition rules will need to be implemented to prevent double taxation. For example, income accrued on a transaction

---

[16]Even if losses can be used under the new system, their value may be reduced if the rate of tax is reduced. For a more general discussion of accounting issues under a new consumption tax, see Chapter 17, also see Gann and Strowd (1995).

[17]When the investment tax credit was repealed by the Tax Reform Act of 1986, credits carried forward to taxable years after enactment were reduced by 35 percent.

prior to the effective date of a cash method consumption tax but subsequently determined uncollectable might not be allowed a bad debt deduction because such deductions are inconsistent with the cash method.[18]

Impact Over the Business Cycle and Over the Life Cycle of a Firm

Business Cycles

Because profits are highly procyclical, taxes on profits have served as an "automatic stabilizer" for the economy—disproportionately increasing taxes when the economy is strong and disproportionately reducing taxes during recessions. Under an income tax, when business is bad, many firms can escape income tax entirely. Some are even able to collect refunds.

Although collections from a consumption tax are also likely to follow the business cycle, their variability (in percentage terms) will likely be far less than that of a profits tax. The historical patterns are shown in Chart 9.1. The good news for business is that when profits are high, the burden of the consumption tax will not increase dramatically. On the other hand, because the largest component of value-added is wages, businesses experiencing severe financial difficulties may still be liable for substantial business taxes.

Startup Firms

Lack of profitability is also characteristic of startup firms. Typically, a new business does not generate income tax liability for several years. If the new business is not taxed as a corporation, losses are generally deductible against owners' other income reported on their individual tax returns. For new businesses that are taxed as corporations, losses may not be used on owners' returns, but net operating losses and tax credits generated during the startup years can keep the firm free of income tax years after profitability has been achieved. This is a stark difference to what firms may expect under a value-added tax. New businesses—whether incorporated or not—will have no startup tax holiday under a value-added tax. Unless losses are very large, startup firms are likely to generate tax liabilities right from the beginning of their existence.[19]

Business Reorganizations

Under current law, tax specialists go to great pains to minimize both corporate and individual income tax liability that may be triggered during business reorganizations. Reorganizations involving changes of ownership of a business (e.g., merger, sale of a business) or change in entity (e.g., partnership

---

[18]Not all transition rules need be beneficial to taxpayers. Some might argue that reserves for bad debts accumulated by thrift institutions and certain commercial banks should be taken into income before the expiration of an income tax.

[19]This is another respect in which these taxes are more akin to payroll taxes than income taxes.

to a corporation) will not be taxable events under a new consumption tax. (As noted in Chapter 1, this is a major simplification relative to current law.) If, however, assets—rather than ownership shares— are sold or exchanged, the entire proceeds[20] from the sale of tangible assets (e.g., inventories, plant and equipment) would generally be taxable to the seller[21] and deductible for business purchasers.

Conclusion

Businesses remain unclear about the impact of a consumption tax on their tax liability. They want to know (1) whether they pay more or less under a consumption tax than an income tax, and (2) the relative burden of each consumption tax.

This chapter has tried to introduce the reader to the key factors that make up the strange and new consumption tax landscape. The following two chapters provide some details on the two leading consumption tax plans now under consideration by Congress.

---

[20]Transition rules may allow some or all of the basis of existing assets to be excluded from tax.

[21]In general, the sales of financial assets are exempt from a value-added tax.

Chart 9.1 Growth Rates of Profits and Value-Added, Nonfinancial Corporate Business, 1960–93

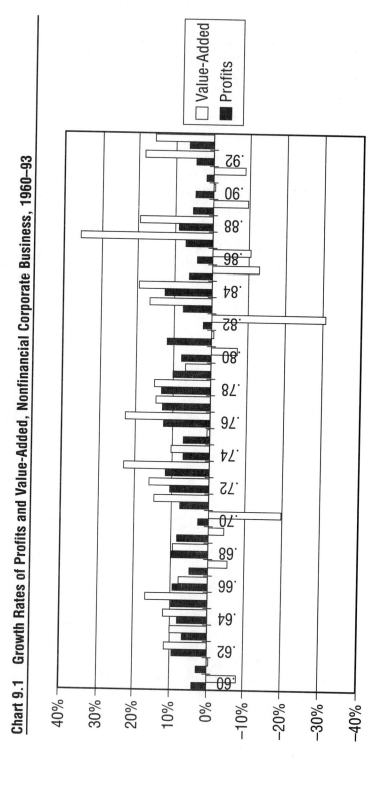

10

The Flat Tax

Summary

- The Flat Tax—proposed by House Majority Leader Dick Armey—is a type of value-added tax collected from both businesses and individuals. (Other value-added taxes are collected only from businesses.) Under the Flat Tax, value added from labor is collected from individuals in the form of a wage tax. All other value added is collected from business using a subtraction-method VAT modified to allow deductions for wages.

- Except for a standard deduction and some additional deductions for dependents, there are no deductions or credits for individuals under the Armey proposal. Most notably, deductions for mortgage interest, charitable contributions, and state and local taxes would not be allowed.

- Unlike almost all other consumption taxes, the Flat Tax does not have border tax adjustments.

Before his ascent to Majority Leader of the House of Representatives, Representative Dick Armey of Texas introduced H.R. 4585, "The Freedom and Fairness Restoration Act of 1994" in June 1994. Majority Leader Armey reintroduced largely the same legislation in the 104th Congress as H.R. 2060 on July 19, 1995. At the same time, Senator Richard Shelby of Alabama introduced the same bill in the Senate as S. 1050.

The proposed legislation provides for a complete overhaul of U.S. economic policy consistent with traditional conservative principles of less regulation and less government spending. In addition, in a few short pages, the bill eliminates the individual income tax and corporate income tax systems[1] and replaces them with a consumption tax system unlike any other that ever

---

[1] The proposal would retain current payroll taxes but not estate and gift taxes, which are specifically removed from the Internal Revenue Code.

has been actually implemented. As a consumption tax, the Flat Tax would not possess the bias against saving that is so prominent in the current U.S. tax system. However, the Flat Tax is more than a switch from an income tax to a consumption tax. If enacted as currently conceived, it would be a massive tax reform that would eliminate dozens of special-interest provisions. It would also be a massive simplification that would eliminate much of the complexity that plagues the current system.

The idea of the Flat Tax is not new. Although the proposal in its current form lacks many details, it is clear that the Armey proposal is a direct descendent of a flat tax proposed by two Hoover Institution scholars, Robert Hall and Alvin Rabushka, in their 1983 book entitled *Low Tax, Simple Tax, Flat Tax*. The Flat Tax has two parts: a tax on individuals and a tax on businesses.[2]

The Individual Tax

Under the Flat Tax individuals pay a wage tax at a flat rate of 17 percent. Pension benefits are included in the wage base, but fringe benefits[3] and income earned abroad are excluded. All capital income—interest, dividends, capital gains, and so on—are untaxed.[4] Large standard deductions and additional large deductions for dependents would remove tens of millions of taxpayers from the tax rolls. The standard deductions and dependent deduction in the Armey bill are shown in Table 10.1 These amounts are for 1996—the first year of the tax according to the proposed statute—and would be indexed for inflation thereafter.

Table 10.1   Standard Deductions Under the Armey Flat Tax

Types of Deduction	Amount
Basic Standard Deduction	
Married Filing Jointly	$21,400
Head of Household	$14,000
Individual	$10,700
Married Filing Separately	$10,700
Additional Deduction Per Dependent	$ 5,000

The Individual Tax is noteworthy for what it is not. *Every* itemized deduction and *every* tax credit allowed under current law would be repealed under the Flat Tax. Most important among these are the mortgage interest deduction, the deduction for state and local taxes, and the deduction for charitable contributions. The major individual tax expenditure items that would be repealed under the Flat Tax are summarized in Table 10.2.

---

[2]The most recent version of the Hall-Rabushka study, *The Flat Tax*, can be found in a 56-page special supplement to the August 4, 1995 edition of *Tax Notes*.

[3]It is important to note, however, that fringe benefits also will not be deductible by employers.

[4]As under current law, "inside buildup" as well as the proceeds of life insurance policies would be tax exempt.

Table 10.2   Special Tax Provisions Repealed Under the Individual Flat Tax

- Deduction for Mortgage Interest
- Deduction for Property Taxes
- Deduction for Income State and Local Taxes
- Deduction for Charitable Contributions
- Exclusion of Scholarship and Fellowship Income
- Exclusion of Employee Awards
- Credit for Child Care and Dependent Expenses
- Earned Income Tax Credit
- Deduction for Casualty and Theft Losses
- Tax Credit for Elderly and Disabled
- Additional Standard Deduction for Blind and Elderly

The basic operation of the Individual Flat Tax is illustrated in the example in Table 10.3. If the currently proposed structure is maintained, the tax would be simpler than the current income tax for many individuals—particularly those taxpayers with itemized deductions and those with significant capital income.

Table 10.3   The Flat Tax on a Family of Four in the Year 2000

A. Flat Tax

Wages		$70,000
Standard Deduction[5]	$29,579	
Dependent Deductions	$11,975	
Total Deductions		$41,554
Tax Base		$28,446
Tax @17%		$ 4,836

B. Current Law

Wages		$70,000
Personal Exemptions	$11,736	
Standard Deduction	$ 7,604	
Total Deductions		$19,340
Taxable Income		$50,660
Tax Paid in 15% Bracket		$ 6,826
Tax Paid in 28% Bracket		$ 1,443
Total Tax		$ 8,269

[5]The estimated inflation adjustments for the years 1996–2000 used in these calculations are those currently used by the Congressional Budget Office in its official revenue estimates. The CBO assumes an inflation rate of approximately 3 percent annually.

Much of the reduced complexity in the individual tax is the result of the elimination of exceptions to general rules. The special rules that exempt certain types of capital income cease to be relevant because all capital income is exempt from tax. It would no longer be necessary to have complex rules to differentiate exempt from nonexempt capital income. This is not, however, good news for everyone. Many political objectives could be seriously frustrated by this change. For example, there would no longer be any tax benefit to investing in municipal bonds. State and local governments would no longer enjoy competitive advantages in capital markets. Likewise, life insurance and annuities would no longer be tax-advantaged vis-à-vis other investments (because other investments would also receive the same tax benefit that life insurance now enjoys). Life insurance companies would no longer have a major tax advantage over their bank and mutual fund competitors. Table 10.4 lists some tax expenditures that would become obsolete under the Flat Tax.[6]

Table 10.4   Items Described as Tax Expenditure Items that Lose Special Emphasis Because All Capital Income Is Exempt

- Exclusion of Investment Income on Life Insurance and Annuity Contracts
- Exclusion of Investment Income from Structured Settlement Accounts
- Deferral of Gain on Sale
- Exclusion of Gain on Home Sales for Person Age 55 and Over
- Exclusion of Interest on State and Local Bonds
- Maximum 28% Tax Rate on Long-Term Capital Gain
- Exclusion of Capital Gains at Death
- Exclusion of Interest on Education Savings Bonds
- Deferral of Interest on Savings Bonds

The Business Tax

The Business Flat Tax would be imposed on all corporate and noncorporate businesses. Thus, under the proposal "flow-through" entities—such as sole proprietorships, partnerships, and Subchapter S corporations, which are not currently subject to an entity-level tax—would be subject to tax along with Subchapter C corporations. The tax base, referred to as *gross active income*, starts with gross business receipts and has deductions for (1) material inputs, (2) wages and compensation paid, including contributions to pension (but not other fringe benefits), and (3) investment in capital. No other deductions would be allowed. Because capital purchases would be expensed, there would no longer be any depreciation deductions (but there is likely to be generous transition relief that allows depreciation on capital in place before

---

[6]The Flat Tax assumes the elimination of specific items described as tax expenditures. Some argue that the need for these programs and indirect expenditures still exist and that these expenditures will be brought back in a different form.

the date of enactment). The basic operation of the Business Flat Tax is illustrated in Table 10.5.

Table 10.5   Basic Operation of the Business Flat Tax

Gross Receipts		100
Less		
Materials Cost	20	
Capital Expenditures	10	
Employee Compensation	40	
Total Costs		70
Equals		
Tax Base		30
Tax @17%		5.10

As with the Individual Flat Tax, the Business Flat Tax is noteworthy for what it excludes. Table 10.6 is a partial list of repealed business tax credits.

Table 10.6   Some Tax Credits Repealed Under the Flat Tax

- Research Tax Credit
- Energy Tax Credits
- Rehabilitation Tax Credit
- Low-Income Housing Credit
- Tax Credit for Orphan Drug Research
- Targeted Jobs Tax Credit

Also, many current tax expenditures would become irrelevant because they would be made obsolete by general provisions of the new tax (Table 10.7). For example, deferral of tax on income generated by businesses operating abroad is no longer an advantage because the business tax is a territorial tax excluding all foreign-source income. Similarly, generous depreciation provisions available under current law no longer provide a tax advantage because all capital expenditures are expensed.

**Table 10.7   Some Current Business Tax Benefits
Made Obsolete Under the Flat Tax**

- Deferral of Income of Controlled Foreign Corporations
- Expensing of Exploration and Development Costs
- Section 179 Expensing
- Expensing of Magazine Circulation Expenses
- Possessions Tax Credit

Equivalence of the Flat Tax to a Subtraction-Method VAT

One way of gaining insight into the operation of the Flat Tax is to view the Business and Individual Taxes as *a single tax collected from two sources.* When combined, the two tax bases approximate a consumption tax base. In fact, if the Individual Tax did not have standard deductions, the Flat Tax base would exactly replicate the tax base of a subtraction-method value-added tax. The two taxes are compared in Table 10.8.

Under a subtraction-method VAT, all tax is collected from businesses. From gross receipts, deductions are allowed for purchases of material and for capital expenditures but not for employee compensation and interest. The Flat Tax allows business to deduct employee compensation but then taxes employees directly on this compensation.

Table 10.8   Comparison of the Flat Tax and a Subtraction-Method VAT

Subtraction-Method VAT			The Flat Tax		
A. Business Tax			**A. Business Tax**		
Gross Receipts		**100**	**Gross Receipts**		**100**
Less			Less		
Materials Cost	20		Materials Cost	20	
Capital Expenditures	10		Capital Expenditures	10	
			Employee Compensation	**40**	
Total Costs		30	Total Costs		70
Equals			Equals		
Tax Base		70	Tax Base		30
Tax @17%		11.90	Tax @17%		5.10
B. Individual Tax			**B. Individual Tax**		
– None –			**Employee Compensation**		40
			Less		
			Standard Deductions		15
			Equals		
			Tax Base		25
Tax @17%		0.00	Tax @17%		4.25
Total Tax		**11.90**	Total Tax		9.35
			Note:		
			Total Tax Without Standard Deductions		**11.90**

Economic Effects

Because of its equivalence to a subtraction-method value-added tax, many of the economic effects of the Flat Tax are the same as those of a broad-based consumption tax. For example, because the corporate income tax is eliminated, the proposal eliminates the bias against capital formation in the corporate sector. Because the tax does not apply to income from capital, the bias against capital formation in general under current law is entirely eliminated. To the extent the current tax system is an impediment to saving and capital formation, the Flat Tax could foster increases in productivity, wages, competitiveness, and economic growth.

The major impediment to passage of the Flat Tax in its current form—as with most consumption taxes—is that these taxes are generally considered regressive. This is the case because it is generally assumed that consumption taxes are passed forward in prices and low-income households spend more in proportion to their incomes than do high-income households. Although there is much dispute about how to measure the distributional effects of consumption taxes, it is noteworthy that a recent Treasury study[7] showed that the Armey Flat Tax would hurt families with incomes below $200,000 and help those with incomes above $200,000.[8]

One notable difference between the Flat Tax and other consumption tax proposals is that the tax is not imposed on imports and there is no tax relief for exports. Such "border tax adjustments" are common to consumption taxes currently in place around the world and common to all current consumption tax proposals. (Chapter 9 presents some calculations showing that the absence of border tax adjustments makes a large difference to exporters.)

Political Prospects

A key attraction of the Flat Tax is its simplicity relative to current law. Under the proposal, corporate income taxation would be eliminated, the minimum tax would be eliminated, taxation of overseas earnings would be eliminated, documentation of depreciation, interest, and charitable contributions would no longer be necessary, and there would be no taxation of interest, dividends, and capital gains. Proponents claim that under the proposal both individuals and businesses would file tax returns the size of a postcard. There can be little doubt that this proposal in its current form is simpler than current law for a large number of taxpayers.

It is unlikely, however, that the tax would be so absolutely simple as proponents claim. First of all, many issues under current law would remain problematic under the Flat Tax. For example, under either tax there is no bright line between business expenses and personal consumption in the case of self-employed individuals. Second, new issues arise that are not present

---

[7]See Toder (1995).

[8]With regard to distributional issues, it is important to note that the proposal would repeal the earned income tax credit.

under current law. For example, the value of employee fringe benefits, which business cannot deduct under the Flat Tax, must be calculated. Finally, it is often remarked that it is not really fair to compare a tax system functioning in the real world to an idealized system that has not yet been subjected to the political maneuvering necessary for passage into law. If history is any indicator, it seems likely that in the name of political expediency the proposal would rapidly be burdened with special exceptions and adjustments as it moved through the legislative process.

Of course, the tax must also raise sufficient revenue. The Treasury Department claims that the 17 percent Armey Flat Tax would reduce tax collections by nearly $250 billion annually. Given the low probability of reductions in government spending by this amount, and given the current intolerance for larger federal deficits,[9] it seems likely that any Flat Tax enacted into law would have a tax rate greater than 17 percent. The Treasury Department estimates[10] that the Armey proposal would require a rate of approximately 24 percent to raise the same revenues as the corporate and individual income taxes it would replace.[11]

---

[9]Early in the 104th Congress, a balanced-budget amendment passed the House of Representative and missed obtaining the necessary two-thirds majority in the Senate by one vote.

[10]See Toder (1995).

[11]If current revenue-estimating methodologies were altered to take into account possible economic growth resulting from the proposal (i.e., so called *dynamic* revenue estimates), the revenue neutral rate could be lower. At this time, it is unclear whether the new Congress will adopt this new approach and how significant its impact might be.

Nunn-Domenici USA Tax

Summary

- The Nunn-Domenici USA Tax proposal eliminates the individual and corporate income taxes and imposes a new consumption tax on individuals and a new consumption tax on businesses.

- The Individual Tax is a personal consumption tax with a progressive rate structure and a top rate of 40 percent. Unlike the Armey plan, favorable treatment is retained for housing, charitable contributions, and state and local income taxes.

- The Business Tax is a subtraction-method consumption tax with a rate of 11 percent. The tax applies to all businesses, not just corporations.

- The Nunn-Domenici proposal contains complicated transition rules under both the Individual and Business Taxes for deducting basis of assets acquired before the effective date of the new system.

After years of preparation, Senator Sam Nunn of Georgia and Senator Pete Domenici of New Mexico introduced the 293-page "USA Tax Act of 1995" (S. 722). Like flat tax proposals, the Nunn-Domenici plan would completely eliminate the individual and corporate income taxes[1] and would replace them with a system of consumption taxes levied on both individuals and business.

There are important differences, however, between the Armey Flat Tax and the Nunn-Domenici USA Tax. For example, unlike the individual portion of the Flat Tax, the Nunn-Domenici Individual Tax would have progressive rates and would allow deductions for mortgage interest, charitable contributions, and state and local taxes. Unlike the business portion of the Flat Tax, the Nunn-Domenici Business Tax would not allow deductions for wages. The Nunn-Domenici proposal, however, would allow all employer and most

---

[1] The Nunn-Domenici proposal would retain the current estate and gift taxes and current payroll taxes, but subject to a carryover in tax basis at death.

employee payroll taxes to be credited against the new tax. Furthermore—unlike the Flat Tax, but like most consumption taxes—the proposal imposes tax on imports and exempts exports, that is, the tax is border adjusted.

The Individual Tax

In General

The Individual Tax under the Nunn-Domenici plan is an individual consumption tax. Under the tax, individuals would file annual returns much as they do under current law. Moreover, they would include on this return their "gross income" that is similar to adjusted gross income under current law, and they would deduct itemized deductions and allowances for personal exemptions in order to arrive at taxable income. The key difference between the current individual income tax and the Nunn-Domenici Individual Tax is a deduction for additional saving. In fact, the "USA" in the proposal's title refers to Unlimited Savings Allowance.

Under the proposal, gross income includes wages, salaries, interest, dividends, distributions from proprietorships and partnerships, pension benefits, proceeds from life insurance and annuity contracts[2], and—with some important exceptions—the entire proceeds of asset sales. In order to arrive at taxable income, individuals would first deduct generous "Family Living Allowances" and personal exemption amounts. These are summarized in Table 11.1.

Table 11.1   Personal Exemptions and Family Living Allowances Under the Nunn-Domenici Plan

Personal Exemption	
All Returns	$2,250
Family Living Allowance	
Form of Return	
Joint	$7,400
Surviving spouse	$7,400
Head of Household	$5,400
Individual	$4,400
Married filing separately	$3,700

Thus, a family of four would not be liable for individual tax unless their gross income exceeded $16,400.[3] All of these amounts are for 1996 and would thereafter be indexed for inflation. It is interesting to note there is no standard deduction.

---

[2]As under current law and the Flat Tax, the inside buildup on life insurance would be exempt from tax. Under current law and the Flat Tax, proceeds from life insurance policies are exempt from tax.

[3]Of the approximately 115 million individual income tax returns filed in 1990, 47 million were for households with adjusted gross income of less than $15,000.

Itemized Deductions

The Nunn-Domenici proposal would allow fi_ following purposes:

1. Mortgage interest
2. Charitable contributions
3. Tuition for education and training
4. Additional savings
5. Transition basis

The deductions for mortgage interest and operate under the same rules as apply unde_ ... tax system. The deduction for education expenses would be a new itemized deduction. The deduction would allow for tuition relating to postsecondary education. It would be limited to $2,000 per year per eligible student and could not exceed $8,000 per household annually. As noted above, the Nunn-Domenici plan includes a deduction for saving. This deduction is similar to the deduction for contributions to individual retirement accounts, except there would be no limitations on the amounts that could be contributed and no restrictions on withdrawals.

Except for the transition-basis deduction and the deduction for new saving (both discussed below), no other deductions would be allowed under the new Individual Tax. In particular, deductions would not be allowed for state and local property taxes, moving expenses, casualty losses, and medical expenses.

Tax Rates

The tax rates under the Nunn-Domenici plan are summarized in Table 11.2.

Table 11.2   Individual Tax Rates Under the Nunn-Domenici Plan

| Taxable Income by Filing Status | | | | Tax Rate in Each Year | | | | |
Married Filing Jointly	Head of House-hold	Unmarried Individual	Married Filing Separately	1996	1997	1998	1999	2000 and after
Up to $5,400	Up to $4,750	Up to $3,200	Up to $2,700	19%	15%	13%	10%	8%
$5,400- $24,000	$4,750-$21,100	$3,200-$14,400	$2,700-$12,000	27%	26%	25%	20%	19%
Over $24,000	Over $21,100	Over $14,400	Over $12,000	40%	40%	40%	40%	40%

As noted above, individuals can always lower their taxes by saving instead of spending. Nevertheless, the low thresholds for the top tax brackets mean that a large number of middle-class taxpayers would be subject to the 40 percent tax rate.

Tax Credits

As under current law (and unlike under the Flat Tax), a refundable earned income tax credit would be available under the Nunn-Domenici plan. An innovation of this provision of the Nunn-Domenici plan is the credit for the employee portion of payroll taxes. Under current law, the employee portion of payroll taxes equals 7.65 percent of the first $61,200 (1995 level) of wages and 1.45 percent on all wages above that amount. No other tax credits would be allowed.

Example

Table 11.3 presents a simple example that illustrates the basic operation of the tax and compares it to current law.[4] Under the Nunn-Domenici proposal, this family with wages income of $70,000 can deduct a living allowance and itemized deductions, and taxes are reduced by a payroll tax credit. Under the Nunn-Domenici proposal, however, this family is subject to a higher rate of tax.

Table 11.3   Computation of Individual Tax Under the Nunn-Domenici Plan for a Family of Four in the Year 2000

A. Nunn-Domenici Individual Tax

Wages	$70,000
Less Personal Exemptions	10,199
Less Living Allowance	8,386
Less Itemized Deductions	7,000
Equals Taxable Income	44,415
Tax at 8%	490
Tax at 19%	4,005
Tax at 40%	6,888
Total Tax	11,383
Less Payroll Credit	5,355
Net Tax	6,028

B. Current Individual Income Tax

Wages	70,000
Less Personal Exemptions	11,736
Less Standard Deduction	7,604
Equals Taxable Income	50,660
Tax at 15%	6,826
Tax at 28%	1,443
Total Tax	8,269

---

[4]See Chapter 13 for more examples of the operation of the Nunn-Domenici proposal.

Treatment of Saving

General Rules

At the core of the Nunn-Domenici proposal is its treatment of personal savings. The following section summarizes the basic mechanics. Before getting mired in the details, it may be helpful to keep in mind four main points:

1. Net additions to savings are deductible.
2. New borrowing is included in income (but most mortgage, automobile, and credit card indebtedness is exempt from this rule).
3. Withdrawals from accounts and proceeds from sales are included in income.
4. There are deductions for basis of assets held before January 1, 1997. For investors with less than $50,000 of basis, basis may be deducted ratably over three years. For other investors, basis may be deducted only when there is net dissaving, generally during retirement.

Deductible additions to savings include deposits in all types of banks, mutual funds, brokerage and retirement accounts as well as the purchase or investment in stock, bonds, certificates of deposits, ownership interests in partnerships and proprietorships, life insurance, and annuities. Conversely, withdrawals from these accounts and sales of these assets are included in the tax base. Purchases of land (whether directly or indirectly) and collectibles are not deductible.

New borrowing increases tax but not if borrowing is "exempt." Exempt borrowing includes:

1. Up to $1 million of mortgage indebtedness
2. Up to $25,000 of debt used to purchase a consumer durable
3. Credit card charges paid within the first billing cycle
4. Any other debt up to $10,000

Needless to say these exceptions remove most personal indebtedness from consideration. It is unclear what in the statute or in practice will prevent taxpayers from borrowing and using the loan proceeds for deductible saving. For example, under the proposal, an individual could get a $25,000 deduction by taking out a second mortgage with a principal of $15,000 and borrowing $10,000 secured against a new $10,000 certificate of deposit. This would result in large revenue losses for the government with no net increase in private saving.

Pre-effective-Date Basis

Under the general rules of a personal consumption tax, all new savings are deductible and the entire amount withdrawn (in the case of an account) and the entire proceeds of a sale (in the case of a savings asset) are subject to tax. Thus, there is no need to distinguish between principal and interest or between gain and basis.

This cash-flow approach creates serious difficulties during the transition from an income tax to a consumption tax. Without transition relief, assets purchased before the effective date of the new consumption tax are penalized. From the perspective of an income tax, these assets are overtaxed because basis as well as gain is subject to tax. From the perspective of a consumption tax, these assets are overtaxed because no deduction was received when the original investment was made. In effect, assets whose holding period straddles the effective date are whipsawed between the two systems—subject to more tax than they would be under either system when fully phased in. This is illustrated in Table 11.4.

Table 11.4 Return on an Investment of $10,000 Is Earnings Under an Income Tax, Under Consumption Tax, and During the Transition from an Income Tax to a Consumption Tax

A. Income Tax

	1995	1996	1997	1998	1999
(1) Beginning Basis	7200.00	7614.72	8053.33	8517.20	9007.79
(2) Income	576.00	609.18	644.27	681.38	720.62
(3) Tax	161.28	170.57	180.39	190.79	201.77
(4) Ending Basis (1) + (2) − (3)	7614.72	8053.33	8517.20	9007.79	9526.64

B. Fully Phased-in Consumption Tax

	1995	1996	1997	1998	1999
(1) Beginning Basis	10000.00	10800.00	11664.00	12597.12	13604.89
(2) Income	800.00	864.00	933.12	1007.77	1088.39
(3) Tax	0.00	0.00	0.00	0.00	4114.12
(4) Ending Basis (1) + (2) − (3)	10800.00	11664.00	12597.12	13604.89	10579.16

C. Switch to Consumption Tax in 1996, without Transition Relief

	1995	1996	1997	1998	1999
(1) Beginning Basis	7200.00	7614.72	8223.90	8881.81	9592.35
(2) Income	576.00	609.18	657.91	710.54	767.39
(3) Tax	161.28	0.00	0.00	0.00	2900.73
(4) Ending Basis (1) + (2) − (3)	7614.72	8223.90	8881.81	9592.35	**7459.01**

Note: The assumed tax rate is 28 percent and the assumed pretax rate of return is 8 percent.

In Panel A of the table, the taxpayer earns $10,000 that is subject to tax at 28 percent which leaves $7,200 available for investment. Earnings are subject to tax annually but are plowed back into investment. At the end of five years, the taxpayer has $9,526.64. In Panel B the taxpayer also earns $10,000 and this entire amount is available for investment under an individual consumption tax where saving is deductible. Over the life of the investment (in this case, five years) the income is not subject to tax. In the last year, however, the *entire* proceeds of the investment ($13,604 plus $1,088) are subject to tax, leaving the taxpayer with $10,579.16. Thus, after five years, a taxpayer in the 28 percent bracket who is saving $10,000 of earnings is more than a thousand dollars richer under a consumption tax than he or she would be under an income tax.

In Panel C the taxpayer is caught between an income tax and a consumption tax and gets the worst of both. When the taxpayer makes the initial investment there is no deduction for saving, but when the taxpayer liquidates the investment the entire proceeds are subject to tax. This leaves the taxpayer with only $7,459.01—a far worse outcome than under the *income* tax.

In order to provide relief to "old capital" most proposals for a personal consumption tax provide transition relief for pre-effective-date assets in the form of deductions for pre-effective-date basis. Before explaining the particular basis deduction rules under the Nunn-Domenici plan, two points are worth noting.

First, the entire reason for providing such relief is to provide equity between old and new savers. It provides no benefits to the economy. (In fact, by requiring higher tax rates in a revenue-neutral setting it is detrimental to growth.) It is true that old saving would be unduly penalized without transition rules but providing relief to existing assets does little to encourage new investment and economic growth.

Second, the problem of overtaxation of existing assets is prevalent under all consumption taxes. Under a retail sales tax or a VAT, relief in the form of basis adjustment is not practical. (Remember, under these options all tax collections are from businesses, and individuals do not even file returns.) Thus, under other types of consumption taxes, the additional burden on taxpayers who have already saved is ignored or relief is directed toward the elderly (for example, by exempting prescription drugs).

Under the Nunn-Domenici plan, there are two methods for recovering pre-effective-date basis. The first is available only to investors with no more than $50,000 of pre-effective-date basis. These taxpayers will be eligible to ratably include basis over the first three years the consumption tax is in effect. This is referred to as the transition basis deduction.

This option is not realistic for all taxpayers because of the severe revenue losses that would result. (Existing aggregate basis in the economy is probably greater than an entire year's taxable income.) Thus, under the Nunn-Domenici proposal, savers would be allowed to deduct basis only when there are net withdrawals to savings. The practical effect of this rule is that many who must use their savings will get some tax relief.[5]

---

[5]The statutory language is difficult to follow. In each year in which there is a sale of a pre-effective-date asset, "withdrawals" (which are deducted from net deductible saving) are reduced by basis and net deductible saving is also reduced by basis. The net result of this is that pre-effective basis does not generally figure into any one year's deduction for saving, as shown in the following formula:

Net Saving = Additions – (Proceeds – Basis) – Basis – Borrowing

For example, if a taxpayer deposits $100 in a bank account, borrows $50, and sells an asset for $30 with a basis of $20, the taxpayer's net deduction for saving is $20 = $100 – ($30 – $20) – $20 – $50).

It is only when saving (which is generally deductible) turns negative (and therefore potentially taxable) that pre-effective-date basis can be helpful to the taxpayer. Pre-effective-date

The Business Tax

In General

The Nunn-Domenici Business Tax is a subtraction-method VAT levied at an 11 percent rate. As is common to all subtraction-method VAT proposals, exports are excluded from gross receipts and imports are subject to a duty at a rate equal to the tax rate. The tax is territorial so there is no taxation of foreign subsidiaries. All businesses, not just corporations, must pay the tax. Wages and interest are not deductible, but capital may be expensed.

There are two important features of the Nunn-Domenici Business Tax that are not necessarily part of a standard subtraction-method VAT. First, there is the treatment of state and local taxes. Under the Nunn-Domenici proposal, all taxes paid by businesses to state and local governments are deductible. Second, there is the credit against the business tax for the employer portion of payroll taxes.

Many of the key features of the Nunn-Domenici Business Tax can be illustrated with the example in Table 11.5.

Table 11.5   Comparison of the Corporate Income Tax and the Nunn-Domenici Business Tax

	Current Corporate Income Tax	Nunn-Domenici Business Tax
Business Receipts—Domestic	90	90
Business Receipts—Exports	10	
Interest Income	5	
Total Gross Receipts	*105*	*90*
Business Purchases	55	55
Wages	25	—
Interest Cost	10	—
Depreciation	10	—
Capital Spending	—	15
Total Deductions	*100*	*70*
Tax Base	5	20
Tax @ 35% , 11%	1.75	2.2
Wages Below Wage Cap		20
Payroll Tax Credit	0	1.60
Net Tax	1.75	0.60

basis is included in the "general basis account." This account may be used to reduce or eliminate otherwise taxable withdrawals:

Net Taxable Withdrawal = Net Negative Saving – General Basis Account

Returning to the prior example, except that the taxpayer makes a deposit of only $10 (instead of $100), net negative saving is $40. This taxable amount may be reduced by the $20 of basis so that there is $20 of net taxable withdrawal.

The Payroll Tax Credit

The payroll tax credit deserves careful attention for two reasons. First, it is important to understand how it works in order to gauge the tax's overall impact on wage costs. As noted, wages are not deductible under the general 11 percent tax. However, this is substantially offset by the availability of a tax credit for the employer portion of the payroll tax. The employer portion of the payroll tax is 7.65 percent up to a per-employee annual ceiling ($61,200 in 1995, indexed to wage growth) and an additional 1.45 percent tax on all wages without limit. As illustrated in Table 11.6, the net burden of the tax on labor is larger for firms that pay high salaries.

Table 11.6   The Differential Benefit of the Payroll Credit on Low-Wage and High-Wage Firms

Total payroll	1,000,000	1,000,000	1,000,000	1,000,000
Average salary	**50,000**	**75,000**	**100,000**	**200,000**
# of employees	20	13	10	5
Tax at 6.2 % , per employee	3,100	3,794	3,794	3,794
Tax at 1.45% per employee	725	1,088	1,450	2,900
Total tax per employee	3,825	4,882	5,244	6,694
Total payroll tax credit (# of employees *times* per employee tax)	**76,500**	**63,446**	**52,440**	**33,470**
VAT cost @ 11%	110,000	110,000	110,000	110,000
Net increase in wage cost (VAT *less* payroll credit)	33,500	46,554	57,560	76,530
Percentage increase	3.35%	4.66%	5.76%	7.65%

The second issue is the impact of the payroll tax credit on the international competitiveness of domestically produced goods. The ability to credit the entire employer portion of the payroll tax against the Nunn-Domenici Business Tax is equivalent to repealing the employer portion of the payroll tax and using the business tax to restore the lost revenues. Under the rules of the General Agreements on Tariffs and Trade (GATT) border adjustments are permitted for "indirect" sales and value-added taxes but are not allowed for "direct" taxes on wages and profits. By replacing payroll tax revenue with VAT revenues, the Nunn-Domenici proposal effectively replaces a non-border-adjustable tax with a border-adjustable tax. This will be true to the extent the burden of payroll taxes is passed forward to consumers in higher prices (and not backward to employees in lower after-tax wages). In general, economists believe that the burden of wage taxes is born by labor in the form of lower after-tax wages.

Because the payroll tax is not repealed outright, however, some commentators strongly contend that the payroll tax credit violates GATT rules on border adjustability.[6]

---

[6]See McLure (1987), pp. 86–88.

Amortization of Pre-effective Date-Basis and Other Transition Rules

The Nunn-Domenici Business Tax provides a large incentive for capital formation by allowing all purchases of new capital to be expensed. If, however, no depreciation deductions are allowed for the remaining basis of existing capital, this capital will be subject to a tax penalty. To prevent the imposition of an undue burden on existing capital, the Nunn-Domenici proposal allows a *transition basis deduction* for the amortization of remaining basis on the effective date for any assets placed into service before the effective date. The amount of the deduction is determined according to the schedule shown in Table 11.7.

Table 11.7   Transition Basis Recovery Periods Under the Nunn-Domenici Plan

Type of Property	Remaining Amortization On Effective Date Under Current Law	Amortization Period Under Nunn-Domenici
Category I basis	Less than 15 yrs.	10 years
Category II basis	More than 15 yrs.	30 years
Category III basis	Not depreciable	40 years

In addition, unrecovered inventory costs would be deducted ratably over three years.

Carryforwards of net operating losses, alternative minimum tax credit, and other business credits—including the R&E tax credit—generated under the existing income tax could not be carried forward to reduce liability under the new Business Tax. This will impose a particularly large burden on startup firms.

Conclusion

The Nunn-Domenici proposal is not as simple as the Flat Tax nor is it as sweeping in its elimination of tax preferences. The argument can be made, however, the plan contains the most important elements of consumption taxation but at the same time makes realistic accommodations that may be necessary to ensure sufficient political support for enactment. Table 11.8 summarizes some of the key differences between current law and the two leading consumption tax alternatives.

Table 11.8   Summary Comparison of Current Law, The Nunn-Domenici Proposal, and the Flat Tax

	Biased Against Capital Formation?	Simpler Than Current Law?	Distribution of Tax Burden	Border Tax Adjustments?
Current Law	Yes, but numerous special rules provide relief.	—	Progressive.	No.
Nunn-Domenici	No.	In some matters, Yes. In some matters, No.	Approximately as progressive as current law.	Yes.
Flat Tax	No.	Yes.	Less progressive than current law.	No.

The following two chapters provide much more detailed, numerical comparisons of the Nunn-Domenici proposal and the Flat Tax.

Impact of Consumption Taxes on Various Business Sectors

Summary

- About two thirds of total value added in the economy is employee compensation. Therefore, an ordinary VAT primarily is a tax on wages.

- The business components of the Flat Tax and the Nunn-Domenici proposal are similar to value-added taxes except that the Flat Tax allows a deduction for wages and the Nunn-Domenici proposal provides a tax credit for wages. Although this relief is substantial, these proposals in general still favor capital-intensive relative to labor-intensive industries.

- The exclusion of exports from gross receipts provides large tax benefits to those firms with exports. For a typical manufacturing exporter, the availability of border tax adjustments under the Nunn-Domenici proposal can easily cut a business's tax bill in half. In contrast, the Flat Tax does not have border tax adjustments.

The primary objective of the study is to provide insight to businesses and policymakers about the impacts of consumption taxes. Along these lines, this chapter uses real data to estimate the effects of real proposals on various sectors of the economy. This is tricky business because proposals are always changing. Also, data are incomplete. Economic impacts are complex and uncertain.

Moreover, generalizations can be misleading: Any conclusion derived from the industry calculations should not necessarily be interpreted as applicable to all businesses within an industry. The effects of new consumption tax proposals will often depend on each business's *unique* circumstances. For example, a firm with high profits might prefer a consumption tax to the current corporate income tax, but this firm's highly leveraged competitor might prefer current law. A third competitor—even if it is paying relatively little corporate income tax—might prefer a border-adjustable consumption tax if it is able to entirely eliminate its tax liability (or even generate refunds) by exporting a small fraction of its total sales.

Chapter 9 developed concepts to help readers think about consumption taxes. Chapters 10 and 11 provided an overview of the two proposals currently receiving the most attention on Capitol Hill. This chapter builds on all this information and combines it with information from Commerce Department economic data on value added in different industry segments.

The Importance of Wages

Official statistics published by the Commerce Department provide an excellent starting point for evaluating and comparing consumption tax proposals. From these statistics, value added can be computed as the sum of total employee compensation (including wages and fringe benefits), corporate profits, net interest paid, net nonincome taxes paid by business, and net income received by owners of noncorporate business.[1] (It is not possible to differentiate between "wages" and "profits" that owners of closely held businesses pay to themselves, so no distinction is made between the two in official statistics.) These components are shown in Table 12.1.

Table 12.1   Total Private Sector Value Added, Commerce Department Data, 1993 (billions of dollars)

Wages	$2,517	51.2%
Fringe Benefits	$ 498	10.1%
Corporate Profits	$ 391	7.9%
Net Interest	$ 460	9.4%
Payments to Owners of Noncorporate Business	$ 520	10.6%
Net Indirect Business Taxes	$ 529	10.8%
Total	$4,915	100.0%

This small table makes a big point. *Employee compensation (wages plus fringe benefits) is at least 60 percent of all private-sector value added.* Considering that some significant portion of payments to owners of noncorporate business is also wages, it is reasonable to assume that about two-thirds of all private-sector value added are payments for labor services. Thus, in a plain

---

[1]This is the addition method of calculating value added. Most proposals for value-added taxation use the subtraction method (or some variant of the concept). See the beginning of Chapter 3 for a comparison.

vanilla value-added tax, employee compensation is the dominant factor determining business tax liability.

Table 12.2 shows the ratio of employee compensation to total value added for 13 major industry groups. The main point of this table is that not only is employee compensation an important component of value added for the economy as a whole, it is also important for most major industry groups. Only for three of the 13 industries—agriculture, utilities, and real estate—is the ratio of employee compensation to total value added less than 50 percent. (Except for utilities, these ratios are low because much of the return to labor is in the form of payments to owners of noncorporate business.) Even for such industries that are commonly considered "capital-intensive"—that is, manufacturing, mining, and construction—wages and fringe benefits are still the largest component of value added.

Table 12.2   Employee Compensation as Percentage of Total Value Added, by Industry, 1993

1. Agriculture	35%
2. Mining	62%
3. Construction	72%
4. Manufacturing—Durables	86%
5. Manufacturing—Nondurables	66%
6. Transportation	76%
7. Communication	53%
8. Utilities	38%
9. Wholesale Trade	64%
10. Retail Trade	63%
11. Finance	62%
12. Real Estate	7%
13. Services	75%
Total Private	61%

Source: U.S. Department of Commerce. See Appendix A for details.

Given these facts, it is not surprising (from a political perspective) that the two leading consumption tax proposals provide substantial relief for the wage component of the consumption tax. The Nunn-Domenici proposal provides a payroll tax credit for the employer portion of payroll taxes (7.65% of wages below the $61,200 and 1.45 percent for all wages above that amount). The Armey Flat Tax exempts wages entirely from the business tax base.

Calculating the Tax Base for the Leading Proposals

Adjustments to the Data

Although the Commerce Department data measure value added, several adjustments must be made to get a reasonable approximation of the aggregate tax base under alternative proposals. Depending on the proposal, adjustments must be made for the following items:

1. Expensing
2. Exports
3. Imports
4. Deductible business taxes

And, although not conceptually related to value added, the following calculations are critically important to determining the impact of some consumption tax proposals:

5. Transition depreciation
6. The payroll tax credit

The details of how these adjustments are made are presented in Appendix B following this chapter.

Using the Data to Calculate Aggregate Tax Liability

Table 12.3 shows the results of all of these adjustments, and uses them to calculate the tax liability for the economy as a whole for (a) a 5 percent broad-based VAT, (b) the Nunn-Domenici Business Tax, and (c) the Armey Flat Tax. The latter two are chosen because they are the two proposals currently receiving the most attention on Capitol Hill. Although not currently in favor, an ordinary VAT serves as a useful benchmark for comparison. A broad-based 5 percent VAT is routinely included in the Congressional Budget Office's annual catalogue of revenue-raising proposals.[2] Five percent is the rate that is approximately revenue neutral to current corporate income tax.

Five Percent Value-Added Tax

In order to calculate the aggregate amount of tax collected under a plain-vanilla VAT, four adjustments must be made to the Commerce Department measure of value added. First, when expensing is allowed instead of depreciation, value added is reduced by the excess of current capital expenditures over current depreciation. Next, because VATs usually operate under the destination principle,[3] the tax base must be reduced by the amount of exports and increased by the amount of imports. Because the United States routinely runs trade deficits, the net effect of implementing the destination principle is to enlarge the tax base. Finally, value added in the Commerce

---

[2]See, for example, Congressional Budget Office (1995).

[3]See Chapter 7 for more explanation.

Table 12.3   Adjusting from Value Added in the 1993 Commerce Department Data to the Business Tax Base Under Three Leading Proposals (billions of dollars)

	5% VAT	11% N-D USA Tax	17% Flat Tax
1993 Value added (in Commerce Dept. Data)	4915	4915	4915
Adjustments			
Wages			−2517
Benefit of Expensing	−205	−205	−205
Benefit of Export Exemption	−457	−457	
Inclusion of Imports	538	538	
Benefit of Excise Tax Deduction	−258	−258	−258
Total Adjustments	382	382	2980
Tax Base	**4533**	**4533**	**1935**
Tax Rate	5%	11%	17%
Gross Tax	227	499	329
Payroll Credit		−177	
Net Tax (w/o Transition Depreciation)	**227**	**322**	**329**
Note: Maximum Transition Depreciation	580	580	580
Note: Tax Benefit of Transition Depreciation	29	64	99
Net Tax (with Transition Depreciation)	**198**	**258**	**230**

Department data includes sales and excise taxes, but these taxes are often deductible in value-added taxes. Thus, the tax base of a broad-based plain-vanilla value-added tax is estimated to be approximately $4.5 trillion in 1993.

Nunn-Domenici Business Tax

As noted previously, the Nunn-Domenici Business Tax is similar to an ordinary broad-based value-added tax. Accordingly, the same adjustments are made to the Commerce Department data to arrive at the Nunn-Domenici tax base, and the Nunn-Domenici tax base is also approximately $4.5 trillion. The big difference between the Nunn-Domenici proposal and an ordinary VAT is the availability of the payroll tax credit, equal to 7.65 percent of most wages. By what percentage this reduces the overall take of a VAT depends on the tax rate. For the Nunn-Domenici proposal with a rate of 11 percent, the amount of revenue raised is reduced from $499 billion to $322 billion, a 35 percent reduction.

The Armey Business Flat Tax

The Armey Flat Tax has two important differences from the Nunn-Domenici proposal. First, it does not have border tax adjustments. Although this will make an enormous difference to individual firms (as discussed below), it results in a net increase of only approximately 2 percent on the overall tax base.[4] The second difference is of such importance it should probably be the defining characteristic of the Flat Tax. Although there are no payroll tax credits under the Flat Tax, wages are entirely deductible. This reduces the tax base to approximately one-half of what it otherwise might be.

The business portion of the Armey Flat Tax has a narrower base than the Nunn-Domenici proposal. The Flat Tax, however, has a higher tax rate (i.e., 17 percent) and no payroll credit. It is striking that these rough calculations show the two taxes raising approximately the same revenue.

Transition Relief Under the Proposals

As noted in Chapter 9, transition relief is a large issue. Table 12.3 underscores its importance. For the regular VAT, the calculations show transition relief reducing total taxes by approximately one-eighth at the beginning of the transition. For the Nunn-Domenici proposal, the reduction in tax revenue is approximately one-seventh. For the Flat Tax, the reduction in tax revenue is approximately one-third. (To offset this reduction in revenue, the Nunn-Domenici proposal has higher individual tax rates during its first four years of existence. The Armey plan would impose a tax rate of 20 percent on individuals and businesses during its first two years.)

Transition relief could be larger than shown in these calculations if, for example, inventories can be written off (as proposed under Nunn-Domenici); if credits (such as the research credit or the alternative minimum tax credit) could be carried forward and credited against the new tax; or if operating losses could be carried forward and deducted against the new tax. Transition relief, however, could be smaller if statutory rules simply reduce the amount of existing capital that may be deducted. In all cases, to the extent there is any transition relief, its importance diminishes over time.

Comparison to the Corporate Income Tax

Estimates of Burden on Corporations

There is interest not only in the differences between various proposals, but also in the differences between proposals and current law. The initial focus here will be on comparing the business components of proposed consumption taxes to the current corporate income tax. (The following chapter will discuss noncorporate business.)

The data are not perfectly suited to this task, so some further assumptions and calculations must be made. In Commerce Department data, the corporate and noncorporate portions of value added are not always separately stated. While corporate profits and corporate depreciation are separate, there is no distinction made, for example, between interest and wages paid by corporations and interest and wages paid by noncorporate businesses.

---

[4]In Table 12.3, the net increase in the tax base due to border adjustments is $119 billion. The total tax base is $4,533 billion.

Therefore, as described in Appendix B, some educated guesses have been made. (Again, none of these calculations should be taken as precise, because they are no more than good-faith estimates given the available data.)

Table 12.4 presents the estimated tax liability incurred by all corporations under (a) the corporation income tax, (b) a 5 percent VAT, (c) the Nunn-Domenici Business Tax, and (d) the Armey Business Flat Tax. Under the corporate income tax only corporate profits are subject to tax.

Table 12.4   Estimated Corporate Tax Liability Under Current Law and Under Alternative Consumption Tax Proposals (1993 data, dollar amounts in billions)

	Current Law	5% VAT	Nunn-Domenici	Armey Flat Tax
Wages	0	2011	2011	0
Fringe Benefits	0	409	409	409
Interest	0	131	131	131
Profit	391	391	391	391
Nondeductible Taxes	0	188	188	188
Benefit of Expensing	0	−139	−139	−139
Imports Less Exports	0	69	69	69
Tax Base	391	3060	3060	1049
Tax Rate	35%	5%	11%	17%
Gross Tax	137	153	337	178
Payroll Credit	0	0	141	0
Net Tax	**137[5]**	**153**	**196**	**178**
Maximum Transition Depreciation	0	394	394	394
Tax Benefit of Transition Depreciation	0	20	43	67
Tax With Transition	137	133	153	111

The calculations show that if all of these tax proposals were fully effective (i.e., no transition) in 1993, they would raise revenues in the same general order of magnitude—between $153 billion and $178 billion. The calculations show that a 5 percent VAT raises a little more than would be needed to replace the revenues lost from repeal of the corporate tax.[6] The Nunn-Domenici tax has a higher rate than the regular VAT (11 percent

---

[5]In 1993 the corporate income tax actually raised $117.5 billion. The lower actual figure is not surprising given the more accelerated depreciation allowed for tax purposes and the availability of tax credits. 1995 Budget, Historical tables, p. 22.

[6]This relationship is consistent with the tabulations presented in Congressional Budget Office (1995). According to the CBO, a 4.3 percent VAT would be needed to raise as much revenue as the corporation tax. The tables presented here are consistent with a 4.5 percent revenue neutral rate.

versus 5 percent), but it also has a generous payroll credit. The calculations indicate that for the corporate sector the benefit of the credit does not compensate for the higher rate: The 11 percent Nunn-Domenici tax imposes a net higher burden than a 5 percent VAT. The Armey proposal does not have a payroll credit, but a full deduction for wages, which is a greater benefit than the Nunn-Domenici credit. To compensate for this lost revenue, the Armey proposal must have a higher tax rate than the Nunn-Domenici proposal.[7]

As noted above, transition rules have the potential to provide substantial temporary relief under all the alternatives. The proportionate benefit of transition relief is related to the tax rate. Thus, transition rules under the Armey plan provide the greatest percentage reduction in tax.

Key Factors Determining Tax Liability

From Table 12.4 (as well as Tables 12.A1 through 12.A11 in Appendix A), a pattern begins to emerge about business consumption taxes. The four most important factors for determining overall liability are:

1. *The amount of each firm's wages and the treatment of wages under the alternative proposal.* For almost all businesses, wage payments are the largest component of the tax base, but treatment of wages can be vastly different (i.e., included in base, deductible, or creditable) under alternative proposals.

2. *Transition rules.* Transition relief can have an enormous impact on tax liabilities. This revenue loss may or may not be offset by temporarily higher tax rates. Transition relief may come in a variety of forms, and it is possible for it to be entirely omitted from the plans.

3. *Tax rates.* The range of possible rates for different reasonable proposals is enormous (as was stressed at the end of Chapter 9). Sometimes the simple impact of differences in tax rates is neglected because so much effort must be devoted to understanding the differences in the tax base.

4. *Exports and imports.* It was noted above that *in the aggregate* the impact of border tax adjustments on the tax base is relatively small— about 2 percent of the total consumption tax burden.Underlying these aggregate figures, however, there lies a wide degree of variation. For example, it is not uncommon for a firm's exports to exceed 10 percent of its sales.[8] For many firms, even with this low exports-to-sale ratio, the deductibility of exports can be a dominant factor in determining tax liability. In many cases, tax liability can be eliminated.[9]

---

[7]A recent empirical study by Price Waterhouse also indicates that both the Nunn-Domenici proposal and a 17% Flat Tax generate more revenue from corporations than does the current corporation tax. See Merrill, Wertz, and Shah (1995), p. 743, Exhibit 2. The calculations in the Price Waterhouse study are based on 1992 Statistics of Income data for nonfinancial corporations, while the calculations presented in this study are based on 1993 Commerce Department data for all corporations.

[8]See Farnham (1987).

[9]The importance of exports was also stressed in the Price Waterhouse study of corporate tax liability. "The single most important factor in determining whether industries would have paid more or less under the USA proposal is net exports: industries with relatively high net exports per dollar of gross receipts pay less tax." Merrill, Wertz, and Shah (1995), p. 744.

Discussion of Exports and Imports

Exports

The example in Table 12.5, based on actual data[10] for manufacturers, demonstrates the importance of border adjustments for firms that export.

Table 12.5   The Impact of the Deduction for Exports on the "Typical" Exporting Manufacturer

	5% VAT	Nunn-Domenici
Total Sales	100.0	100.0
Less Exports	10.0	10.0
Less Business Purchases	64.0	64.0
Equals Tax Base	26.0	26.0
Tax Rate	5%	11%
Gross Tax	1.3	2.9
Wages	27.0	27.0
Wage Credit	0.0	1.9
Net Tax	**1.3**	**1.0**
Note: Net Tax without Deduction for Exports	1.8	2.1
Note: % Reduction in Tax Due to Export Deduction	**28%**	**53%**

For the "typical" manufacturer, the exclusion of exports from the tax base reduces the tax burden of a plain-vanilla VAT by 28 percent. For the Nunn-Domenici proposal, the exclusion of exports from gross receipts reduces the tax burden by 53 percent. The Armey proposal does not provide any such relief for exports. Thus, in general it seems likely that exporters will favor the Nunn-Domenici proposal (and other consumption taxes with border tax adjustments) over the Armey Flat Tax.[11]

Imports

Although the U.S. economy typically imports more than it exports, the impact of import duties has not been included in the industry-by-industry

---

[10]The details are explained in the Appendix B to this chapter.

[11]Under the current income tax, exporters can benefit from either of two provisions: (1) the Foreign Sales Corporation (commonly known as "FSC") rules and the favorable *title-passage* export sourcing rules. The order of magnitude of benefits from these rules is much smaller than that which would be provided with border tax adjustments. Export benefits under current law exempt a certain *portion of income* from exports from tax. Border tax adjustments exempt the *entire* amount of *gross receipts* from exports from tax.

calculations presented in this chapter. This is not because they are unimportant. As noted in Appendix B to this chapter, U.S. imports were $538 billion in 1993. From Table 12.4, it can be seen that this amount accounts for about one-sixth of the revenue collected under a regular VAT and about one-quarter of the revenue collected under the Nunn-Domenici proposal.

The reason for the exclusion of imports is the particular difficulty they pose in presentation. If—as is assumed by economists—the burden of consumption taxes is passed forward in price, businesses purchasing domestically produced inputs will be subject to the same rise in costs as importers. For example, a border-adjustable 10 percent VAT will raise import prices and domestic prices by 10 percent. In this case, there is no special burden borne by importers. If import duties were included in the tables, they would result in a greater tax liability on importers even though their economic burden is no different than that faced by other domestic firms.

Suppose instead, for the sake of argument, that a border-adjustable VAT raised import prices by 10 percent and domestic prices by 6 percent. If the firm is an importer and pays the import duty, including these duties in the calculation of liability would overstate the relative burden borne by the business. That firm would be worse off than the firm with purely domestic sources of supply, but by only 4 percent (and not the 10 percent that would be shown in calculations of pure tax liability).

In addition, a firm that indirectly imports (e.g., a retailer supplied by an importing wholesaler) should not necessarily expect to bear no burden as a result of an import duty (when in fact its import costs may have risen by the full amount of the tax). The bottom line is that import duties can place a significant direct or indirect burden on a business. How different this burden is compared to nonimporting firms is not clear. And no one calculation will do justice to the variety of ways the tax may impact importing sectors. Accordingly, businesses that rely on imports as sources of supply should carefully study the possible impact of import duties on their costs.

Impact on Various Corporate Sectors

The previous section used aggregate corporate data to analyze how consumption tax proposals might affect a "typical" firm in the economy. In this section, the current income tax is compared to consumption tax proposals for a "typical" firm in a variety of business sectors. Of the thirteen components of the total private sector analyzed, two industries—agriculture and real estate—were dropped from the analysis because of the small proportion of business activities undertaken by corporations in those sectors. The estimated proportion of corporate business in each sector is shown in Table 12.6.[12]

---

[12]Appendix A to this chapter explains how the components of value added were allocated between the corporate and noncorporate sectors of each industry group.

Table 12.6   Estimated Proportion of Corporate Business in Each Major Business Sector

	Industry	Corporate Percentage
1.	Manufacturing-Durables	97%
2.	Manufacturing-Nondurables	94%
3.	Mining	86%
4.	Construction	68%
5.	Transportation	86%
6.	Communication	88%
7.	Utilities	92%
8.	Wholesale Trade	97%
9.	Retail Trade	83%
10.	Finance	96%
11.	Services	63%
12.	Agriculture	20%
13.	Real Estate	7%
	Total Private Sector	68%

Source: U.S. Department of Commerce. See Appendix A.

Tables 12.A1 through 12.A11 (in Appendix A to this chapter) present estimates of tax liability under the current law and three consumption tax alternatives. The calculations are made for four different sets of assumptions, as shown in Table 12.7.

Table 12.7   Alternative Assumptions Used in Industry Tables

Assumptions Used in Tables	Legislation Transition Relief	Firms-Export Position
#1	None	No Exports
#2	Maximum Relief	No Exports
#3	None	"Typical" Exporter
#4	Maximum Relief	"Typical" Exporter

These tables provide a great deal of information, and at first it is difficult to discern any patterns. Some industries appear to be winners, and some are losers. Patterns *do* emerge, however, after careful inspection.

No Transition, No Exports

Focusing first on the case of no transition and no exports (assumption #1), industries with percentages of *employee compensation* (wages and fringe benefits) that are *low* relative to other industries do better under the alternatives. This makes sense because consumption tax alternatives tax wages while the current corporate tax does not. Also, industries with relatively *high* levels of *profit* seem to do better under the alternatives. Again, this makes sense because the corporate income tax is a tax exclusively on profits. Under the alternatives, profits are only a small component of the tax base.

To highlight this point, the ratio of profit to employee compensation was calculated for each industry, and then the industries were sorted by this statistic. The estimated ratio of profit to employee compensation for each of the 11 major corporate sectors is shown in Table 12.8.

Table 12.8   Ratio of Profit to Total Employee Compensation for Major Corporate Sectors, 1993

Industry	Profit Divided by Compensation
Utilities	64%
Communications	48%
Finance	42%
Manufacturing-Nondurables	23%
Wholesale	16%
Retail	12%
Mining	10%
Manufacturing-Durables	8%
Transportation	7%
Services	6%
Construction	6%

When tax liabilities are sorted by this ratio a clear pattern emerges: *In general, the higher the ratio of profit-to-employee compensation, the more attractive are consumption tax proposals relative to current law.* In other words, industries with relatively high profits would prefer a consumption tax to an income tax. This can be directly observed in Chart 12.1, which appears at the end of this chapter.

Among industries, utilities, communications, and finance pay less tax under all three alternatives because of their relatively high level of profits and relatively low level of wages. Other industries fare worse under the alternatives (compared to current law) because of low profitability and/or their greater labor intensity.

Peak Transition, No Exports

Whether or not—and in what form—transition relief will be part of consumption tax alternatives is an open issue. The calculations in this study show that transition relief has the potential during the transition period to be important to many firms in a variety of industries. In Chart 12.2, which appears at the end of this chapter, transition benefits are assumed to be available under all three consumption tax alternatives. Two observations can be made. First, of the three consumption alternatives, the relative attractiveness of the Flat Tax improves most due to transition relief. This is because transition depreciation deductions are more valuable under the proposal's 17 percent rate than under the lower rates of the other alternatives (i.e., 11 and 5 percent). Second, transition relief is more beneficial to the more capital-intensive industries, like manufacturing and mining, as shown in Chart 12.2.

No Transition, "Typical" Exporter

Border tax adjustments would be available under a typical VAT and under the Nunn-Domenici proposal. They are not available under the Flat Tax or under current law. Chart 12.3, which appears at the end of this chapter, shows that if a firm in any of these sectors exports as much as a "typical" manufacturer, comparisons of the alternatives change dramatically. The Nunn-Domenici proposal becomes the best alternative for nine of the 11 corporate sectors.

Overview of Results and Caveats

In the long run (i.e., after any transition period), a key factor for determining the relative position before and after imposition of a replacement consumption tax is the ratio of profit to total employee compensation. High-profit/low-wage firms will find alternatives to current law attractive. Transition rules can provide significant relief if the firm is capital intensive. Furthermore, transition deductions will be more valuable as the tax rate climbs. Finally, the availability of border tax adjustments is extremely important to exporters.

It must be stressed that these calculations are only approximations of what particular firms in each industry might experience. All of the calculations assume no tax preferences. Clearly this is not true under current law, and it is yet to be seen how important tax preferences will be under the proposed reforms. Another issue is tax rates. The tax rates used follow the current legislative drafts, but rates are highly susceptible to change—for example, to pay for additional preferences, to pay for transition relief, or to raise additional revenue for deficit reduction.

The data used are based on 1993 data that may no longer be relevant for 1996 or later years. (Cycles and trends in profitability make profit figures particularly suspect.) For each industry, the corporate components of wages, fringe benefits, and interest had to be estimated. How transition relief and "typical" exporters are characterized are only good estimates. Transition relief under actual proposals and export intensity of particular firms are both likely to vary widely.

For this reason it is important for individual firms (and their advisors) to take stock of their (and their client's) own circumstances in assessing the impact of consumption taxes. Toward this end, the worksheets of the following section should provide some useful guidance.

Worksheets for Individual Firm Analysis

The calculations presented thus far hopefully have helped to take abstract discussions of consumption taxes and turn them into reality. To further bring home the reality of these taxes, the following recently published worksheets allow tax and accounting professionals to determine consumption liabilities for their own and their clients' businesses.[13,14]

Under the Armey plan (see Table 12.9), businesses include all receipts from *domestic* business—including exports—in gross active income. Wages are deductible, but fringe benefits are not. Capital purchases are expensed. Interest income is not includable and interest expense is not deductible. There are no deductions for property or state income taxes. There are no tax credits. The tax rate is 17 percent, and payroll taxes are unaffected by the tax.

Under the Nunn-Domenici proposal (see Table 12.10), exports are excluded from the tax base and imports are subject to tax at the border. The rate of tax and rate of import duty are both 11 percent. As under the Armey plan, capital purchases are expensed. As under the Armey plan, interest expense, fringe benefits, and property and state income taxes are not deductible. Wages are not deductible, but the employer portion of the payroll tax is creditable against the tax.

---

[13]The worksheets were developed by Arthur Andersen and were recently reprinted in *Tax Notes* Magazine. See Bernstein, Fogarsi, and Gordon (1995).

[14]The calculations look at the "big picture." They do not examine all gradations and industries. Some generalizations about industries may be misleading because of significant differences in structure within the industry.

Table 12.9   ARMEY FLAT TAX PLAN
Business Tax Worksheet

Gross Active Income:

Gross Receipts from Sales of Goods and Services	_____
Proceeds from Sales of Business Assets	_____

TOTAL INCOME _____

Deductions:

Compensation	_____
Contributions to Qualified Retirement Plans	_____
Capital Equipment	_____
Inventory Items	_____
Real Estate	_____
Other Business Property	_____
Supplies	_____
Services	_____
Travel and Entertainment	_____
Excise Taxes	_____
Transition Deductions	_____

TOTAL DEDUCTIONS (_____)

NET RECEIPTS _____

Business Tax Rate (17%)   x .17

TOTAL TAX LIABILITY _____

Table 12.10   NUNN-DOMENICI USA PLAN
Business Tax Worksheet

Receipts:

Gross Receipts from Domestic Sales
   of Goods and Services   _____

Proceeds from Sales of Business Assets   _____

TOTAL RECEIPTS   _____

Business Purchases: _____

Capital Equipment   _____

Inventory Items   _____

Real Estate   _____

Other Business Property   _____

Rent   _____

Supplies   _____

Services   _____

Bad Debts   _____

Travel and Entertainment   _____

Excise Taxes   _____

Transition Deductions   _____

TOTAL PURCHASES   (_____)

GROSS PROFIT (not less than zero)   _____

Business Tax Rate (11%)   x .11

Tax Liability   _____

Payroll Tax Credit   (_____)

TOTAL BUSINESS TAX DUE (a)   _____

Imports

Total Cost of Imported Products & Services Purchased   _____

Import Tax (11%)   x .11

TOTAL IMPORT TAX DUE (b)   _____

TOTAL TAX LIABILITY   (a)+(b)

Appendix A to Chapter 12

Computation of Corporate Tax Liability for 11 Industry Groups Under Current Law and Three Major Alternatives

The calculations in Tables 12.A1 through 12.A11 are the basis for Charts 12.1, 12.2, and 12.3 at the end of this chapter. Calculations are made for the four sets of assumptions shown in Table 12.7: "#1 Net Tax" assumes no exports and no transition relief; "#2 Tax with Transition" equals Net Tax minus the product of the tax rate and Maximum Transition Depreciation; "#3 Tax for Exporter" equals Net Tax times the product of the tax rate times "Exports"; "#4 Tax for Exporter with Transition" equal "#3 Tax for Exporter" minus the product of the tax rate times Maximum Transition Depreciation. Further, details about the underlying data are found in Appendix B. As noted in the text, many assumptions have been made to produce these tables. The information in the two appendices will allow industrious readers who are uncomfortable with the assumptions made to substitute their own.

Table 12.A1   Comparison of the Corporate Income Tax and Consumption Tax Alternatives: MANUFACTURING-DURABLES

	Current Law	5% VAT	Nunn-Domenici	Armey Flat Tax
Wages	0.0	344.4	344.4	0.0
Fringe Benefits	0.0	88.5	88.5	88.5
Interest	0.0	6.4	6.4	6.4
Profit	36.3	36.3	36.3	36.3
Nondeductible Taxes	0.0	10.6	10.6	10.6
Benefit of Expensing	0.0	−24.6	−24.6	−24.6
Total Tax Base	36.3	461.7	461.7	117.3
Tax Rate	35%	5%	11%	17%
Gross Tax	12.7	23.1	50.8	19.9
Payroll Credit	0.0	0.0	24.2	0.0
#1 Net Tax	**12.7**	**23.1**	**26.6**	**19.9**
Maximum Transition Depreciation	0.0	69.4	69.4	69.4
"Exports"	0.0	166.2	166.2	0.0
# 2 Tax with Transition	12.7	19.6	18.9	8.1
# 3 Tax for "Exporter"	12.7	14.8	8.3	8.1
# 4 Tax for Exporter with Transition	12.7	11.3	0.7	8.1

Table 12.A2   Comparison of the Corporate Income Tax and Consumption Tax Alternatives: MANUFACTURING-NONDURABLES

	Current Law	5% VAT	Nunn-Domenici	Armey Flat Tax
Wages	0.0	224.2	224.2	0.0
Fringe Benefits	0.0	54.7	54.7	54.7
Interest	0.0	30.5	30.5	30.5
Profit	63.0	63.0	63.0	63.0
Nondeductible Taxes	0.0	25.9	25.9	25.9
Benefit of Expensing	0.0	−19.6	−19.6	−19.6
Total Tax Base	63.0	378.7	378.7	154.5
Tax Rate	35%	5%	11%	17%
Gross Tax	22.0	18.9	41.7	26.3
Payroll Credit	0.0	0.0	15.8	0.0
#1 Net Tax	**22.0**	**18.9**	**25.9**	**26.3**
Maximum Transition Depreciation	0.0	55.3	55.3	55.3
"Exports"	0.0	136.3	136.3	0.0
# 2 Tax with Transition	22.0	16.2	19.8	16.9
# 3 Tax for "Exporter"	22.0	12.1	10.9	16.9
# 4 Tax for Exporter with Transition	22.0	9.4	4.8	16.9

Table 12.A3   Comparison of the Corporate Income Tax and Consumption Tax Alternatives: MINING

	Current Law	5% VAT	Nunn-Domenici	Armey Flat Tax
Wages	0.00	22.27	22.27	0.00
Fringe Benefits	0.00	5.36	5.36	5.36
Interest	0.00	1.71	1.71	1.71
Profit	2.86	2.86	2.86	2.86
Nondeductible Taxes	0.00	4.77	4.77	4.77
Benefit of Expensing	0.00	−10.28	−10.28	−10.28
Total Tax Base	2.86	26.69	26.69	4.43
Tax Rate	35%	5%	11%	17%
Gross Tax	1.00	1.33	2.94	0.75
Payroll Credit	0.00	0.00	1.57	0.00
#1 Net Tax	**1.00**	**1.33**	**1.37**	**0.75**
Maximum Transition Depreciation	0.00	29.07	29.07	29.07
"Exports"	0.00	9.61	9.61	0.00
# 2 Tax with Transition	1.00	−0.12	−1.83	−4.19
# 3 Tax for "Exporter"	1.00	0.85	0.31	−4.19
# 4 Tax for Exporter with Transition	1.00	−0.60	−2.88	−4.19

Table 12.A4   Comparison of the Corporate Income Tax and Consumption Tax Alternatives: CONSTRUCTION

	Current Law	5% VAT	Nunn-Domenici	Armey Flat Tax
Wages	0.00	89.66	89.66	0.00
Fringe Benefits	0.00	17.97	17.97	17.97
Interest	0.00	0.68	0.68	0.68
Profit	6.54	6.54	6.54	6.54
Nondeductible Taxes	0.00	2.20	2.20	2.20
Benefit of Expensing	0.00	−2.67	−2.67	−2.67
Total Tax Base	6.54	114.36	114.36	24.71
Tax Rate	35%	5%	11%	17%
Gross Tax	2.29	5.72	12.58	4.20
Payroll Credit	0.00	0.00	6.30	0.00
#1 Net Tax	**2.29**	**5.72**	**6.28**	**4.20**
Maximum Transition Depreciation	0.00	7.55	7.55	7.55
"Exports"	0.00	41.17	41.17	0.00
# 2 Tax with Transition	2.29	5.34	5.45	2.92
# 3 Tax for "Exporter"	2.29	3.66	1.75	2.92
# 4 Tax for Exporter with Transition	2.29	3.28	0.92	2.92

Table 12.A5   Comparison of the Corporate Income Tax and Consumption Tax Alternatives: TRANSPORTATION

	Current Law	5% VAT	Nunn-Domenici	Armey Flat Tax
Wages	0.00	95.03	95.03	0.00
Fringe Benefits	0.00	22.35	22.35	22.35
Interest	0.00	9.24	9.24	9.24
Profit	7.88	7.88	7.88	7.88
Nondeductible Taxes	0.00	5.07	5.07	5.07
Benefit of Expensing	0.00	−7.81	−7.81	−7.81
Total Tax Base	7.88	131.76	131.76	36.73
Tax Rate	35%	5%	11%	17%
Gross Tax	2.76	6.59	14.49	6.24
Payroll Credit	0.00	0.00	6.68	0.00
#1 Net Tax	**2.76**	**6.59**	**7.81**	**6.24**
Maximum Transition Depreciation	0.00	22.08	22.08	22.08
"Exports"	0.00	47.43	47.43	0.00
# 2 Tax with Transition	2.76	5.48	5.38	2.49
# 3 Tax for "Exporter"	2.76	4.22	2.60	2.49
# 4 Tax for Exporter with Transition	2.76	3.11	0.17	2.49

Table 12.A6 Comparison of the Corporate Income Tax and Consumption Tax Alternatives: COMMUNICATION

	Current Law	5% VAT	Nunn-Domenici	Armey Flat Tax
Wages	0.00	45.45	45.45	0.00
Fringe Benefits	0.00	12.92	12.92	12.92
Interest	0.00	11.31	11.31	11.31
Profit	28.02	28.02	28.02	28.02
Nondeductible Taxes	0.00	7.69	7.69	7.69
Benefit of Expensing	0.00	−12.69	−12.69	−12.69
Total Tax Base	28.02	92.69	92.69	47.24
Tax Rate	35%	5%	11%	17%
Gross Tax	9.81	4.63	10.20	8.03
Payroll Credit	0.00	0.00	3.19	0.00
#1 Net Tax	**9.81**	**4.63**	**7.00**	**8.03**
Maximum Transition Depreciation	0.00	35.88	35.88	35.88
"Exports"	0.00	33.37	33.37	0.00
# 2 Tax with Transition	9.81	2.84	3.05	1.93
# 3 Tax for "Exporter"	9.81	2.97	3.33	1.93
# 4 Tax for Exporter with Transition	9.81	1.17	−0.62	1.93

Table 12.A7 Comparison of the Corporate Income Tax and Consumption Tax Alternatives: UTILITIES

	Current Law	5% VAT	Nunn-Domenici	Armey Flat Tax
Wages	0.00	38.52	38.52	0.00
Fringe Benefits	0.00	9.85	9.85	9.85
Interest	0.00	21.05	21.05	21.05
Profit	30.93	30.93	30.93	30.93
Nondeductible Taxes	0.00	12.92	12.92	12.92
Benefit of Expensing	0.00	−12.57	−12.57	−12.57
Total Tax Base	30.93	100.71	100.71	62.19
Tax Rate	35%	5%	11%	17%
Gross Tax	10.83	5.04	11.08	10.57
Payroll Credit	0.00	0.00	2.71	0.00
#1 Net Tax	**10.83**	**5.04**	**8.37**	**10.57**
Maximum Transition Depreciation	0.00	35.54	35.54	35.54
"Exports"	0.00	36.26	36.26	0.00
# 2 Tax with Transition	10.83	3.26	4.46	4.53
# 3 Tax for "Exporter"	10.83	3.22	4.38	4.53
# 4 Tax for Exporter with Transition	10.83	1.45	0.47	4.53

Table 12.A8   Comparison of the Corporate Income Tax and Consumption Tax Alternatives: WHOLESALE TRADE

	Current Law	5% VAT	Nunn-Domenici	Armey Flat Tax
Wages	0.00	199.30	199.30	0.00
Fringe Benefits	0.00	36.89	36.89	36.89
Interest	0.00	6.28	6.28	6.28
Profit	38.35	38.35	38.35	38.35
Nondeductible Taxes	0.00	38.66	38.66	38.66
Benefit of Expensing	0.00	−9.61	−9.61	−9.61
Total Tax Base	38.35	309.87	309.87	110.57
Tax Rate	35%	5%	11%	17%
Gross Tax	13.42	15.49	34.09	18.80
Payroll Credit	0.00	0.00	14.01	0.00
#1 Net Tax	**13.42**	**15.49**	**20.07**	**18.80**
Maximum Transition Depreciation	0.00	27.19	27.19	27.19
"Exports"	0.00	111.55	111.55	0.00
# 2 Tax with Transition	13.42	14.13	17.08	14.17
# 3 Tax for "Exporter"	13.42	9.92	7.80	14.17
# 4 Tax for Exporter with Transition	13.42	8.56	4.81	14.17

Table 12.A9   Comparison of the Corporate Income Tax and Consumption Tax Alternatives: RETAIL TRADE

	Current Law	5% VAT	Nunn-Domenici	Armey Flat Tax
Wages	0.0	245.1	245.1	0.0
Fringe Benefits	0.0	42.6	42.6	42.6
Interest	0.0	10.4	10.4	10.4
Profit	35.3	35.3	35.3	35.3
Nondeductible Taxes	0.0	46.6	46.6	46.6
Benefit of Expensing	0.0	−10.1	−10.1	−10.1
Total Tax Base	35.3	369.9	369.9	124.8
Tax Rate	35%	5%	11%	17%
Gross Tax	12.4	18.5	40.7	21.2
Payroll Credit	0.0	0.0	17.2	0.0
#1 Net Tax	**12.4**	**18.5**	**23.5**	**21.2**
Maximum Transition Depreciation	0.0	28.6	28.6	28.6
"Exports"	0.0	133.2	133.2	0.0
# 2 Tax with Transition	12.4	17.1	20.3	16.3
# 3 Tax for "Exporter"	12.4	11.8	8.8	16.3
# 4 Tax for Exporter with Transition	12.4	10.4	5.7	16.3

Table 12.A10   Comparison of the Corporate Income Tax and Consumption Tax Alternatives: FINANCE

	Current Law	5% VAT	Nunn-Domenici	Armey Flat Tax
Wages	0.0	213.8	213.8	0.0
Fringe Benefits	0.0	38.4	38.4	38.4
Interest	0.0	–0.7	–0.7	–0.7
Profit	106.9	106.9	106.9	106.9
Nondeductible Taxes	0.0	19.2	19.2	19.2
Benefit of Expensing	0.0	–11.4	–11.4	–11.4
Total Tax Base	106.9	366.2	366.2	152.3
Tax Rate	35%	5%	11%	17%
Gross Tax	37.4	18.3	40.3	25.9
Payroll Credit	0.0	0.0	15.0	0.0
#1 Net Tax	**37.4**	**18.3**	**25.2**	**25.9**
Maximum Transition Depreciation	0.0	32.3	32.3	32.3
"Exports"	0.0	131.8	131.8	0.0
# 2 Tax with Transition	37.4	16.7	21.7	20.4
# 3 Tax for "Exporter"	37.4	11.7	10.7	20.4
# 4 Tax for Exporter with Transition	37.4	10.1	7.2	20.4

Table 12.A11   Comparison of the Corporate Income Tax and Consumption Tax Alternatives: SERVICES

	Current Law	5% VAT	Nunn-Domenici	Armey Flat Tax
Wages	0.0	485.6	485.6	0.0
Fringe Benefits	0.0	78.6	78.6	78.6
Interest	0.0	11.0	11.0	11.0
Profit	36.6	36.6	36.6	36.6
Nondeductible Taxes	0.0	10.8	10.8	10.8
Benefit of Expensing	0.0	–13.9	–13.9	–13.9
Total Tax Base	36.6	608.7	608.7	123.1
Tax Rate	35%	5%	11%	17%
Gross Tax	12.8	30.4	67.0	20.9
Payroll Credit	0.0	0.0	34.1	0.0
#1 Net Tax	**12.8**	**30.4**	**32.8**	**20.9**
Maximum Transition Depreciation	0.0	39.2	39.2	39.2
"Exports"	0.0	219.1	219.1	0.0
# 2 Tax with Transition	12.8	28.5	28.5	14.3
# 3 Tax for "Exporter"	12.8	19.5	8.7	14.3
# 4 Tax for Exporter with Transition	12.8	17.5	4.4	14.3

Appendix B to Chapter 12

Additional Notes About Data

The data used in this chapter are unpublished 1993 data from the Bureau of Economic Analysis of the Commerce Department. Value added for each industry was calculated by subtracting depreciation from gross domestic product. The data were provided by the Bureau of Economic Analysis on a diskette labeled, "Gross Product by Industry, 1947–93, USDOC, BEA, NIWD (BE-51)," Washington DC 20230, Release Date May 1995.

Aggregate Tax Liability

The adjustments to the Commerce Department data shown in Table 12.3 were calculated as follows:

1. *Expensing.* The Commerce Department calculates value added by depreciating capital equipment (the *income method*). Most value-added taxes calculate the tax base by expensing capital purchases (the *consumption method*).[15] In 1993, the Commerce Department data show that gross private domestic investment ($882.0 billion) exceeds depreciation ($669.1 billion) by 31.8 percent.[16] As the first step toward adjusting Commerce Department value added to a VAT tax base, depreciation is multiplied by 1.318 and subtracted from Commerce Department value added.

2. *Exports and imports.* Total U.S. exports in 1993 were $456.9 billion. In that year total U.S. imports were $538.0 billion. In the data analyses of this chapter, exports and imports were allocated across industries in proportion to their value added, and then between corporate and noncorporate components of each industry by the proportion of depreciation in the corporate and noncorporate component of each industry.

3. *Indirect business taxes.* Indirect business taxes are composed primarily of excise taxes and property taxes. Under the Armey and the Nunn-Domenici plans, excise taxes are deductible but property taxes are not. In 1993, total state and local excise taxes equaled $212.4 billion and federal excise taxes equaled $45.6 billion. In the aggregate calculations, this amount is subtracted from the value-added tax base. Across industries, this amount is allocated in proportion to indirect business taxes. (In the aggregate, excise taxes were 49 percent of total indirect business taxes in 1993.)

---

[15]See the Appendix to Chapter 3 for further explanation.

[16]U.S. Executive Office of the President (1995), p. 294.

4. *Transition depreciation.* Whether or not transition relief will be granted is a controversial issue. As an illustration of the potential impact of these provisions, the calculations include a downward adjustment of the tax base equal to 90 percent of depreciation allowance in 1993. This is meant to be a proxy for the amount of transition depreciation that would be allowed in the first year after the effective date. Of course in later years (or if transition relief was not complete), the amount would be less. In the aggregate, total private sector depreciation in 1993 was $644 billion, 13.1 percent of value added.

5. *Payroll credit.* A critical component of the Nunn-Domenici proposal is the payroll credit. The payroll credit is 7.65 percent of wages paid to each individual up to $61,200 (in 1995) and 1.45 percent for all amounts above $61,200. In this analysis it is assumed that 90 percent of all wages generate the 7.65 percent tax credit. Thus, the average effective rate of credit is 7.03 percent.

Allocations Between Corporate and Noncorporate Businesses

Corporate profits and payments to owners of noncorporate business were allocated 100 percent to the corporate and noncorporate sectors respectively. Other components of value added—wages, fringe benefits, net interest, rent, and business taxes—were allocated in proportion to the amount of corporate and noncorporate depreciation in each sector. The ratio of corporate to total depreciation in each industry is shown in Table 12.6 and is used in Tables 12A.1 through 12A.11.

Estimate of the "Typical" Exporter

The "typical" exporter for each industry is calculated in the following manner. Based on the observation that large exporters typically export between five and fifteen percent of their sales,[17] it is assumed that a "typical" exporter has exports equal to 10 percent of sales. Total sales by manufacturers in 1993 was $3,015 billion.[18] Total value added (as measured under a regular VAT tax base) for the manufacturing sector is $840 billion.[19] Thus, the ratio of value added to sales is approximately 28 percent and the ratio of exports to value added is approximately 36 percent. These estimates are used in Table 12.5 and Tables 12.A1 through 12.A11.

---

[17]Fortune (1987), p. 80.

[18]U.S. Executive Office of the President (1995), p. 382.

[19]See Table 12.9 of this chapter.

**Chart 12.1   Percent Increase (or Decrease) in Tax Liability Under Three Alternatives:
No Exports, No Transition**

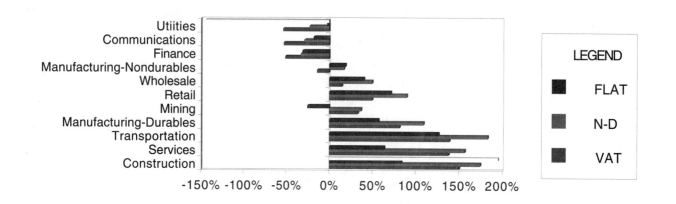

Chart 12.2   Percent Change in Tax Liability Under Three Alternatives: No Exports, With Transition

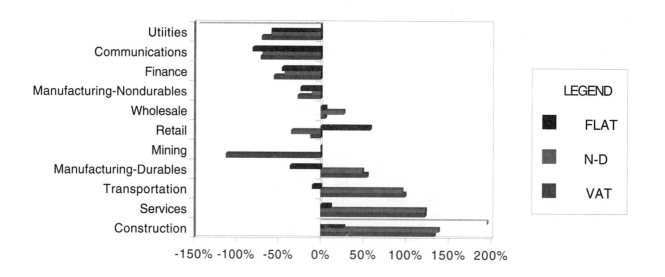

Not Shown: Mining 282% decrease under Nunn-Domenici and 518% decrease under Flat Tax

Chart 12.3   Percent Increase in Tax Liability Under Three Alternatives: "Typical Exporter", No Transition

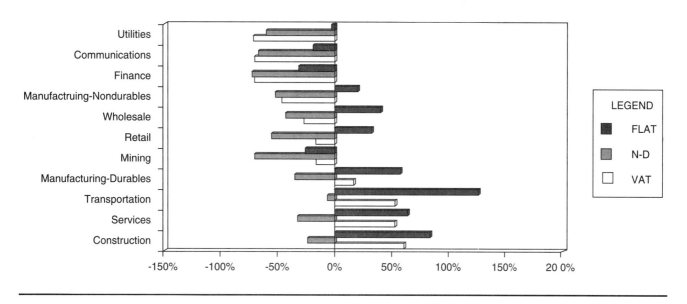

13

The Impact of Consumption Taxes on Individuals and on Noncorporate Businesses

Summary

- Under current law, the individual tax burden per dollar of income is largest for upper-income households.

- Relative to current law, the Nunn-Domenici proposal appears to provide tax relief to the lowest and highest income classes, and a modest tax increase to middle-income taxpayers.

- The individual component of the Flat Tax appears to provide tax relief for nearly all individual taxpayers. It is likely, therefore, that with a 17-percent rate, the Flat Tax raises significantly less revenue than the current individual income tax.

- Under the Flat Tax, the individual tax burden per dollar of income is largest for middle-income taxpayers. Higher-income households enjoy substantial relief under the tax because capital income is exempt.

- Both the Nunn-Domenici proposal and the Flat Tax impose new tax burdens on noncorporate business. For a "typical" small business, the Nunn-Domenici proposal imposes a greater business burden than the Flat Tax.

- For owners of unincorporated businesses, the combined individual and business tax burden under the Flat Tax appears to be less than the burden under current law. Under the Nunn-Domenici proposal, the combined burden appears to be greater than current law except in the case of low-income business owners (particularly when business income is only a small component of total family income). In contrast, high-income owners of unincorporated businesses generally appear to pay a much greater amount of taxes under the Nunn-Domenici proposal than under current law.

The focus of this study so far has been on business taxes. In this chapter attention is shifted to individual taxes. First is a comparative study of the individual tax burden under (1) current law, (2) the Flat Tax, and (3) the Nunn-Domenici tax. Next, the combined individual and business tax burdens of the owners of noncorporate business under these same three alternatives are examined. To acquaint readers with the details of each alternative, numerous examples are presented. In all cases, care has been taken to present examples that are realistic. This is achieved by basing the calculations on the extensive data collected by the IRS from individual and business tax returns.

The Impact of Consumption Taxes on Individuals

Background

Before delving into the calculations, it is useful to review some basic facts about the current individual income tax. In 1993 (the latest year for which comprehensive data are available), $632 billion of federal individual income tax revenue was collected, and more than 115 million individual income tax returns were filed. As shown in Chart 13.1, which appears at the end of this chapter, more than half of these returns showed adjusted gross income (AGI) of less than $30,000. These returns accounted for only about 10 percent of total individual income tax collected. In contrast, more than one-third of total individual income tax revenue is collected from the 4 percent of tax returns with adjusted gross income in excess of $100,000. It is also worth noting that only 29 percent of all individual tax filings included itemized deductions.[1]

Preview of Calculations

The factual basis for the calculations presented in this chapter are the data collected by the Statistics of Income (SOI) Division of the IRS. Because of the likely lag in enactment of any major consumption tax proposal, all data were adjusted to levels that would prevail in the year 2000 based on currently available Congressional Budget Office estimates of inflation. Data for each income class (e.g., those returns with adjusted gross income between $10,000 and $25,000) were then averaged and adjusted so AGI classifications were round numbers. The resulting data used in the calculations are intended to be reasonable approximations of what tax returns for a given amount of AGI might be in the year 2000. It is extremely important to remember, however, that there can be substantial variance within each income category. For example, some high-income individuals who are renters will have no mortgage deductions even though the average mortgage deduction in their income category may be quite large.

---

[1]The 1993 individual income tax return data that serve as the basis of the comments in this paragraph, as well as the basis for individual tax return calculations in Tables 13.1 through 13.7 are shown in Table 13.A1 in the Appendix to this chapter.

In addition to adjusting the data, computer models were developed for each of the three alternatives examined. For current law, it was assumed that 1993 law would prevail in the year 2000. Current law and the two consumption tax alternatives have numerous adjustments for inflation (e.g., for the standard deductions, exemption amounts, and tax brackets). All of these adjustments were calculated for levels that would prevail in the year 2000 given current projections about future inflation.

The Results of the Calculations

The Current Individual Income Tax

Table 13.1 presents calculations depicting the tax burden for a couple with two children and a single individual in the year 2000 under current law. Personal exemptions and the standard deduction allow most low-income households to entirely escape tax. Many low-income households with children receive refunds as a result of the earned income tax credit (EITC). As income increases, so do itemized deductions, and therefore most taxpayers with adjusted gross income in excess of $50,000 itemize deductions.[2] In general, the larger amounts of itemized deductions are on average not enough to offset the impact of the progressive rate structure enacted into law in 1993 (and to a lesser extent, the phaseout of itemized deductions and personal exemptions enacted into law in 1990). On the whole, tax as a percentage of AGI rises as income rises, that is, the current tax system is progressive.

The Nunn-Domenici Individual Tax

Table 13.2 presents calculations depicting the tax burden for a couple with two children and a single individual in the year 2000 under the individual tax of the Nunn-Domenici proposal. In addition to the earned income credit, the *refundable* payroll tax credit provides substantial tax relief to low-income working households. Under the Nunn-Domenici proposal, personal exemption amounts are slightly lower than current law (but they do not phaseout for high-bracket taxpayers as under current law). On the other hand, the family allowance (which can be considered the equivalent to the standard deduction under current law) is slightly larger than the standard deduction available under current law. Moreover, unlike the itemized deduction, the family allowance is available to all taxpayers (and, therefore, low-income taxpayers will get some benefits from itemized deductions).

Unlike current law, where the top 39.6 percent bracket is not imposed until taxable income reaches $250,000, the Nunn-Domenici proposal imposes its top 40 percent rate on middle-income households. As a general rule, most saving is done by the wealthiest individuals, and low-income households in general do little or no saving. The great benefit to high-income households is the deduction for new saving. But this benefit varies widely because the rate of saving among high-income households can vary greatly.

---

[2]As shown in Table 13.A1, the three largest itemized deductions are deductions for state and local taxes, deductions for mortgage interest, and deductions for charitable contributions.

In general, the Nunn-Domenici proposal seems to place tax burdens on middle-income taxpayers that are comparable to current law and provides some relief to low- and high-income taxpayers.

The Individual Flat Tax

Table 13.3 presents calculations depicting the tax burden for a couple with two children and a single individual in the year 2000 under the individual component of the Flat Tax. Perhaps the most prominent feature of the individual Flat Tax is the size of the personal allowances. They are far larger than the combined standard deduction and personal exemptions available under current law or the Nunn-Domenici proposal. For a family of four, these allowances are estimated to sum to $35,250 by the year 2000. These large personal allowances permit lower-income taxpayers to escape tax in far greater numbers than current law. Moreover, unlike current law, taxpayers may claim refunds for negative tax (i.e., for an amount equal to the tax rate times any excess of deductions over adjusted gross income). To some extent, this offsets the impact of the repeal of the earned income tax credit under the proposal.

The Flat Tax has a single low rate that provides a significant advantage to high-income taxpayers relative to current law and relative to the Nunn-Domenici proposal. Moreover, because high-income taxpayers receive a far greater fraction of their income from capital than low-income taxpayers, high-income taxpayers enjoy significant tax relief under the Flat Tax despite the *complete* elimination of itemized deductions.

Comparison of the Alternatives

The three alternatives can be compared at a glance with the summary presented in Chart 13.2, which appears at the end of this chapter. This graph shows tax as a percent of AGI for married couples with two children for different income levels. With regard to overall amount of tax paid, the most striking feature of the diagram is the significantly lower amounts of individual tax collected under the Flat Tax compared to current law. It is likely that the Flat Tax's 17 percent rate would have to be increased substantially to raise as much revenue as the current individual income tax.

With regard to the distribution of the tax burden, both the current individual income tax and the individual Nunn-Domenici tax appear to maintain progressivity through all income levels. Compared to current law, the Nunn-Domenici proposal provides more relief for the poor—primarily through the refundable payroll credit—and more relief for the wealthy—primarily through the deduction for savings. The individual component of the Flat Tax provides substantial relief to the poor—despite the repeal of the EITC—by allowing refunds when taxable compensation is negative. The highest income categories actually may have lower effective tax rates than upper-middle-income taxpayers because income from capital is exempt from tax.

The Impact of Consumption Taxes on Noncorporate Businesses

Background

In the previous chapter, business taxes were analyzed by comparing the business consumption taxes to the *corporate* income tax. The focus there was purely on entity-level taxes. In this section, the impacts of consumption taxes on noncorporate business are analyzed by comparing current law to the combined impact of individual and business-level taxes under the proposed alternatives.

The Statistics of Income (SOI) Division of the Internal Revenue Service collects and publishes extensive amounts of data on sole proprietorships and partnerships.[3] The data were carefully inspected to identify some realistic and representative examples of noncorporate business.

Chart 13.3 shows that partnership income is heavily concentrated among those businesses providing highly skilled professional services—such as lawyers (36 percent of total partnership income), physicians (9 percent), and accountants (8 percent). Chart 13.4 shows that partners in these professions on average generate far greater income from their partnerships than do other partners in other lines of business. Chart 13.5 shows that partnership and S corporation income is highly concentrated in the upper-income brackets.[4]

In contrast to the case of partnerships, sole proprietorship income is more evenly spread throughout different types of business. This is shown in Chart 13.6. This is because sole proprietorship data are dominated by numerous small businesses generating relatively low levels of income. Chart 13.7 shows that as in the case of partnerships the highly skilled professionals still generate higher than average returns. Chart 13.8 indicates that sole proprietorship income is spread much more uniformly across income classes than partnership income.[5]

Case Studies of Noncorporate Business

With these data as points of reference, case studies of four noncorporate businesses and their owners were constructed and analyzed. The data and the results of the calculations are described below.

Case 1: Mom and Pop Retail Store

Although not important in terms of income generated, truly small businesses are quite numerous in the Unites States. In 1992, there were 2.8 million sole proprietorships in retail and wholesale trade. The average income

---

[3]The underlying partnership and sole proprietorship data are presented in more detail in the Appendix to this chapter in Tables 13.A2 and 13.A3.

[4]The data source for this chart is Michael E. Weber, "Individual Income Tax Returns, 1993: Early Tax Estimates," *Statistics of Income Bulletin*, Internal Revenue Service, Fall 1994, Washington D.C.

[5]The data source for this chart is the same as for Chart 13.5.

generated by each of these businesses was just under $5,000. In the first case study (Table 13.4), a family of four has total adjusted gross income of $21,000 in the year 2000 of which $20,000 is from their small business. They have two part-time employees whom they pay $12,500 each.

Under current law, this family takes the standard deduction. This deduction, along with four personal exemptions, nearly eliminates their entire income tax liability. There is no entity-level business tax.

Under the Nunn-Domenici proposal, the family benefits relative to current law because they can deduct their mortgage interest payments and charitable contributions, and their small addition to saving. This approximately offsets the personal exemption deductions that are somewhat smaller than current law. The biggest difference, however, between the Nunn-Domenici Individual Tax and the current individual income tax is the availability of the refundable payroll credit under the new system, which provides a substantial benefit to this family. These benefits on the individual side, however, are more than offset on the business side. While the business pays no income tax under current law, there is an 11 percent tax on the small business's value-added (primarily wages to employees and payments to the owner). Despite the availability of the payroll credit, this results in a significant new tax burden on the family business, and a much greater total burden on its proprietors.

Under the Flat Tax, the family has a significant negative tax liability because of the large family and dependency deductions allowed. Because negative tax liability is refundable under the proposal, this results in a large refund to the family. This large refund offsets the business tax burden and leaves the family with a somewhat smaller total tax burden than current law. (The business tax burden is significantly less than under the Nunn-Domenici proposal because salaries and payments to owners are deductible under the Flat Tax.)

Overall, for this family with a small business, both consumption tax alternatives provide substantial individual tax relief relative to current law. In the case of Nunn-Domenici, this benefit is overwhelmed by a large new business tax burden. In the case of the Flat Tax, the new business tax burden is almost entirely negated by individual tax benefit.

Case 2: Two-Earner Couple with One Earner Owning Small Business

In the second case study (Table 13.5), a family of four has two breadwinners. One is an employee with an annual salary of $33,000, and the second has a small business clearing $15,000. Thus, unlike the first case study, a much smaller portion of family income is business income. The business pays about $11,000 in wages to its single employee.

As in the first case, with regard to the individual tax, the family does better than under current law. In the case of the Nunn-Domenici proposal, this is due to the availability of the family allowance and personal deductions in addition to itemized deductions and the deduction for new saving. In the case of the Flat Tax, this is due to the generous family and dependency deductions.

Also, as in the first case, the benefits under the individual consumption tax alternatives are countered by a higher business tax. In this case, however, business income and business taxes are not as dominant in the family finances, and under both plans the family has a reduced tax burden relative to current law.

Case 3: Sole Practitioner Physician

In the third case study (Table 13.6), a family of four has $145,000 of income in the year 2000 from two sources. $120,000 is generated by one spouse with a medical practice, and the remainder is income from investments. Part of the medical practice expenses are $22,000 of salary to its sole employee.

Under current law, the $14,500 of itemized deductions is used instead of the standard deduction. Under the Nunn-Domenici proposal, tax rates are generally higher, but the family benefits from the availability of a family allowance and a deduction for additional saving. The net result is that this family pays virtually the same individual tax under current law and the Nunn-Domenici proposal. Under the Flat Tax, despite the denial of itemized deductions, the family is far better off than under current law because of family and dependency deductions and because of the lower tax rate imposed.

The Nunn-Domenici business tax provides a large new tax burden for the medical practice and overall leaves the family with a larger tax burden than under current law. The business component of the Flat Tax also provides a new burden, but it is small relative to that under Nunn-Domenici and insufficient to completely offset the individual benefits under the Flat Tax.

Case 4: Partner at Law Firm

This fourth case (Table 13.7) is in many ways similar to the prior case except income levels are higher. The family of four generates $230,000 of income—most of it from one parent's share of law partnership profits. If the law partnership's salaries to employees were allocated in proportion to partners' income, this partner's share would be about $150,000.

Under current law, this family itemizes deductions. Under Nunn-Domenici, the family gets a family allowance and savings deduction in addition to itemized deductions, but these benefits do not offset the burdens of higher rates. The family pays significantly more individual tax than under current law. The family pays less individual tax under the Flat Tax than under current law, primarily due to the lower rates available under the new plan.

Consideration of business taxes make the Nunn-Domenici proposal even less attractive. Not only does the Nunn-Domenici individual tax impose a greater burden than current law, but in addition a substantial new business tax is incurred. The business tax disallows deductions for employment costs, so salaries and benefits of hired labor as well as of the partners are all taxed. The net result is that under the Nunn-Domenici proposal the total individual and business tax burden for this family increases by nearly 80 percent relative to current law. The Flat Tax imposes a much smaller business tax burden, and (as in the case of the physician's family, above), this new business burden does not completely offset the benefits enjoyed (relative to current law) under the individual tax. Thus, for these professionals the burden of the Flat Tax is less than that of current law.

A Note About the Taxation of Estates, Trusts, and Gifts

Under current law, bequests at death are taxed under a separate federal *estate* tax. A federal *gift* tax is imposed on lifetime transfers. Also, income generated by trusts and estates are subject to *income* tax after reflecting a flow-through deduction for distributions to beneficiaries.

The administration of estate and gift taxes is separable from the administration of consumption taxes. Thus, a new retail sales tax, value-added tax, or individual consumption tax could be implemented with or without existing estate and gift taxes.[6] The proposed Flat Tax eliminates these transfer taxes while the Nunn-Domenici tax system retains estate and gift taxes and provides for carryover basis at death. As a matter of policy, some might argue that estate and gift taxes are more important than ever if a consumption tax replaces the income tax because estate and gift taxes are highly progressive taxes that would be necessary to offset the regressivity of consumption taxes. On the other hand, others argue that estate and gift taxes—like income taxes—penalize the accumulation of saving and wealth that is necessary for capital formation.

With regard to the income from trusts and estates, it seems likely that under any retail sales tax or value-added tax (which are only collected from businesses) their gross receipts would be exempt from tax unless these receipts were business receipts (i.e., these receipts were generated by business transactions where the business's legal entity is the trust itself and did not flow through a taxable business entity). However, it does seem that trusts could be considered taxable businesses if they engage in an active trade or business. Under the Flat Tax, individuals do not pay tax on gifts, inheritances, or income from trusts.

Without specific legislative markup language or commentary, it is assumed that the current system for taxing fiduciaries and beneficiaries would continue under a flat tax. However since most receipts and disbursements, especially distributions to beneficiaries, reflect investment activities (dividends interest, gains and losses on sales of investment assets, passive income and loss from partnerhips/S corporation and similar investment entities like REITs, RICs, etc.), most fiduciary activities would not be subject to a flat tax at either the fiduciary or beneficiary level.

Under the Nunn-Domenici proposal, an entirely new set of rules have been developed to govern the tax treatment of distributions to beneficiaries. In general, under these rules, the trust is treated as a flow-through entity. Principles similar to those governing the operation of the unlimited saving allowance seem to be in operation, that is, assets in trust on the date of enactment have basis, but distribution of the entire proceeds of postenactment trust assets, which have no basis, may be subject to tax upon distribution.

How this concept will interrelate with state law and governing instruments that utilize fiduciary accounting income concepts is very problematic.

---

[6]Bequests and inheritance could be brought into the system through accessions.

Conclusion

The data presented in this chapter show that consumption tax alternatives will substantially redistribute the tax burden. Under the Nunn-Domenici proposal, individual taxes will be less for low-income households primarily because of a deductible payroll tax credit. High-income households will pay less primarily because of the deduction for new saving.

Under the Flat Tax, all individual taxpayers appear to pay less. This is particularly true for low-income households that could receive refunds for negative tax liability—which would be commonplace under the proposal because of the generous family deduction and dependency deductions. It would also be particularly true for high-income households that no longer face a progressive rate structure and only pay tax on wage income.

Under current law, noncorporate businesses pay no entity-level income tax as they would under both consumption tax alternatives. For noncorporate businesses, the business taxes proposed under both Nunn-Domenici and the Flat Tax would pose substantial new tax burdens. The Nunn-Domenici tax is particularly harsh for "typical" noncorporate businesses because these business are labor-intensive and wages are not deductible under the tax (as they are under the Flat Tax).

Table 13.1   Individual Income Tax Burden for Various Income Classes Under Current Law

A. FAMILY OF FOUR

Adjusted Gross Income	$10,000	$25,000	$50,000	$75,000	$100,000	$150,000	$600,000
Standard Deduction	$ 7,600	$ 7,600	$ 7,600	$ 0	$ 0	$ 0	$ 0
Itemized Deductions	$ 0	$ 0	$ 0	$10,923	$ 16,536	$ 24,637	$ 72,831
Personal Exemptions	$11,800	$11,800	$11,800	$11,800	$ 11,800	$ 11,800	$ 0
Taxable Income	($ 9,400)	$ 5,600	$30,600	$52,277	$ 71,665	$113,563	$527,169
Tax at 15%	$ 0	$ 840	$ 4,590	$ 6,825	$ 6,825	$ 6,825	$ 6,825
Tax at 28%	$ 0	$ 0	$ 0	$ 1,898	$ 7,326	$ 18,060	$ 18,060
Tax at 31%	$ 0	$ 0	$ 0	$ 0	$ 0	$ 1,105	$ 17,871
Tax at 36%	$ 0	$ 0	$ 0	$ 0	$ 0	$ 0	$ 47,430
Tax at 39.6%	$ 0	$ 0	$ 0	$ 0	$ 0	$ 0	$ 90,197
Total Tax (Less EITC)	($ 2,080)	$ 100	$ 4,590	$ 8,723	$ 14,151	$ 25,990	$180,383
Tax as % of AGI	−20.8%	0.4%	9.2%	11.6%	14.2%	17.3%	30.1%

B. SINGLE

Adjusted Gross Income	$10,000	$25,000	$50,000	$75,000	$100,000	$150,000	$600,000
Standard Deduction	$ 4,550	$ 4,550	$ 0	$ 0	$ 0	$ 0	$ 0
Itemized Deductions	$ 0	$ 0	$ 5,213	$10,923	$ 16,536	$ 24,638	$ 72,831
Personal Exemptions	$ 2,950	$ 2,950	$ 2,950	$ 2,950	$ 2,950	$ 2,570	$ 0
Taxable Income	$ 2,500	$17,500	$41,837	$61,127	$ 80,514	$122,792	$527,169
Tax at 15%	$ 375	$ 2,405	$ 4,087	$ 4,087	$ 4,087	$ 4,087	$ 4,087
Tax at 28%	$ 0	$ 411	$ 4,084	$ 9,486	$ 10,850	$ 10,850	$ 10,850
Tax at 31%	$ 0	$ 0	$ 0	$ 0	$ 4,499	$ 17,606	$ 22,227
Tax at 36%	$ 0	$ 0	$ 0	$ 0	$ 0	$ 0	$ 58,212
Tax at 39.6%	$ 0	$ 0	$ 0	$ 0	$ 0	$ 0	$ 90,196
Total Tax	$ 375	$ 2,816	$ 8,172	$13,573	$ 19,437	$ 32,543	$185,573
Tax as % of AGI	3.8%	11.3%	16.3%	18.1%	19.4%	21.7%	30.9%

Table 13.2   Individual Income Tax Burden for Various Income Classes Under the Nunn-Domenici Plan[7]

A. FAMILY OF FOUR

Adjusted Gross Income	$10,000	$25,000	$50,000	$75,000	$100,000	$150,000	$600,000
Family Allowance	$ 8,400	$ 8,400	$ 8,400	$ 8,400	$ 8,400	$ 8,400	$ 8,400
Personal Exemptions	$10,200	$10,200	$10,200	$10,200	$ 10,200	$ 10,200	$ 10,200
Itemized Deductions	$ 408	$ 1,006	$ 3,466	$ 6,889	$ 10,011	$ 14,347	$ 43,031
Taxable Income	($ 9,145)	$ 3,181	$24,175	$43,951	$ 62,736	$ 96,620	$391,719
Tax at 8%	$ 0	$ 254	$ 488	$ 488	$ 488	$ 488	$ 488
Tax at 19%	$ 0	$ 0	$ 3,434	$ 4,009	$ 4,009	$ 4,009	$ 4,009
Tax at 40%	$ 0	$ 0	$ 0	$ 6,700	$ 14,214	$ 27,768	$145,807
Total Tax	$ 0	$ 254	$ 3,922	$11,197	$ 18,711	$ 32,265	$150,304
Less Payroll Credit	$ 743	$ 1,554	$ 3,217	$ 4,838	$ 6,148	$ 6,512	$ 9,166
Less EITC	$ 2,040	$ 740	$ 0	$ 0	$ 0	$ 0	$ 0
Net Tax	($ 2,783)	($ 2,040)	$ 705	$ 6,359	$ 12,564	$ 25,754	$141,138
Tax as % of AGI	−27.8%	−8.2%	1.4%	8.5%	12.6%	17.2%	23.5%

B. SINGLE

Adjusted Gross Income	$10,000	$25,000	$50,000	$75,000	$100,000	$150,000	$600,000
Family Allowance	$ 5,000	$ 5,000	$ 5,000	$ 5,000	$ 5,000	$ 5,000	$ 5,000
Personal Exemptions	$ 2,550	$ 2,550	$ 2,550	$ 2,550	$ 2,550	$ 2,550	$ 2,550
Itemized Deductions	$ 408	$ 1,006	$ 3,466	$ 6,889	$ 10,011	$ 14,347	$ 43,031
Taxable Income	$ 1,906	$14,231	$35,226	$55,001	$ 73,787	$107,671	$402,769
Tax at 8%	$ 152	$ 290	$ 290	$ 290	$ 290	$ 290	$ 290
Tax at 19%	$ 0	$ 2,015	$ 2,411	$ 2,411	$ 2,411	$ 2,411	$ 2,411
Tax at 40%	$ 0	$ 0	$ 7,563	$15,473	$ 22,988	$ 36,541	$154,580
Total Tax	$ 152	$ 2,305	$10,265	$18,175	$ 25,689	$ 39,243	$157,282
Less Payroll Credit	$ 743	$ 1,554	$ 3,217	$ 4,838	$ 6,148	$ 6,512	$ 9,166
Less EITC	$ 0	$ 0	$ 0	$ 0	$ 0	$ 0	$ 0
Net Tax	($ 590)	$ 751	$ 7,048	$13,337	$ 19,541	$ 32,731	$148,116
Tax as % of AGI	−5.9%	3.0%	14.1%	17.8%	19.5%	21.8%	24.7%

---

[7]Taxable income equals adjusted gross income less personal exemptions, itemized deductions, and the deduction for net new saving (not shown on table).

Table 13.3   Individual Income Tax Burden for Various Income Classes Under the Flat Tax[8]

A. FAMILY OF FOUR

Adjusted Gross Income	$10,000	$25,000	$50,000	$75,000	$100,000	$150,000	$600,000
Wages	$ 9,712	$20,320	$42,052	$63,242	$ 81,702	$106,790	$289,876
Personal Allowance	$24,250	$24,250	$24,250	$24,250	$ 24,250	$ 24,250	$ 24,250
Dependents Allowance	$11,300	$11,300	$11,300	$11,300	$ 11,300	$ 11,300	$ 11,300
Taxable Compensation	($25,838)	($15,230)	$ 6,502	$27,692	$ 46,152	$ 71,240	$254,326
Tax Rate	17%	17%	17%	17%	17%	17%	17%
Tax	($ 4,393)	($ 2,589)	$ 1,105	$ 4,708	$ 7,846	$ 12,111	$ 43,235
Tax as % of AGI	−43.9%	−10.4%	2.2%	6.3%	7.8%	8.1%	7.2%

B. SINGLE

Adjusted Gross Income	$10,000	$25,000	$50,000	$75,000	$100,000	$150,000	$600,000
Wages	$ 9,712	$20,320	$42,052	$63,242	$ 81,702	$106,790	$289,876
Personal Allowance	$12,150	$12,150	$12,150	$12,150	$ 12,150	$ 12,150	$ 12,150
Dependents Allowance	$ 0	$ 0	$ 0	$ 0	$ 0	$ 0	$ 0
Taxable Compensation	($ 2,438)	$ 8,170	$29,902	$51,092	$ 69,552	$ 94,640	$277,726
Tax Rate	17%	17%	17%	17%	17%	17%	17%
Tax	($ 415)	$ 1,389	$ 5,083	$ 8,686	$ 11,824	$ 16,089	$ 47,213
Tax as % of AGI	−4.1%	5.6%	10.2%	11.6%	11.8%	10.7%	7.9%

---

[8]Taxable compensation equals wages less the personal allowance and the dependents allowance.

Table 13.4   Tax Burden for Owners of Unincorporated Businesses Under Current Law, Nunn-Domenici, and the Flat Tax — Case 1: Mom and Pop Retail Store[9]

INDIVIDUAL TAX

	CURRENT LAW	NUNN-DOMENICI	FLAT TAX
Income from Noncorporate Business	$20,000	$20,000	$20,000
Other Wage Income	$ 0	$ 0	$ 0
Other Capital Income	$ 1,000	$ 1,000	$ 0
Total Gross Income	$21,000	$21,000	$20,000
Standard Deduction/Family Allowance	$ 7,600	$ 8,400	$24,250
Personal/Dependency Deduction—Number	4	4	2
Personal/Dependency Deduction—Amount	$11,800	$10,200	$11,300
Charitable Deduction	$ 0	$ 200	$ 0
Mortgage Deduction	$ 0	$ 800	$ 0
Deduction for Net Saving	$ 0	$ 500	$ 0
Tax Base	$ 1,600	$ 900	($15,550)
Tax	$ 240	$ 72	($ 2,643)
Payroll Credit	$ 0	$ 1,530	$ 0
Net Tax	**$ 240**	**($ 1,458)**	**($ 2,643)**

BUSINESS TAX

	CURRENT LAW	NUNN-DOMENICI	FLAT TAX
Wages to Employees		$25,000	$ 0
Fringe Benefits		$ 9,000	$ 9,000
Interest		$ 4,750	$ 4,750
Income to Owner		$20,000	$ 0
Tax Base		$58,750	$13,750
Tax Rate		11%	17%
Gross Tax		$ 6,463	$ 2,338
Payroll Credit		$ 1,750	$ 0
Net Tax	**– none –**	**$ 4,713**	**$ 2,338**
TOTAL INDIVIDUAL AND BUSINESS TAX	**$ 240**	**$ 3,255**	**($ 306)**

---

[9]The cash flow to the individual owner will be affected where money from the business is not available to pass through.

Table 13.5   Tax Burden for Owners of Unincorporated Businesses Under Current Law, Nunn-Domenici, and the Flat Tax — Case 2: Two Earner Couple, One Owning a Small Business

INDIVIDUAL TAX

	CURRENT LAW	NUNN-DOMENICI	FLAT TAX
Income from Noncorporate Business	$15,000	$15,000	$15,000
Other Wage Income	$33,000	$33,000	$33,000
Other Capital Income	$ 2,000	$ 2,000	$ 0
Total Gross Income	$50,000	$50,000	$48,000
Standard Deduction/Family Allowance	$ 7,600	$ 8,400	$24,250
Personal/Dependency Deduction—Number	4	4	2
Personal/Dependency Deduction—Amount	$11,800	$10,200	$11,300
Charitable Deduction	$ 0	$ 700	$ 0
Mortgage Deduction	$ 0	$ 2,700	$ 0
Deduction for Net Saving	$ 0	$ 3,000	$ 0
Tax Base	$30,600	$25,000	$12,450
Tax	$ 4,590	$ 4,079	$ 2,117
Payroll Credit	$ 0	$ 3,672	$ 0
Net Tax	**$ 4,590**	**$ 407**	**$ 2,117**

BUSINESS TAX

	CURRENT LAW	NUNN-DOMENICI	FLAT TAX
Wages to Employees		$10,950	$ 0
Fringe Benefits		$ 5,190	$ 5,190
Interest		$ 548	$ 548
Income to Owner		$15,000	$ 0
Tax Base		$31,688	$ 5,738
Tax Rate		11%	17%
Gross Tax		$ 3,486	$ 975
Payroll Credit		$ 1,530	$ 0
Net Tax	– none –	**$ 1,956**	**$ 975**
TOTAL INDIVIDUAL AND BUSINESS TAX	**$ 4,590**	**$ 2,363**	**$ 3,092**

Table 13.6   Tax Burden for Owners of Unincorporated Businesses Under Current Law, Nunn-Domenici, and the Flat Tax — Case 3: Sole Practitioner Physician

INDIVIDUAL TAX

	CURRENT LAW*	NUNN-DOMENICI	FLAT TAX
Income from Noncorporate Business	$120,000	$120,000	$120,000
Other Wage Income	$ 0	$ 0	$ 0
Other Capital Income	$ 30,000	$ 30,000	$ 0
Total Gross Income	$150,000	$150,000	$120,000
Standard Deduction/Family Allowance	$ 0	$ 8,400	$ 24,250
Personal/Dependency Deduction—Number	4	4	2
Personal/Dependency Deduction—Amount	$ 11,800	$ 10,200	$ 11,300
Charitable Deduction	$ 3,500	$ 3,500	$ 0
Mortgage Deduction	$ 11,000	$ 11,000	$ 0
Deduction for Net Saving	$ 0	$ 20,000	$ 0
Tax Base	$112,961	$ 96,900	$ 84,450
Tax	$ 25,803	$ 32,377	$ 14,357
Payroll Credit	$ 0	$ 6,703	$ 0
Net Tax	**$ 25,803**	**$ 25,674**	**$ 14,357**

BUSINESS TAX

	CURRENT LAW	NUNN-DOMENICI	FLAT TAX
Wages to Employees		$ 21,600	$ 0
Fringe Benefits		$ 28,320	$ 28,320
Interest		$ 432	$ 432
Income to Owner		$120,000	$ 0
Tax Base		$170,352	$ 28,752
Tax Rate		11%	17%
Gross Tax		$ 18,739	$ 4,888
Payroll Credit		$ 8,215	$ 0
Net Tax	– none –	**$ 10,524**	**$ 4,888**
TOTAL INDIVIDUAL AND BUSINESS TAX	**$ 25,803**	**$ 36,198**	**$ 19,244**

*Not shown are an $11,000 deduction for state and local income taxes and property taxes, and a $261 deduction disallowance for high income taxpayers.

Table 13.7   Tax Burden for Owners of Unincorporated Businesses Under Current Law, Nunn-Domenici, and the Flat Tax — Case 4: Law Partner

INDIVIDUAL TAX

	CURRENT LAW*	NUNN-DOMENICI	FLAT TAX
Income from Noncorporate Business	$180,000	$180,000	$180,000
Other Wage Income	$ 0	$ 0	$ 0
Other Capital Income	$ 50,000	$ 50,000	$ 0
Total Gross Income	$230,000	$230,000	$180,000
Standard Deduction/Family Allowance	$ 0	$ 8,400	$ 24,250
Personal/Dependency Deduction—Number	4	4	2
Personal/Dependency Deduction—Amount	$ 11,800	$ 10,200	$ 11,300
Charitable Deduction	$ 5,000	$ 5,000	$ 0
Mortgage Deduction	$ 14,000	$ 14,000	$ 0
Deduction for Net Saving	$ 0	$ 30,000	$ 0
Tax Base	$188,618	$162,400	$144,450
Tax	$ 42,756	$ 58,577	$ 24,557
Payroll Credit	$ 0	$ 7,573	$ 0
Net Tax	**$ 42,756**	**$ 51,004**	**$ 24,557**

BUSINESS TAX

	CURRENT LAW	NUNN-DOMENICI	FLAT TAX
Wages to Employees		$153,000	$ 0
Fringe Benefits		$ 66,600	$ 66,600
Interest		$ 1,530	$ 1,530
Income to Owner		$180,000	$ 0
Tax Base		$401,130	$ 68,130
Tax Rate		11%	17%
Gross Tax		$ 44,124	$ 11,582
Payroll Credit		$ 18,283	$ 0
Net Tax	– none –	**$ 25,841**	**$ 11,582**
TOTAL INDIVIDUAL AND BUSINESS TAX	**$ 42,756**	**$ 76,845**	**$ 36,139**

*Not shown are a $16,000 deduction for state and local income taxes and property taxes, a $2,757 reduction in personal exemptions for high-income taxpayers, and a $2,661 reduction in itemized deductions for high-income taxpayers.

Appendix to Chapter 13

This appendix contains statistical data for the tax returns, average incomes, and income distributions, of individuals, partnership, and sole proprietorship.

Table 13A.1   Individual Tax Return Data, 1993
(All data are in thousands)

	All Individual Returns	<15	15<AGI<30	30<AGI<50	50<AGI<75	75<AGI<100	100<AGI<200	AGI>200
# of Returns	115061	44527	28660	21204	12273	4278	3108	1011
Adjusted Gross Income	3720662	261340	622374	828312	741080	365231	407329	494946
Salary and Wages	2880338	245154	496844	690222	621808	297636	289601	239073
Tax'ble Pen & Annuities	192215	28590	50468	46661	34075	14200	12780	5441
Un. Compensation	28367	8648	9009	6414	3090	767	389	49
Itemizers—Returns	33482	2144	5078	9499	9065	3815	2924	956
Taxes—Paid Returns	32896	1911	4920	9390	9013	3797	2911	952
Taxes—Amount	175377	5649	11517	28946	39861	23829	29258	36118
Interest—Returns	27832	1267	3759	8036	8051	3393	2529	796
Interest—Amount	203920	9247	19452	45106	53169	28170	29118	19659
Contributions—Returns	29973	1338	4230	8508	8501	3661	2812	923
Contributions—Amount	68305	1428	5591	12313	14901	8394	9841	15837
Earned Income Credit—Returns	15301	10173	5128	0	0	0	0	0
Earned Income Credit—Amount	15674	12396	3279	0	0	0	0	0

Source: Statistics of Income Division, Internal Revenue Service, Fall 1994, Washington, D.C.

Table 13A.2 Partnership Tax Return Data, 1992
(All data except ratios and averages are in thousands)

	Partner-ships	Avg. # of Partners	Receipts	Payroll	Guaranteed Partner Payments	Interest	Net Income	Avg. Partner Income	Ratio of Employee Payroll to Income
Finance	135	22.3	18755	3519	1126	6478	5263	$ 1,749	0.88
Real Estate	658	11.1	31627	1985	510	3674	–5585	($ 766)	–0.45
Physicians	9	4.3	10132	2316	580	60	4446	$116,390	0.65
Law	24	5.6	47173	13577	1666	292	17991	$134,028	0.85
Accounting	11	4.4	17622	6370	1207	155	4194	$ 86,358	1.81
Other Services	209	9.3	106675	24282	1951	7039	4236	$ 2,177	6.19
Other Nonservice Businesses	440	7.4	282842	24539	2906	7393	7729	$ 2,361	3.55
Total	**1485**	**10.6**	**514827**	**76588**	**9945**	**25091**	**38274**	**$ 2,432**	**2.26**

Source: Timothy D. Wheeler, "Partnership Returns, 1992," *Statistics of Income Bulletin*, Internal Revenue Service, Fall 1994, Washington D.C.

Table 13A.3 Sole Proprietorship Tax Return Data, 1992
(All data except ratios and averages are in thousands)

	Returns	Receipts	Interest	Payroll	Income	Avg. Income	Ratio of Employee Payroll Income
Skilled Construction	1573	$ 66,928	$ 653	$ 9,706	$ 13,299	$ 8,457	0.73
Wholesale & Retail Trade	2835	$247,261	$ 2,557	$17,452	$ 13,937	$ 4,915	1.25
Insurance Agents	361	$ 15,939	$ 251	$ 1,271	$ 7,086	$19,654	0.18
Real Estate Agents	672	$ 17,293	$ 303	$ 372	$ 7,097	$10,565	0.05
Business Services	1974	$ 47,339	$ 504	$ 3,815	$ 14,441	$ 7,315	0.26
Physicians	193	$ 29,815	$ 219	$ 3,063	$ 16,759	$87,039	0.18
Dentists	97	$ 19,524	$ 334	$ 3,786	$ 7,074	$73,112	0.54
Lawyers	281	$ 23,576	$ 246	$ 2,824	$ 11,184	$39,808	0.25
Accountants	307	$ 7,158	$ 121	$ 849	$ 2,953	$ 9,612	0.29
Consultants	619	$ 16,979	$ 114	$ 574	$ 9,418	$15,203	0.06
Other Services	4152	$115,536	$ 2,254	$12,254	$ 31,316	$ 7,543	0.39
Other Nonservice Business	2432	$129,736	$ 2,851	$15,188	$ 19,397	$ 7,975	0.78
Total	**15495**	**$737,082**	**$10,406**	**$71,155**	**$153,960**	**$ 9,936**	**0.46**

Source: Michael Strudler and Marty Shiley, "Sole Proprietorship Returns, 1992," *Statistics of Income Bulletin,* Internal Revenue Service, Fall 1994, Washington D.C.

Chart 13.1

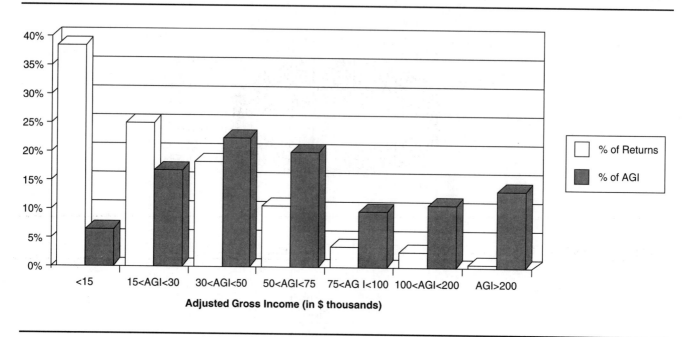

Chart 13.2   Comparison of Individual Taxes—Family of Four

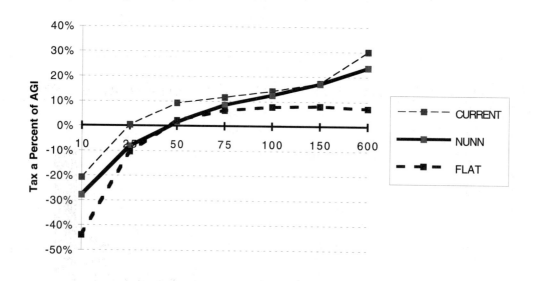

Chart 13.3   Distribution of Partnership Income Across Types of Business, 1992

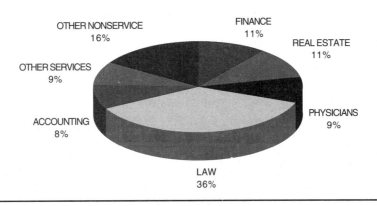

Chart 13.4   Average Partnership Income Across Types of Business, 1992

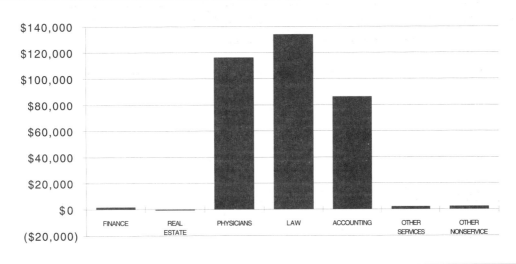

Chart 13.5   Distribution of Partnership and S Corporation Income Across Income Classes, 1992

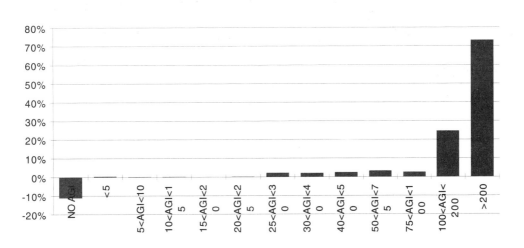

Chart 13.6   Distribution of Sole Proprietorship Income Across Types of Business, 1992

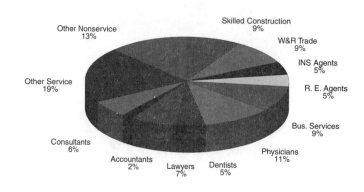

Chart 13.7   Average Income of Sole Proprietor By Type of Business, 1992

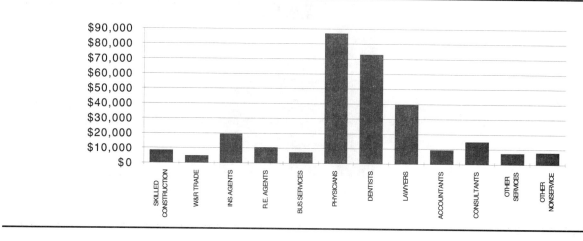

Chart 13.8   Distribution of Sole Proprietorship Income Across Income Classes, 1992

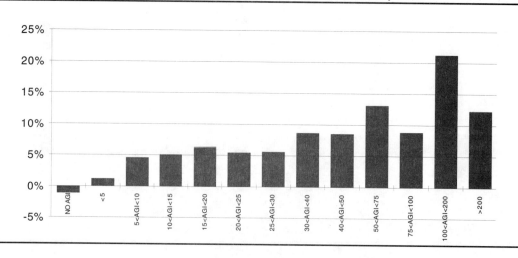

Treatment of Housing and Other Consumer Durables Under a Consumption Tax

Summary

- In theory, the rental value of homes should be subject to a consumption tax, but formidable administrative and compliance problems block this approach. As an alternative to taxing rents, tax may be "prepaid" by taxing the purchase price of homes.

- In most other countries with consumption taxes, new housing is taxed and existing housing is exempt.

- Under an individual consumption tax, housing receives preferential treatment if both mortgage interest is deductible and additions to mortgage debt are not included in gross income.

The taxation of consumer durables under a consumption tax poses substantial theoretical, administrative, and political problems. Appliances, furniture, tools, computing equipment, and automobiles— when used for personal consumption—are all examples of consumer durables. Of course, the most important consumer durable is housing. This chapter will focus on this "special case" of housing, but most of the analysis applies to consumer durables in general.

There are basically two ways of taxing housing under a consumption tax. One is to tax annual rental value. The other is to tax the purchase price. Economists consider taxing annual rental values is the more theoretically pure approach. In practice, however, taxing the purchase price of housing is more common.

There is the threshold issue of whether housing should be taxed at all. In particular, tax relief for housing is often under consideration because such relief can help alleviate some of the inherent regressivity of a consumption tax. Moreover, the deduction for mortgage interest is the most cherished of middle-class tax preferences, and there is no particular reason to expect the switch from an income tax to a consumption tax will obviate the political need to maintain housing prices and the happiness of homeowners.

It is likely that housing will receive preferential treatment under any consumption tax that has a realistic chance of being enacted. The relief can take a variety of forms, and it is likely that any relief granted will be uneven. As under the income tax, the tax benefits for housing can depend on whether housing is debt- or equity-financed and on whether housing is owner-occupied or for rent. In addition, as with changes under an income tax, there is likely to be differential treatment for housing built before and after the date a consumption tax becomes effective.

Taxing Rent

By definition, a consumer durable provides services to consumers for more than one year. Economists assert that the correct *theoretical* treatment of housing and other consumer durables is straightforward: Tax the consumption provided by these durables as measured by their annual rental values.[1] For rental housing, owners can be taxed directly on the market rents charged to residents. For owner-occupied housing, however, rental value must be imputed and then taxed. This poses major valuation problems. The necessary imputations would present issues at least as difficult as those surrounding the valuation of property for local property taxation. Valuation disputes would be particularly contentious when one considers the high rates of tax (e.g., 25 percent) being contemplated for a national consumption tax. In addition, most homeowners would be unfamiliar with and hostile to the notion that their homes generate "services" that should be taxed.

Even if valuation were not an issue, other administrative concerns make taxation of rent unattractive. Under a value-added or retail sales tax, almost all revenues would be collected from businesses. Taxation of rents would necessitate the collection of tax from tens of millions of households that would otherwise be exempt from business tax. Compliance would appear to be a major problem not only for owners who occupy their own homes but also for the numerous landlords who rent only one or two dwellings.

If small residential property owners remain untaxed, it would be difficult politically to tax only rents collected by large landlords (even though major compliance or valuation issues would likely be more manageable). Singling out rentals of multifamily residential housing units would be perceived as unfair because of the high proportion of low-income families in this type of housing.

---

[1]Consumption services should not be confused with depreciation, which is sometimes referred to as *capital consumption*. In an otherwise outstanding volume, the study by Tait (1988) seems to make this mistake. In economic theory, rental value equals depreciation *plus* the carrying cost of capital. Tait makes the claim that land should not be taxed because it is not consumed. This conclusion can be challenged because land certainly does provide consumption services (as is evident by rental changes), even if it does not depreciate.

It seems reasonable to conclude that the taxation of rents will not be the primary mechanism for the treatment of housing under any realistic consumption tax. The issues are summarized in the Table 14.1.

Table 14.1   Summary of the Problems with Taxing Rents

Type of Owner	Imputation Problem?	High Administrative Cost/ Low Compliance?	Political Problems?
Owner-Occupiers	yes	yes	yes
Small Landlords	no	yes	yes
Large Landlords	no	no	yes

Taxing the Purchase Price

The alternative treatment of housing under a consumption tax is to include the purchase price in the tax base. In fact, under certain circumstances the taxation of rent and the taxation of purchase price are economically equivalent. It is a basic tenet of economics and appraisal that the purchase price of a home equals the present value of expected future rents. (This is illustrated in Table 14.2.) Thus, if tax rates are equal over time, taxation of the purchase price of a home is equivalent to taxing all the future rents.[2] For this reason, tax imposed on the purchase price of a home is sometimes referred to as a "prepayment" of tax.

Table 14.2   Example Showing Home Value is Equivalent to the Present Value of Future Rents

	Year 1	Year 2	Year 3	Year 4
1. Value at Beginning of Year	**100.0**	75.0	50.0	25.0
2. Rent	35.0	32.5	30.0	27.5
3. Depreciation	25.0	25.0	25.0	25.0
4. Net Rental Income [(2) *minus* (3)]	10.0	7.5	5.0	2.5
5. Value at End of Year [(1) *minus* (3)]	75.0	50.0	25.0	0.0
Present Value of Rents	**100.0**			

Notes: Rate of return is 10 percent. Depreciation is straight-line. Rent equals owner's income plus depreciation.

While removing the need to impute rental values of owner-occupied housing, the prepayment approach opens up a Pandora's box of new issues. For example, imposing tax all in one year can create cash flow problems for home buyers (who are often cash constrained even without a new tax). The

---

[2]There are some additional technical issues about this equivalence that are not appropriate for this discussion. The interested reader can consult Graetz (1979) for further details.

major difficulty arises with regard to the taxation of existing housing. Equitable treatment of existing and new homes would necessitate that owners of existing houses be taxed on the value of their homes at the time of enactment. Existing homes, however, cannot be taxed under this method without severe administrative and political problems.

Exemption for Existing Housing

Neither the rental-value nor purchase-price approaches provide good ways of taxing existing housing.[3] For this reason, most industrialized countries with consumption taxes do not tax existing homes, and it is unlikely the United States would break new ground in this area. These countries impose tax only on new homes— and improvements to existing homes— and leave existing housing exempt from tax. Under this approach, all rental payments are exempt from tax.

Economists contend that exemption of existing housing would provide a windfall to existing owners: Prices of existing houses would rise along with the new housing subject to tax. Moreover, this favoritism does nothing to spur new housing starts. These concerns have hardly deterred most other countries that have implemented this system. The remainder of this chapter will focus on the taxation of new housing.

Taxation of Newly Constructed Owner-Occupied Housing

Newly Constructed Owner-Occupied Housing

When a builder sells a newly constructed home to a final consumer, the proceeds of that sale should be included in the builder's taxable receipts. Under a retail sales tax or a VAT, exclusion (or zero-rating) of these proceeds would exempt this housing from tax. Under any real-world consumption tax, the homeowner is "outside of the system."[4] Thus, it is the treatment of the *seller*, not the *purchaser*, which generally determines whether or not owner-occupied housing receives preferential treatment. Most countries with a consumption tax require full inclusion of sales by builders. One notable exception is the United Kingdom, which allows zero-rating on the sales of new residential houses.

Newly Constructed Rental Housing

The taxation of new rental housing is a bit more complex. One possibility would be to treat owners of rental housing like any other business: Purchases

---

[3]One method of taxing existing housing would be tax the market value of existing homes on the date of enactment of a consumption tax. As shall be shown in the next section, the market value of any home should be equal to the present discounted value of future rentals. The other would be to tax existing housing on the first sale after the date of enactment. This would result in a lock-in effect as homeowners could avoid tax as long as they did not sell. See Conrad (1990).

[4]Thus, purchasers effectively do not deduct their investment in housing nor do they include their rental returns in gross receipts. Equivalently, purchasers could be allowed to deduct their investment and include their rents—a much more complex regime.

of building (like other capital purchases) would be fully deductible and rents collected from the lessee would be included in taxable receipts. The problem with this approach, as noted above, is that taxation of small landlords would impose large compliance and administrative costs.

This has prompted most industrialized countries to entirely exempt owners of residential rental real estate from tax. In the case of a retail sales tax, builders selling homes are considered retailers (instead of building owners collecting rent). And in the case of a VAT, the last link in the chain subject to tax are sales to owners of housing, not the provision of housing to renters. This creates the problem of excluding from tax any value added by owners (e.g., services—such as maintenance—provided by owners' employees).

Mortgage Interest

Under a VAT or a retail sales tax, deductibility of mortgage interest is not at issue for individual taxpayers because only businesses pay taxes. Under general rules of interest payments under a VAT, businesses that own residential real estate are not allowed deductions (or credits, in the case of a credit-invoice VAT) for interest costs.

Under an individual consumption tax system, the situation is more complex. In order to understand the implications of mortgage deductibility it is necessary to review the general treatment of indebtedness under the tax. Under an individual consumption tax, *net* additions to saving are deductible. Under a standard individual consumption tax, (1a) increases in indebtedness are included in the tax base (because they present opportunities for increased consumption) and (1b) payment of interest and principal are deductible (because this is income that is not consumed). Equivalent treatment of debt can be achieved by (2a) not including increases in indebtedness in the tax base and (2b) not allowing deductions of interest and principal (Table 14.3).[5]

Table 14.3   Treatment of Consumer Debt Under a Personal Consumption Tax

	New Indebtedness	Payments of Interest and Principal
Standard Approach	(1a) Include	(1b) Deduct
Equivalent Approach	(2a) Exclude	(2b) Do Not Deduct

[5]As shown in the example in Table 14.3 (which assumes a 10 percent rate of interest), the value of a loan on its beginning date equals the present discounted value of future interest and principal payments. Therefore, the inclusion in taxable income of either the loan amount at the beginning of the loan or interest and principal are over the life of the loan economically equivalent.

	Year 1	Year 2	Year 3	Year 4
Principal at Beginning of Year	**100**	75	50	25
Principal Payment	25	25	25	25
Interest Payment	10	7.5	5	2.5
Principal at End of Year	75	50	25	0

Present Value of Interest and Principal Payments
100

Therefore, whether or not mortgage-financed housing is favorably treated under a personal consumption tax does not hinge entirely on whether mortgage interest is deductible,[6] but depends as well on the treatment of new debt and retirement of existing debt. Under the Nunn-Domenici proposal, mortgage-financed housing is favored because new debt is not included in income and mortgage interest (but not principal) is deductible.

Existing Housing and Used Goods

Under a consumption tax, if the entire purchase price is taxed, the present value of all future rentals is taxed. This holds true even if the consumer durable is sold. Therefore, if tax has been paid on the purchase price of a new consumer durable, sales of used goods that had been subject to tax when new should not be subject to tax on resale. Therefore, housing built after the effective date of a consumption tax and then resold should not be subject to tax. This should not create major administrative problems. For other consumer durables, the recordkeeping and other compliance costs might be large in comparison to the amount of tax collected. Dealers in used goods would be required to keep records of which used goods are subject to tax.[7]

Conclusion

It seems that if housing is not entirely exempt from a retail sales tax or a VAT, only new housing would be subject to tax. For housing to receive preferential treatment under the individual consumption tax, it is not sufficient for mortgage interest to be exempt from tax; mortgage debt must be exempted from the general rule that new indebtedness be included in income.

---

[6]In fact, if mortgage is deductible and principal is not, and mortgage indebtedness is included in income, mortgage-financed debt would be a penalized form of investment.

[7]It should be noted that a used good, originally purchased before the effective date and then sold after the effective date and subject to tax, should not be taxed if it is resold again. Thus, if a consumption tax came into effect, for example, in 1999, it would not be sufficient to merely know the vintage of an automobile (e.g., 1996) to determine if that vehicle should be taxed on resale.

Taxation of Financial Institutions Under a Consumption Tax

Summary

- Because it is difficult to identify and value services provided by financial institutions, no country with a consumption tax has been able to tax financial services in a manner consistent with consumption tax principles.

- Exemption of financial institutions from consumption tax generally results in overtaxation of financial services provided to businesses and undertaxation of services provided to consumers.

Countries with consumption taxes have experienced significant difficulties in finding an acceptable method of taxing banks, insurance companies, and other financial service companies. These difficulties have caused most countries to simply leave financial services untaxed. This hands-off policy has, however, led to other problems. The first part of this section describes the problem of taxing financial intermediaries. The second part describes the problems that result when financial services are untaxed. The third part discusses possible methods of imposing tax on financial services.

Problems Under the Credit-Invoice Method VAT

There are three major difficulties under the credit-invoice method VAT with respect to taxation of financial intermediaries. The first is identifying the correct amount of tax for each financial intermediary. The second is identifying the correct amount of tax credit for each of the intermediaries' business customers. Because it is likely that special rules should apply to financial intermediaries, the third difficulty is determining a workable definition of a financial intermediary to which the special rules would apply. (This chapter initially focuses on issues related to banking. Consumption tax issues relating to insurance companies are discussed immediately afterward.)

In general, under a value-added tax, interest income is not included in the tax base and interest expense is not deductible. This makes sense in the case of most businesses (e.g., a manufacturer) because interest income does not emanate from any value generated by the business (i.e., it is just income flowing through the business) while interest expense is a payment to providers of capital used to generate value. This general rule, however, makes little or no sense in the case of a traditional financial intermediary, as shown in the simple example in Table 15.1.

Table 15.1   The Problem with Measuring the Value Added of a Financial Institution Under Conventional Methods
(Total Bank Assets = $100 Loans
Total Bank Liabilities = $90 Deposits *plus* $10 Equity)

Income Statement:	
Interest Income @ 8%	$8.00
Interest Expense @ 6%	($5.40)
Gross Profit	$2.60
Salaries	($0.80)
Materials	($0.20)
Net Profit	$1.60
Subtraction Method:	
Business Receipts	$0.00
Business Purchases	($0.20)
Value added	($0.20)

Naive application of standard VAT methods in this case leaves the bank with a tax base of *negative* $0.20. As shall be shown later (in Table 14.6), the bank in this example actually has value added of $1.60. The gross inaccuracy of standard VAT rules has lead most countries with value-added taxes to remove financial institutions from the VAT system, but this leads to other problems as discussed below.

Problems with Placing Financial Institutions Outside the VAT System

The main problem of removing financial institutions from the VAT system is that this special treatment will usually result in economic distortions. Some bank customers will be favored and others penalized, and certain types of financial institutions may be given a competitive advantage. Moreover, the nature of the distortion will depend on the type of VAT (credit-invoice or sub-traction), the method of relief (zero-rating or exemption), and the type of bank customer (business or consumer).

In the case of the credit-invoice VAT, the problems of exemption and zero-rating for financial institutions are largely the same as those discussed for taxpayers generally in Chapter 3. Under the credit-invoice method, exemption does provide some relief in the case of financial services provided to consumers, but at the same time can result in overtaxation of (or cascad-ing of tax on) services provided to business customers. Zero-rating solves the overtaxation problem of business customers under the credit-invoice VAT, but it exacerbates the distortions on consumer financial services by entirely eliminating tax.

Under the subtraction method, business customers are unable to deduct implicit fees for financial services because these fees cannot be identified. This offsets any benefit to the bank from exemption, so the net result is that business services with implicit charges are fully taxed.[1] (Financial services for explicit charges still enjoy the benefit of exemption.) In the case of finan-cial services provided to consumers, exemption eliminates the tax associ-ated with bank value added. The discussion in this paragraph is summarized in Table 15.2.

Table 15.2   Summary of Problems with Relief for Financial Institutions

	Business Customer	**Consumer Customer**
Credit-Invoice Method:		
Exemption	Overtaxation of Financial Services Due to Cascading (No credits for business customers)	Undertaxation of Financial Services Because *Bank's* Value Added Not Taxed
Zero-Rating	Full Taxation (Bank's undertaxation offset by customer's overtaxation)	Undertaxation of Financial Services Because *Total* Value Added Not Taxed
Subtraction Method:		
Exemption	Full Taxation (Bank's undertaxation offset by customer's overtaxation)	Undertaxation of Financial Services Because *Bank's* Value Added Not Taxed

---

[1]Note that this differs from the effect discussed in Chapter 4 of exemption of a business pro-viding services to other business. In the case of exemption of a nonfinancial firm providing services to other businesses, that firm's value added is excluded from the tax base and its cus-tomer is able to deduct the cost of those services.

Methods of Including Financial Institutions in a VAT System

Most countries have abandoned attempts to include financial institutions in their VAT systems. There are, however, many aspects of the new consumption taxes currently under consideration in the United States that differ from the experience of other countries. It is likely that any serious attempt to enact a consumption tax will include efforts to put financial intermediaries on a level playing field with other businesses. It is possible in theory to calculate bank value added under either the subtraction or addition method. This section explores the viability of either of these alternatives in practice.

The reasons for the enormous errors in the calculation of bank value added under standard approaches (see Table 15.2) is that implicit fees for financial services are often embedded in interest charges and netted against interest payments. For example, banks provide a range of services (e.g., free checking) to depositors without explicit charges. Banks receive payment for these services by *paying* depositors *lower* rates of interest than would be charged on financial exchanges for more convenient sources of funds, such as commercial paper. Banks also provide services to borrowers (e.g., processing, assumption of risk) often without explicit fees. In these cases banks receive payment for these services by *charging* borrowers *higher* rates of interest than would be paid for less cumbersome investments, such as corporate bonds.[2]

These implicit fees for financial services provided to customers should be included in gross receipts when calculating VAT liability. The central problem concerning the treatment of banks under a consumption tax is that these charges usually are not separately identified. These points are illustrated in the example of Table 15.3. In this example, the bank charges its borrowers 0.5 percent annually per dollar of loan principal and therefore can charge 8 percent instead of the simple market rate of 7.5 percent. Similarly, the bank charges its depositors a rate of 1.5 percent for each dollar of account balance. The bank nets this charge against a simple market rate of interest of 7.5 percent and therefore pays its depositors 6 percent.

As noted above, the problem with straightforward calculation of the credit-invoice method is that it is invariably inaccurate. Under this method, interest income is not included in gross receipts and interest paid is not deductible. It is in interest charges, however, that bank fees are included. (Note that in the example in Table 15.3 only the items in **bold** are observable.) Thus, the credit-invoice method does not take into account the major source of bank value added. In this example, the credit-invoice method would measure bank value added as minus $0.20 when it is actually $1.65.[3]

---

[2]It should be noted that there is an increasing trend for banks to separately state fees for specific financial services.

[3]Under the *subtraction* method, and assuming implicit fees were made explicit, value-added ($1.65) equals total fees ($0.50 plus $1.35) minus business purchases ($0.20). Under the *addition* method, value added ($1.65) equals net profit ($1.60) plus salaries ($0.80) minus net interest paid ($6.75 minus $7.50).

Table 15.3   Taxing Implicit Fees Charged by Financial Institutions

1. Interest Income @8%		**$8.00**
2. Implicit Service Charge @0.5%	$0.50	
3. Pure Interest @7.5%	$7.50	
4. Interest Expense @6%		**($5.40)**
5. Implicit Service Charge @1.5%	$1.35	
6. Pure Interest @7.5%	($6.75)	
7. Gross Profit		**$2.60**
8. Operating Expenses		**($1.00)**
9. Salaries	($0.80)	
10. Materials	($0.20)	
11. Net Profit		**$1.60**

Notes:	
Value Added Applying Normal Credit-Invoice Rules (zero *less* line 10)	($0.20)
Note: Actual Valued Added Using the Subtraction Method and Making Service Charge Explicit (line 2 plus line 5 *less* line 10)	$1.65
Actual Value Added Using the Addition Method (line 11 *plus* line 9 *plus* line 6 *minus* line 3)	$1.65

Under the subtraction and credit-invoice methods the problem could be solved if the implicit fees charged by banks all would be made explicit. In this case, fees would be included in gross receipts (just as with any other service business) and interest paid and charged would be excluded entirely from the calculation. (Of course, many bank fees—e.g., for safe deposit boxes—are explicit and these are already correctly treated under the credit-invoice method.) Bank fees could be estimated by trying to disentangle service fees from "pure" interest.

This estimate might be accomplished by taking the difference between a market rate of interest and actual bank interest charges and assuming that the difference is implicit bank charges that should be included in gross receipts. The administrative problems with this approach are formidable. A market or "standard" rate of interest would have to be chosen that would have to vary with the estimated maturity of the corresponding loan or deposit. In a period of volatile interest rates, these rates would have to be adjusted frequently. Because tax liability depends on spreads between interest rates, small measurement errors could result in large errors in tax liability. And, of course, the compliance burden involved would hardly represent tax simplification.

Under the addition method,[4] bank value added is equal to profit plus wages plus net interest paid. In this case, an imputation would need to be made to calculate net interest paid because net interest calculated should not include charges for financial services. Thus, under both the addition and subtraction method, estimates must be made of a "pure" rate of interest. It turns out that, given a standard rate of interest, both methods yield the same results, and so neither is more accurate than the other. Some sample calculations shown in the Appendix to this chapter indicate that one of these methods might be acceptable when used under a general subtraction method if administrative and compliance costs are not prohibitive and if the standard rate of interest can be estimated with reasonable accuracy.

Taxing Insurance Companies Under a Consumption Tax

The problems with taxation of insurance companies under a consumption tax are analogous to those which arise with the taxation of banks. Application of standard VAT rules yield highly inaccurate measures of true VAT liability. If insurance companies are exempted from a credit-invoice VAT, insurance services provided to business customers will be overtaxed, and insurance services provided to consumers will be undertaxed. If insurance companies are exempted under the subtraction method, undertaxation results for services provided to both businesses and consumers.

Any attempts to bring insurance companies into the system are thwarted by measurement problems. Premiums paid to insurance companies often have three elements: (1) funding for current and future claims, (2) savings for the policyholder, and (3) compensation for the owners of the insurance companies (profits), their lenders (net interest), and their employees (wages). Only the last element is value added. Because of the difficulty in identifying pure interest, it is difficult to measure net interest under the addition method. Because of the difficulty in identifying the value of implicit fees, it is difficult to measure gross receipts under the subtraction method. Thus, taxation of insurance under a VAT is largely similar to the problems of taxing other financial services.

Definition of Financial Intermediary

If financial intermediaries are going to be exempt or zero-rated (and perhaps, subject to a special separate tax), the term *financial institution* would need to be defined for tax purposes. Clearly, banks and insurance companies fit that definition, but questions may arise in the case of other financial intermediaries and service providers such as finance companies, mortgage com-

---

[4]If the addition method is found to have acceptable results for financial institutions, it is possible to implement the addition method for financial institutions even when all other taxpayers use the subtraction method. If financial institutions use the addition method when all other taxpayers are using the credit-invoice method, this would result in overtaxation of financial services to businesses that is even larger than the overtaxation from exemption.

panies, and securities dealers and brokers. Special problems may also arise in the case of financing subsidiaries of nonfinancial corporations and self-insurance by nonfinancial corporations.

Conclusion

Financial intermediation poses special problems for the design of value-added taxes. Most other nations with VATs simply exempt financial institutions (or most of their value added) from tax.[5] It may be possible, however, to implement some rules that reasonably approximate the correct amount of VAT liability for financial services. Unfortunately, such rules would almost certainly be complex and cumbersome.

---

[5]There are indications that these countries are reconsidering this position. See Organization for Economic Cooperation and Development (1994).

Appendix to Chapter 15

Financial institutions may be taxed under either the subtraction or addition method in a system where taxpayers are generally subject to the subtraction method. Both methods, however, require estimates and imputations to approximate the correct amount of liability.

Under the addition method, a bank's tax base would equal wages plus profit plus net interest paid. In this case, an imputation would need to be made to calculate net interest paid. Under the subtraction method, bank liability would equal explicit and implicit fee income less purchases from other business. In this case, an imputation would be needed to calculate implicit fee income. In both cases, imputation would depend on the choice of the pure rate of deposit interest and a pure rate of loan interest.

A sensitivity analysis was conducted in the following table to determine which method would generally be more accurate and how large errors could be under either method. In this example, a bank has $100 of loans and $95 of deposits. The bank charges its borrowers 8.5 percent and earns annual implicit fees equal to 1.0 percent of loan balances. The bank pays its depositors 5.5 percent and charges depositors implicit fees equal to 2.0 percent of deposit balances. The "pure" rate of interest is 7.5 percent.[6]

In the first column, it is assumed that the pure rate of interest and implicit fees can be identified. Under the subtraction method, the tax base is $1.90, the *sum* of implicit fees ($2.90) and explicit fees ($1.00) *less* purchases from other businesses ($2.00). Under the addition method, the tax base is also $1.90, the sum of net interest paid calculated using the pure rate of interest ($7.13 - $7.50 = -$0.37), salaries ($2.00), and net profit (0.28).

The six columns in Table 15.A1 calculate the error in calculation of the correct tax base when the pure rate of interest is not estimated correctly. Even when the pure interest rate is in error by 100 basis points, the error in the calculation of tax liability is less than 3 percent.

Thus, the table shows that for a given estimate of a pure rate of interest both methods provide the same result, so neither is more accurate than the other. It shows that if pure interest estimates are not grossly inaccurate, the margin of error due to inaccurate imputations may be acceptable.

---

[6]The "pure" rate of interest is the rate of interest that would prevail if no financial services were provided with transaction. The rates of interest on a marketable security is an example of a pure rate of interest.

Table 15A.1   Error in Measured VAT Liability Due to Inaccurate Imputation of "Pure" Interest Rate

Error in "Pure" Rate	0.00%	0.25%	−0.25%	0.5%	−0.5%	1.0%	−1.0%
Bank Assets	100	100	100	100	100	100	100
Bank Deposits	95	95	95	95	95	95	95
Loan Rate	8.50%	8.50%	8.50%	8.50%	8.50%	8.50%	8.50%
Implicit Fee	1.00%	1.25%	0.75%	1.50%	0.50%	2.00%	0.00%
Pure Interest	7.50%	7.25%	7.75%	7.00%	8.00%	6.50%	8.50%
Deposit Rate	5.50%	5.50%	5.50%	5.50%	5.50%	5.50%	5.50%
Implicit Fee	2.00%	1.75%	2.25%	1.50%	2.50%	1.00%	3.00%
Pure Interest	7.50%	7.25%	7.75%	7.00%	8.00%	6.50%	8.50%
Interest Earned	8.50	8.50	8.50	8.50	8.50	8.50	8.50
Implicit Fee	1.00	1.25	0.75	1.50	0.50	2.00	0.00
Pure Interest	7.50	7.25	7.75	7.00	8.00	6.50	8.50
Interest Charged	5.23	5.23	5.23	5.23	5.23	5.23	5.23
Implicit Fee	1.90	1.66	2.14	1.43	2.38	0.95	2.85
Pure Interest	7.13	6.89	7.36	6.65	7.60	6.18	8.08
Explicit Fees	1.00	1.00	1.00	1.00	1.00	1.00	1.00
Gross Profit	4.28	4.28	4.28	4.28	4.28	4.28	4.28
Material	2.00	2.00	2.00	2.00	2.00	2.00	2.00
Salaries	2.00	2.00	2.00	2.00	2.00	2.00	2.00
Operating Expense	4.00	4.00	4.00	4.00	4.00	4.00	4.00
Net Profit	0.28	0.28	0.28	0.28	0.28	0.28	0.28
Value Added — Subtraction Method	1.90	1.91	1.89	1.93	1.88	1.95	1.85
Value Added — Addition Method	1.90	1.91	1.89	1.93	1.88	1.95	1.85
Error in Calculation of VAT	0.00	−0.01	0.01	−0.03	0.02	−0.05	0.05

The Treatment of State and Local Governments and Charitable Organizations Under a Consumption Tax

Summary

- State and local governments could be subject to large, new financial burdens as a result of a new federal consumption tax.

- State and local governments have several concerns. They would suffer financial hardship if their taxes were not deductible against federal taxable income and if their services were subject to tax under a comprehensive consumption tax. State and local governments are also particularly worried that a federal VAT or sales tax might encroach on their ability to levy their own sales taxes.

- In many respects, the potential burdens of charitable organizations under a consumption tax are comparable to those of state and local governments. Charitable organizations would suffer if charitable contributions were not deductible, and services provided by charitable organizations might be subject to tax under a comprehensive consumption tax.

State and Local Governments

Introduction

State and local governments would be affected by the replacement of the current income tax with a consumption tax in a variety of ways. The five most important potential effects of a replacement consumption tax are:

1. Infringement on state and local governments sales tax base
2. Loss of federal income tax deduction to state and local citizens and residents for state and local property and income taxes
3. Taxation of government activities
4. Loss of tax-favored status to investors in state and local government debt
5. Loss of ability of state income tax systems to piggyback on federal system once federal income tax system is repealed

For state and local governments, any one of these changes could pose a major new burden. The impact of the loss of all five of these benefits could be devastating. It is therefore likely that a consumption tax that did not provide relief from these problems would face stiff opposition from state and local governments. If state and local governments keep existing income tax systems, taxpayers will still have the cost of complying with multiple systems.

Infringement on Sales Tax Base

As noted in Chapters 2 and 3, a retail sales tax and credit-invoice VAT would pose problems for state and local governments in a variety of ways. First, as a political matter, it may be more difficult for these governmental units to raise additional revenue through sales tax increases if the combined federal and state tax rate is high. For example, there may be less tolerance for a sales tax increase from 5 to 6 percent if the federal government has just imposed a 15 percent—let alone a 25 percent—federal sales tax. Second, it is widely believed by tax administrators that enforcement problems begin to be unmanageable when retail tax rates get into double digits. Third, state and local governments would be under much pressure to conform to federal sales tax rules in order to simplify taxpayer compliance. This would, however, greatly lessen the ability of state and local governments to achieve policy objectives through adjustments in the sales tax base. Finally, even with total conformity in the tax base, there must be some coordination of the tax rates between the federal and local tax bases: It must be decided whether, for example, the federal tax will include local tax in the federal tax base.

Almost all of these problems disappear under a subtraction-method VAT or an individual consumption tax. Concerns only remain if public perception likens them to a sales tax. Although the equivalence of consumption taxes is widely recognized by economists, this is not the case for the public at large—particularly if the tax is not separately stated at the cash register. Thus, while the infringement issue looms as a large problem for the states in the case of a federal sales tax or a federal VAT, it does not appear to be a major problem for a subtraction-method VAT or an individual consumption tax.

Loss of Federal Income Tax Deduction for Income and Property Taxes

In 1993 individuals deducted $175 billion of state and local income and property taxes from their federal income taxes. If the average marginal federal income tax rate is 30 percent, this deduction provides taxpayers a benefit of approximately $50 billion annually. Taxpayers in high-tax states—such as New York and California—would face a larger burden.

Individuals would not be able to deduct local taxes under a retail sales tax or a VAT. Although it would be possible to do so under a Flat Tax, no such proposal has yet been offered. Just as under the individual income tax, the deductibility of local taxes under an individual consumption tax can be made available. Under the Nunn-Domenici proposal, deductions for state and local taxes are allowed. Moreover, it is likely under this tax that there may be greater federal tax benefits for local tax payments than under current law for two reasons. First, the value of these deductions is greater for a larger number of taxpayers because most state and local taxes are likely to be paid by taxpayers in the 40 percent bracket. (Under the Nunn-Domenici plan, taxpayers with taxable income as low as $12,000—in the case of a single individual—face a 40 percent rate while under current law only taxpayers with taxable income in excess of $250,000 pay tax at a 39.6 percent rate.) Second, under the Nunn-Domenici proposal, all taxpayers—not just itemizers as under current law—may deduct taxes paid to state and local governments.

Taxation of Government Activities

In theory there is no reason that goods and services provided by governments should not be subject to a retail sales tax or a VAT at the same rate as goods and services provided by the private sector. In practice, however, government goods and services are almost always excluded from tax. This gives government an unfair competitive advantage over private industry. Political pressures from private firms that compete with governments, as well as need for revenue, mean that this issue is likely to be revisited during any debate about a federal consumption tax.

If governments are provided relief under a credit-invoice VAT, the issue arises as to whether they should be exempt from tax or zero-rated. As noted in Chapter 3, zero-rating is likely to provide more relief, and it is possible that exemption may result in overtaxation of governments relative to private business.

An individual consumption tax effectively taxes all government services. Relief is provided, however, to the extent state and local services are financed by income and property taxes and the individual consumption tax does allow them to be deducted. It is also relevant to note that the Flat Tax is partially effective in taxing governments because wages are subject to tax under the individual component of the Flat Tax and—because government is extremely labor-intensive—wages paid are a relatively accurate measure of value-added in the government sector.

Loss of Tax-Favored Status for State and Local Debt

Under a retail sales tax, value-added tax, and the Flat Tax, *all* interest income would be exempt from tax. Thus, state and local governments, and investors in their securities, would not lose the benefit of tax exemption of interest on their indebtedness (and, in fact, they would benefit from removal of regulations and restrictions dictated by federal tax rules). However, under these taxes, state and local governments would lose the special status that allows them to issue securities providing yields approximately 35 percent less than yields on taxable securities of comparable maturity and risk. The interest on all debt would be tax-exempt, so there would no longer be large interest-rate spreads between yields on private bonds and state and local bonds. How much this lack of distinction hurts state and local government depends on how much interest rates in general decline as a result of a new tax regime. It is likely that interest rates will decline, but it is unlikely that they will decline to such a level that would be available to state and local governments if they were the only type of tax-exempt security. Moreover, it removes the competitive advantage governments currently enjoy over various private offerings.

The impact of an individual consumption tax on the municipal bond market can be more problematic. Under the general principles of individual consumption taxation, all interest income would be subject to tax, but purchases of new securities—if they represented new saving—would be deductible. (In contrast, all interest income is exempt under the Flat Tax, but purchases of securities are not deductible.) Without special transition rules retaining tax-exemption for the interest income they generate, previously issued bonds—now facing the prospects of taxation—would decline in value.[1] Because purchased newly issued securities could be deducted, they would effectively be tax exempt.[2]

The individual consumption tax included in the Nunn-Domenici proposal retains tax-exemption for all state and local government bond interest and, *in addition*, allows purchases of newly issued securities to be deductible. Thus, state and local bonds retain a special status under the Nunn-Domenici proposal despite the general relief from taxation on all capital income.

Relationship Between Federal and State Income Taxes

Most states that collect income taxes rely heavily on the federal income tax. Taxable income for state income tax purposes often is based on taxable income for federal tax purposes. States also benefit indirectly from federal enforcement efforts. The elimination of federal income taxation will increase the complexity of state income taxation. The likely heightened dissatisfaction with state income taxes will likely increase pressure on states to reduce or reform their income taxes.

Conclusion About State and Local Governments

Consumption taxes can result in a real challenge for state and local governments. Yet, it is possible to design consumption taxes that do not impose new hardships on state and local governments. It is even possible, as exemplified by the Nunn-Domenici proposal, to design a consumption tax that in many respects makes state and local governments better off than under current law.

---

[1]This decline in value would begin once the markets perceived the *possibility* of loss of deductions for interest might occur. Value would rise and fall as the prospects for overall legislation and the particular details changed through the legislative process.

[2]The equivalence of tax-exemption of interest and tax deductibility of the purchase price of bonds is discussed in Chapter 6.

Charitable Organizations

Possible Elimination of the Deduction for Charitable Contributions

The elimination of the deduction for charitable contributions could be a serious blow to the charitable sector. In 1993 deductions against the individual income tax for charitable contributions totaled approximately $100 billion. If the average marginal tax rate is 30 percent, this could represent a loss in value of approximately $30 billion annually to the charitable sector. The imposition of this burden could be particularly burdensome at this time when it seems likely there will be less government spending for social services and a corresponding increase in demand for privately funded charity. It may be the case that charitable contributions would not change as a result of this change in tax benefits (i.e., such contributions are "inelastic" with respect to tax changes). It is the feeling among those working in the charitable sector, however, that recent experience with changes in the tax rates and in tax rules regarding the alternative minimum tax treatment of appreciated property has had a significant impact on the timing and amounts of charitable giving.

As noted in the case of deductions for state and local taxes, a replacement retail sales tax or VAT would entirely eliminate this deduction for individuals. It could be made available under the individual component of the Flat Tax (but no version of the Flat Tax has yet been offered that does so). The deduction is optional under the individual consumption tax (as it is under the individual *income* tax). In the tax case of the Nunn-Domenici version of the individual consumption tax, the deduction is available and is, in fact, enhanced because of the generally higher marginal tax rates and the availability to taxpayers who currently are precluded from taking the charitable deduction because they use the standard deduction.

Possible Taxation of Activities of Charitable Organizations

Under current law, charitable organizations' business activities that are unrelated to their exempt purpose are subject to unrelated business income tax (UBIT). These unrelated activities would almost certainly continue to be subject to tax under any consumption tax imposed on businesses. The real question is whether activities related to charitable purposes (e.g., educational services provided by universities, medical services provided by hospitals) would be included in the new consumption tax base. Economists assert that it would be more efficient to tax all services—whether provided by an exempt organization or a private firm—equally. This proposition is, however, also true under the current income tax, but has had little impact on policy. Tax-exempt hospitals, for example, continue to enjoy a competitive advantage over taxable hospitals. It is unclear whether the political dynamics of a new consumption tax would result in inclusion of all charitable activities in the consumption tax base.

Even if all activities of all charitable organizations are not subject to tax, some curtailment of tax advantages to certain types of tax-exempt organizations may be on the horizon. For example, the Nunn-Domenici proposal repeals the tax exemption for certain types of educational organizations (more commonly known as "think tanks") as well as certain organizations whose activities may be in the public interest but are not considered to be purely charitable.

Other Issues for Charitable Organizations

Many charitable organizations, like hospitals and universities, have been able to issue tax-exempt securities. As noted above in the discussion relating to state and local government debt, a new consumption tax may result in some new burdens for entities currently issuing—and investors currently holding—tax-exempt debt.

The Nunn-Domenici proposal includes a deduction for postsecondary tuition (limited to $2,000 annually per eligible student). This may provide some relief to universities and other institutions of higher learning that wish to raise tuition.

Conclusion for Charitable Organizations

As in the case of state and local governments, organizations that are currently tax exempt could be severely affected by the imposition of a federal consumption tax. This would be a particularly onerous burden in light of possibly reduced direct government support to these institutions and potentially increased needs for their services given other government cutbacks. Nevertheless, as demonstrated by the Nunn-Domenici proposal, it is possible to design a federal consumption tax that is generally favorable to tax exempt organizations.

17

Financial Statement Implications

Summary

- Investors, bankers, appraisers, and regulators rely heavily on financial statements to evaluate the financial health of businesses. Replacing the current system of income taxation with a new system of consumption taxation can have a major impact on both income statements and balance sheets.

- Without transition relief, the impact of a new consumption tax on the income and net worth reported on financial statements in many cases would be highly adverse. This could have a detrimental or even disruptive impact on financial markets. Without transition, very large special charges to income statements and reduction in shareholder equity may result.

The financial reporting impacts of new consumption taxes are likely to be an issue of major importance to the business community. There are many aspects of a replacement consumption tax that have the potential to adversely affect the financial health of the firm as reported on financial statements. Because financial reporting is of critical importance to investors, creditors, bankers, appraisers, and regulators evaluating the financial soundness of firms, these impacts deserve careful consideration before adoption of any replacement consumption tax.

In order to provide the reader with a better understanding of these issues, the discussion is divided into two parts: (1) the financial reporting involved in repealing the income tax and (2) the financial reporting involved in adopting a new consumption tax.

Accounting

The Benefit from Eliminating Deferred Tax Liability

If the corporate income tax rate is 35 percent, and book profits are $100, the after-tax book profits on a business are $65. If the availability of accelerated depreciation for tax purposes reduces taxable income to $90 and the actual current tax liability to $31.50, after-tax profits of a business are still recorded at $65. The $3.50 of tax reduction is really only a deferral of tax. Accountants record this $3.50 tax effect of the temporary difference of $10 in taxable income which results from the excess of tax over book depreciation as a *deferred tax liability*.

Another example of tax deferral is the treatment of repatriated foreign-source income for tax purposes. Corporations with overseas subsidiaries recognize foreign-source income for book purposes as it accrues, but generally foreign-source income from overseas subsidiaries is subject to U.S. tax only when paid out in dividends to the U.S. parent company. Thus, if there is an expectation that income will be repatriated, unrepatriated income in foreign subsidiaries can generate a deferred tax liability on financial statements (to the extent it is expected to be reinvested overseas indefinitely, no such liability need be reflected).

A reduction in the rate of income tax reduces deferred tax liabilities. Similarly, without transition provisions, total elimination of the income tax reduces deferred tax liabilities. Under the accounting rules for the treatment of income taxes—*Financial Accounting Standard Board Statement 109: Accounting for Income Taxes*—businesses would eliminate their deferred tax liabilities and increase their recorded book income (and resultant shareholders' equity) by the amount of deferred tax liability all in the accounting period in which the tax was repealed.

The Burden of Eliminating Tax Assets

Sometimes taxable income of businesses exceeds their book income. For example, a large commercial bank may record $100 of book income and $65 of after-tax profit. The nondeductibility of bad debt reserves for tax purposes can cause that same bank to have taxable income of $120. The $20 excess of tax over book income gives rise to $7 more tax actually paid than recorded on the financial statements (i.e., 35% of book income). This is considered a $7 deferred tax asset on the bank's balance sheet which will be realized in tax reductions in the future when the bank loan is written off. Similar tax assets result to corporate America when other expenses are recognized earlier in financial statements than is allowed for tax purposes.

Without transition provisions, the elimination of the income tax would eliminate deferred tax assets. In the year in which the income tax was eliminated, businesses would be required to eliminate their deferred tax assets and decrease their recorded book income by the amount of deferred tax assets. This tax asset elimination would then be a dollar-for-dollar reduction in book income and shareholders' equity.

Other Tax Assets: Carryforwards of Losses and Credits

Besides deferred tax assets arising from temporary differences, businesses may carry other tax assets on their books. These arise from unused net operating losses, alternative minimum tax credits, foreign tax credits, research tax credits, and other business credits. If it is more likely than not that these credits can be utilized against future tax liability, these unused tax benefits are book assets. Elimination of the income tax assets for unused losses and credits, without special transition rules that allow that use of these losses[1] and credits against any new tax, would result in the write-off of those assets and an immediate reduction in book income and shareholders' equity by the amount of the writeoff.

Conclusion About Elimination of the Income Tax

For firms that have accumulated a net deferred tax liability, the elimination of the income tax taken in isolation would result in a large improvement to balance sheets and a one-shot improvement to the income statement as these liabilities were eliminated. Over the long term, the impact on income statements of the elimination from the income tax could be favorable: A firm that previously would record $100 of before-tax and $65 of after-tax income might now record considerably more than $65 of after-tax income, depending on the new consumption tax rate and mix of factors comprising the tax base. Those with tax assets would be detrimental. Still on an overall basis, business would benefit since tax liabilities significantly exceed tax assets. Yet for any specific firm, the change could be of crucial importance.

Imposition of a New Consumption Tax

Introduction

The accounting treatment of any new consumption tax depends critically on whether the new tax would be considered an income tax or a sales tax for accounting purposes. If the new business tax is considered an income (or profits) tax, FASB Statement No. 109 would apply. In this case, permanent differences between book and tax income—such as the lack of deductions for wages under a value-added tax—would be reflected in the income statement every year. Temporary differences—such as immediate tax deductions for items capitalized for financial statements—would be reflected on the balance sheet.

As a collection agent, the business would establish a liability account for any taxes collected until such time as they are remitted to the government. There would be no impact on revenue or expenses. As a sales tax the new

---

[1]Even if net operating losses could be deducted under a new consumption tax, their value would have to be reduced if the rate of tax were reduced. For example, a $100 net operating loss for a corporation could result in a $35 deferred tax asset under current law. Under the Nunn-Domenici proposal, net operating loss generated under the income tax cannot be deducted against the new business tax, but even if they could, their value in this example would have to be reduced from $35 to $11 given the 11 percent rate of tax under the plan.

consumption tax would not give rise to deferred tax assets or deferred tax liabilities. If the new consumption tax enacted is a retail sales tax or a credit-invoice VAT, it seems probable that this tax will not be considered an income tax. Conversely, the FASB could provide that some of the FASB Statement No. 109 concepts be applied as described below.

Although in many ways similar to a credit-invoice VAT, the case might be made that a subtraction-method VAT is akin to a business income tax, and that the principles of FASB Statement No. 109 should apply. Certainly there is a legitimate question about whether a tax that disallows deductions for interest expenses, wages, salaries, and fringe benefits is an income tax. On the other hand, proponents of subtraction-method VAT (and related proposals) stress that the tax is based on income concepts and accounting, and they often refer to the tax base as *gross profit*. (It should also be noted that, because the Flat Tax allows deductions for wages and salaries, the Flat Tax is even more likely to be categorized as an income tax than would be a regular subtraction-method VAT.)

If the new tax is accounted for under the principles of FASB Statement No. 109, there would be numerous important effects on financial statements. Some of the more notable effects are listed below. The first of these effects has potentially significant implications for financial statements.

Treatment of Transition Basis

Loosely speaking, the term *basis* refers to that portion of the cost of an asset that will not be subject to tax. For depreciable assets, the remaining basis may be deducted over the useful life of the asset. For assets that are sold, only sale proceeds in excess of basis are income and therefore subject to tax. In contrast, under a consumption tax *without transition relief*, all of the book basis *in existence on the date of enactment* would eventually be subject to tax. Without transition relief, deductions for depreciation of *existing* assets would not be allowed under the new tax, and the entire proceeds from a theoretical sale of assets at the end of the reporting year for the initial application of the new tax law would be included in the tax base. These future tax payments would be booked as deferred tax liabilities equal in amount to the book value of these assets times the new tax rate.

Data from the Statistics of Income Division of the IRS indicate that U.S. corporations have approximately $20 *trillion* dollars in book basis. If the new business tax had a tax rate of 10 percent, and no transition relief (i.e., deductions for existing depreciable assets over their useful life and deductions for basis upon sale) were allowed under the new system, it is possible that $2 *trillion* of deferred tax liabilities would be created upon the enactment of this new tax! Under the principles of FASB Statement 109, this entire amount would be reflected on the income statement in the year of enactment. This amount would be reflected net of all tax liabilities and tax assets that also would have to be "written off" as discussed above. Precise information on these latter two items is not readily available from statistical sources. If one assumes tax liabilities of $600 billion and tax assets of $100 billion, the net charge to income statements and shareholders' equity would be $1.5 trillion ($2 trillion less $.6 trillion plus $.1 trillion). This would more than wipe out total corporate profits in any one year and severely reduce the amount of shareholders' equity.[2] Thus, financial statements would have to reflect the enormous increase in future taxes that results from lost depreciation deductions or taxable gain on sales due to the elimination of tax basis. The majority of major U.S. corporations would likely reflect substantial losses in the year of enactment.

Treatment of Expensing and Other Temporary Differences

As just noted, in the absence of transition rules, old assets might be treated harshly under a new consumption tax. In contrast, new asset purchases receive favorable treatment because these costs may be deducted entirely in the year of purchase, that is, they may be "expensed." Under income tax accounting principles, expensing allows tax payment to be deferred on an equal sum of value added or consumption tax base. This tax liability is like a loan from the government and, like a loan, is recorded as a liability on the balance sheet since the assets are capitalized for financial statement purposes.

Treatment of Permanent Differences

Under a subtraction-method VAT like the Nunn-Domenici business tax, interest expense, wages, and employee benefits are not deductible. (Under the Flat Tax wages are deductible, but interest and employee benefits are not deductible.) For most firms, the inability to deduct these result in the tax base being far in excess of book income. In this case, the firm's effective tax rate (i.e., the ratio of tax to book income) will far exceed the statutory rate of the new tax (e.g., 17 percent under the proposed Armey Flat Tax). Whether or not the firm's effective tax rate will exceed the statutory corporate rate of 35 percent under current law will depend on how many of expenses for financial purposes are not deductible and also—on the plus side—on how much of gross receipts (for example, exports and interest income) is excluded from the tax base.

Conclusion

In order to determine the impact of elimination of the income tax on financial statements, businesses need to determine (1) the net balance of their deferred tax assets and liabilities on their balance sheet, (2) the new tax rate, and (3) the amount of transition relief (if any).

In order to determine the impact of the enactment of a new consumption tax, firms need to determine (1) the book basis of their existing assets, (2) the new tax rate, (3) the amount of transition relief (if any), (4) the net balance of their existing deferred taxes, and (5) whether the new tax would be considered an income tax for accounting purposes, in which case FASB Statement No. 109 applies. If there is no transition relief and FASB 109 applies, there could be significant financial reporting effects in the year the new tax was enacted. These issues are summarized Table 17.1.

---

[2]In 1993, total corporate profits were measured at approximately $486 billion. See U.S. Executive Office of the President (1995), Table B-25, p. 303.

Table 17.1   Summary of Major Impacts on Financial Statement Resulting From Repeal of Income Tax and Enactment of New Consumption Tax

I. Repeal of Current Income Tax	W/ NO TRANSITION Results in . . .	W/ FULL TRANSITION Results in . . .
A. Transition Depreciation and Other Temporary Differences	. . . Elimination of Deferred Tax Liability (Assets) that Increases (Reduced) Equity and Income in Year of Enactment	. . . Reduction in Deferred Tax Liability (Assets) Value Due to Reduction in Tax Rate
B.1 Carryforwards: Losses	. . . Elimination of Tax Asset that Reduces Equity and Income in Year of Enactment	. . . Reduction in Tax Asset Amount Due to Reduction in Tax Rate
B.2 Carryforwards: Tax Credits	. . . Elimination of Tax Asset that Reduces Equity and Income in Year of Enactment	. . . No Impact on Financial Statement
C.1 Unremitted Foreign Earnings: Remittance Assumed	. . . Elimination of Deferred Tax Liability that Increases Equity and Income in Year of Enactment	. . . Reduction in Tax Liability Amount Due to Reduction in Tax Rate
C.2 Unremitted Foreign Earnings: Indefinite Reinvestment Overseas	No Impact	No Impact
II. Imposition of Consumption Tax *(Assuming FASB 109 Applies)* **Existing Assets**	W/ NO TRANSITION Results in . . .	W/ FULL TRANSITION Results in . . .
A. Book Basis of *Existing* Assets	. . . Creation of Deferred Tax Liability that Reduces Equity and Income in Year of Enactment	. . . No Impact on Financial Statement

Conclusion

Some Remaining Questions

This book has attempted to introduce readers to some issues that are likely to receive attention in the upcoming consumption tax debate. The preceding seventeen chapters, however, do not do justice to the enormous issues involved in totally revising federal tax policy. As a conclusion to this volume, this chapter lists some questions about consumption taxes that deserve further attention and, in some cases, further research.

Questions of Tax Administration

- Will the Internal Revenue Service administer the new tax? Will its budget over the transition have to be increased?

- What are the additional administrative costs of transitioning into a new consumption tax?

- How much time is needed after enactment to prepare for administration of the new tax?

- How will tax administrators be trained? Over what time period?

- What new audit procedures need to be developed? How will they be coordinated with state audits? How will they be coordinated with ongoing income tax audits?

- What new forms and instructions will have to be produced?

- What new regulations will need to be written? How quickly can these regulations be written?

- What implications does a replacement consumption tax have for existing tax treaties and new tax treaties?

- Should the new system be phased in over a number of years?

Questions for State and Local Governments

- Would a national sales tax force states to conform to federal rules?

- How would states administer their income taxes in absence of the federal income tax? How would taxes be calculated without reference to the federal return? Would states need to increase their income tax audits? (Indeed, how much simplification is there for taxpayers who must still file state income tax returns?)

- If a replacement consumption tax reduces property values, what effect will this have on property tax revenue?
- What activities and services of state and local governments will be subject to this new tax?

Questions for Businesses

- What will be the new recordkeeping and reporting requirements? How should computer software and information be changed? How will tax staffing requirements change? How will tax staff be retrained? What are the costs of these changes?
- Should businesses reconfigure their multinational operations that are currently structured around current rules?
- How are plans for business reorganizations affected by the change to a replacement consumption tax?
- Given that interest is unlikely to be deductible under these taxes, should businesses be reducing their indebtedness?
- Given that fringe benefits are unlikely to be deductible, should businesses continue to provide health insurance to their employees?
- Should partnerships and sole proprietorships consider incorporating now that they are subject to the same tax as corporations?
- With all forms of savings tax favored under a consumption tax, should pension plans be altered?

Questions for Households

- How should financial planning be adjusted in anticipation of this tax? Will there be an estate and gift tax under the new system? Could the returns on existing investments be adversely affected by incomplete transition relief?
- Should some types of investments not favored under the current system (e.g., stock with high dividends, certificates of deposit) be given additional weight in personal portfolios?
- Should some types of investments currently tax favored (municipal bonds, whole life insurance) receive less weight in personal investment portfolios?
- If there are no deductions for charitable giving, should contributions be accelerated before the effective date? Should charitable giving be reduced over the long term?
- If there are no deductions for state and local income and property taxes, should relocation decisions be reconsidered because cost differences between low- and high-tax jurisdictions will increase?

Economic Questions

- Will consumption taxes have adverse pre-enactment effects? For example, will taxpayers delay capital purchases until the date the new system takes effect in order to expense their purchases? Will taxpayers delay exports, and rush imports, before border-adjustable taxes take effect? Will taxpayers defer recognition of capital gains until the effective date?

- What quantitative effect will consumption taxes have on employment, wages, inflation, and productivity? How long will it take for any positive effects to take hold?

- What effect will these consumption taxes have on the distribution of income?

- What effect will a replacement consumption tax have on federal revenues? If there is a shortfall or excess in revenue from predicted levels will there be automatic adjustments in tax rates? Will pre-enactment behavioral responses significantly reduce revenues in the early years of the tax?

- What effect will a replacement consumption tax have on real estate values?

Political Questions

- Should revenue estimates include "dynamic" revenue effects, that is, the impacts on revenue from any changes in economic growth that result from the tax? If yes, which economic models will be used? How will differences in estimates between the executive and legislative branches be reconciled?

- What are the benefits in terms of compliance and administrative costs of switching to a new system? Among the widely varying estimates of the compliance costs of the current system, which should be used as a guide for policymakers in the current debate? How will the compliance costs of the new consumption tax system be estimated?

- What is to prevent the political process from weighing down any replacement consumption tax proposal with amendments that result in additional complexity? (This applies not only to the original legislation, but also to actions by subsequent Congresses.)

- Will likely "losers" under a consumption tax (e.g., realtors, insurance companies, state governments, unincorporated businesses, retailers, etc.) be accommodated with special tax relief? If so, how?

- Is there any room for compromise on the notion of totally replacing the current income tax system? Could a new consumption tax be used to reduce income tax rates? Or perhaps just eliminate the corporation income tax?

- Can a replacement consumption tax be enacted without strong presidential leadership?

104th Congress

Names, Addresses, and Telephone Numbers

Rep. Neil Abercrombie (D), Representative from Hawaii, District 1

DC Office: 1233 Longworth House Office Building, Washington, DC 20515, 202-225-2726.

District Offices: 300 Ala Moana Blvd., Honolulu 96850, 808-541-2570.

Sen. Spencer Abraham (R), Senator from Michigan

DC Office: 245 Dirksen Senate Office Building, Washington, DC 20510, 202-224-4822; Fax: 202-224-8834.

State Offices: 30800 Van Dyke Ave., Warren 48093, 810-573-9017; and 720 Fed. Bldg., 110 Michigan Ave., NW, Grand Rapids 49503, 616-456-2592.

Rep. Gary L. Ackerman (D), Representative from New York, District 5

DC Office: 2243 Rayburn House Office Building, Washington, DC 20515, 202-225-2601; Fax: 202-225-1589.

District Offices: 218-14 Northern Blvd., Bayside 11361, 718-423-2154; and 229 Main St., Huntington 11743, 516-423-2154.

Sen. Daniel K. Akaka (D), Senator from Hawaii

DC Office: 720 Hart Senate Office Building, Washington, DC 20510, 202-224-6361; Fax: 202-224-2126.

State Offices: 3104 Prince Kuhio Fed. Bldg., 300 Ala Moana Blvd., Honolulu 96850, 808-541-2534.

Rep. Wayne Allard (R), Representative from Colorado, District 4

DC Office: 422 Cannon House Office Building, Washington, DC 20515, 202-225-4676; Fax: 202-225-8630.

District Offices: Greeley Natl. Plz., 822 7th St., Greeley 80631, 303-351-7582; 315 W. Oak, Ft. Collins 80521, 303-493-9132; 212 E. Kiowa, Ft. Morgan 80701, 303-867-8909; and 19 W. 4th Ave., La Junta 81050, 719-384-7370.

Rep. Robert E. Andrews (D), Representative from New Jersey, District 1

DC Office: 2439 Rayburn House Office Building, Washington, DC 20515, 202-225-6501; Fax: 202-225-6583; e-mail: randrews@hr.house.gov.

District Offices: 16 Somerdale Sq., Somerdale 08063, 609-627-9000; and 63 N. Broad St., Woodbury 08096, 609-848-3900.

Rep. Bill Archer (R), Representative from Texas, District 7

DC Office: 1236 Longworth House Office Building, Washington, DC 20515, 202-225-2571; Fax: 202-225-4381.

District Offices: 1003 Wirt Rd., Houston 77055, 713-467-7493.

———————

Rep. Richard K. (Dick) Armey (R), Representative from Texas, District 26

DC Office: 301 Cannon House Office Building, Washington, DC 20515, 202-225-7772; Fax: 202-225-7614.

District Offices: 9901 Valley Ranch Pkwy. E., Irving 75063, 214-556-2500.

———————

Sen. John Ashcroft (R), Senator from Missouri

DC Office: 170 Russell Senate Office Building, Washington, DC 20510, 202-224-6154; Fax: 202-228-0998; e-mail: john_ashcroft@ashcroft.senate.gov.

State Offices: 1736 Sunshine, Springfield 65804, 417-881-7068; 339 Broadway, Cape Girardeau 63701, 314-334-7044; 600 Broadway, Kansas City 64105, 816-471-7141; 312 Monroe St., Jefferson City 65101, 314-634-2488; and 8000 Maryland Ave., St. Louis 63105, 314-727-7773.

———————

Rep. Spencer Bachus (R), Representative from Alabama, District 6

DC Office: 127 Cannon House Office Building, Washington, DC 20515, 202-225-4921; Fax: 202-225-2082; e-mail: sbachus@hr.house.gov.

District Offices: 1900 Intl. Park Dr., Birmingham 35243, 205-969-2296; and 3500 McFarland Blvd., P.O. Drawer 569, Northport 35476, 205-333-9894.

———————

Rep. Scotty Baesler (D), Representative from Kentucky, District 6

DC Office: 113 Cannon House Office Building, Washington, DC 20515, 202-225-4706; Fax: 202-225-2122.

District Offices: 401 W. Main St., Lexington 40507, 606-253-1124.

———————

Rep. Bill Baker (R), Representative from California, District 10

DC Office: 1724 Longworth House Office Building, Washington, DC 20515, 202-225-1880; Fax: 202-225-1868.

District Offices: 1801 N. California Blvd., Walnut Creek 94596, 510-932-8899; and Dublin City Hall, 100 Civic Plz., Dublin 94568, 510-829-0813.

———————

Rep. Richard H. Baker (R), Representative from Louisiana, District 6

DC Office: 434 Cannon House Office Building, Washington, DC 20515, 202-225-3901; Fax: 202-225-7313.

District Offices: 5555 Hilton Ave., Baton Rouge 70808, 504-929-7711; 3406 Rosalino St., Alexandria 71301, 318-445-5504.

———————

Rep. John Elias Baldacci (D), Representative from Maine, District 2

DC Office: 1740 Longworth House Office Building, Washington, DC 20515, 202-225-6306.

District Offices: 202 Harlow St., P.O. Box 858, Bangor 04402, 207-942-6935; 157 Main St., Lewiston 04240, 207-782-3704; and 445 Main St., Presque Isle 04769, 207-764-1036.

Rep. Cass Ballenger (R), Representative from North Carolina, District 10

DC Office: 2238 Rayburn House Office Building, Washington, DC 20515, 202-225-2576; Fax: 202-225-0316; e-mail: cassmail@hr.house.gov.

District Offices: P.O. Box 1830, Hickory 28603, 704-327-6100; and P.O. Box 1881, Clemmons 27012, 919-766-9455.

Rep. James A. Barcia (D), Representative from Michigan, District 5

DC Office: 1410 Longworth House Office Building, Washington, DC 20515, 202-225-8171; Fax: 202-225-2168.

District Offices: 503 N. Euclid, Bay City 48706, 517-667-0003; 5409 Pierson Rd., Flushing 48433, 313-732-7501; and 301 E. Genessee St., Saginaw 48607, 517-754-6075.

Rep. Bob Barr (R), Representative from Georgia, District 7

DC Office: 1607 Longworth House Office Building, Washington, DC 20515, 202-225-2931; Fax: 202-225-2944.

District Offices: 1001 Whitlock Ave., Marietta 30061, 404-429-1776; 200 Ridley Ave., LaGrange 30240, 706-812-1776; 600 E. 1st St., Rome 30161, 706-290-1776; and 423 College St., Carrollton 30117, 404-836-1776.

Rep. William (Bill) Barrett (R), Representative from Nebraska, District 3

DC Office: 1213 Longworth House Office Building, Washington, DC 20515, 202-225-6435; Fax: 202-225-0207.

District Offices: 312 W. 3d St., Grand Island 68801, 308-381-5555; and 1502 2d Ave., Scottsbluff 69361, 307-632-3333.

Rep. Thomas M. Barrett (D), Representative from Wisconsin, District 5

DC Office: 1224 Longworth House Office Building, Washington, DC 20515, 202-225-3571; Fax: 202-225-2185.

District Offices: 135 W. Wells St., Milwaukee 53203, 414-297-1331.

Rep. Roscoe G. Bartlett (R), Representative from Maryland, District 6

DC Office: 322 Cannon House Office Building, Washington, DC 20515, 202-225-2721; Fax: 202-225-2193.

District Offices: 5831 Buckeystown Pk., Frederick 21701, 301-694-3030; 15 E. Main St., Westminster 21157, 410-857-1115; 100 W. Franklin St., Hagerstown 21740, 301-797-6043; and 50 Broadway, Frostburg 21532, 301-689-0034.

Rep. Joe L. Barton (R), Representative from Texas, District 6

DC Office: 2264 Rayburn House Office Building, Washington, DC 20515, 202-225-2002; Fax: 202-225-3052; e-mail: barton06@hr.house.gov.

District Offices: 2019 E. Lamar Blvd., Arlington 76006, 817-543-1000.

———————

Rep. Charles F. Bass (R), Representative from New Hampshire, District 2

DC Office: 1728 Longworth House Office Building, Washington, DC 20515, 202-225-5206; Fax: 202-225-2946.

District Offices: 142 N. Main St., Concord 03301, 603-226-0249.

———————

Rep. Herbert H. Bateman (R), Representative from Virginia, District 1

DC Office: 2350 Rayburn House Office Building, Washington, DC 20515, 202-225-4261; Fax: 202-225-4382.

District Offices: 739 Thimble Shoals Blvd., Newport News 23606, 804-873-1132; 4712 Southpoint Pkwy., Fredericksburg 22407, 703-898-2975; and P.O. Box 447, Accomac 23301, 804-787-7836.

———————

Sen. Max Baucus (D), Senator from Montana

DC Office: 511 Hart Senate Office Building, Washington, DC 20510, 202-224-2651; e-mail: max@baucus.senate.gov.

State Offices: Granite Bldg., 23 S. Last Chance Gulch, Helena 59601, 406-449-5480; 202 Fratt Bldg., 2817 2d Ave. N., Billings 59101, 406-657-6970; Fed. Bldg., 32 E. Babcock, P.O. Box 1689, Bozeman 59715, 406-586-6104; Silver Bow Ctr., 125 W. Granite, Butte 59701, 406-782-8700; 107 5th St. N., Great Falls 59401, 406-761-1574; 715 Main St., Kalispell 59901; and 211 N. Higgins, Missoula 59802, 406-329-3123.

———————

Rep. Xavier Becerra (D), Representative from California, District 30

DC Office: 1119 Longworth House Office Building, Washington, DC 20515, 202-225-6235; Fax: 202-225-2202.

District Offices: 2435 Colorado Blvd., Los Angeles 90041, 213-550-8962.

———————

Rep. Anthony C. Beilenson (D), Representative from California, District 24

DC Office: 2465 Rayburn House Office Building, Washington, DC 20515, 202-225-5911; Fax: 202-225-0092.

District Offices: 21031 Ventura Blvd., Woodland Hills 91364, 818-999-1990; and 200 N. Westlake Blvd., Thousand Oaks 91362, 805-496-4333.

———————

Sen. Robert F. Bennett (R), Senator from Utah

DC Office: 431 Dirksen Senate Office Building, Washington, DC 20510, 202-224-5444.

State Offices: 4225 Wallace F. Bennett Fed. Bldg., Salt Lake City 84138, 801-524-5933; 51 S. University Ave., Provo 84601, 801-379-2525; 324 24th St., Ogden 84401, 801-625-5676; and Fed. Bldg., 196-E Tabernacle St., St. George 84770, 801-628-5514.

———————

Rep. Ken Bentsen (D), Representative from Texas, District 25

DC Office: 128 Cannon House Office Building, Washington, DC 20515, 202-225-7508; Fax: 202-225-2947.

District Offices: 515 Rusk St., Houston 77002, 713-229-2244; and 100 E. Southmore St., Pasadena 77502, 713-473-4334.

_____

Rep. Doug Bereuter (R), Representative from Nebraska, District 1

DC Office: 2348 Rayburn House Office Building, Washington, DC 20515, 202-225-4806; Fax: 202-226-1148.

District Offices: 1045 K St., Lincoln 68508, 402-438-1598; and 502 N. Broad St., Fremont 68025, 402-727-0888.

_____

Rep. Howard L. Berman (D), Representative from California, District 26

DC Office: 2231 Rayburn House Office Building, Washington, DC 20515, 202-225-4695.

District Offices: 10200 Sepulveda Blvd., Mission Hills 91345, 818-891-0543.

_____

Rep. Tom Bevill (D), Representative from Alabama, District 4

DC Office: 2302 Rayburn House Office Building, Washington, DC 20515, 202-225-4876; Fax: 202-225-1604.

District Offices: 107 Fed. Bldg., Gadsden 35901, 205-546-0201; 1710 Alabama Ave. Fed. Bldg., Jasper 35501, 205-221-2310; and 102 Fed. Bldg., Cullman 35055, 205-734-6043.

_____

Sen. Joseph R. Biden, Jr. (D), Senator from Delaware

DC Office: 221 Russell Senate Office Building, Washington, DC 20510, 202-224-5042; Fax: 202-224-0139; e-mail: senator@biden.senate.gov.

State Offices: Fed. Bldg., 844 King St., Wilmington 19801, 302-573-6345; 1101 Fed. Bldg, 300 S. New St., Dover 17901, 302-678-9483; and Box 109, The Circle, Georgetown 19947, 302-856-9275.

_____

Rep. Brian P. Bilbray (R), Representative from California, District 49

DC Office: 1004 Longworth House Office Building, Washington, DC 20515, 202-225-2040; Fax: 202-225-2948.

District Offices: 1011 Camino de Rio South, San Diego 92108, 619-291-1430.

_____

Rep. Michael Bilirakis (R), Representative from Florida, District 9

DC Office: 2240 Rayburn House Office Building, Washington, DC 20515, 202-225-5755; Fax: 202-225-4085.

District Offices: 1100 Cleveland St., Clearwater 34615, 813-441-3721; and 4111 Land O'Lakes Blvd., Land O'Lakes 34639, 813-996-7441.

_____

Sen. Jeff Bingaman (D), Senator from New Mexico

DC Office: 703 Hart Senate Office Building, Washington, DC 20510, 202-224-5521; Fax: 202-224-2852; e-mail: senator_bingaman@bingaman.senate.gov.

State Offices: 119 E. Marcy St., Santa Fe 87501, 505-988-6647; 625 Wilver Ave., SW, Albuquerque 87102, 505-766-3636; 505 S. Main St., Las Cruces 88001, 505-523-6561; and 114 E. 4th St., Roswell 88201, 505-622-7113.

———

Rep. Sanford D. Bishop, Jr. (D), Representative from Georgia, District 2

DC Office: 1632 Longworth House Office Building, Washington, DC 20515, 202-225-3631; Fax: 202-225-2203.

District Offices: 225 Pine St., Albany 31701, 912-439-8067; 17 10th St., Columbus 31901, 706-323-6894; City Hall, Dawson 31742, 912-995-3991; 682 Cherry St., Macon 31201, 912-741-2221; and 401 N. Patterson St., Valdosta 31601, 912-247-9705.

———

Rep. Thomas J. Bliley, Jr. (R), Representative from Virginia, District 7

DC Office: 2241 Rayburn House Office Building, Washington, DC 20515, 202-225-2815.

District Offices: 4914 Fitzhugh Ave., Richmond 23230, 804-771-2809.

———

Rep. Peter I. Blute (R), Representative from Massachusetts, District 3

DC Office: 1029 Longworth House Office Building, Washington, DC 20515, 202-225-6101; Fax: 202-225-2217.

District Offices: 100 Front St., Worcester 01608, 508-752-6789; 1039 S. Main St., Fall River 02724, 508-675-3400; and 7 N. Main St., Attleboro 02703, 508-223-3100.

———

Rep. Sherwood Boehlert (R), Representative from New York, District 23

DC Office: 2246 Rayburn House Office Building, Washington, DC 20515, 202-225-3665; Fax: 202-225-1891; e-mail: boehlert@hr.house.gov.

District Offices: 10 Broad St., Utica 13501, 315-793-8146; 41 S. Main St., Oneonta 13820, 607-432-5524; and 42 S. Broad St., Norwich 13815 607-336-7160.

———

Rep. John A. Boehner (R), Representative from Ohio, District 8

DC Office: 1011 Longworth House Office Building, Washington, DC 20515, 202-225-6205; Fax: 202-225-0704.

District Offices: 5617 Liberty-Fairfield Rd., Hamilton 45011, 513-894-6003; and 12 S. Plum St., Troy 45373, 513-339-1524.

———

Sen. Christopher S. (Kit) Bond (R), Senator from Missouri

DC Office: 293 Russell Senate Office Building, Washington, DC 20510, 202-224-5721; Fax: 202-224-8149.

State Offices: 1736 Sunshine, Springfield 65804, 417-881-7068; 339 Broadway, Cape Girardeau 63701, 314-334-7044; 600 Broadway, Kansas City 64105, 816-471-7141; 312 Monroe St., Jefferson City 65101, 314-634-2488; and 8000 Maryland Ave., St. Louis 63105, 314-727-7773.

———

Rep. Henry Bonilla (R), Representative from Texas, District 23

DC Office: 1427 Longworth House Office Building, Washington, DC 20515, 202-225-4511; Fax: 202-225-2237.

District Offices: 11120 Wurzbach, San Antonio 78230, 210-697-9055; 1300 Matamoros St., Laredo 78040, 210-726-4682; 100 E. Broadway, Del Rio 78840, 210-774-6547; 4400 N. Big Spring, Midland 79705, 915-686-8833.

_____

Rep. David E. Bonior (D), Representative from Michigan, District 10

DC Office: 2207 Rayburn House Office Building, Washington, DC 20515, 202-225-2106; Fax: 202-226-1169.

District Offices: 59 N. Walnut, Mt. Clemens 48043, 313-469-3232; and 526 Water St., Port Huron 48060, 313-987-8889.

_____

Rep. Sonny Bono (R), Representative from California, District 44

DC Office: 512 Cannon House Office Building, Washington, DC 20515, 202-225-5330; Fax: 202-225-2961.

District Offices: 1555 S. Palm Canyon Dr., Palm Springs 92264, 619-320-1076; and 23119-A Cottonwood Ave., Moreno Valley 92553, 909-653-4466.

_____

Rep. Robert A. Borski (D), Representative from Pennsylvania, District 3

DC Office: 2182 Rayburn House Office Building, Washington, DC 20515, 202-225-8251; Fax: 202-225-4628.

District Offices: 7141 Frankford Ave., Philadelphia 19135, 215-335-3355; and 2630 Memphis St., Philadelphia 19125, 215-426-4616.

_____

Rep. Rick Boucher (D), Representative from Virginia, District 9

DC Office: 2245 Rayburn House Office Building, Washington, DC 20515, 202-225-3861; Fax: 202-225-0442; e-mail: ninthnet@hr.house.gov.

District Offices: 188 E. Main St., Abingdon 24210, 703-628-1145; 311 Shawnee Ave., Big Stone Gap 24219, 703-523-5450; and 112 N. Washington Ave., Pulaski 24301, 703-980-4310.

_____

Sen. Barbara Boxer (D), Senator from California

DC Office: 112 Hart Senate Office Building, Washington, DC 20510, 202-224-3553; Fax: 202-228-0026; e-mail: senator@boxer.senate.gov.

State Offices: 1700 Montgomery St., San Francisco 94111, 415-403-0100; and 2250 E. Imperial Hwy., El Segundo 90245, 310-414-5700.

_____

Sen. Bill Bradley (D), Senator from New Jersey

DC Office: 731 Hart Senate Office Building, Washington, DC 20510, 202-224-3224; Fax: 202-224-8567; e-mail: senator@bradley.senate.gov.

State Offices: 1 Newark Ctr., Newark 07102, 201-639-2860; and 1 Greentree Ctr., Rte. Marlton 08053, 609-983-4143.

_____

Sen. John B. Breaux (D), Senator from Louisiana

DC Office: 516 Hart Senate Office Building, Washington, DC 20510, 202-224-4623; Fax: 202-224-4268; e-mail: senator@breaux.senate.gov.

State Offices: 705 Jefferson, Lafayette 70501, 318-264-6871; Hale Boggs Fed. Bldg., 501 Magazine St., New Orleans 70130, 504-589-2531; and 211 N. 3d St., Monroe 71201, 318-325-3320.

Rep. Bill Brewster (D), Representative from Oklahoma, District 3

DC Office: 1727 Longworth House Office Building, Washington, DC 20515, 202-225-4565; Fax: 202-225-9029.

District Offices: 201 Post Office Bldg., Ada 74820, 405-436-1980; 118 Fed. Bldg., McAlester 74501, 918-423-5951; 123 W. 7th Ave., Stillwater 74074, 405-743-1400; and 101 W. Main St., Ardmore 73401, 405-266-6300.

Rep. Glen Browder (D), Representative from Alabama, District 3

DC Office: 2344 Rayburn House Office Building, Washington, DC 20515, 202-225-3261; Fax: 202-225-9020.

District Offices: 107 Fed. Bldg., Opelika 36801, 205-745-6221; P.O. Box 2042, Anniston 36202, 205-236-5655; and 115 E. Northside, Tuskegee 36083, 205-727-6490.

Sen. Hank Brown (R), Senator from Colorado

DC Office: 716 Hart Senate Office Building, Washington, DC 20510, 202-224-5941; Fax: 202-224-6471; e-mail: senator_brown@brown.senate.gov.

State Offices: 1200 17th St., Denver 80202, 303-844-2600; 1100 10th St., Greeley 80631, 303-352-4112; 228 N. Cascade, Colorado Springs 80903, 719-634-6071; 411 Thatcher Bldg., Pueblo 81003, 719-545-9751; and 215 Fed. Bldg., 400 Rood Ave., Grand Junction 81501, 303-245-9553.

Rep. George E. Brown, Jr. (D), Representative from California, District 42

DC Office: 2300 Rayburn House Office Building, Washington, DC 20515, 202-225-6161; Fax: 202-225-8671.

District Offices: 657 La Cadena Dr., Colton 92324, 909-825-2472.

Rep. Corrine Brown (D), Representative from Florida, District 3

DC Office: 1610 Longworth House Office Building, Washington, DC 20515, 202-225-0123; Fax: 202-225-2256.

District Offices: 815 S. Main St., Jacksonville 32207, 904-398-8567; 250 N. Beach St., Daytona Beach 32114, 904-254-4622; 75 Ivanhoe Blvd., Orlando 32806, 407-872-0656; and 401 SE First Ave., Gainesville 32601, 904-375-6003.

Rep. Sherrod Brown (D), Representative from Ohio, District 13

DC Office: 1019 Longworth House Office Building, Washington, DC 20515, 202-225-3401; Fax: 202-225-2266.

District Offices: 5201 Abbe Rd., Elyria 44035, 216-934-5100.

_____

Rep. Sam Brownback (R), Representative from Kansas, District 2

DC Office: 1313 Longworth House Office Building, Washington, DC 20515, 202-225-6601; Fax: 202-225-2983; e-mail: brownbak@hr.house.gov.

District Offices: 612 S. Kansas St., Topeka 66603, 913-233-2503; 1001 N. Broadway, Pittsburg 66762, 316-231-6040.

_____

Sen. Richard H. Bryan (D), Senator from Nevada

DC Office: 364 Russell Senate Office Building, Washington, DC 20510, 202-224-6244; Fax: 202-224-1867.

State Offices: 300 Las Vegas Blvd. S., Las Vegas 89101, 702-388-6605; 300 Booth St., Reno 89509, 702-784-5007; and 600 E. William St., Carson City 89701, 702-885-9111.

_____

Rep. Ed Bryant (R), Representative from Tennessee, District 7

DC Office: 1516 Longworth House Office Building, Washington, DC 20515, 202-225-2811; Fax: 202-225-2989.

District Offices: 5909 Shelby Oaks Dr., Memphis 38134, 901-382-5811; 330 N. 2nd St., Clarksville 37040, 615-503-0391; and 810 1/2 S. Garden St., Columbia 38401, 615-381-8100.

_____

Rep. John Bryant (D), Representative from Texas, District 5

DC Office: 2330 Rayburn House Office Building, Washington, DC 20515, 202-225-2231; Fax: 202-225-0327.

District Offices: 8035 E. R.L.Thornton Freeway, Dallas 75228, 214-767-6554.

_____

Sen. Dale Bumpers (D), Senator from Arkansas

DC Office: 229 Dirksen Senate Office Building, Washington, DC 20510, 202-224-4843; Fax: 202-224-6435; e-mail: senator_bumpers.senate.gov.

State Offices: 2527 Fed. Bldg., 700 W. Capitol, Little Rock 72201, 501-324-6286.

_____

Rep. Jim Bunn (R), Representative from Oregon, District 5

DC Office: 1517 Longworth House Office Building, Washington, DC 20515, 202-225-5711; Fax: 202-225-2994.

District Office: 738 Hawthorne Ave. NE, Salem 97301, 503-588-9100.

_____

Rep. Jim Bunning (R), Representative from Kentucky, District 4

DC Office: 2437 Rayburn House Office Building, Washington, DC 20515, 202-225-3465; Fax: 202-225-0003; e-mail; bunning4@hr.house.gov.

District Offices: 1717 Dixie Hwy., Ft. Wright 41011, 606-341-2602; 1408 Greenup Ave., Ashland 41101, 606-325-9898; and 704 W. Jefferson St., La Grange 40031, 502-222-2188.

————————

Sen. Conrad Burns (R), Senator from Montana

DC Office: 187 Dirksen Senate Office Building, Washington, DC 20510, 202-224-2644; Fax: 202-224-8594; e-mail; conrad_burns@burns.senate.gov.

State Offices: 2708 First Ave. N., Billings 59101, 406-252-0550; 208 N. Montana Ave., Helena 59601, 406-449-5401; 415 N. Higgins, Missoula 59802, 406-329-3528; 321 1st Ave. N, Great Falls 59401, 406-252-9585; 324 W. Towne, Glendive 59330, 406-365-2391; 10 E. Babcock, Fed. Bldg. Bozeman 59715, 406-586-4450; 125 W. Granite, Butte 59701, 406-723-3277; and 575 Sunset Blvd., Kalispell 59901, 406-257-3360.

————————

Rep. Richard M. Burr (R), Representative from North Carolina, District 5

DC Office: 1431 Longworth House Office Building, Washington, DC 20515, 202-225-2071; Fax: 202-225-2995; e-mail: mail2nc5@hr.house.gov.

District Offices: 2000 W. 1st St., Winston-Salem 27104, 910-631-5125.

————————

Rep. Dan Burton (R), Representative from Indiana, District 6

DC Office: 2411 Rayburn House Office Building, Washington, DC 20515, 202-225-2276; Fax: 202-225-0016.

District Offices: 8900 Keystone-at-the-Crossing, Indianapolis 46240, 317-848-0201; and 435 E. Main St., Greenwood 46142, 317-882-3640.

————————

Rep. Steve Buyer (R), Representative from Indiana, District 5

DC Office: 326 Cannon House Office Building, Washington, DC 20515, 202-225-5037.

District Offices: 120 E. Mulberry St., Kokomo 46901, 317-454-7551; 204-A N. Main St., Monticello 47960, 219-583-9819.

————————

Sen. Robert C. Byrd (D), Senator from West Virginia

DC Office: 311 Hart Senate Office Building, Washington, DC 20510, 202-224-3954; Fax: 202-228-0002.

State Offices: Fed. Bldg., 500 Quarrier St., Charleston 25301, 304-342-5855.

————————

Rep. H. L. (Sonny) Callahan (R), Representative from Alabama, District 1

DC Office: 2418 Rayburn House Office Building, Washington, DC 20515, 202-225-4931; Fax: 202-225-0562.

District Offices: 2970 Cottage Hill Rd., Mobile 36606, 334-690-2811.

————————

Rep. Ken Calvert (R), Representative from California, District 43

DC Office: 1034 Longworth House Office Building, Washington, DC 20515, 202-225-1986; Fax: 202-225-2004.

District Offices: 3400 Central Ave., Riverside 92506, 909-784-4300.

————————

Rep. Dave Camp (R), Representative from Michigan, District 4

DC Office: 137 Cannon House Office Building, Washington, DC 20515, 202-225-3561; Fax: 202-225-9679; e-mail: davecamp@hr.house.gov.

District Offices: 135 Ashman St., Midland 48640, 517-631-2552; 308 W. Main St., Owosso 48867, 517-723-6759; and 3508 W. Houghton Lake Dr., Houghton Lake 48629, 517-366-4922.

————————

Rep. Tom Campbell (R), Representative from California, District 15

DC Office: 2221 Rayburn House Office Building, Washington, DC 20515; 202-225-2631; Fax: 202-225-6788.

District Offices: 100 N. Winchester Blvd., Santa Clara CA 95050, 408-983-1291.

————————

Sen. Ben Nighthorse Campbell (R), Senator from Colorado

DC Office: 380 Russell Senate Office Building, Washington, DC 20510, 202-224-5852; Fax: 202-224-1933.

State Offices: 1129 Pennsylvania St., Denver 80203, 303-866-1900; 720 N. Main St., Pueblo 81003, 719-542-6987; 105 E. Vermijo, Colorado Springs 80903, 719-636-9092; 743 Horizon Ct., Grand Junction 81506, 303-241-6631; 835 2nd Ave., Durango 81301, 303-247-1609; and 19 Old Town Sq, Ft. Collins 80524, 303-224-1909.

————————

Rep. Charles T. Canady (R), Representative from Florida, District 12

DC Office: 1222 Longworth House Office Building, Washington, DC 20515, 202-225-1252.

District Offices: Fed. Bldg., 124 S. Tennessee Ave., Lakeland 33801, 813-688-2651.

————————

Rep. Benjamin L. Cardin (D), Representative from Maryland, District 3

DC Office: 104 Cannon House Office Building, Washington, DC 20515, 202-225-4016; Fax: 202-225-9219; e-mail: cardin@hr.house.gov.

District Offices: 540 E. Belvedere Ave., Baltimore 21212, 410-433-8886.

————————

Rep. Michael N. Castle (R), Representative from Delaware, District 1

DC Office: 1207 Longworth House Office Building, Washington, DC 20515, 202-225-4165; Fax: 202-225-2291; e-mail: delaware@hr.house.gov.

District Offices: 3 Christina Ctr., 201 N. Walnut St., Wilmington 19801, 302-428-1902; and Freer Fed. Bldg., 300 S. New St., Dover 19901, 302-736-1666.

————————

Rep. Steve Chabot (R), Representative from Ohio, District 1

DC Office: 1641 Longworth House Office Building, Washington, DC 20515, 202-225-2216; Fax: 202-225-3012.

District Offices: 105 W. 4th St., Cincinnati 45202, 513-684-2723.

Sen. John H. Chafee (R), Senator from Rhode Island

DC Office: 505 Dirksen Senate Office Building, Washington, DC 20510, 202-224-2921; e-mail: senator_chafee@chafee.senate.gov.

State Offices: 10 Dorrance St., Providence 02903, 401-528-5294.

Rep. Saxby Chambliss (R), Representative from Georgia, District 8

DC Office: 1708 Longworth House Office Building, Washington, DC 20515, 202-225-6531; Fax: 202-225-3013; e-mail: saxby@hr.house.gov.

District Offices: 3312 Northside Dr., Macon 31210, 912-475-0665; 1707 1st. Ave. SE, Moultrie 31768, 912-891-3474.

Rep. Jim Chapman, Jr. (D), Representative from Texas, District 1

DC Office: 2417 Rayburn House Office Building, Washington, DC 20515, 202-225-3035; Fax: 202-225-7265; e-mail: jchapman@hr.house.gov.

District Offices: P.O. Box 538, Sulphur Springs 75482, 903-885-8682; Fed. Bldg., 100 E. Houston St., Marshall 75670, 903-938-8386; and P.O. Box 248, New Boston 75510, 903-628-5594.

Rep. Helen Chenoweth (R), Representative from Idaho, District 1

DC Office: 1722 Longworth House Office Building, Washington, DC 20515, 202-225-6611.

District Offices: 304 N. 8th St., Boise 83702, 208-336-9831; 118 N. 2nd St., Coeur d'Alene 83814, 208-667-0127; and 621 Main St., Lewiston 83501, 208-746-4613.

Rep. Jon Christensen (R), Representative from Nebraska, District 2

DC Office: 1020 Longworth House Office Building, Washington, DC 20515, 202-225-4155; Fax: 202-225-3032.

District Offices: 8712 Dodge St., Omaha 68114, 402-397-9944.

Rep. Dick Chrysler (R), Representative from Michigan, District 8

DC Office: 327 Cannon House Office Building, Washington, DC 20515, 202-225-4872; Fax: 202-225-3034; e-mail: chrysler@hr.house.gov.

District Offices: 721 N. Capitol, Lansing 48906, 514-484-1770; 10049 E. Grand River Ave. Brighton 48116, 810-220-1002.

Rep. William (Bill) Clay (D), Representative from Missouri, District 1

DC Office: 2306 Rayburn House Office Building, Washington, DC 20515, 202-225-2406; Fax: 202-225-1725.

District Offices: 5261 Delmar Blvd., St. Louis 63108, 314-367-1970; and 49 Central City Shopping Ctr. N., St. Louis 63136, 314-388-0321.

_____

Rep. Eva M. Clayton (D), Representative from North Carolina, District 1

DC Office: 222 Cannon House Office Building, Washington, DC 20515, 202-225-3101; Fax: 202-225-3354.

District Offices: 400 W. 5th St., Greenville 27834, 800-274-8672; and P.O. Box 676, Warrenton 27589, 919-257-4800.

_____

Rep. Bob Clement (D), Representative from Tennessee, District 5

DC Office: 2229 Rayburn House Office Building, Washington, DC 20515, 202-225-4311; Fax: 202-226-1035.

District Offices: 552 U.S. Crthse., Nashville 37203, 615-736-5295; 2701 Jefferson St., N. Nashville 37208, 615-320-1363; and 101 5th Ave. W., Springfield 37172, 615-384-6600.

_____

Rep. William F. (Bill) Clinger, Jr. (R), Representative from Pennsylvania, District 5

DC Office: 2160 Rayburn House Office Building, Washington, DC 20515, 202-225-5121; Fax: 202-225-4681.

District Offices: 315 S. Allen St., State College 16801, 814-238-1776; and 605 Integra Bank Bldg., Warren 16365, 814-726-3910.

_____

Rep. James E. Clyburn (D), Representative from South Carolina, District 6

DC Office: 319 Cannon House Office Building, Washington, DC 20515, 202-225-3315; Fax: 202-225-2313.

District Offices: 1703 Gervais St., Columbia 29201, 803-799-1100; 181 E. Evans St., Florence 29502, 803-622-1212; and 4900 LaCrosse Rd., N. Charleston 29418, 803-747-9660.

_____

Sen. Daniel R. Coats (R), Senator from Indiana

DC Office: 404 Russell Senate Office Building, Washington, DC 20510, 202-224-5623; Fax: 202-228-4137.

State Offices: 1180 Market Tower, 10 W. Market St., Indianapolis 46204, 317-226-5555; Fed. Bldg., 1300 S. Harrison St., Fort Wayne 46802, 219-422-1505; 103 Fed. Ctr., 1201 E. 10th St., Jeffersonville 47132, 812-288-3377; 122 Fed. Bldg., 101 NW M.L.K. Blvd., Evansville 47708, 812-465-6313; and 5530 Sohl Ave., Hammond 46320, 219-937-5380.

_____

Rep. Howard Coble (R), Representative from North Carolina, District 6

DC Office: 403 Cannon House Office Building, Washington, DC 20515, 202-225-3065; Fax: 202-225-8611.

District Offices: 324 W. Market St., Greensboro 27401, 919-333-5005; P.O. Box 1813, 1404 Piedmont Dr., Lexington 27293, 704-246-8230; P.O. Box 814, 124 W. Elm St., Graham 27253, 919-228-0159; 241 Sunset Ave., Asheboro 27203, 919-626-3060; and 1912 Eastchester Dr., High Point 27265, 919-886-5106.

Rep. Tom Coburn (R), Representative from Oklahoma, District 2

DC Office: 511 Cannon House Office Building, Washington, DC 20515, 202-225-2701; Fax: 202-225-3038.

District Offices: 215 State St., Muskogee 74401, 918-687-2533.

Sen. Thad Cochran (R), Senator from Mississippi

DC Office: 326 Russell Senate Office Building, Washington, DC 20510, 202-224-5054; e-mail: senator@cochran.senate.gov.

State Offices: 188 E. Capitol St., Jackson 39201, 601-965-4459; and 911 Jackson St., Oxford 38655, 601-236-1018.

Sen. William S. Cohen (R), Senator from Maine

DC Office: 322 Hart Senate Office Building, Washington, DC 20510, 202-224-2523; Fax: 202-224-2693; e-mail: billcohen@cohen.senate.gov.

State Offices: 150 Capitol St., P.O. Box 347, Augusta 04332, 207-622-8414; Fed. Bldg., 202 Harlow St., Bangor 04402, 207-945-0417; 109 Alfred St., Biddeford 04005, 207-283-1101; 11 Lisbon St., Lewiston 04240, 207-784-6969; 10 Moulton St., P.O. Box 1938, Portland 04104, 207-780-3575; and 169 Academy St., Presque Isle 04769, 207-764-3266.

Rep. Ronald D. Coleman (D), Representative from Texas, District 16

DC Office: 2312 Rayburn House Office Building, Washington, DC 20515, 202-225-4831; Fax: 202-225-4825.

District Offices: Fed. Bldg., 700 E. San Antonio St., El Paso 79901, 915-534-6200; and P.O. Bldg., Pecos 79772, 915-445-6218.

Rep. Mac Collins (R), Representative from Georgia, District 3

DC Office: 1130 Longworth House Office Building, Washington, DC 20515, 202-225-5901; Fax: 202-225-2515.

District Offices: 173 N. Main St., Jonesboro 30236, 404-603-3395; and 5704 Beallwood Connector, Columbus 31904, 706-327-7728.

Rep. Cardiss Collins (D), Representative from Illinois, District 7

DC Office: 2308 Rayburn House Office Building, Washington, DC 20515, 202-225-5006; Fax: 202-225-8396.

District Offices: 230 S. Dearborn St., Chicago 60604, 312-353-5754; and 328 Lake St., Oak Park 60302, 708-383-1400.

Rep. Barbara-Rose Collins (D), Representative from Michigan, District 15

DC Office: 401 Cannon House Office Building, Washington, DC 20515,
202-225-2261; Fax: 202-225-6645.

District Offices: 1155 Brewery Park Blvd., Detroit 48207, 313-567-2233.

———————

Rep. Larry Combest (R), Representative from Texas, District 19

DC Office: 1511 Longworth House Office Building, Washington, DC 20515,
202-225-4005.

District Offices: 1205 Texas Ave., Lubbock 79401, 806-763-1611; 5809 S. Western,
Amarillo 79110, 806-353-3945; and 3800 E. 42d St., Odessa 79762, 915-362-2631.

———————

Rep. Gary A. Condit (D), Representative from California, District 18

DC Office: 2444 Rayburn House Office Building, Washington, DC 20515,
202-225-6131; Fax: 202-225-0819.

District Offices: 415 W. 18th St., Merced 95340, 209-383-4455;
and 920 16th St., Modesto 95354, 209-527-1914.

———————

Sen. Kent Conrad (D), Senator from North Dakota

DC Office: 724 Hart Senate Office Building, Washington, DC 20510, 202-224-2043;
Fax: 202-224-7776.

State Offices: Fed. Bldg., 3d & Rosser Ave., Bismarck 58501, 701-258-4648;
657 2d Ave. N., Fargo 58102, 701-232-8030; 100 1st St. SW, Minot 58701,
701-852-0703; and Fed. Bldg., 102 N. 4th St., Grand Forks 58201, 701-775-9601.

———————

Rep. John Conyers, Jr. (D), Representative from Michigan, District 14

DC Office: 2426 Rayburn House Office Building, Washington, DC 20515,
202-225-5126; Fax: 202-225-0072; e-mail: jconyers@hr.house.gov.

District Offices: 669 Fed. Bldg., 231 W. Lafayette St., Detroit 48226, 313-961-5670.

———————

Rep. Wes Cooley (R), Representative from Oregon, District 2

DC Office: 1609 Longworth House Office Building, Washington, DC 20515,
202-225-6730; Fax: 202-225-3046.

District Offices: 259 Barnett Rd., Medford 97501, 503-776-4646.

———————

Rep. Jerry F. Costello (D), Representative from Illinois, District 12

DC Office: 2454 Rayburn House Office Building, Washington, DC 20515,
202-225-5661; Fax: 202-225-0285; e-mail: jfcil12@hr.house.gov.

District Offices: 327 W. Main St., Belleville 62221, 618-233-8026.

———————

Sen. Paul Coverdell (R), Senator from Georgia

DC Office: 200 Russell Senate Office Building, Washington, DC 20510,
202-224-3643; Fax: 202-228-3783; e-mail: senator_coverdell@coverdell.senate.gov.

State Offices: 100 Colony Sq., 1175 Peachtree St., NE, Atlanta 30361, 404-347-2202.

———————

Rep. Christopher Cox (R), Representative from California, District 47

DC Office: 2402 Rayburn House Office Building, Washington, DC 20515, 202-225-5611; Fax: 202-225-9177.

District Offices: 4000 MacArthur Blvd., Newport Beach 92660, 714-756-2244.

_____

Rep. William J. Coyne (D), Representative from Pennsylvania, District 14

DC Office: 2455 Rayburn House Office Building, Washington, DC 20515, 202-225-2301; Fax: 202-225-1844.

District Offices: 2009 Fed. Bldg., 1000 Liberty Ave., Pittsburgh 15222, 412-644-2870.

_____

Sen. Larry Craig (R), Senator from Idaho

DC Office: 313 Hart Senate Office Building, Washington, DC 20510, 202-224-2752; Fax: 202-224-2573; e-mail: larry_craig@craig.senate.gov.

State Offices: 304 N. 8th St., Boise 83702, 208-342-7985; 103 N. 4th St., Coeur d'Alene 83814, 208-667-6130; 846 Main St., Lewiston 83501, 208-743-0792; 1292 Addison Ave. E., Twin Falls 83301, 202-734-6780; 250 S. 4th Ave., Pocatello 83201, 208-236-6817; and 2539 Channing Way, Idaho Falls 83404, 208-523-5541.

_____

Rep. Robert E. (Bud) Cramer (D), Representative from Alabama, District 5

DC Office: 236 Cannon House Office Building, Washington, DC 20515, 202-225-4801; Fax: 202-225-4392; e-mail: budmail@hr.house.gov.

District Offices: 737 E. Avalon Ave., Muscle Shoals 35661, 205-381-3450; 403 Franklin St., Huntsville 35801, 205-551-0190; and Morgan Cnty. Crthse., P.O. Box 668, Decatur 35602, 205-355-9400.

_____

Rep. Philip M. Crane (R), Representative from Illinois, District 8

DC Office: 233 Cannon House Office Building, Washington, DC 20515, 202-225-3711; Fax: 202-225-7830.

District Offices: 1450 S. New Wilke Rd., Arlington Heights 60005, 708-394-0790; and 300 N. Milwaukee Ave., Lake Villa 60046, 708-265-9000.

_____

Rep. Michael Crapo (R), Representative from Idaho, District 2

DC Office: 437 Cannon House Office Building, Washington, DC 20515, 202-225-5531; Fax: 202-225-8216.

District Offices: 304 N. 8th St., Boise 83702, 208-334-1953; 250 S. 4th St., Pocatello 83201, 208-236-6734; 628 Blue Lakes Blvd., N., Twin Falls 83301, 208-734-7219; and 2539 Channing Way, Idaho Falls 83404, 208-523-6701.

_____

Rep. Frank A. Cremeans (R), Representative from Ohio, District 6

DC Office: 1630 Longworth House Office Building, Washington, DC 20515, 202-225-5705; Fax: 202-225-3054.

District Offices: 200 Putnam St., Marietta 45750, 614-373-2120; 301 N. High St., Hillsboro 45133, 513-393-8688; and 308 Bank One Plz., Portsmouth 45662, 614-353-4006.

_____

Rep. Barbara Cubin (R), Representative from Wyoming, District 1

DC Office: 1114 Longworth House Office Building, Washington, DC 20515, 202-225-2311; Fax: 202-225-3057.

District Offices: 4003 Fed. Bldg., 100 E. B St., Casper 82601, 307-261-5595; 2015 Fed. Bldg., 2120 Capitol Ave., Cheyenne 82001, 307-772-2595; and 2515 Foothills Blvd., Rock Springs 82901, 307-362-4095.

───────────

Rep. Randy (Duke) Cunningham (R), Representative from California, District 51

DC Office: 227 Cannon House Office Building, Washington, DC 20515, 202-225-5452; Fax: 202-225-2558.

District Offices: 613 W. Valley Pkwy., Escondido 92025, 619-737-6960.

───────────

Sen. Alfonse M. D'Amato (R), Senator from New York

DC Office: 520 Hart Senate Office Building, Washington, DC 20510, 202-224-6542; Fax: 202-224-5871.

State Offices: 420 Fed. Bldg., Albany 12207, 518-472-4343; Fed. Bldg., 111 W. Huron, Buffalo 14202, 716-846-4111; 7 Penn Plz., 7th Ave., New York 10001, 212-947-7390; 1259 Fed. Bldg., 100 S. Clinton St., Syracuse 13260, 315-423-5471; and 100 State St., 304 Fed. Bldg., Rochester 14614, 716-263-5866.

───────────

Rep. Pat Danner (D), Representative from Missouri, District 6

DC Office: 1323 Longworth House Office Building, Washington, DC 20515, 202-225-7041; Fax: 202-225-8221.

District Offices: 5754 N. Broadway, Bldg. 3, Kansas City 64118, 816-455-2256; and 201 S. 8th St., St. Joseph 64501, 816-233-9818.

───────────

Sen. Thomas A. Daschle (D), Senator from South Dakota

DC Office: 509 Hart Senate Office Building, Washington, DC 20510, 202-224-2321; Fax: 202-224-2047; e-mail: tom_daschle@daschle.senate.gov.

State Offices: P.O. Box 1274, Sioux Falls 57101, 605-334-9596; P.O. Box 1536, Aberdeen 57401, 605-225-8823; and P.O. Box 8168, Rapid City 57709, 605-348-3551.

───────────

Rep. Tom Davis (R), Representative from Virginia, District 11

DC Office: 415 Cannon House Office Building, Washington, DC 20515, 202-225-1492; Fax: 202-225-3071; e-mail: tomdavis@hr.house.gov.

District Offices: 7018 Evergreen Ct., Annandale 22003, 703-916-9610.

───────────

Rep. E (Kika) de la Garza (D), Representative from Texas, District 15

DC Office: 1401 Longworth House Office Building, Washington, DC 20515, 202-225-2531; Fax: 202-225-2534.

District Offices: 1418 Beech St., McAllen 78501, 210-682-5545; and Alice Fed. Bldg., 401 E. 2d St., Alice 78332, 512-664-2215.

───────────

Rep. Nathan Deal (R), Representative from Georgia, District 9

DC Office: 1406 Longworth House Office Building, Washington, DC 20515, 202-225-5211; Fax: 202-225-8272.

District Offices: P.O. Box 1015, Gainesville 30503, 404-535-2592; 415 E. Walnut Ave., Dalton 30720, 706-226-5320; and 109 N. Main St., La Fayette 30728, 706-638-7042.

———————

Rep. Peter A. DeFazio (D), Representative from Oregon, District 4

DC Office: 2134 Rayburn House Office Building, Washington, DC 20515, 202-225-6416; Fax: 202-225-0373; e-mail: pdefazio@hr.house.gov.

District Offices: P.O. Box 1557, Coos Bay 97420, 503-269-2609; 151 W. 7th Ave., Eugene 97401, 503-465-6732; and P.O. Box 2460, Roseburg 97470, 503-440-3523.

———————

Rep. Rosa L. DeLauro (D), Representative from Connecticut, District 3

DC Office: 436 Cannon House Office Building, Washington, DC 20515, 202-225-3661; Fax: 202-225-4890.

District Offices: 265 Church St., New Haven 06510, 203-562-3718.

———————

Rep. Tom DeLay (R), Representative from Texas, District 22

DC Office: 203 Cannon House Office Building, Washington, DC 20515, 202-225-5951; Fax: 202-225-5241.

District Offices: 12603 Southwest Frwy., Stafford 77477, 713-240-3700.

———————

Rep. Ronald V. Dellums (D), Representative from California, District 9

DC Office: 2108 Rayburn House Office Building, Washington, DC 20515, 202-225-2661; Fax: 202-225-9817.

District Offices: 1301 Clay St., Oakland 94612, 510-763-0370.

———————

Rep. Peter Deutsch (D), Representative from Florida, District 20

DC Office: 204 Cannon House Office Building, Washington, DC 20515, 202-225-7931; Fax: 202-225-8456; e-mail: pdeutsch@hr.house.gov.

District Offices: 10100 Pines Blvd., Pembroke Pines 33025, 305-437-3936.

———————

Sen. Mike DeWine (R), Senator from Ohio

DC Office: 140 Russell Senate Office Building, Washington, DC 20510, 202-224-2315; Fax: 202-224-6519; e-mail: senator_dewine@dewine.senate.gov.

State Offices: 200 N. High St., Columbus 43215, 614-469-6774; 550 Main St., Cincinnati 45202, 513-684-3894; 234 N. Summit St., Toledo 43604, 419-259-7535; 1240 E. 9th St., Cleveland 44199, 216-522-7272; and 200 Putnam St., Marietta 45750, 614-373-2120.

———————

Rep. Lincoln Diaz-Balart (R), Representative from Florida, District 21

DC Office: 431 Cannon House Office Building, Washington, DC 20515, 202-225-4211; Fax: 202-225-8576.

District Offices: 8525 N.W. 53d Terr., Miami 33166, 305-470-8555.

_____

Rep. Jay Dickey (R), Representative from Arkansas, District 4

DC Office: 230 Cannon House Office Building, Washington, DC 20515, 202-225-3772; Fax: 202-225-1314; e-mail: jdickey@hr.house.gov.

District Offices: 100 E. 8th St., Pine Bluff 71601, 501-536-3376; 100 Reserve, Hot Springs 71913, 501-623-5800; and 100 S. Jackson, El Dorado 71730, 501-862-0236.

_____

Rep. Norm Dicks (D), Representative from Washington, District 6

DC Office: 2467 Rayburn House Office Building, Washington, DC 20515, 202-225-5916; Fax: 202-226-1176.

District Offices: 1717 Pacific Ave., Tacoma 98402, 206-593-6536; and 500 Pacific Ave., Bremerton 98310, 206-479-4011.

_____

Rep. John D. Dingell (D), Representative from Michigan, District 16

DC Office: 2328 Rayburn House Office Building, Washington, DC 20515, 202-225-4071.

District Offices: 5465 Schaefer Rd., Dearborn 48126, 313-846-1276; and 23 E. Front St., Monroe 48161, 313-243-1849.

_____

Rep. Julian C. Dixon (D), Representative from California, District 32

DC Office: 2252 Rayburn House Office Building, Washington, DC 20515, 202-225-7084; Fax: 202-225-4091.

District Offices: 5100 W. Goldleaf Cir., Los Angeles 90056, 213-678-5424.

_____

Sen. Christopher J. Dodd (D), Senator from Connecticut

DC Office: 444 Russell Senate Office Building, Washington, DC 20510, 202-224-2823; Fax: 202-224-1083; e-mail: sen_dodd@dodd.senate.gov.

State Offices: 100 Great Meadow Rd., Wethersfield 06109, 203-240-3470.

_____

Rep. Lloyd Doggett (D), Representative from Texas, District 10

DC Office: 126 Cannon House Office Building, Washington, DC 20515, 202-225-4865; Fax: 202-225-3073; e-mail: doggett@hr.house.gov.

District Offices: 763 Fed. Bldg., 300 E. 8th St., Austin 78701, 512-482-5921.

_____

Sen. Robert Dole (R), Senator from Kansas

DC Office: 141 Hart Senate Office Building, Washington, DC 20510, 202-224-6521; Fax: 202-228-1245.

State Offices: 500 State Ave., Kansas City 66101, 913-371-6108; 444 S.E. Quincy, Topeka 66683, 913-295-2745; 100 N. Broadway, Wichita 67202, 316-263-4956.

_____

Sen. Pete V. Domenici (R), Senator from New Mexico

DC Office: 328 Hart Senate Office Building, Washington, DC 20510, 202-224-6621; e-mail: senator_domenici@domenici.senate.gov.

State Offices: 625 Silver SW, Albuquerque 87102, 505-766-3481; New Postal Bldg., 120 S. Federal Pl., Santa Fe 87501, 505-988-6511; Sun Belt Plz., 1065 S. Main St., Bldg. Las Cruces 88005, 505-526-5475; and Fed. Bldg. Roswell 88201, 505-623-6170.

———————

Rep. Calvin Dooley (D), Representative from California, District 20

DC Office: 1227 Longworth House Office Building, Washington, DC 20515, 202-225-3341; Fax: 202-225-9308.

District Offices: 224 W. Lacey Blvd., Hanford 93230, 209-585-8171.

———————

Rep. John T. Doolittle (R), Representative from California, District 4

DC Office: 1526 Longworth House Office Building, Washington, DC 20515, 202-225-2511; Fax: 202-225-5444.

District Offices: 2130 Professional Dr., Roseville 95661, 916-786-5560.

———————

Sen. Byron L. Dorgan (D), Senator from North Dakota

DC Office: 713 Hart Senate Office Building, Washington, DC 20510, 202-224-2551; Fax: 202-224-1193; e-mail: senator@dorgan.senate.gov.

State Offices: 312 Fed. Bldg., 3rd & Rosser Ave., Bismarck 58502, 701-250-4618; 112 Robert St., Fargo 58107, 701-239-5389.

———————

Rep. Robert K. (Bob) Dornan (R), Representative from California, District 46

DC Office: 1201 Longworth House Office Building, Washington, DC 20515, 202-225-2965; Fax: 202-225-2762.

District Offices: 300 Plaza Alicante, Garden Grove 92642, 714-971-9292.

———————

Rep. Mike Doyle (D), Representative from Pennsylvania, District 18

DC Office: 1218 Longworth House Office Building, Washington, DC 20515, 202-225-2135; Fax: 202-225-3084.

District Offices: 11 Duff Rd., Pittsburgh 15235, 412-241-6055; 541 5th Ave., McKeesport 15132, 412-664-4049.

———————

Rep. David Dreier (R), Representative from California, District 28

DC Office: 411 Cannon House Office Building, Washington, DC 20515, 202-225-2305; Fax: 202-225-7018.

District Offices: 112 N. 2d Ave., Covina 91723, 818-339-9078.

———————

Rep. John J. Duncan, Jr. (R), Representative from Tennessee, District 2

DC Office: 2400 Rayburn House Office Building, Washington, DC 20515, 202-225-5435; Fax: 202-225-6440.

District Offices: 501 W. Main St., Knoxville 37902, 615-523-3772; 200 E. Broadway, Maryville 37801, 615-984-5464; and Crthse., Athens 37303, 615-745-4671.

———————

Rep. Jennifer B. Dunn (R), Representative from Washington, District 8

DC Office: 432 Cannon House Office Building, Washington, DC 20515, 202-225-7761; Fax: 202-225-8673; e-mail: dunnwa08@hr.house.gov.

District Offices: 50-116th Ave., SE, Bellevue 98004, 206-460-0161.

_____

Rep. Richard J. Durbin (D), Representative from Illinois, District 20

DC Office: 2463 Rayburn House Office Building, Washington, DC 20515, 202-225-5271; Fax: 202-225-0170; e-mail: durbin@hr.house.gov.

District Offices: 525 S. 8th St., Springfield 62703, 217-492-4062; 221 E. Broadway, Centralia 62801, 618-532-4265; and 400 St. Louis St., Edwardsville 62025, 618-492-1082.

_____

Rep. Chet Edwards (D), Representative from Texas, District 11

DC Office: 328 Cannon House Office Building, Washington, DC 20515, 202-225-6105; Fax: 202-225-0350.

District Offices: 710 University Tower, 700 S. University Parks Dr., Waco 76706, 817-752-9600.

_____

Rep. Vernon J. Ehlers (R), Representative from Michigan, District 3

DC Office: 1717 Longworth House Office Building, Washington, DC 20515, 202-225-3831; Fax: 202-225-5144; e-mail: congehlr@hr.house.gov.

District Offices: 166 Fed. Bldg., 110 Michigan St. NW, Grand Rapids 49503, 616-451-8383.

_____

Rep. Robert L. Ehrlich, Jr. (R), Representative from Maryland, District 2

DC Office: 315 Cannon House Office Building, Washington, DC 20515, 202-225-3061; Fax: 202-225-3094.

District Offices: 1407 York Rd., Lutherville 21093, 410-337-7222; and 45 N. Main St., Bel Air 21014, 410-838-2517.

_____

Rep. Bill Emerson (R), Representative from Missouri, District 8

DC Office: 2268 Rayburn House Office Building, Washington, DC 20515, 202-225-4404; e-mail: bemerson@hr.house.gov.

District Offices: 339 Broadway, Cape Girardeau 63701, 314-335-0101; and 612 Pine, Rolla 65401, 314-364-2455.

_____

Rep. Eliot L. Engel (D), Representative from New York, District 17

DC Office: 1433 Longworth House Office Building, Washington, DC 20515, 202-225-2464; e-mail: engeline@hr.house.gov.

District Offices: 3655 Johnson Ave., Bronx 10463, 718-796-9700.

_____

Rep. Philip S. English (R), Representative from Pennsylvania, District 21

DC Office: 1721 Longworth House Office Building, Washington, DC 20515, 202-225-5406.

District Offices: 310 French St., Erie 16507, 814-456-2038; 306 Chestnut St., Meadville 16335, 814-724-8414; City Annex Bldg., Hermitage 16148, 412-342-6132; 327 N. Main St., Butler 16001, 412-285-5616.

————————

Rep. John Ensign (R), Representative from Nevada, District 1

DC Office: 414 Cannon House Office Building, Washington, DC 20515, 202-225-5965; Fax: 202-225-3119.

District Offices: 1000 E. Sahara Ave., Las Vegas 89104, 702-731-1801.

————————

Rep. Anna G. Eshoo (D), Representative from California, District 14

DC Office: 308 Cannon House Office Building, Washington, DC 20515, 202-225-8104; Fax: 202-225-8890; e-mail: annagram@hr.house.gov.

District Offices: 698 Emerson St., Palo Alto 94301, 415-323-2984.

————————

Rep. Lane Evans (D), Representative from Illinois, District 17

DC Office: 2335 Rayburn House Office Building, Washington, DC 20515, 202-225-5905; Fax: 202-225-5396.

District Offices: 1535 47th Ave., Moline 61265, 309-793-5760; and 1640 N. Henderson St., Galesburg 61401, 309-342-4411.

————————

Rep. Terry Everett (R), Representative from Alabama, District 2

DC Office: 208 Cannon House Office Building, Washington, DC 20515, 202-225-2901; e-mail: everett@hr.house.gov.

District Offices: 3500 Eastern Blvd., Montgomery 36116, 334-277-9113; 100 W. Troy St., Dothan 36303, 334-794-9680; and City Hall Bldg., Opp 36487, 334-493-9253.

————————

Rep. Thomas W. Ewing (R), Representative from Illinois, District 15

DC Office: 1317 Longworth House Office Building, Washington, DC 20515, 202-225-2371; Fax: 202-225-8071.

District Offices: P.O. Box 20, Pontiac 61764, 815-844-7660; 2401 E. Washington St., Bloomington 61704, 309-662-9371; 102 E. Madison, Urbana 61801, 217-328-0165; and 120 N. Vermillion, Danville 61832, 217-431-8230.

————————

Sen. J. James Exon (D), Senator from Nebraska

DC Office: 528 Hart Senate Office Building, Washington, DC 20510, 202-224-4224; Fax: 202-224-5213.

State Offices: 1623 Farnam St., Omaha 68102, 402-341-1776; 287 Fed. Bldg., 100 Centennial Mall N., Lincoln 68508, 402-437-5591; 2106 1st St., Scottsbluff 69361, 308-632-3595; and 275 Fed. Bldg., North Platte 69101, 308-534-2006.

————————

Sen. Lauch Faircloth (R), Senator from North Carolina

DC Office: 317 Hart Senate Office Building, Washington, DC 20510, 202-224-3154; Fax: 202-224-7406.

State Offices: Fed. Bldg., 310 New Bern Ave., Raleigh 27601, 919-856-4791; Fed. Bldg., 401 W. Trade St., Charlotte 28202, 704-375-1993; Fed. Bldg., 151 Patton Ave., Asheville 28801, 704-244-3099; and Fed. Bldg., 251 Main St., Winston-Salem 27101, 919-631-5313.

—————————

Rep. Sam Farr (D), Representative from California, District 17

DC Office: 1117 Longworth House Office Building, Washington, DC 20515, 202-225-2861; e-mail:samfarr@hr.house.gov.

District Offices: 380 Alvarado St., Monterey 93940, 408-649-3555; 701 Ocean Ave., Santa Cruz 95060, 408-429-1976; and 100 W. Alisal St., Salinas 93901, 408-424-2229.

—————————

Rep. Chaka Fattah (D), Representative from Pennsylvania, District 2

DC Office: 1205 Longworth House Office Building, Washington, DC 20515, 202-225-4001.

District Offices: 4104 Walnut St., Philadelphia 19104, 215-387-6404.

—————————

Rep. Harris W. Fawell (R), Representative from Illinois, District 13

DC Office: 2159 Rayburn House Office Building, Washington, DC 20515, 202-225-3515; Fax: 202-225-9420; e-mail: hfawell@hr.house.gov.

District Offices: 115 W. 55th St., Clarendon Hills 60514, 708-655-2052.

—————————

Rep. Vic Fazio (D), Representative from California, District 3

DC Office: 2113 Rayburn House Office Building, Washington, DC 20515, 202-225-5716; Fax: 202-225-5141; e-mail: dcaucus@hr.house.gov.

District Offices: 722-B Main St., Woodland 95695, 916-666-5521; and 332 Pine St., Red Bluff 96080, 916-529-5629.

—————————

Sen. Russell D. Feingold (D), Senator from Wisconsin

DC Office: 502 Hart Senate Office Building, Washington, DC 20510, 202-224-5323; Fax: 202-224-2725; e-mail: senator_feingold@feingold.senate.gov.

State Offices: 517 E. Wisconsin Ave., Milwaukee 53202, 414-276-7282; 8383 Greenway Blvd., Middleton 53562, 608-828-1200; 317 1st St., Wausau 54403, 715-848-5660; and 425 State St., LaCrosse 54603, 608-782-5585.

—————————

Sen. Dianne Feinstein (D), Senator from California

DC Office: 331 Hart Senate Office Building, Washington, DC 20510, 202-224-3841; Fax: 202-228-3954; e-mail: senator@feinstein.senate.gov.

State Offices: 1700 Montgomery St., San Francisco 94111, 415-249-4777; 750 B St., San Diego 92101, 619-231-9712; 11111 Santa Monica Blvd., Los Angeles 90025, 310-914-7300; and 1130 O St., Fresno 93721, 209-485-7430.

—————————

Rep. Cleo Fields (D), Representative from Louisiana, District 4

DC Office: 218 Cannon House Office Building, Washington, DC 20515, 202-225-8490; Fax: 202-225-8959.

District Offices: 700 N. 10th St., Baton Rouge 70802, 504-343-9773; 301 N. Main St., Opelousas 70570, 318-942-9691; and 610 Texas St., Shreveport 71101, 318-221-9924; 515 Murrey St., Alexandria 71301, 318-445-0632.

————

Rep. Jack M. Fields, Jr. (R), Representative from Texas, District 8

DC Office: 2228 Rayburn House Office Building, Washington, DC 20515, 202-225-4901; Fax: 202-225-2772.

District Offices: 111 E. University Dr., College Station 77840, 409-846-6068; 300 W. Davis, Conroe 77301, 409-756-8044; and 9810 FM1960 Bypass W., Deerbrook Plz., Humble 77338, 409-540-8000.

————

Rep. Bob Filner (D), Representative from California, District 50

DC Office: 504 Cannon House Office Building, Washington, DC 20515, 202-225-8045; Fax: 202-225-9073; e-mail: dfogle@hr.house.gov.

District Offices: 333 F St., Chula Vista 91910, 619-422-5963.

————

Rep. Floyd H. Flake (D), Representative from New York, District 6

DC Office: 1035 Longworth House Office Building, Washington, DC 20515, 202-225-3461; Fax: 202-226-4169.

District Offices: 196-06 Linden Blvd., St. Albans 11412, 718-849-5600; and 20-80 Seagirt Blvd., Far Rockaway 11691, 718-327-9791.

————

Rep. Michael Patrick Flanagan (R), Representative from Illinois, District 5

DC Office: 1407 Longworth House Office Building, Washington, DC 20515, 202-225-4061; Fax: 202-225-3128.

District Offices: 3538 W. Irving Park Rd., Chicago 60618, 312-588-2288.

————

Rep. Thomas M. Foglietta (D), Representative from Pennsylvania, District 1

DC Office: 341 Cannon House Office Building, Washington, DC 20515, 202-225-4731; Fax: 202-225-0088.

District Offices: Green Fed. Bldg., 600 Arch St., Philadelphia 19106, 215-925-6840; 1806 S. Broad St., Philadelphia 19125, 215-463-8702; and 2630 Memphis St., Philadelphia 19125, 215-426-4616.

————

Rep. Mark Foley (R), Representative from Florida, District 16

DC Office: 506 Cannon House Office Building, Washington, DC 20515, 202-225-5792; Fax: 202-225-3132.

District Offices: 4440 PGA Blvd., Palm Beach Gardens 33410, 407-627-6192; and 250 NW Country Club Dr., Port St. Lucie 34986, 407-878-3181.

————

Rep. Michael P. Forbes (R), Representative from New York, District 1

DC Office: 502 Cannon House Office Building, Washington, DC 20515, 202-225-3826; Fax: 202-225-3143; e-mail: mpforbes@hr.house.gov.

District Office: 1500 William Floyd Pkwy., Shirley 11967, 516-345-9000.

Sen. Wendell H. Ford (D), Senator from Kentucky

DC Office: 173-A Russell Senate Office Building, Washington, DC 20510, 202-224-4343; Fax: 202-224-0046; e-mail: wendell_ford@ford.senate.gov.

State Offices: 1072 New Fed. Bldg., Louisville 40202, 502-582-6251; 305 Fed. Bldg., Owensboro 42301, 502-685-5158; 343 Waller Ave., Lexington 40504, 606-233-2484; and 19 U.S. P.O. and Crthse., Covington 41011, 606-491-7929.

Rep. Harold E. Ford (D), Representative from Tennessee, District 9

DC Office: 2111 Rayburn House Office Building, Washington, DC 20515, 202-225-3265; Fax: 202-225-9215.

District Offices: 369 Fed. Bldg., 167 N. Main St., Memphis 38103, 901-544-4131.

Rep. Tillie K. Fowler (R), Representative from Florida, District 4

DC Office: 413 Cannon House Office Building, Washington, DC 20515, 202-225-2501; Fax: 202-225-9318.

District Offices: 4452 Hendricks Ave., Jacksonville 32207, 904-739-6600; and 533 N. Nova Rd., Ormond Beach 32174, 904-672-0754.

Rep. Jon D. Fox (R), Representative from Pennsylvania, District 13

DC Office: 510 Cannon House Office Building, Washington, DC 20515, 202-225-6111; Fax: 202-225-3155; e-mail: jonfox@hr.house.gov.

District Offices: 1768 Markley St., Norristown 19401, 610-272-8400; and Easton & Edge Hill Rds., Abington 19001, 215-885-3500.

Rep. Barney Frank (D), Representative from Massachusetts, District 4

DC Office: 2210 Rayburn House Office Building, Washington, DC 20515, 202-225-5931; Fax: 202-225-0182.

District Offices: 29 Crafts St., Newton 02158, 617-332-3920; 558 Pleasant St., New Bedford 02740, 508-999-6462; 222 Milliken Pl., Fall River 02721, 508-674-3551; and 89 Main St., Bridgewater 02324, 508-697-9403.

Rep. Gary A. Franks (R), Representative from Connecticut, District 5

DC Office: 133 Cannon House Office Building, Washington, DC 20515, 202-225-3822; Fax: 202-225-5085.

District Offices: 135 Grand St., Waterbury 06701, 203-573-1418; 30 Main St., Danbury 06810, 203-790-1263; 1 First St., Seymour Town Hall, Seymour 06483, 800-556-5089; 142 E. Main St., Meriden City Hall, Meriden 06450, 203-630-4130.

Rep. Bob Franks (R), Representative from New Jersey, District 7

DC Office: 429 Cannon House Office Building, Washington, DC 20515, 202-225-5361; Fax: 202-225-9460; e-mail: franksnj@hr.house.gov.

District Offices: 2333 Morris Ave., Union 07083, 908-686-5576; and 73 Main St., Woodbridge 07095, 908-602-0075.

———————

Rep. Rodney P. Frelinghuysen (R), Representative from New Jersey, District 11

DC Office: 514 Cannon House Office Building, Washington, DC 20515, 202-225-5034; Fax: 202-225-3186.

District Offices: 1 Morris St., Morristown 07960, 201-984-0711; 18 W. Blackwell St., Dover 07801, 201-328-7413; and 3 Fairfield Ave., W. Caldwell 07006, 201-228-9262.

———————

Rep. Dan Frisa (R), Representative from New York, District 4

DC Office: 1529 Longworth House Office Building, Washington, DC 20515, 202-225-5516; Fax: 202-225-3187.

District Office: 250 Old Country Rd., Mineola 11501, 516-739-1800.

———————

Sen. William H. Frist (R), Senator from Tennessee

DC Office: 565 Dirksen Senate Office Building, Washington, DC 20510, 202-224-3344; Fax: 202-228-1264; e-mail: senate_frist@frist.senate.gov.

State Offices: U.S. Cthse., 801 Broadway, Nashville 37203, 615-736-7353.

———————

Rep. Martin Frost (D), Representative from Texas, District 24

DC Office: 2459 Rayburn House Office Building, Washington, DC 20515, 202-225-3605; Fax: 202-225-4951; e-mail: frost@hr.house.gov.

District Offices: 3020 S.E. Loop 820, Ft. Worth 76140, 817-293-9231; 400 S. Zang Blvd., Dallas 75208, 214-948-3401; and 100 N. Main St., Corsicana 75110, 903-874-0760.

———————

Rep. David Funderburk (R), Representative from North Carolina, District 2

DC Office: 427 Cannon House Office Building, Washington, DC 20515, 202-224-4531; Fax: 202-225-3191.

District Office: 1207 W. Cumberland St., Dunn 28334, 910-891-1114; e-mail: funnc02@hr.house.gov.

———————

Rep. Elizabeth Furse (D), Representative from Oregon, District 1

DC Office: 316 Cannon House Office Building, Washington, DC 20515, 202-225-0855; Fax: 202-225-9497; e-mail: furseor1@hr.house.gov.

District Offices: 2701 NW Vaughn, Portland 97210, 503-326-2901.

———————

Rep. Elton Gallegly (R), Representative from California, District 23

DC Office: 2441 Rayburn House Office Building, Washington, DC 20515, 202-225-5811; Fax: 202-225-1100.

District Offices: 300 Esplanade Dr., Oxnard 93030, 805-485-2300.

———————

Rep. Greg Ganske (R), Representative from Iowa, District 4

DC Office: 1108 Longworth House Office Building, Washington, DC 20515, 202-225-4426; Fax: 202-225-3193.

District Offices: Fed. Bldg., 210 Walnut St., Des Moines 50309, 515-284-4634; and 40 Pearl St., Council Bluffs 51503, 712-323-5976.

———————

Rep. Samuel Gejdenson (D), Representative from Connecticut, District 2

DC Office: 2416 Rayburn House Office Building, Washington, DC 20515, 202-225-2076; Fax: 202-225-4977; e-mail: bozrah@hr.house.gov

District Offices: 74 W. Main, Norwich 06360, 203-886-0139; and 94 Court St., Middletown 06457, 203-346-1123.

———————

Rep. George W. Gekas (R), Representative from Pennsylvania, District 17

DC Office: 2410 Rayburn House Office Building, Washington, DC 20515, 202-225-4315; Fax: 202-225-8440.

District Offices: 3605 Vartan Way, Harrisburg 17110, 717-541-5507; 222 S. Market St., Elizabethtown 17022, 717-367-6731; and 108-B Municipal Bldg., 400 S. 8th St., Lebanon 17042, 717-273-1451.

———————

Rep. Richard A. Gephardt (D), Representative from Missouri, District 3

DC Office: 1226 Longworth House Office Building, Washington, DC 20515, 202-225-2671; Fax: 202-225-7452; e-mail: gephardt@hr.house.gov.

District Offices: 11140 S. Towne Sq., St. Louis 63123, 314-894-3400.

———————

Rep. Pete Geren (D), Representative from Texas, District 12

DC Office: 2448 Rayburn House Office Building, Washington, DC 20515, 202-225-5071; Fax: 202-225-2786.

District Offices: 1600 W. 7th St., Ft. Worth 76102, 817-338-0909.

———————

Rep. Sam M. Gibbons (D), Representative from Florida, District 11

DC Office: 2204 Rayburn House Office Building, Washington, DC 20515, 202-225-3376; Fax: 202-225-8016.

District Offices: 2002 N. Lois Ave., Tampa 33607, 813-870-2101.

———————

Rep. Wayne T. Gilchrest (R), Representative from Maryland, District 1

DC Office: 332 Cannon House Office Building, Washington, DC 20515, 202-225-5311; Fax: 202-225-0254.

District Offices: 1 Plaza E., Salisbury 21801, 410-749-3184; 521 Washington Ave., Chestertown 21620, 410-778-9407; and 101 Crain Hwy., NW, Glen Burnie 21061, 410-760-3372.

———————

Rep. Paul E. Gillmor (R), Representative from Ohio, District 5

DC Office: 1203 Longworth House Office Building, Washington, DC 20515, 202-225-6405; Fax: 202-225-1985.

District Offices: 120 Jefferson St., Port Clinton 43452, 800-541-6446; and 148 E. South Boundary St., Perrysburg 43551, 419-872-2500.

Rep. Benjamin A. Gilman (R), Representative from New York, District 20

DC Office: 2449 Rayburn House Office Building, Washington, DC 20515, 202-225-3776; Fax: 202-225-2541.

District Offices: 407 E. Main St., P.O. Box 358, Middletown 10940, 914-343-6666; 377 Rte. 59, Monsey 10952, 914-357-9000; and 32 Main St., Hastings-on-Hudson 10706, 914-478-5550.

Rep. Newt Gingrich (R), Representative from Georgia, District 6

DC Office: 2428 Rayburn House Office Building, Washington, DC 20515, 202-225-4501; Fax: 202-225-4656; e-mail: georgia6@hr.house.gov.

District Offices: 3823 Roswell Rd., Marietta 30062, 404-565-6398.

Sen. John H. Glenn Jr. (D), Senator from Ohio

DC Office: 503 Hart Senate Office Building, Washington, DC 20510, 202-224-3353; Fax: 202-224-7983.

State Offices: 200 N. High St., Columbus 43215, 614-469-6697; 1240 E. 9th St., Cleveland 44199, 216-522-7095; 550 Main St., Cincinnati 45202, 513-684-3265; and 234 N. Summit St., Toledo 43604, 419-259-7592.

Rep. Henry B. Gonzalez (D), Representative from Texas, District 20

DC Office: 2413 Rayburn House Office Building, Washington, DC 20515, 202-225-3236.

District Offices: 727 E. Durango St., San Antonio 78206, 512-229-6195.

Rep. Bob Goodlatte (R), Representative from Virginia, District 6

DC Office: 123 Cannon House Office Building, Washington, DC 20515, 202-225-5431; Fax: 202-225-9681; e-mail: talk2bob@hr.house.gov.

District Offices: 540 Crestar Plz., 10 Franklin Rd., SE, Roanoke 24011, 703-857-2672; 114 N. Central Ave., Staunton 24401, 703-885-3861; 2 S. Main St., Harrisonburg 22801, 703-432-2391; and 916 Main St., 804-845-8306.

Rep. Bill Goodling (R), Representative from Pennsylvania, District 19

DC Office: 2263 Rayburn House Office Building, Washington, DC 20515, 202-225-5836.

District Offices: Fed. Bldg., 200 S. George St., York 17405, 717-843-8887; 212 N. Hanover St., Carlisle 17013, 717-243-5432; 140 Baltimore St., Gettysburg 17325, 717-334-3430; 2020 Yale Ave., Camp Hill 17011, 717-763-1988; and 44 Frederick St., Hanover 17331, 717-632-7855, 800-631-1811.

Rep. Bart Gordon (D), Representative from Tennessee, District 6

DC Office: 2201 Rayburn House Office Building, Washington, DC 20515, 202-225-4231; Fax: 202-225-6887.

District Offices: P.O. Box 1986, 106 S. Maple St., Murfreesboro 37133, 615-896-1986; and 17 S. Jefferson, Cookeville 38501, 615-528-5907.

———————

Sen. Slade Gorton (R), Senator from Washington

DC Office: 730 Hart Senate Office Building, Washington, DC 20510, 202-224-3441; Fax: 202-224-9393; e-mail: senator_gorton@gorton.senate.gov.

State Offices: 1350 Grandridge Blvd., Kennewick 99336, 509-783-0640; 15600 Redmond Wy., Redmond 98052, 206-883-6072; and 402 E. Yakima Ave., Box 4083, Yakima 98901, 509-248-8084.

———————

Rep. Porter Johnston Goss (R), Representative from Florida, District 14

DC Office: 108 Cannon House Office Building, Washington, DC 20515, 202-225-2536; Fax: 202-225-6820.

District Offices: 2000 Main St., Fort Myers 33901, 813-332-4677; and 3301 Tamiami Trail E., Bldg. F, Naples 33962, 813-774-8060.

———————

Rep. Lindsey Graham (R), Representative from South Carolina, District 3

DC Office: 1429 Longworth House Office Building, Washington, DC 20515, 202-225-5301.

District Offices: P.O. Box 4126, Anderson 29622, 803-224-7401; 5 Fed. Bldg., 211 York St., NE, Aiken 29801, 803-649-5571; and 129 Fed. Bldg., 120 Main St., Greenwood 29646, 803-223-8251.

———————

Sen. Bob Graham (D), Senator from Florida

DC Office: 524 Hart Senate Office Building, Washington, DC 20510, 202-224-3041; Fax: 202-224-2237; e-mail: bob_graham@graham.senate.gov.

State Offices: 44 W. Flagler St., Miami 33130, 305-536-7293; and 325 John Knox Rd., Bldg. 600, Tallahassee 32303, 904-422-6100; and 101 E. Kennedy Blvd., Tampa 33602, 813-228-2476.

———————

Sen. Phil Gramm (R), Senator from Texas

DC Office: 370 Russell Senate Office Building, Washington, DC 20510, 202-224-2934; Fax: 202-228-2856.

State Offices: 2323 Bryan, Dallas 75201, 214-767-3000; 222 E. Van Buren., Harlingen 78550, 512-423-6118; 712 Main, Houston 77002, 713-229-2766; 113 Fed. Bldg., 1205 Texas Ave., Lubbock 79401, 806-743-7533; 123 Pioneer Plz., El Paso 79901, 915-534-6896; 9311 San Pedro, San Antonio 78216, and InterFirst Plz., 102 N. College St., Tyler 75702, 903-593-0902.

———————

Sen. Rod Grams (IR), Senator from Minnesota

DC Office: 261 Dirksen Senate Office Building, Washington, DC 20510, 202-224-3244; Fax: 202-228-0956; e-mail: mail_grams@grams.senate.gov.

State Offices: 2013 2nd Ave., N., Anoka 55303, 612-427-5921.

———————

Sen. Charles E. Grassley (R), Senator from Iowa

DC Office: 135 Hart Senate Office Building, Washington, DC 20510, 202-224-3744; Fax: 202-224-6020.

State Offices: 721 Fed. Bldg., 210 Walnut St., Des Moines 50309, 515-284-4890; 210 Waterloo Bldg., 531 Commercial St., Waterloo 50701, 319-232-6657; 116 Fed. Bldg., 131 E. 4th St., Davenport 52801, 319-322-4331; 103 Fed. Bldg., 320 6th St., Sioux City 51101, 712-233-3331; 307 Fed. Bldg., 8 S. 6th St., Council Bluffs 51501, 712-322-7103; and 206 Fed. Bldg., 101 1st St., SE, Cedar Rapids 52401, 319-399-2555.

———————

Rep. Gene Green (D), Representative from Texas, District 29

DC Office: 1024 Longworth House Office Building, Washington, DC 20515, 202-225-1688; Fax: 202-225-9903; e-mail: ggreen@hr.house.gov.

District Offices: 5502 Lawndale, Houston 77023, 713-923-9961; and 420 N. 19th St., Houston 77008, 713-880-4364.

———————

Rep. Jim Greenwood (R), Representative from Pennsylvania, District 8

DC Office: 430 Cannon House Office Building, Washington, DC 20515, 202-225-4276; Fax: 202-225-9511.

District Offices: 69 E. Oxford Ave., Doylestown 18901, 215-348-7511; and One Oxford Valley, Langhorne 19047, 215-752-7711.

———————

Sen. Judd Gregg (R), Senator from New Hampshire

DC Office: 393 Russell Senate Office Building, Washington, DC 20510, 202-224-3324; Fax: 202-224-4952; e-mail: mailbox@gregg.senate.gov.

State Offices: 125 N. Main St., Concord 03301, 603-225-7115; 28 Webster St., Manchester 03104, 603-622-7979; 136 Pleasant St., Berlin 03570, 603-752-2604; and 99 Pease Blvd., Portsmouth 03801, 603-431-2171.

———————

Rep. Steve Gunderson (R), Representative from Wisconsin, District 3

DC Office: 2185 Rayburn House Office Building, Washington, DC 20515, 202-225-5506; Fax: 202-225-6195.

District Offices: P.O. Box 247, 622 E. State Hwy. 54, Black River Falls 54615, 715-284-7431.

———————

Rep. Luis V. Gutierrez (D), Representative from Illinois, District 4

DC Office: 408 Longworth House Office Building, Washington, DC 20515, 202-225-8203; Fax: 202-225-7810; e-mail: louisg@hr.house.gov.

District Offices: 3181 N. Elston Ave., Chicago 60618, 312-509-0999; 1751 W. 47th St., Chicago 60609, 312-247-9020; 3659 Halsted, Chicago 60609, 312-254-0797; and 2132 W. 21st St., Chicago 60608, 312-579-0886.

———————

Rep. Gil Gutknecht (IR), Representative from Minnesota, District 1

DC Office: 425 Cannon House Office Building, Washington, DC 20515, 202-225-2472; Fax: 202-225-0051; e-mail: gil@hr.house.gov.

District Offices: 1530 Greenview Dr., Rochester 55902, 507-252-9841.

———————

Rep. Tony P. Hall (D), Representative from Ohio, District 3

DC Office: 1432 Longworth House Office Building, Washington, DC 20515, 202-225-6465; Fax: 202-225-9272.

District Offices: 501 Fed. Bldg., 200 W. 2d St., Dayton 45402, 513-225-2843.

———————

Rep. Ralph M. Hall (D), Representative from Texas, District 4

DC Office: 2236 Rayburn House Office Building, Washington, DC 20515, 202-225-6673; Fax: 202-225-3332.

District Offices: 104 N. San Jacinto St., Rockwall 75087, 214-771-9118; 119 N. Fed. Bldg., Sherman 75090, 214-892-1112; 211 Fed. Bldg., Tyler 75702, 214-597-3729; and Cooke Cnty. Cthse., Gainesville 76240, 819-668-6370.

———————

Rep. Lee H. Hamilton (D), Representative from Indiana, District 9

DC Office: 2314 Rayburn House Office Building, Washington, DC 20515, 202-225-5315; Fax: 202-225-1101; e-mail: hamilton@hr.house.gov.

District Offices: 107 Fed. Ctr., 1201 E. 10th St., Jeffersonville 47130, 812-288-3999.

———————

Rep. Mel Hancock (R), Representative from Missouri, District 7

DC Office: 438 Cannon House Office Building, Washington, DC 20515, 202-225-6536; Fax: 202-225-7700.

District Offices: 2840 E. Chestnut Expwy., Springfield 65802, 417-862-4317; and 302 Fed. Bldg., Joplin 64801, 417-781-1041.

———————

Rep. James V. Hansen (R), Representative from Utah, District 1

DC Office: 2466 Rayburn House Office Building, Washington, DC 20515, 202-225-0453; Fax: 202-225-5857.

District Offices: 1017 Fed. Bldg., 324 25th St., Ogden 84401, 801-625-5677; and 435 E. Tabernacle, St. George 84770, 801-628-1071.

———————

Sen. Tom Harkin (D), Senator from Iowa

DC Office: 531 Hart Senate Office Building, Washington, DC 20510, 202-224-3254; Fax: 202-224-9369; e-mail: tom_harkin@harkin.senate.gov.

State Offices: 733 Fed. Bldg., 210 Walnut St., Des Moines 50309, 515-284-4574; Fed. Bldg., Council Bluffs 51501, 712-325-0036; 150 1st Ave., NE, Cedar Rapids 52401, 319-365-4504; 131 E. 4th St., 314B Fed. Bldg., Davenport, 52801, 319-322-1338; 350 W. 6th St., Dubuque 52001, 319-588-2130; and 110 Federal Bldg., 320 6th St., Sioux City 51101, 712-252-1550.

———————

Rep. Jane Harman (D), Representative from California, District 36

DC Office: 325 Cannon House Office Building, Washington, DC 20515, 202-225-8220; Fax: 202-225-0684; e-mail: jharman@hr.house.gov.

District Offices: 5200 W. Century Blvd., Los Angeles 90045, 310-348-8220; 3031 Torrance Blvd., Torrance 90503, 310-787-0767.

––––––––––

Rep. Dennis Hastert (R), Representative from Illinois, District 14

DC Office: 2453 Rayburn House Office Building, Washington, DC 20515, 202-225-2976; Fax: 202-225-0697; e-mail: dhastert@hr.house.gov.

District Offices: 27 N. River St., Batavia 60510, 708-406-1114.

––––––––––

Rep. Alcee L. Hastings (D), Representative from Florida, District 23

DC Office: 1039 Longworth House Office Building, Washington, DC 20515, 202-225-1313; Fax: 202-226-0690; e-mail: hastings@hr.house.gov.

District Offices: 2701 W. Oakland Park Blvd., Ft. Lauderdale 33311, 305-733-2800.

––––––––––

Rep. Doc Hastings (R), Representative from Washington, District 4

DC Office: 1229 Longworth House Office Building, Washington, DC 20515, 202-225-5816; Fax: 202-225-3251.

District Offices: 320 N. Johnson, Kennewick 99336, 509-783-0310; 302 E. Chestnut, Yakima 98901, 509-452-3243; and 25 N. Wenatchee Ave., Wenatchee 98801, 509-662-4294.

––––––––––

Sen. Orrin G. Hatch (R), Senator from Utah

DC Office: 131 Russell Senate Office Building, Washington, DC 20510, 202-224-5251; Fax: 202-224-6331.

State Offices: 8402 Fed. Bldg., Salt Lake City 84138, 801-524-4380; 109 Fed. Bldg., 51 S. University Ave., Provo 84601, 801-375-7881; 1410 Fed. Bldg., 325 25th St., Ogden 84401, 801-625-5672; and 10 N. Main, P.O. Box 99, Cedar City 84720, 801-586-8435.

––––––––––

Sen. Mark O. Hatfield (R), Senator from Oregon

DC Office: 711 Hart Senate Office Building, Washington, DC 20510, 202-224-3753; Fax: 202-224-0276.

State Offices: 727 Center St., NE, Salem 97301; and One World Trade Ctr., 121 SW Salmon St., Portland 97204.

––––––––––

Rep. James A. (Jimmy) Hayes (R), Representative from Louisiana, District 7

DC Office: 2432 Rayburn House Office Building, Washington, DC 20515, 202-225-2031; Fax: 202-225-1175.

District Offices: 100 E. Vermilion, Lafayette 70501, 318-233-4773; and 901 Lake Shore Dr., Lake Charles 70601, 318-433-1613.

––––––––––

Rep. J. D. Hayworth (R), Representative from Arizona, District 6

DC Office: 1023 Longworth House Office Building, Washington, DC 20515, 202-225-2190; Fax: 202-225-3263.

District Offices: 1818 E. Southern Ave., Mesa 85204, 602-926-4151; and 1300 S. Milton, Flagstaff 85001, 520-556-8760.

———————

Rep. Joel Hefley (R), Representative from Colorado, District 5

DC Office: 2351 Rayburn House Office Building, Washington, DC 20515, 202-225-4422; Fax: 202-225-1942.

District Offices: 104 S. Cascade Ave., Colorado Springs 80903, 719-520-0055; and 9605 Maroon Cir., Englewood 80112, 303-792-3923.

———————

Sen. Howell T. Heflin (D), Senator from Alabama

DC Office: 728 Hart Senate Office Building, Washington, DC 20510, 202-224-4124; Fax: 202-224-3149.

State Offices: B-29 Fed. Crthse., 15 Lee St., Montgomery 36104, 334-832-7287; 104 W. 5th St., P.O. Box 228, Tuscumbia 35674, 205-381-7060; 341 Fed. Bldg., 1800 5th Ave., N., Birmingham 35203, 205-731-1500; and 437 Fed. Crthse., Mobile 36602, 334-690-3167.

———————

Rep. W. G. (Bill) Hefner (D), Representative from North Carolina, District 8

DC Office: 2470 Rayburn House Office Building, Washington, DC 20515, 202-225-3715; Fax: 202-225-4036.

District Offices: P.O. Box 385, 101 Union St. S., Concord 28025, 704-786-1612; P.O. Box 4220, 507 W. Innes St., Salisbury 28144, 704-636-0635; and P.O. Box 1503, 230 E. Franklin St., Rockingham 28379, 910-997-2070.

———————

Rep. Fred Heineman (R), Representative from North Carolina, District 4

DC Office: 1440 Longworth House Office Building, Washington, DC 20515, 202-225-1784; Fax: 202-225-3269; e-mail: thechief@hr.house.gov.

District Offices: 16 E. Rowan St., Raleigh 27609, 919-856-4611.

———————

Sen. Jesse A. Helms (R), Senator from North Carolina

DC Office: 403 Dirksen Senate Office Building, Washington, DC 20510, 202-224-6342; Fax: 202-224-7588.

State Offices: P.O. Box 2888, Raleigh 27602, 919-856-4630; and P.O. Box 2944, Hickory 28601, 704-322-5170.

———————

Rep. Wally Herger (R), Representative from California, District 2

DC Office: 2433 Rayburn House Office Building, Washington, DC 20515, 202-225-3076; Fax: 202-225-3245.

District Offices: 55 Independence Cir., Chico 95926, 916-893-8363; and 410 Hemsted Dr., Redding 96002, 916-223-5898.

———————

Rep. Van Hilleary (R), Representative from Tennessee, District 4

DC Office: 114 Cannon House Office Building, Washington, DC 20515, 202-225-6831; Fax: 202-225-3272.

District Offices: 1502 N. Main St., Crossville 38555, 615-484-1114; 400 W. Main St., Morristown 37814, 615-587-0396; and 300 S. Jackson St., Tullahoma 37388, 615-393-4764.

_____

Rep. Earl F. Hilliard (D), Representative from Alabama, District 7

DC Office: 1007 Longworth House Office Building, Washington, DC 20515, 202-225-2665; Fax: 202-226-0772.

District Offices: Vance Fed. Bldg., 1800 5th Ave., Birmingham 35203, 205-328-2841; P.O. Box 2627, Tuscaloosa 35403, 205-752-3578; Fed. Bldg., Selma 36701, 205-872-2684; and Fed. Bldg., 15 Lee St., Montgomery 36104, 334-262-4724.

_____

Rep. Maurice D. Hinchey (D), Representative from New York, District 26

DC Office: 1524 Longworth House Office Building, Washington, DC 20515, 202-225-6335; Fax: 202-226-0774.

District Offices: 291 Wall St., Kingston 12401, 914-331-4466; 100A Fed. Bldg., Binghamton 13901, 607-773-2768; and 114 Prospect St., Ithaca 14850, 607-273-1388.

_____

Rep. David L. Hobson (R), Representative from Ohio, District 7

DC Office: 1514 Longworth House Office Building, Washington, DC 20515, 202-225-4324; Fax: 202-225-1984.

District Offices: 220 P.O. Bldg., 150 N. Limestone St., Springfield 45501, 513-325-0474; and 212 S. Broad St., Lancaster 43130, 614-654-5149.

_____

Rep. Peter Hoekstra (R), Representative from Michigan, District 2

DC Office: 1122 Longworth House Office Building, Washington, DC 20515, 202-225-4401; Fax: 202-226-0779; e-mail: tellhoek@hr.house.gov.

District Offices: 42 W. 10th St., Holland 49423, 616-395-0030; 900 Third St., Muskegon 49440, 616-722-8386; and 120 W. Harris St., Cadillac 49601, 616-775-0050.

_____

Rep. Martin R. Hoke (R), Representative from Ohio, District 10

DC Office: 212 Cannon House Office Building, Washington, DC 20515, 202-225-5871; e-mail: hokemail@hr.house.gov.

District Offices: 21270 Lorraine Rd., Fairview Park 44126, 216-356-2010.

_____

Rep. Tim Holden (D), Representative from Pennsylvania, District 6

DC Office: 1421 Longworth House Office Building, Washington, DC 20515, 202-225-5546; Fax: 202-226-0996.

District Offices: Berks Cnty. Ctr., 633 Court St., Reading 19801, 610-371-9931; Meridian Bank Bldg., 101 N. Centre St., Pottsville 17901, 717-662-4212; and Northumberland Cnty. Cthse., Market Sq., Sunbury 17801, 717-988-1902.

_____

Sen. Ernest F. (Fritz) Hollings (D), Senator from South Carolina

DC Office: 125 Russell Senate Office Building, Washington, DC 20510, 202-224-6121; Fax: 202-224-4293; e-mail: senator@hollings.senate.com.

State Offices: 1835 Assembly St., Columbia 29201, 803-765-5731; 112 Custom House, 200 E. Bay St., Charleston 29401, 803-727-4525; and 126 Fed. Bldg., Greenville 29304, 803-233-5366; 103 Fed. Bldg., Spartanburg 29301, 803-585-3702.

Rep. Stephen Horn (R), Representative from California, District 38

DC Office: 129 Cannon House Office Building, Washington, DC 20515, 202-225-6676; Fax: 202-225-1012.

District Offices: 4010 Watson Plaza Dr., Lakewood 90712, 310-425-1336.

Rep. John N. Hostettler (R), Representative from Indiana, District 8

DC Office: 1404 Longworth House Office Building, Washington, DC 20515, 202-225-4636; Fax: 202-225-3284; e-mail: johnhost@hr.house.gov.

District Offices: 101 M.L.K. Blvd., Evansville 47708, 812-465-6484; and 120 W. 7th St., Bloomington 47404, 812-334-1111.

Rep. Amo Houghton (R), Representative from New York, District 31

DC Office: 1110 Longworth House Office Building, Washington, DC 20515, 202-225-3161; Fax: 202-225-5574.

District Offices: 700 W. Gate Plz., W. State St., Olean 14760, 716-372-2127; 32 Denison Pkwy. W., Corning 14830, 607-937-3333; and Fed. Bldg., Prendergast & 3d Sts., Jamestown 14701, 716-484-0252.

Rep. Steny H. Hoyer (D), Representative from Maryland, District 5

DC Office: 1705 Longworth House Office Building, Washington, DC 20515, 202-225-4131; Fax: 202-225-4300.

District Offices: 6500 Cherrywood Ln., Greenbelt 20770, 301-474-0119; and 21-A Industrial Park Dr., Waldorf 20602, 301-843-1577.

Rep. Duncan Hunter (R), Representative from California, District 52

DC Office: 2265 Rayburn House Office Building, Washington, DC 20515, 202-225-5672; Fax: 202-225-0235.

District Offices: 366 S. Pierce St., El Cajon 92020, 619-579-3001; and 1101 Airport Rd., Imperial 92251, 619-353-5420.

Rep. Tim Hutchinson (R), Representative from Arkansas, District 3

DC Office: 1005 Longworth House Office Building, Washington, DC 20515, 202-225-4301.

District Offices: 30 S. 6th St., Ft. Smith 72901, 501-782-7787; 422 Fed. Bldg., 35 E. Mountain, Fayetteville 72701, 501-442-5258; and 210 Fed. Bldg., 425 N. Walnut, Harrison 72601, 501-741-6900.

Sen. Kay Bailey Hutchison (R), Senator from Texas

DC Office: 283 Russell Senate Office Building, Washington, DC 20510, 202-224-5922; Fax: 202-224-0776; e-mail: senator@hutchison.senate.gov.

State Offices: 10440 N. Central Expressway, Dallas 75231, 214-361-3500; 8023 Vantage Dr., San Antonio 78230, 210-340-2885; and 500 Chestnut St., Abilene 79602, 915-676-2839.

————————

Rep. Henry J. Hyde (R), Representative from Illinois, District 6

DC Office: 2110 Rayburn House Office Building, Washington, DC 20515, 202-225-4561; Fax: 202-225-1166.

District Offices: 50 E. Oak St., Addison 60101, 312-832-5950.

————————

Rep. Bob Inglis (R), Representative from South Carolina, District 4

DC Office: 1237 Longworth House Office Building, Washington, DC 20515, 202-225-6030; Fax: 202-226-1177.

District Offices: 201 Magnolia St., Spartanburg 29301, 803-582-6422; 300 E. Washington St., Greenville 29601, 803-232-1141; and 405 W. Main St., Union 29379, 803-427-2205.

————————

Sen. James M. Inhofe (R), Senator from Oklahoma

DC Office: 453 Russell Senate Office Building, Washington, DC 20510, 202-224-4721; Fax: 202-228-0380.

State Offices: 1924 S. Utica St., Tulsa 74104, 918-748-5111; and 204 N. Robinson, Oklahoma City 73102, 405-231-4381.

————————

Sen. Daniel K. Inouye (D), Senator from Hawaii

DC Office: 722 Hart Senate Office Building, Washington, DC 20510, 202-224-3934; Fax: 202-224-6747.

State Offices: 7325 Prince Kuhio Fed. Bldg., 300 Ala Moana Blvd., Honolulu 96850, 808-541-2542.

————————

Rep. Ernest J. Istook, Jr. (R), Representative from Oklahoma, District 5

DC Office: 119 Cannon House Office Building, Washington, DC 20515, 202-225-2132; Fax: 202-226-1463; e-mail: istook@hr.house.gov.

District Offices: 5400 N. Grand Blvd., Oklahoma City 73112, 405-942-3636; First Court Pl., Bartlesville 74003, 918-336-5546; and 5th and Grand Sts., Ponca City 74601, 405-762-6778.

————————

Rep. Jesse L. Jackson, Jr. (D), Representative from Illinois, District 2

DC Office: 312 Cannon House Office Building, Washington, DC 20515, 202-225-0773; Fax: 202-225-0899.

District Offices: 11133 S. Halsted St., Chicago, IL, 312-785-1996.

————————

Rep. Sheila Jackson Lee (D), Representative from Texas, District 18

DC Office: 1520 Longworth House Office Building, Washington, DC 20515, 202-225-3816; Fax: 202-225-3317.

District Offices: 1919 Smith St., Mickey Leland Bldg., Houston 77002, 713-655-0050.

_____

Rep. Andy Jacobs, Jr. (D), Representative from Indiana, District 10

DC Office: 2313 Rayburn House Office Building, Washington, DC 20515, 202-225-4011; Fax: 202-226-4093.

District Offices: 441-A Fed. Bldg., 46 E. Ohio St., Indianapolis 46204, 317-226-7331.

_____

Rep. William J. Jefferson (D), Representative from Louisiana, District 2

DC Office: 240 Cannon House Office Building, Washington, DC 20515, 202-225-6636; Fax: 202-225-1988.

District Offices: 501 Magazine St., New Orleans 70130, 504-589-2274.

_____

Sen. James M. Jeffords (R), Senator from Vermont

DC Office: 513 Hart Senate Office Building, Washington, DC 20510, 202-224-5141; e-mail: vermont@jeffords.senate.gov.

State Offices: P.O. Box 676, 138 Main St., Montpelier 05601, 802-223-5273; 95 St. Paul St., Burlington 05401, 802-658-6001; and P.O. Box 397, 2 S. Main St., Rutland 05702, 802-773-3875.

_____

Rep. Nancy L. Johnson (R), Representative from Connecticut, District 6

DC Office: 343 Cannon House Office Building, Washington, DC 20515, 202-225-4476; Fax: 202-225-4488.

District Offices: 480 Myrtle St., New Britain 06051, 203-223-8412.

_____

Rep. Tim Johnson (D), Representative from South Dakota, District 1

DC Office: 2438 Rayburn House Office Building, Washington, DC 20515, 202-225-2801; Fax: 202-225-2427.

District Offices: 515 S. Dakota Ave., Sioux Falls 57102, 605-332-8896; 809 South St., Rapid City 57701, 605-341-3990; and 20 6th Ave., SW, Aberdeen 57401, 605-226-3440.

_____

Rep. Eddie Bernice Johnson (D), Representative from Texas, District 30

DC Office: 1123 Longworth House Office Building, Washington, DC 20515, 202-225-8885; Fax: 202-226-1477.

District Offices: 2525 McKinney Ave., Dallas 75201, 214-922-8885.

_____

Rep. Sam Johnson (R), Representative from Texas, District 3

DC Office: 1030 Longworth House Office Building, Washington, DC 20515, 202-225-4201; Fax: 202-225-1485; e-mail: samtx03@hr.house.gov.

District Offices: 9400 N. Central Expressway, Dallas 75231, 214-767-4848.

_____

Sen. J. Bennett Johnston (D), Senator from Louisiana

DC Office: 136 Hart Senate Office Building, Washington, DC 20510, 202-224-5824; Fax: 202-224-2952; e-mail: senator@johnston.senate.gov.

State Offices: 1010 Hale Boggs Fed. Bldg., 501 Magazine St., New Orleans 70130, 504-589-2427; 300 Fannin St., Shreveport 71101, 318-676-3085; and 1 American Pl., Baton Rouge 70825, 504-389-0395.

Rep. Harry A. Johnston (D), Representative from Florida, District 19

DC Office: 2458 Rayburn House Office Building, Washington, DC 20515, 202-225-3001; Fax: 202-225-8791.

District Offices: 1501 Corporate Dr., Boynton Beach 33426, 407-732-4000.

Rep. Walter B. Jones, Jr. (R), Representative from North Carolina, District 3

DC Office: 214 Cannon House Office Building, Washington, DC 20515, 202-225-3415; Fax: 202-225-3286.

District Offices: 102-C Eastbrook Dr., Greenville 27858, 919-931-1003.

Rep. Paul E. Kanjorski (D), Representative from Pennsylvania, District 11

DC Office: 2429 Rayburn House Office Building, Washington, DC 20515, 202-225-6511; e-mail: kanjo@hr.house.gov.

District Offices: 10 E. South St., Wilkes-Barre 18701, 717-825-2200.

Rep. Marcy Kaptur (D), Representative from Ohio, District 9

DC Office: 2104 Rayburn House Office Building, Washington, DC 20515, 202-225-4146; Fax: 202-225-7711.

District Offices: Fed. Bldg., 234 Summit St., Toledo 43604, 419-259-7500.

Rep. John R. Kasich (R), Representative from Ohio, District 12

DC Office: 1131 Longworth House Office Building, Washington, DC 20515, 202-225-5355; Fax: 202-225-7695.

District Offices: 200 N. High St., Columbus 43215, 614-469-7318.

Sen. Nancy Landon Kassebaum (R), Senator from Kansas

DC Office: 302 Russell Senate Office Building, Washington, DC 20510, 202-224-4774; Fax: 202-224-3514.

State Offices: 444 S.E. Quincy, Box 51, Topeka 66683, 913-295-2888; 911 N. Main, Garden City 67846, 316-276-3423; 4200 Somerset, Prairie Village 66208, 913-648-3103; and 111 N. Market, Wichita 67202, 316-269-6251.

Rep. Sue W. Kelly (R), Representative from New York, District 19

DC Office: 1037 Longworth House Office Building, Washington, DC 20515, 202-225-5441; Fax: 202-225-3289; e-mail: dearsue@hr.house.gov.

District Offices: 21 Old Main St., Fishkill 12524, 914-897-5200.

Sen. Dirk Kempthorne (R), Senator from Idaho

DC Office: 367 Dirksen Senate Office Building, Washington, DC 20510, 202-224-6142; Fax: 202-224-5893; e-mail: dirk_kempthorne@kempthorne.senate.gov.

State Offices: 304 N. 8th St., Boise 83701, 208-334-1776; 118 N. 2d St., Coeur d'Alene 83814, 208-664-5490; 633 Main St., Lewiston 83501, 208-743-1492; 401 2d St. N., Twin Falls 83301, 208-734-2515; 250 S. 4th, Pocatello 83201, 208-236-6775; 2539 Channing Way, Idaho Falls 83404, 208-522-9779; 704 Blaine St., Caldwell 83605, 208-955-0360; and 220 E. 5th St., 208-883-9783.

Rep. Patrick J. Kennedy (D), Representative from Rhode Island, District 1

DC Office: 1505 Longworth House Office Building, Washington, DC 20515, 202-225-4911; Fax: 202-225-3290.

District Offices: 286 Main St., Pawtucket 02860, 401-729-5600; 320 Thames St., Newport 02840, 401-841-0440; also, 127 Social St., Woonsocket 02895, 401-762-2288.

Sen. Edward M. Kennedy (D), Senator from Massachusetts

DC Office: 315 Russell Senate Office Building, Washington, DC 20510, 202-224-4543; Fax: 202-224-2417; e-mail: senator@kennedy.senate.gov.

State Offices: 2400 JFK Fed. Bldg., Boston 02203, 617-565-3170.

Rep. Joseph P. Kennedy, II (D), Representative from Massachusetts, District 8

DC Office: 2242 Rayburn House Office Building, Washington, DC 20515, 202-225-5111; Fax: 202-225-9322.

District Offices: Schrafft Ctr., 529 Main St., Charlestown 02129, 617-242-0200.

Rep. Barbara B. Kennelly (D), Representative from Connecticut, District 1

DC Office: 201 Cannon House Office Building, Washington, DC 20515, 202-225-2265; Fax: 202-225-1031.

District Offices: One Corporate Ctr., Hartford 06103, 203-278-8888.

Sen. Robert Kerrey (D), Senator from Nebraska

DC Office: 303 Hart Senate Office Building, Washington, DC 20510, 202-224-6551; Fax: 202-224-7645; e-mail: bob@kerrey.senate.gov.

State Offices: 7602 Pacific St. Omaha 68114, 402-391-3411; and 100 Centennial Mall N., Fed. Bldg, Lincoln 68508, 402-437-5246.

Sen. John F. Kerry (D), Senator from Massachusetts

DC Office: 421 Russell Senate Office Building, Washington, DC 20510, 202-224-2742; Fax: 202-224-8525: e-mail: john_kerry@kerry.senate.gov.

State Offices: One Bowdoin Sq., Boston 02114, 617-565-8519; 222 Milliken Pl., Fall River 02722, 508-677-0522; and 145 State St., Springfield 01103, 413-785-4619.

Rep. Dale E. Kildee (D), Representative from Michigan, District 9

DC Office: 2187 Rayburn House Office Building, Washington, DC 20515, 202-225-3611; Fax: 202-225-6393.

District Offices: 316 W. Water St., Flint 48503, 313-239-1437; and 1829 N. Perry St., Pontiac 48340, 313-373-9337.

———————

Rep. Jay Kim (R), Representative from California, District 41

DC Office: 435 Cannon House Office Building, Washington, DC 20515, 202-225-3201; Fax: 202-225-1485.

District Offices: 1131 W. 6th St., Ontario 91762, 909-988-1055; and 18200 Yorba Linda Blvd., Yorba Linda 92686, 714-572-8574.

———————

Rep. Peter T. King (R), Representative from New York, District 3

DC Office: 224 Cannon House Office Building, Washington, DC 20515, 202-225-7896; Fax: 202-226-2279.

District Office: 1003 Park Blvd., Massapequa Park 11762, 516-541-4225.

———————

Rep. Jack Kingston (R), Representative from Georgia, District 1

DC Office: 1507 Longworth House Office Building, Washington, DC 20515, 202-225-5831; Fax: 202-226-2269.

District Offices: Enterprise Bldg., 6605 Abercorn St., Savannah 31405, 912-352-0101; Statesboro Fed. Bldg., Statesboro 30458, 912-489-8797; Thomas Henry Clarke Bldg., 208 Tebeau St., Waycross 31501, 912-287-1180; and Brunswick Fed. Bldg., 805 Gloucester St., Brunswick 31520, 912-265-9010.

———————

Rep. Gerald D. Kleczka (D), Representative from Wisconsin, District 4

DC Office: 2301 Rayburn House Office Building, Washington, DC 20515, 202-225-4572; Fax: 202-225-8135.

District Offices: 5032 W. Forest Home Ave., Milwaukee 53219, 414-297-1140; and 414 W. Moreland Blvd., Waukesha 53188, 414-549-6360.

———————

Rep. Ron Klink (D), Representative from Pennsylvania, District 4

DC Office: 125 Cannon House Office Building, Washington, DC 20515, 202-225-2565; Fax: 202-226-2274.

District Offices: 11279 Center Hwy., N. Huntingdon 15642, 412-864-8681; Beaver Trust Bldg., 250 Insurance St., Beaver 15009, 412-728-3005; Cranberry Municipal Bldg., 2525 Rochester Rd., Cranberry Township 16066, 412-772-6080; 2692 Leechburg Rd., Lower Burrell 15068, 412-335-4518; and 134 N. Mercer St., New Castle 16101, 412-654-9036.

———————

Rep. Scott Klug (R), Representative from Wisconsin, District 2

DC Office: 1113 Longworth House Office Building, Washington, DC 20515, 202-225-2906; Fax: 202-225-6942; e-mail: badger02@hr.house.gov.

District Offices: 16 N. Carroll St., Madison 53703, 608-257-9200.

———————

Rep. Joe Knollenberg (R), Representative from Michigan, District 11

DC Office: 1221 Longworth House Office Building, Washington, DC 20515, 202-225-5802; Fax: 202-226-2356.

District Offices: 30833 Northwestern Hwy., Farmington Hills 48334, 313-851-1366; and 15439 Middlebelt St., Livonia 48514, 313-425-7557.

––––––––––

Sen. Herb Kohl (D), Senator from Wisconsin

DC Office: 330 Hart Senate Office Building, Washington, DC 20510, 202-224-5653; Fax: 202-224-9787; e-mail: senator_kohl@kohl.senate.gov.

State Offices: 310 W. Wisconsin Ave., Milwaukee 53202, 414-297-4451; 14 W. Mifflin St., Madison 53703, 608-264-5338; 402 Graham Ave., Eau Claire 54701, 715-832-8424; and 4321 W. College Ave., Appleton 54914, 414-738-1640.

––––––––––

Rep. Jim Kolbe (R), Representative from Arizona, District 5

DC Office: 205 Cannon House Office Building, Washington, DC 20515, 202-225-2542; e-mail: jimkolbe@hr.house.gov.

District Offices: 1661 N. Swan Rd., Tucson 85712, 520-881-3588; and 77 Calle Portal, Sierra Vista 85635, 520-459-3115.

––––––––––

Sen. Jon Kyl (R), Senator from Arizona

DC Office: 702 Hart Senate Office Building, Washington, DC 20510, 202-224-4521; Fax: 202-224-2207; e-mail: info_kyl.senate.gov.

State Offices: 2200 E. Camelback, Phoenix 85016, 602-840-1891; and 7315 N. Oracle, Tucson 85704, 520-575-8633.

––––––––––

Rep. John J. LaFalce (D), Representative from New York, District 29

DC Office: 2310 Rayburn House Office Building, Washington, DC 20515, 202-225-3231; Fax: 202-225-8693.

District Offices: Fed. Bldg., 111 W. Huron St., Buffalo 14202, 716-846-4056; Main P.O. Bldg., 615 Main St., Niagara Falls 14302, 716-284-9976; and 409 S. Union St., Spencerport 14559, 716-352-4777.

––––––––––

Rep. Ray LaHood (R), Representative from Illinois, District 18

DC Office: 329 Cannon House Office Building, Washington, DC 20515, 202-225-6201; Fax: 202-225-9249.

District Offices: 100 N.E. Monroe, Peoria 61602, 309-671-7027; 3050 Montvale Dr., Springfield 62704, 217-793-0808; and 236 W. State St., Jacksonville 62650, 217-245-1431.

––––––––––

Rep. Tom Lantos (D), Representative from California, District 12

DC Office: 2217 Rayburn House Office Building, Washington, DC 20515, 202-225-3531; Fax: 202-225-7900; e-mail: talk2tom@hr.gov.

District Offices: 400 El Camino Real, San Mateo 94402, 415-342-0300.

––––––––––

Rep. Steve Largent (R), Representative from Oklahoma, District 1

DC Office: 410 Cannon House Office Building, Washington, DC 20515, 202-225-2211; Fax: 202-225-9817.

District Offices: 2424 E. 21st St., Tulsa 74114, 918-749-0014.

Rep. Tom Latham (R), Representative from Iowa, District 5

DC Office: 516 Cannon House Office Building, Washington, DC 20515, 202-225-5476; Fax: 202-225-3301.

District Offices: 123 Albany Ave., SE. Orange City 51041, 712-737-8708; 526 Pierce St., Sioux City 51101, 712-277-2114; 1411 1st Ave., S. Fort Dodge 50501, 515-573-2738; and 217 Grand Ave., Spencer 51301, 712-262-6480.

Rep. Steven C. LaTourette (R), Representative from Ohio, District 19

DC Office: 1508 Longworth House Office Building, Washington, DC 20515, 202-225-5731; Fax: 202-225-3307.

District Offices: 1 Victoria Pl., Painesville 44077, 216-352-3939.

Rep. Greg Laughlin (R), Representative from Texas, District 14

DC Office: 442 Cannon 20515, 202-225-2831; Fax: 202-225-1108.

District Offices: 312 S. Main St., Victoria 77901, 512-576-1231; and 221 E. Main St., Round Rock 78664, 512-244-3765.

Sen. Frank R. Lautenberg (D), Senator from New Jersey

DC Office: 506 Hart Senate Office Building, Washington, DC 20510, 202-224-4744; Fax: 202-224-9707; e-mail: frank_lautenberg@lautenberg.senate.gov.

State Offices: Barrington Commons, 208 Whitehorse Pk., Barrington 08007, 609-757-5353; and 1 Gateway Ctr., Newark 07102, 201-645-3030.

Rep. Rick A. Lazio (R), Representative from New York, District 2

DC Office: 314 Cannon House Office Building, Washington, DC 20515, 202-225-3335; Fax: 202-225-4669; e-mail: lazio@hr.house.gov.

District Offices: 126 W. Main St., Babylon 11702, 516-893-9010.

Rep. James A. Leach (R), Representative from Iowa, District 1

DC Office: 2186 Rayburn House Office Building, Washington, DC 20515, 202-225-6576; Fax: 202-226-1278.

District Offices: 209 W. 4th St., Davenport 52801, 319-326-1841; 102 S. Clinton, Iowa City 52240, 319-351-0789; and 309 10th St., SE, Cedar Rapids 52403, 319-363-4773.

Sen. Patrick J. Leahy (D), Senator from Vermont

DC Office: 433 Russell Senate Office Building, Washington, DC 20510, 202-224-4242; Fax: 202-224-3595; e-mail: senator_leahy@leahy.senate.gov.

State Offices: 199 Main St., Burlington 05401, 802-863-2525; and Fed. Bldg., Box 933, Montpelier 05602, 802-229-0569.

Sen. Carl Levin (D), Senator from Michigan

DC Office: 459 Russell Senate Office Building, Washington, DC 20510, 202-224-6221; Fax: 202-224-1388; e-mail: senator@levin.senate.gov.

State Offices: 1860 McNamara Bldg., 477 Michigan Ave., Detroit 48226, 313-226-6020; Fed. Bldg., 145 Water St., Alpena 49707, 517-354-5520; 623 Ludington St., Escanaba 49829, 517-789-0052; Gerald R. Ford Fed. Bldg., 110 Michigan Ave. N.W., Grand Rapids 49503, 616-456-2531; 1810 Michigan Natl. Tower, 124 Allegan St., Lansing 48933, 517-377-1508; P.O. Box 817, Saginaw 48606, 517-754-2494; 15100 Northline Rd., Southgate 48195, 313-285-8596; 24580 Cunningham, Warren 48091, 313-759-0477; and 207 Grandview Pkwy., Traverse City 49685, 616-947-9569.

Rep. Sander M. Levin (D), Representative from Michigan, District 12

DC Office: 2230 Rayburn House Office Building, Washington, DC 20515, 202-225-4961; Fax: 202-226-1033.

District Offices: 2107 E. 14 Mile Rd., Sterling Heights 48310, 810-268-4444.

Rep. Jerry Lewis (R), Representative from California, District 40

DC Office: 2112 Rayburn House Office Building, Washington, DC 20515, 202-225-5861; Fax: 202-225-6498.

District Offices: 1150 Brookside Ave., Redlands 92374, 909-862-6030.

Rep. John Lewis (D), Representative from Georgia, District 5

DC Office: 229 Cannon House Office Building, Washington, DC 20515, 202-225-3801; Fax: 202-225-0351.

District Offices:100 Peachtree St., NW, 404-659-0116.

Rep. Ron Lewis (R), Representative from Kentucky, District 2

DC Office: 412 Cannon House Office Building, Washington, DC 20515, 202-225-3501.

District Offices: 312 N. Mulberry St., Elizabethtown 42701, 502-765-4360; B-18 Fed. Bldg., 241 W. Main St., Bowling Green 42101, 502-842-9896; and B-17 Fed. Bldg., 423 Frederica St., Owensboro 42303, 502-688-8858.

Sen. Joseph I. Lieberman (D), Senator from Connecticut

DC Office: 316 Hart Senate Office Building, Washington, DC 20510, 202-224-4041; Fax: 202-224-9750; e-mail: senator_lieberman@lieberman-dc.senate.gov.

State Offices: One Commercial Plz., Hartford 06103, 203-240-3566.

Rep. Jim Ross Lightfoot (R), Representative from Iowa, District 3

DC Office: 2161 Rayburn House Office Building, Washington, DC 20515, 202-225-3806; Fax: 202-225-6973.

District Offices: 501 W. Lowell, Shenandoah 51601, 712-246-1984; 413 Kellogg, Ames 50010, 515-232-1288; 220 W. Salem, Indianola 50125, 515-961-0591; 347 E. 2d St., Ottumwa 52501, 515-683-3551; and 311 N. 3d St., Burlington 52601, 319-753-6415.

———————

Rep. Blanche Lambert Lincoln (D), Representative from Arkansas, District 1

DC Office: 1204 Longworth House Office Building, Washington, DC 20515, 202-225-4076; Fax: 202-225-4654.

District Offices: 615 S. Main, Jonesboro 72401, 501-972-4600.

———————

Rep. John Linder (R), Representative from Georgia, District 4

DC Office: 1318 Longworth House Office Building, Washington, DC 20515, 202-225-4272; Fax: 202-225-4696; e-mail: jlinder@hr.house.gov.

District Offices: 3003 Chamblee-Tucker Rd., Atlanta 30341, 404-936-9400.

———————

Rep. William O. Lipinski (D), Representative from Illinois, District 3

DC Office: 1501 Longworth House Office Building, Washington, DC 20515, 202-225-5701; Fax: 202-225-1012.

District Offices: 5832 S. Archer Ave., Chicago 60638, 312-886-0481; and 12717 W. Ridgeland Ave., Palos Heights 60463, 708-371-7460.

———————

Rep. Robert L. (Bob) Livingston (R), Representative from Louisiana, District 1

DC Office: 2406 Rayburn House Office Building, Washington, DC 20515, 202-225-3015; Fax: 202-225-0739.

District Offices: 111 Veterans Blvd., Metairie 70005, 504-589-2753.

———————

Rep. Frank A. LoBiondo (R), Representative from New Jersey, District 2

DC Office: 513 Cannon House Office Building, Washington, DC 20515, 202-225-6572; Fax: 202-225-3318.

District Offices: 222 New Rd., Linwood 08221, 609-927-4442.

———————

Rep. Zoe Lofgren (D), Representative from California, District 16

DC Office: 118 Cannon House Office Building, Washington, DC 20515, 202-225-3072; Fax: 202-225-3336; e-mail: zoegram@hr.house.gov.

District Offices: 635 N. 1st St., San Jose 95112, 408-271-8700.

———————

Rep. James B. Longley, Jr. (R), Representative from Maine, District 1

DC Office: 226 Cannon House Office Building, Washington, DC 20515, 202-225-6116; Fax: 202-225-3353.

District Offices: 4 Moulton St., Portland 04101, 207-774-5019; and 168 Capitol St., Augusta 04330, 207-626-3608.

———————

Sen. Trent Lott (R), Senator from Mississippi

DC Office: 487 Russell Senate Office Building, Washington, DC 20510, 202-224-6253; Fax: 202-224-2262.

State Offices: 1 Gov. Plaza, Gulfport 39501, 601-863-1988; 245 E. Capitol St., Jackson 39201, 601-965-4644; 3100 S. Pascagoula St., Pascagoula 39567, 601-762-5400; P.O. Box 1474, Oxford 38655, 601-234-3774; and 200 E. Washington St., Greenwood 38930, 601-453-5681.

———————

Rep. Nita M. Lowey (D), Representative from New York, District 18

DC Office: 2421 Rayburn House Office Building, Washington, DC 20515, 202-225-6506; Fax: 202-225-0546.

District Offices: 222 Mamaroneck Ave., White Plains 10605, 914-428-1707; and 97-45 Queens Blvd., Rego Park 11374, 718-897-3602.

———————

Rep. Frank D. Lucas (R), Representative from Oklahoma, District 6

DC Office: 107 Cannon House Office Building, Washington, DC 20515, 202-225-5565; Fax: 202-225-8698.

District Offices: 215 Dean A. McGee, Oklahoma City 73102, 405-231-5511; P.O. Box 3612, Enid 73701, 405-237-9224; and 1007 Main St., Woodward 73802, 405-256-5752.

———————

Sen. Richard G. Lugar (R), Senator from Indiana

DC Office: 306 Hart Senate Office Building, Washington, DC 20510, 202-224-4814.

State Offices: 1180 Market Tower, 10 W. Market St., Indianapolis 46204, 317-226-5555; Fed. Bldg., 1300 S. Harrison St., Fort Wayne 46802, 219-422-1505; 122 Fed. Bldg., 101 NW M.L.K. Blvd., Evansville 47708, 812-465-6313; 103 Fed. Ctr., 1201 E. 10th St., Jeffersonville 47132, 812-288-3377; and 8585 Broadway, Merrillville 46410, 219-937-5380.

———————

Rep. Bill Luther (DFL), Representative from Minnesota, District 6

DC Office: 1419 Longworth House Office Building, Washington, DC 20515, 202-225-2271; Fax: 202-225-3368.

District Offices: 1811 Weir Dr., Woodbury 55125, 612-730-4940.

———————

Sen. Connie Mack III (R), Senator from Florida

DC Office: 517 Hart Senate Office Building, Washington, DC 20510, 202-224-5274; Fax: 202-224-8022.

State Offices: 600 N. Westshore Blvd., Tampa 33609, 813-225-7483.

———————

Rep. Carolyn B. Maloney (D), Representative from New York, District 14

DC Office: 1504 Longworth House Office Building, Washington, DC 20515, 202-225-7944; Fax: 202-225-4709.

District Offices: 110 E. 59th St., 2d Fl., New York 10022, 212-832-6531; 28-11 Astoria Blvd., Long Island City 11102, 718-932-1804; and 619 Lorimer St., Brooklyn 11211, 718-349-1260.

———————

Rep. Thomas J. Manton (D), Representative from New York, District 7

DC Office: 2235 Rayburn House Office Building, Washington, DC 20515, 202-225-3965; Fax: 202-225-1909; e-mail: tmanton@hr.house.gov

District Offices: 46-12 Queens Blvd., Sunnyside 11104, 718-706-1400; and 2114 Williamsbridge Rd., Bronx 10461, 718-931-1400.

———————

Rep. Donald Manzullo (R), Representative from Illinois, District 16

DC Office: 426 Cannon House Office Building, Washington, DC 20515, 202-225-5676; Fax: 202-225-5284.

District Offices: 415 S. Mulford Rd., Rockford 61108, 815-394-1231; and 191 Virginia Ave., Crystal Lake 60014, 815-356-9800.

———————

Rep. Edward J. Markey (D), Representative from Massachusetts, District 7

DC Office: 2133 Rayburn House Office Building, Washington, DC 20515, 202-225-2836; Fax: 202-225-1716.

District Offices: 5 High St., Medford 02155, 617-396-2900.

———————

Rep. Matthew G. (Marty) Martinez (D), Representative from California, District 31

DC Office: 2239 Rayburn House Office Building, Washington, DC 20515, 202-225-5464; Fax: 202-225-5467.

District Offices: 320 S. Garfield Ave., Alhambra 91801, 818-458-4524.

———————

Rep. Bill Martini (R), Representative from New Jersey, District 8

DC Office: 1513 Longworth House Office Building, Washington, DC 20515, 202-225-5751; Fax: 202-225-3372.

District Offices: 200 Fed. Plz., Paterson 07505, 201-523-5152.

———————

Rep. Frank R. Mascara (D), Representative from Pennsylvania, District 20

DC Office: 1531 Longworth House Office Building, Washington, DC 20515, 202-225-4665; Fax: 202-225-3377.

District Offices: 96 N. Main St., Washington 15301, 412-228-4326; 47 E. Penn St., Uniontown 15401, 412-437-5078; and 93 E. High St., Waynesburg 15370, 412-852-2182.

———————

Rep. Robert T. Matsui (D), Representative from California, District 5

DC Office: 2311 Rayburn House Office Building, Washington, DC 20515, 202-225-7163; Fax: 202-225-0566.

District Offices: 8058 Fed. Bldg., 650 Capitol Mall, Sacramento 95814, 916-498-5600.

———————

Sen. John McCain (R), Senator from Arizona

DC Office: 241 Russell Senate Office Building, Washington, DC 20510, 202-224-2235; Fax: 202-228-2862; e-mail: senator_mccain@mccain.senate.gov.

State Offices: 1839 S. Alma School Rd., Mesa 85210, 602-491-4300; 450 W. Pasco Redondo, Tucson 85701, 520-670-6334; and 2400 E. Arizona Biltmore Cir., Phoenix 85016, 602-952-2410.

Rep. Karen McCarthy (D), Representative from Missouri, District 5

DC Office: 1232 Longworth House Office Building, Washington, DC 20515, 202-225-4535; Fax: 202-225-4403.

District Offices: 811 Grand Ave., Kansas City 64106, 816-842-4545; and 301 W. Lexington, Independence 64050, 816-833-4545.

Rep. Bill McCollum (R), Representative from Florida, District 8

DC Office: 2266 Rayburn House Office Building, Washington, DC 20515, 202-225-2176; Fax: 202-225-0999.

District Offices: 605 E. Robinson Orlando 32801, 407-872-1962.

Sen. Mitch McConnell (R), Senator from Kentucky

DC Office: 120 Russell Senate Office Building, Washington, DC 20510, 202-224-2541; Fax: 202-224-2499.

State Offices: 601 W. Broadway, Louisville 40202, 502-582-6304; 1185 Dixie Hwy., Fort Wright 41011, 606-578-0188; Irvin Cobb Bldg., 602 Broadway, Paducah 42001, 502-442-4554; 1501-N S. Main St., London 40741, 606-864-2026; Fed. Bldg., 241 E. Main St., Bowling Green 42101; and 155 E. Main St., Lexington 40508, 606-252-1781.

Rep. Jim McCrery (R), Representative from Louisiana, District 5

DC Office: 225 Cannon House Office Building, Washington, DC 20515, 202-225-2777; Fax: 202-225-8039.

District Offices: 6425 Youree Dr., Shreveport 71105, 318-798-2254; and 1900 N. 18th St., Monroe 71201, 318-388-6105.

Rep. Joseph M. McDade (R), Representative from Pennsylvania, District 10

DC Office: 2107 Rayburn House Office Building, Washington, DC 20515, 202-225-3731; Fax: 202-225-9594.

District Offices: 514 Scranton Life Bldg., Scranton 18503, 717-346-3834; and 240 W. Third St., Williamsport 17701, 717-327-8161.

Rep. Jim McDermott (D), Representative from Washington, District 7

DC Office: 2349 Rayburn House Office Building, Washington, DC 20515, 202-225-3106.

District Offices: 1212 Tower Bldg., 1809 7th Ave., Seattle 98101, 206-553-7170.

Rep. Paul McHale (D), Representative from Pennsylvania, District 15

DC Office: 217 Cannon House Office Building, Washington, DC 20515, 202-225-6411; Fax: 202-225-5320; e-mail: mchale@hr.house.gov.

District Offices: 26 E. 3d St., Bethlehem 18015, 215-866-0916; Hamilton Financial Ctr., One Center Sq., Allentown 18101, 215-439-8861; and 168 Main St., Pennsburg 18073, 215-541-0614.

———————

Rep. John M. McHugh (R), Representative from New York, District 24

DC Office: 416 Cannon House Office Building, Washington, DC 20515, 202-225-4611.

District Offices: 404 Key Bank Bldg., 200 Washington St., Watertown 13601, 315-782-3150.

———————

Rep. Scott McInnis (R), Representative from Colorado, District 3

DC Office: 215 Cannon House Office Building, Washington, DC 20515, 202-225-4761; Fax: 202-225-0622.

District Offices: 327 N. 7th St., Grand Junction 81501, 303-245-7107; 134 W. B St., Pueblo 81003, 719-543-8200; 1060 Main Ave., Durango 81301, 303-259-2754; and 526 Pine St., Glenwood Springs 81601, 303-928-0637.

———————

Rep. David M. McIntosh (R), Representative from Indiana, District 2

DC Office: 1208 Longworth House Office Building, Washington, DC 20515, 202-225-3021. Fax: 202-225-3382; e-mail: mcintosh@hr.house.gov.

District Offices: 2900 W. Jackson St., Muncie 47304, 317-747-5566.

———————

Rep. Howard P. (Buck) McKeon (R), Representative from California, District 25

DC Office: 307 Cannon House Office Building, Washington, DC 20515, 202-225-1956; Fax: 202-225-0683; e-mail: tellbuck@hr.house.gov.

District Offices: 23929 W. Valencia Blvd., Santa Clarita 91355, 805-254-2111; and 1008 West Ave., Palmdale 93551, 805-948-7833.

———————

Rep. Cynthia A. McKinney (D), Representative from Georgia, District 11

DC Office: 124 Cannon House Office Building, Washington, DC 20515, 202-225-1605.

District Offices: 1 S. DeKalb Ctr., 2853 Candler Rd., Decatur 30034, 404-244-9902; 120 Barnard St., Savannah 31401, 912-652-4118; and 505 Courthouse La., Augusta 30901, 706-722-7551.

———————

Rep. Michael R. McNulty (D), Representative from New York, District 21

DC Office: 2442 Rayburn House Office Building, Washington, DC 20515, 202-225-5076; Fax: 202-225-5077.

District Offices: U.S. Post Office, Jay St., Schenectady 12305, 518-374-4547; O'Brien Fed. Bldg., 518-465-0700; 9 Market St., Amsterdam 12010, 518-843-3400; and 33 2d St., Troy 12180, 518-271-0822.

———————

Rep. Martin T. (Marty) Meehan (D), Representative from Massachusetts, District 5

DC Office: 318 Cannon House Office Building, Washington, DC 20515, 202-225-3411; Fax: 202-226-0771.

District Offices: 11 Kearney Sq., Lowell 01852, 508-459-0101; Bay State Bldg., 11 Lawrence St., Lawrence 01840, 508-681-6200; and Walker Bldg., 255 Main St., Marlborough 01752, 508-460-9292.

Rep. Carrie P. Meek (D), Representative from Florida, District 17

DC Office: 404 Cannon House Office Building, Washington, DC 20515, 202-225-4506.

District Offices: 25 W. Flagler St., Miami 33130, 305-381-9541.

Rep. Robert Menendez (D), Representative from New Jersey, District 13

DC Office: 1730 Longworth House Office Building, Washington, DC 20515, 202-225-7919; Fax: 202-226-0792.

District Offices: 911 Bergen Ave., Jersey City 07306, 201-222-2828; and 654 Ave. C, Bayonne 07002, 201-823-2900.

Rep. Jack Metcalf (R), Representative from Washington, District 2

DC Office: 507 Cannon House Office Building, Washington, DC 20515, 202-225-2605; Fax: 202-225-4420.

District Offices: 2930 Wetmore Ave., Everett 98201, 206-252-3188; and 322 N. Commercial St., Bellingham 98225, 206-733-4500.

Rep. Jan Meyers (R), Representative from Kansas, District 3

DC Office: 2303 Rayburn House Office Building, Washington, DC 20515, 202-225-2865; Fax: 202-225-0554.

District Offices: 182 Fed. Bldg., Kansas City 66101, 913-621-0832; 7133 W. 95th St., Overland Park 66212, 913-383-2013; and 708 W. 9th St., Lawrence 66044, 913-842-9313.

Rep. Kweisi Mfume (D), Representative from Maryland, District 7

DC Office: 2419 Rayburn House Office Building, Washington, DC 20515, 202-225-4741; Fax: 202-225-3178.

District Offices: 3000 Druid Park Dr., Baltimore 21215, 410-367-1900; and 1825 Woodlawn Dr., Baltimore 21207, 410-298-5997.

Rep. John L. Mica (R), Representative from Florida, District 7

DC Office: 336 Cannon House Office Building, Washington, DC 20515, 202-225-4035; Fax: 202-226-0821; e-mail: mica2hr.house.gov.

District Offices: 1211 Semoran Blvd., Casselberry 32707, 407-657-8080; 840 Deltona Blvd., Deltona 32725, 407-866-1499; and 1396 Dunlawton Blvd., Port Orange 32127, 904-756-9798.

Sen. Barbara A. Mikulski (D), Senator from Maryland

DC Office: 709 Hart Senate Office Building, Washington, DC 20510, 202-224-4654; Fax: 202-224-8858; e-mail: senator@mikulski.senate.gov.

State Offices: 253 World Trade Ctr., 401 E. Pratt St., Baltimore 21202, 410-962-4510; 60 West St., Annapolis 21401, 410-263-1805; 9658 Baltimore Ave., College Park 20740, 301-345-5517; 1201 Pemberton, Salisbury 21801, 410-546-7711; and 82 W. Washington St., Hagerstown 21740, 301-797-2826.

Rep. George Miller (D), Representative from California, District 7

DC Office: 2205 Rayburn House Office Building, Washington, DC 20515, 202-225-2095; Fax: 202-225-5609; e-mail: gmiller@hr.house.gov

District Offices: 367 Civic Dr., Pleasant Hill 94523, 510-602-1880; and 3220 Blume Dr., Richmond 94806, 510-262-6500.

Rep. Dan Miller (R), Representative from Florida, District 13

DC Office: 117 Cannon House Office Building, Washington, DC 20515, 202-225-5015; Fax: 202-226-0828.

District Offices: 2424 Manatee Ave., Bradenton 34205, 813-747-9081; 1751 Mound St., Sarasota 34236, 813-951-6643.

Rep. David Minge (DFL), Representative from Minnesota, District 2

DC Office: 1415 Longworth House Office Building, Washington, DC 20515, 202-225-2331; Fax: 202-226-0836; e-mail: dminge@hr.house.gov.

District Offices: 542 1st St., Montevideo 56265, 612-269-9311; 405 E. 2nd St., Chaska 55318, 612-448-6567; and 938 4th Ave., Windom 56101, 507-831-0115.

Rep. Patsy T. Mink (D), Representative from Hawaii, District 2

DC Office: 2135 Rayburn House Office Building, Washington, DC 20515, 202-225-4906; Fax: 202-225-4987.

District Offices: 5104 Prince Kuhio Fed. Bldg., P.O. Box 50124, Honolulu 96850, 808-541-1966.

Rep. John Joseph (Joe) Moakley (D), Representative from Massachusetts, District 9

DC Office: 235 Cannon House Office Building, Washington, DC 20515, 202-225-8273; Fax: 202-225-3984; e-mail: jmoakley@hr.house.gov.

District Offices: 4 Court St., Taunton 02780, 617-824-6676; and World Trade Ctr., Boston 02210, 617-565-2920.

Rep. Susan Molinari (R), Representative from New York, District 13

DC Office: 2435 Rayburn House Office Building, Washington, DC 20515, 202-225-3371; Fax: 202-226-1272; e-mail: smolinari@hr.house.gov.

District Offices: 14 New Dorp Ln., Staten Island 10306, 718-987-8400; and 9818 4th Ave., Brooklyn 11209, 718-630-5277.

Rep. Alan B. Mollohan (D), Representative from West Virginia, District 1

DC Office: 2427 Rayburn House Office Building, Washington, DC 20515, 202-225-4172; Fax: 202-225-7564.

District Offices: 213 Fed. Bldg., Morgantown 26505, 304-292-3019; 1117 Fed. Bldg., Parkersburg 26101, 304-428-0493; 316 Fed. Bldg., Wheeling 26003, 304-232-5390; and 209 P.O. Bldg., Clarksburg 26301, 304-623-4422.

_____

Rep. G. V. (Sonny) Montgomery (D), Representative from Mississippi, District 3

DC Office: 2184 Rayburn House Office Building, Washington, DC 20515, 202-225-5031; Fax: 202-225-3375.

District Offices: Fed. Bldg., Meridian 39301, 601-693-6681; 110-D Airport Rd., Pearl 39208, 601-932-2410; and Golden Triangle Airport, Columbus 39701, 601-327-2766.

_____

Rep. Carlos J. Moorhead (R), Representative from California, District 27

DC Office: 2346 Rayburn House Office Building, Washington, DC 20515, 202-225-4176; Fax: 202-225-1279.

District Offices: 420 N. Brand Blvd., Glendale 91203, 818-247-8445.

_____

Rep. James P. Moran, Jr. (D), Representative from Virginia, District 8

DC Office: 405 Cannon House Office Building, Washington, DC 20515, 202-225-4376; Fax: 202-225-0017.

District Offices: 5115 Franconia Rd., Alexandria 22310, 703-971-4700.

_____

Rep. Constance A. Morella (R), Representative from Maryland, District 8

DC Office: 106 Cannon House Office Building, Washington, DC 20515, 202-225-5341; Fax: 202-225-1389.

District Offices: 51 Monroe St., Rockville 20850, 301-424-3501.

_____

Sen. Carol Moseley-Braun (D), Senator from Illinois

DC Office: 320 Hart Senate Office Building, Washington, DC 20510, 202-224-2854; Fax: 202-224-1318; e-mail: senator@moseley-braun.senate.gov.

State Offices: Kluczynski Fed. Bldg., 230 S. Dearborn, Chicago 60604, 312-353-5420; 117 Fed. Bldg., 600 E. Monroe St., Springfield 62701, 217-492-4126; and Fed. Bldg., 105 S. 6th St., Mt Vernon 62864, 618-383-7920.

_____

Sen. Daniel Patrick Moynihan (D), Senator from New York

DC Office: 464 Russell Senate Office Building, Washington, DC 20510, 202-224-4451.

State Offices: 405 Lexington Ave., New York 10174, 212-661-5150; Guaranty Bldg., 28 Church St., Buffalo 14202, 716-846-4097; and 214 Main St., Oneonta 13820, 607-433-2310.

_____

Sen. Frank H. Murkowski (R), Senator from Alaska

DC Office: 706 Hart Senate Office Building, Washington, DC 20510, 202-224-6665; Fax: 202-224-5301.

State Offices: 222 W. 7th Ave., Box 1, Anchorage 99513, 907-271-3735; 101 12th Ave., Fairbanks 99701, 907-456-0233; Box 21647 Fed. Bldg, Juneau 99802, 907-586-7400; 130 Trading Bay Rd., Kenai 99611, 907-283-5808; and 109 Main St., Ketchikan 99901, 907-225-6880.

———————

Sen. Patty Murray (D), Senator from Washington

DC Office: 111 Russell Senate Office Building, Washington, DC 20510, 202-224-2621; Fax: 202-224-0238; e-mail: senator_murray@murray.senate.gov.

District Offices: 2988 Jackson Fed. Bldg., 915 2nd Ave., Seattle 98174, 206-553-5545; 601 1st Ave., Spokane 99201, 509-624-9515; and 140 Fed. Bldg., 500 W. 12th St., Vancouver 98660, 206-696-7797.

———————

Rep. John P. Murtha (D), Representative from Pennsylvania, District 12

DC Office: 2423 Rayburn House Office Building, Washington, DC 20515, 202-225-2065; Fax: 202-225-5709; e-mail: murtha@hr.house.gov.

District Offices: Vine and Walnut Sts., Centre Town Mall, Johnstown 15907, 814-535-2642.

———————

Rep. John T. Myers (R), Representative from Indiana, District 7

DC Office: 2372 Rayburn House Office Building, Washington, DC 20515, 202-225-5805; Fax: 202-225-1649.

District Offices: 107 Fed. Bldg., Terre Haute 47808, 812-238-1619; and 107 Halleck Fed. Bldg., Lafayette 47901, 317-423-1661.

———————

Rep. Sue Myrick (R), Representative from North Carolina, District 9

DC Office: 509 Cannon House Office Building, Washington, DC 20515, 202-225-1976; Fax: 202-225-3389; e-mail: myrick@hr.house.gov.

District Offices: 1901 Roxborough Rd., Charlotte 28211, 704-362-1060; and 224 S. New Hope Rd., Gastonia 28054, 704-861-1976.

———————

Rep. Jerrold Nadler (D), Representative from New York, District 8

DC Office: 109 Cannon House Office Building, Washington, DC 20515, 202-225-5635; Fax: 202-225-6923.

District Offices: 1841 Broadway, New York 10023, 212-489-3530; and 2875 W. 8th St., Brooklyn 11224, 718-373-3198.

———————

Rep. Richard E. Neal (D), Representative from Massachusetts, District 2

DC Office: 2431 Rayburn House Office Building, Washington, DC 20515, 202-225-5601; Fax: 202-225-8112.

District Offices: Fed. Office Bldg., 1550 Main St., Springfield 01103, 413-785-0325; and 4 Congress St., Milford 01757, 508-634-8198.

———————

Rep. George R. Nethercutt, Jr. (R), Representative from Washington, District 5

DC Office: 1527 Longworth House Office Building, Washington, DC 20515, 202-225-2006; Fax: 202-225-3392; e-mail: grnwa05@hr.house.gov.

District Offices: W. 920 Riverside, Spokane 99201, 509-353-2374.

—————

Rep. Mark W. Neumann (R), Representative from Wisconsin, District 1

DC Office: 1725 Longworth House Office Building, Washington, DC 20515, 202-225-3031; Fax: 202-225-3393; e-mail: mneumann@hr.house.gov.

District Offices: 1 Parker Pl., Janesville 53525, 608-752-4050.

—————

Rep. Bob Ney (R), Representative from Ohio, District 18

DC Office: 1605 Longworth House Office Building, Washington, DC 20515, 202-225-6265; Fax: 202-225-3394.

District Offices: 3201 Belmont St., Bellaire 43906, 614-676-1960; 152 2nd St., NE, New Philadelphia 44663, 216-364-6380; 500 Market St., Steubenville 43952, 614-283-1915; and 225 Underwood St., Zanesville 43701, 614-452-8598.

—————

Sen. Don Nickles (R), Senator from Oklahoma

DC Office: 133 Hart Senate Office Building, Washington, DC 20510, 202-224-5754; Fax: 202-224-6008.

State Offices: 1820 Liberty Tower, 100 N. Broadway, Oklahoma City 73102, 405-231-4941; 3310 Mid-Continent Tower, 401 S. Boston, Tulsa 74103, 918-581-7651; 1916 Lake Rd., Ponca City 74601, 405-767-1270; and American Natl. Bank Bldg., 601 D Ave., Lawton 73501, 405-357-9878.

—————

Rep. Charlie Norwood (R), Representative from Georgia, District 10

DC Office: 1707 Longworth House Office Building, Washington, DC 20515, 202-225-4101; Fax: 202-225-3397; e-mail: ga10@hr.house.gov.

District Offices: 1056 Clausson Rd., Augusta 30807, 706-733-7066.

—————

Sen. Sam Nunn (D), Senator from Georgia

DC Office: 303 Dirksen Senate Office Building, Washington, DC 20510, 202-224-3521; Fax: 202-224-0072.

State Offices: 75 Spring St. SW, Atlanta 30303, 404-331-4811; 915 Main St., Perry 31069, 912-987-1458; 130 Fed. Bldg., Gainesville 30501, 404-532-9976; 600 E. 1st St., Rome 30161, 404-291-5696; and 120 Barnard St., Savannah 31069, 912-944-4300.

—————

Rep. Jim Nussle (R), Representative from Iowa, District 2

DC Office: 303 Cannon House Office Building, Washington, DC 20515, 202-225-2911; Fax: 202-225-9129.

District Offices: 2300 JFK Rd., Dubuque 52002, 319-557-7740; 3356 Kimball Ave., Waterloo 50702, 310-235-1109; 1825 4th St., SW, Mason City 50401, 515-423-0303; and 223 W. Main St., Manchester 52057, 319-927-5141.

—————

Rep. James L. Oberstar (DFL), Representative from Minnesota, District 8

DC Office: 2366 Rayburn House Office Building, Washington, DC 20515, 202-225-6211; Fax: 202-225-0699; e-mail: oberstar@hr.house.gov.

District Offices: 231 Fed. Bldg., Duluth 55802, 218-727-7474; Chisolm City Hall, 316 Lake St., Chisholm 55719, 218-254-5761; City Hall, 13065 Orono Pkwy., Elk River 55330, 612-241-0188; and Brainerd City Hall, 501 Laurel St., Brainerd 56401, 218-828-4400.

———————

Rep. David R. Obey (D), Representative from Wisconsin, District 7

DC Office: 2462 Rayburn House Office Building, Washington, DC 20515, 202-225-3365.

District Offices: Fed. Bldg., 317 First St., Wausau 54401, 715-842-5606.

———————

Rep. John Olver (D), Representative from Massachusetts, District 1

DC Office: 1027 Longworth House Office Building, Washington, DC 20515, 202-225-5335; Fax: 202-226-1224.

District Offices: 78 Center St. Arterial, Pittsfield 02101, 413-442-0946; 881 Main St., Philbin Fed. Bldg., Fitchburg 01420, 508-342-8722; and 187 High St., Holyoke 01040, 413-584-8108.

———————

Rep. Solomon P. Ortiz (D), Representative from Texas, District 27

DC Office: 2136 Rayburn House Office Building, Washington, DC 20515, 202-225-7742; Fax: 202-225-1134.

District Offices: 3649 Leopard St., Corpus Christi 78408, 512-883-5868; and 3505 Boca Chica Blvd., Brownsville 78521, 512-541-1242.

———————

Rep. William H. Orton (D), Representative from Utah, District 3

DC Office: 440 Cannon House Office Building, Washington, DC 20515, 202-225-7751; Fax: 202-226-7683; e-mail: ortonut3@hr.house.gov.

District Offices: 51 S. University Ave., Provo 84601, 801-379-2500; and 3540 S. 40th St., West Valley City 84119, 801-964-5828.

———————

Rep. Major R. Owens (D), Representative from New York, District 11

DC Office: 2305 Rayburn House Office Building, Washington, DC 20515, 202-225-6231; Fax: 202-226-0112.

District Offices: 289 Utica Ave., Brooklyn 11213, 718-773-3100; and 1310 Cortelyon Rd., Brooklyn 11226, 718-940-3213.

———————

Rep. Michael G. Oxley (R), Representative from Ohio, District 4

DC Office: 2233 Rayburn House Office Building, Washington, DC 20515, 202-225-2676.

District Offices: 3121 W. Elm Plz., Lima 45805, 419-999-6455; 24 W. 3d St., Mansfield 44902, 419-522-5757; and 100 E. Main Cross St., Findlay 45840, 419-423-3210.

———————

Rep. Ron Packard (R), Representative from California, District 48

DC Office: 2162 Rayburn House Office Building, Washington, DC 20515,
202-225-3906; Fax: 202-225-0134; e-mail: rpackard@hr.house.gov.

District Offices: 221 E. Vista Way, Vista 92084, 619-631-1364;
and 629 Camino del los Mares, San Clemente 92672, 714-496-2343.

Sen. Bob Packwood (R), Senator from Oregon

DC Office: 259 Russell Senate Office Building, Washington, DC 20510,
202-224-5244; Fax: 202-228-3576; e-mail: senator_packwood@packwood.senate.gov.

State Offices: 101 SW Main St., Portland 97204-3210, 503-326-3370.

Rep. Frank Pallone, Jr. (D), Representative from New Jersey, District 6

DC Office: 420 Cannon House Office Building, Washington, DC 20515,
202-225-4671; Fax: 202-225-9665.

District Offices: IEI Airport Plz., Hazlet 07703, 908-264-9104; 67/69 Church St.,
New Brunswick 08901, 908-249-8892; and 540 Broadway Ave., Long Branch 07740,
201-571-1140.

Rep. Mike Parker (R), Representative from Mississippi, District 4

DC Office: 2445 Rayburn House Office Building, Washington, DC 20515,
202-225-5865; Fax: 202-225-5886.

District Offices: 245 E. Capitol, Jackson 39201, 601-352-1355; 230 S. Whitworth St.,
Brookhaven 39601, 601-835-0706; 118 N. Pearl St., Natchez 39120, 601-446-7250;
Chancery Ct. Annex, Columbia 39429, 601-731-1622; 728 Sawmill Rd., Laurel 39440,
601-425-4999; and 176 W. Court St., Mendenhall 39114, 601-847-0873.

Rep. Ed Pastor (D), Representative from Arizona, District 2

DC Office: 223 Cannon House Office Building, Washington, DC 20515,
202-225-4065; Fax: 202-225-1655; e-mail: edpastor@hr.house.gov.

District Offices: 802 N. Third Ave., Phoenix 85003, 602-256-0551;
2432 E. Broadway, Tucson 85719, 520-624-9986; and 281 W. 24th St., Yuma 85364,
520-726-2234.

Rep. Bill Paxon (R), Representative from New York, District 27

DC Office: 2436 Rayburn House Office Building, Washington, DC 20515,
202-225-5265; Fax: 202-225-5910; e-mail: bpaxon@hr.house.gov.

District Offices: 5500 Main St., Williamsville, 14221, 716-634-2324;
and 10 E. Main St., Victor 14564, 716-742-1600, 800-453-8330.

Rep. Donald M. Payne (D), Representative from New Jersey, District 10

DC Office: 2244 Rayburn House Office Building, Washington, DC 20515,
202-225-3436; Fax: 202-225-4160.

District Offices: 50 Walnut St., Newark 07102, 201-645-3213; and 333 N. Broad St.,
Elizabeth 07208, 908-629-0222.

Rep. L. F. Payne (D), Representative from Virginia, District 5

DC Office: 2412 Longworth House Office Building, Washington, DC 20515, 202-225-4711; Fax: 202-226-1147.

District Offices: 301 P.O. Bldg., 700 Main St., Danville 24541, 804-792-1280; Abbitt Fed. Bldg., 103 S. Main St., Farmville 23901, 804-392-8331; and 103 E. Water St., Charlottesville 22902, 804-295-6372.

Sen. Claiborne Pell (D), Senator from Rhode Island

DC Office: 335 Russell Senate Office Building, Washington, DC 20510, 202-224-4642; Fax: 202-224-4680.

State Offices: 418 Fed. Bldg., Providence 02903, 401-528-5456.

Rep. Nancy Pelosi (D), Representative from California, District 8

Rep. Douglas (Pete) Peterson (D), Representative from Florida, District 2

DC Office: 306 Cannon House Office Building, Washington, DC 20515, 202-225-5235; Fax: 202-225-1586.

District Offices: 930 Thomasville Rd., Tallahassee 32303, 904-561-3979; 30 W. Government St., Panama City 32401, 904-785-0812.

Rep. Collin C. Peterson (DFL), Representative from Minnesota, District 7

DC Office: 1314 Longworth House Office Building, Washington, DC 20515, 202-225-2165; Fax: 202-225-1593; e-mail: tocollin@hr.house.gov.

District Offices: 714 Lake Ave., Detroit Lakes 56501, 218-847-5056; 110 2nd St., Waite Park 56387, 612-259-0559; and 2603 Wheat Dr., Red Lake Falls 56750, 218-253-4356.

Rep. Tom Petri (R), Representative from Wisconsin, District 6

DC Office: 2262 Rayburn House Office Building, Washington, DC 20515, 202-225-2476; Fax: 202-225-2356.

District Offices: 845 S. Main St., Fond du Lac 54935, 414-922-1180; and 115 Washington Ave., Oshkosh 54901, 414-231-6333.

Rep. Owen Pickett (D), Representative from Virginia, District 2

DC Office: 2430 Rayburn House Office Building, Washington, DC 20515, 202-225-4215; Fax: 202-225-4218; e-mail: opickett@hr.house.gov.

District Offices: 112 E. Little Creek Rd., Norfolk 23505, 804-583-5892; and 2710 VA Beach Blvd., Virginia Beach 23452, 804-486-3710.

Rep. Richard W. Pombo (R), Representative from California, District 11

DC Office: 1519 Longworth House Office Building, Washington, DC 20515, 202-225-1947; Fax: 202-225-0861.

District Offices: 2495 W. March La., Stockton 95207, 209-951-3091.

Rep. Earl Pomeroy (D), Representative from North Dakota, District 1

DC Office: 1533 Longworth House Office Building, Washington, DC 20515, 202-225-2611; Fax: 202-226-0893; e-mail: epomeroy@hr.house.gov.

District Offices: Fed. Bldg., 657 2nd Ave., Fargo 58102, 701-235-9760; Fed. Bldg., 220 East Rosser Ave., Bismarck 58501, 701-224-0355.

_____

Rep. John E. Porter (R), Representative from Illinois, District 10

DC Office: 2373 Rayburn House Office Building, Washington, DC 20515, 202-225-4835.

District Offices: 102 Wilmot Rd., Deerfield 60015, 708-940-0202; and 18 N. County St., Waukegan 60085, 708-662-0101.

_____

Rep. Rob Portman (R), Representative from Ohio, District 2

DC Office: 238 Cannon House Office Building, Washington, DC 20515, 202-225-3164; Fax: 202-225-1992; e-mail: portmail@hr.house.gov.

District Offices: 8010 Fed. Bldg., 550 Main St., Cincinatti 45202, 513-684-2456.

_____

Rep. Glenn Poshard (D), Representative from Illinois, District 19

DC Office: 2334 Rayburn House Office Building, Washington, DC 20515, 202-225-5201; Fax: 202-225-1541.

District Offices: 201 E. Nolan St., W. Frankfort 62896, 618-937-6402; New Rte. Marion 62959, 618-953-8532; 363 S. Main St., Decatur 62521, 217-362-9011; 800 Airport Rd., Mattoon 61938, 217-234-7032; 444 S. Willow St., Effingham 62401, 217-342-7220; and 606 N. 13th St., Lawrenceville 62439, 618-943-6036.

_____

Sen. Larry Pressler (R), Senator from South Dakota

DC Office: 243 Russell Senate Office Building, Washington, DC 20510, 202-224-5842; e-mail: larry_pressler@pressler.senate.gov.

State Offices: 1923 6th Ave., Aberdeen 57402, 605-226-7471; 112 Rushmore Mall, Rapid City 57701, 605-341-1185; and 309 Minnesota Ave., Sioux Falls 57102, 605-335-1990.

_____

Rep. Deborah Pryce (R), Representative from Ohio, District 15

DC Office: 221 Cannon House Office Building, Washington, DC 20515, 202-225-2015; Fax: 202-226-0986.

District Offices: 200 N. High St., Columbus, OH 43215, 614-469-5614.

_____

Sen. David Pryor (D), Senator from Arkansas

DC Office: 267 Russell Senate Office Building, Washington, DC 20510, 202-224-2353; Fax: 202-228-3973.

State Offices: 3030 Fed. Bldg., Little Rock 72201, 501-378-6336.

_____

Rep. James H. (Jimmy) Quillen (R), Representative from Tennessee, District 1

DC Office: 102 Cannon House Office Building, Washington, DC 20515, 202-225-6356; Fax: 202-225-7812.

District Offices: Fed. P.O. Bldg., Kingsport 37662, 615-247-8161.

———————

Rep. Jack Quinn (R), Representative from New York, District 30

DC Office: 331 Cannon House Office Building, Washington, DC 20515, 202-225-3306; Fax: 202-226-0347.

District Offices: 403 Main St., Buffalo 14203, 716-845-5257.

———————

Rep. George P. Radanovich (R), Representative from California, District 19

DC Office: 313 Cannon House Office Building, Washington, DC 20515, 202-225-4540; Fax: 202-225-3402; e-mail: george@hr.house.gov.

District Offices: 2377 W. Shaw, Fresno 93711, 209-248-0800.

———————

Rep. Nick J. Rahall (D), Representative from West Virginia, District 3

DC Office: 2269 Rayburn House Office Building, Washington, DC 20515, 202-225-3452; Fax: 202-225-9061.

District Offices: 110 Main St., Beckley 25801, 304-252-5000; 815 5th Ave., Huntington 25701, 304-522-6425; 1005 Fed. Bldg., Bluefield 24701, 304-325-6222; R.K. Bldg., 45 Washington Ave., Logan 25601, 304-752-4934; and P.O. Box 5, 101 N. Court St., Lewisburg 24901, 304-647-3228.

———————

Rep. Jim Ramstad (IR), Representative from Minnesota, District 3

DC Office: 103 Cannon House Office Building, Washington, DC 20515, 202-225-2871; Fax: 202-225-6351; e-mail: mn03@hr.house.gov.

District Offices: 8120 Penn Ave. S., Bloomington 55431, 612-881-4600.

———————

Rep. Charles B. Rangel (D), Representative from New York, District 15

DC Office: 2354 Rayburn House Office Building, Washington, DC 20515, 202-225-4365; Fax: 202-225-0816.

District Offices: 163 W. 125th St., New York 10027, 212-663-3900; 601 W. 181st St., New York 10033, 212-927-5333; and 2110 1st Ave., New York 10029, 212-348-9830.

———————

Rep. Jack Reed (D), Representative from Rhode Island, District 2

DC Office: 1510 Longworth House Office Building, Washington, DC 20515, 202-225-2735; Fax: 202-225-9580.

District Offices: Garden City Ctr., 100 Midway Place, Cranston 02920, 401-943-3100.

———————

Rep. Ralph S. Regula (R), Representative from Ohio, District 16

DC Office: 2309 Rayburn House Office Building, Washington, DC 20515, 202-225-3876; Fax: 202-225-3059.

District Offices: 4150 Belden Village St., NW, Canton 44718, 216-489-4414.

———————

Sen. Harry Reid (D), Senator from Nevada

DC Office: 324 Hart Senate Office Building, Washington, DC 20510, 202-224-3542; Fax: 202-224-7327; e-mail: senator_reid@reid.senate.gov.

State Offices: 245 E. Liberty St., Reno 89501, 702-784-5568; 500 E. Charleston Blvd., Las Vegas 89104, 702-474-0041; and 600 E. Williams St., Carson City 89701, 702-882-7343.

Rep. Bill Richardson (D), Representative from New Mexico, District 3

DC Office: 2209 Rayburn House Office Building, Washington, DC 20515, 202-225-6190.

District Office: 1494 S. St. Francis Dr., Santa Fe 87505, 505-988-7230; Gallup City Hall, 2d & Aztec, Gallup 87301, 505-722-6522; San Miguel Cnty. Crthse., P.O. Box 1805, Las Vegas 87701, 505-425-7270; and P.O. Box 1108, Clovis 88102, 505-769-3380.

Rep. Frank D. Riggs (R), Representative from California, District 1

DC Office: 1714 Longworth House Office Building, Washington, DC 20515, 202-225-3311; Fax: 202-225-3403; e-mail: repriggs@hr.house.gov.

District Offices: 1700 2nd St., Napa 94559, 707-254-7308; and 710 E St., Eureka 95501, 707-441-8701.

Rep. Lynn N. Rivers (D), Representative from Michigan, District 13

DC Office: 1116 Longworth House Office Building, Washington, DC 20515, 202-225-6261; Fax: 202-225-3404; e-mail: lrivers@hr.house.gov.

District Offices: 106 E. Washington, Ann Arbor 48104, 313-741-4210; 3716 Newberry, Wayne 48184, 313-722-1411.

Sen. Charles S. Robb (D), Senator from Virginia

DC Office: 154 Russell Senate Office Building, Washington, DC 20510, 202-224-4024; Fax: 202-224-8689; e-mail: senator_robb@robb.senator.gov.

State Offices: 1001 E. Broad St., Richmond 23219, 804-771-2221; 310 1st St., SW, Roanoke 24011, 703-985-0103; Signet Bank Bldg., 530 Main St., Danville 24541, 804-791-0330; Dominion Towers, 999 Waterside Dr., Norfolk 23510, 804-441-3124; 8229 Boone Blvd., Vienna 22182, 703-356-2006; and First Union Bank Bldg., Main St., Clintwood 24288, 703-926-4104.

Rep. Pat Roberts (R), Representative from Kansas, District 1

DC Office: 1126 Longworth House Office Building, Washington, DC 20515, 202-225-2715; Fax: 202-225-5375; e-mail: emailpat@hr.house.gov

District Offices: P.O. Box 550, Dodge City 67801, 316-227-2244; P.O. Box 128, Norton 67654, 913-877-2454; P.O. Box 1128, Hutchinson 67502, 316-665-6138; and P.O. Box 1334, Salina 67402, 913-825-5409.

Sen. John D. (Jay) Rockefeller IV (D), Senator from West Virginia

DC Office: 109 Hart Senate Office Building, Washington, DC 20510, 202-224-6472; Fax: 202-224-7665; e-mail: senator@rockefeller.senate.gov.

State Offices: 405 Capitol St., Charleston 25301, 304-347-5372; 115 S. Kanawha St., Beckley 25801, 304-253-9704; and 200 Adams St., Fairmont 26554, 304-367-0122.

Rep. Tim Roemer (D), Representative from Indiana, District 3

DC Office: 407 Cannon House Office Building, Washington, DC 20515, 202-225-3915; Fax: 202-225-6798.

District Offices: 217 N. Main St., South Bend 46601, 219-288-3301.

Rep. Harold D. Rogers (R), Representative from Kentucky, District 5

DC Office: 2468 Rayburn House Office Building, Washington, DC 20515, 202-225-4601; Fax: 202-225-0940.

District Offices: 203 E. Mount Vernon St., Somerset 42501, 606-679-8346; 601 Main St., Hazard 41701, 606-439-0794; and 806 Hambley Blvd., Pikeville 41501, 606-432-4388.

Rep. Dana Rohrabacher (R), Representative from California, District 45

DC Office: 2338 Rayburn House Office Building, Washington, DC 20515, 202-225-2415; Fax: 202-225-0145.

District Offices: 16162 Beach Blvd., Huntington Beach 92647, 714-847-2433.

Rep. Charlie Rose (D), Representative from North Carolina, District 7

DC Office: 242 Cannon House Office Building, Washington, DC 20515, 202-225-2731; Fax: 202-225-0345; e-mail: crose@hr.house.gov.

District Offices: 208 P.O. Bldg., Wilmington 28401, 919-343-4959; and 218 Fed. Bldg., Fayetteville 28301, 919-323-0260.

Rep. Ileana Ros-Lehtinen (R), Representative from Florida, District 18

DC Office: 2440 Rayburn House Office Building, Washington, DC 20515, 202-225-3931; Fax: 202-225-5620.

District Offices: 5757 Blue Lagoon Dr., Miami 33126, 305-262-1800.

Rep. Toby Roth (R), Representative from Wisconsin, District 8

DC Office: 2234 Rayburn House Office Building, Washington, DC 20515, 202-225-5665; Fax: 202-225-0087; e-mail: roth@hr.house.gov.

District Offices: 2301 S. Oneida St., Green Bay 54304, 414-494-2800; and 126 N. Oneida St., Appleton 54911, 414-739-4167.

Sen. William V. Roth, Jr. (R), Senator from Delaware

DC Office: 104 Hart Senate Office Building, Washington, DC 20510, 202-224-2441; Fax: 202-224-0354.

State Offices: 3021 Fed. Bldg., 844 King St., Wilmington 19801, 302-573-6291; 2215 Fed. Bldg., 300 S. New St., Dover 19901, 302-674-3308; and 12 The Circle, Georgetown 19947, 302-856-7690.

Rep. Marge Roukema (R), Representative from New Jersey, District 5

DC Office: 2469 Rayburn House Office Building, Washington, DC 20515, 202-225-4465; Fax: 202-225-9048.

District Offices: 1200 E. Ridgewood Ave., Ridgewood 07450, 201-447-3900; and 1500 Rte. 517, Hackettstown 07840, 908-850-4747.

Rep. Lucille Roybal-Allard (D), Representative from California, District 33

DC Office: 324 Cannon House Office Building, Washington, DC 20515, 202-225-1766.

District Offices: Edward Roybal Fed. Bldg., 255 E. Temple St., Los Angeles 90012, 213-628-9230.

Rep. Edward R. Royce (R), Representative from California, District 39

DC Office: 1133 Longworth House Office Building, Washington, DC 20515, 202-225-4111; Fax: 202-225-0335.

District Offices: 305 N. Harbor Blvd., Fullerton 92632, 714-992-8081.

Rep. Bobby Rush (D), Representative from Illinois, District 1

DC Office: 131 Cannon House Office Building, Washington, DC 20515, 202-225-4372; Fax: 202-226-0333; e-mail: brush@hr.house.gov.

District Offices: 655 E. 79th St., Chicago 60619, 312-224-6500; and 9730 S. Western Ave., Evergreen Park 60643, 708-422-4055.

Rep. Martin Olav Sabo (DFL), Representative from Minnesota, District 5

DC Office: 2336 Rayburn House Office Building, Washington, DC 20515, 202-225-4755.

District Offices: 462 Fed. Courts Bldg., 110 S. 4th St., Minneapolis 55401, 612-348-1649.

Rep. Matt Salmon (R), Representative from Arizona, District 1

DC Office: 115 Cannon House Office Building, Washington, DC 20515, 202-225-2635; Fax: 202-225-3405.

District Offices: 401 W. Baseline Rd., Tempe 85282, 602-831-2900.

Rep. Bernard Sanders (I), Representative from Vermont, District 1

DC Office: 213 Cannon House Office Building, Washington, DC 20515, 202-225-4115; Fax: 202-225-6790; e-mail: bsanders@hr.house.gov

District Offices: 1 Church St., Burlington 05401, 802-862-0697.

———————

Rep. Marshall (Mark) Sanford, Jr. (R), Representative from South Carolina, District 1

DC Office: 1223 Longworth House Office Building, Washington, DC 20515, 202-225-3407; e-mail: sanford@hr.house.gov.

District Offices: 640 Federal Bldg., Charleston 29043, 803-727-4175; 206 Laurel St., Conway 29526, 803-248-2660; 829-E Frost St., Georgetown 29440, 803-527-6868.

———————

Sen. Rick Santorum (R), Senator from Pennsylvania

DC Office: 120 Russell Senate Office Building, Washington, DC 20510, 202-224-6324.

State Offices: 130 Fed. Bldg., Erie 16501, 814-454-7114; 221 Strawberry Sq., Harrisburg 17101, 717-231-7540; 2019 Industrial Dr., Bethlehem 18017, 610-865-1874; 1 S. Penn Sq, Philadelphia 19107, 215-597-9914; 1 Station Sq., Pittsburgh 15219, 412-562-0533, and 527 Linden St., Scranton 18503, 717-344-8799.

———————

Sen. Paul S. Sarbanes (D), Senator from Maryland

DC Office: 309 Hart Senate Office Building, Washington, DC 20510, 202-224-4524; Fax: 202-224-1651: e-mail: senator@sarbanes.senate.gov.

State Offices: 100 S. Charles St., Baltimore 21201, 410-962-4436; 1110 Bonifant St., Silver Spring 20910, 301-589-0797; 111 Baptist St., Salisbury 21801, 410-860-2131; 47 S.E. Crain Hwy., Box 331, Cobb Island 20625, 301-259-2404; and 141 Baltimore St., Cumberland 21502, 301-724-4660.

———————

Rep. Tom Sawyer (D), Representative from Ohio, District 14

DC Office: 1414 Longworth House Office Building, Washington, DC 20515, 202-225-5231; Fax: 202-225-5278.

District Offices: 411 Wolf Ledges Pkwy., Akron 44311, 216-375-5710; and 250 Chestnut St., Ravenna 44266, 216-296-9810.

———————

Rep. H. James Saxton (R), Representative from New Jersey, District 3

DC Office: 339 Cannon House Office Building, Washington, DC 20515, 202-225-4765; Fax: 202-225-0778.

District Offices: 100 High St., Mt. Holly 08060, 609-261-5800; 1 Maine Ave., Cherry Hill 08002, 609-428-0520; and 7 Hadley Ave., Toms River 08753, 908-914-2020.

———————

Rep. Joe Scarborough (R), Representative from Florida, District 1

DC Office: 1523 Longworth House Office Building, Washington, DC 20515, 202-225-4136; Fax: 202-225-3414.

District Offices: 4300 Bayou Blvd., Pensacola 32503, 904-479-1183; and 348 S.W. Miracle Strip Hwy., Ft. Walton Beach 32548, 904-664-1266.

Rep. Dan Schaefer (R), Representative from Colorado, District 6

DC Office: 2353 Rayburn House Office Building, Washington, DC 20515, 202-225-7882; Fax: 202-225-7885; e-mail: schaefer@hr.house.gov.

District Offices: 3615 S. Huron, Englewood 80110, 303-762-8890.

Rep. Steven H. Schiff (R), Representative from New Mexico, District 1

DC Office: 2404 Rayburn House Office Building, Washington, DC 20515, 202-225-6316; Fax: 202-225-4975.

District Offices: 625 Silver Ave. SW, Albuquerque 87102, 505-766-2538.

Rep. Patricia Schroeder (D), Representative from Colorado, District 1

DC Office: 2307 Rayburn House Office Building, Washington, DC 20515, 202-225-4431; Fax: 202-225-5842.

District Offices: 1600 Emerson St., Denver 80218, 303-866-1230.

Rep. Charles E. Schumer (D), Representative from New York, District 9

DC Office: 2211 Rayburn House Office Building, Washington, DC 20515, 202-225-6616; Fax: 202-225-4183.

District Offices: 1628 Kings Hwy., Brooklyn 11229, 718-627-9700.

Rep. Robert C. (Bobby) Scott (D), Representative from Virginia, District 3

DC Office: 501 Cannon House Office Building, Washington, DC 20515, 202-225-8351; Fax: 202-225-8354.

District Offices: 2700 Washington Ave., Newport News 23607, 804-380-1000.

Rep. Andrea Seastrand (R), Representative from California, District 22

DC Office: 320 Cannon House Office Building, Washington, DC 20515, 202-225-3601; Fax: 202-225-3426; e-mail: andrea22@hr.house.gov.

District Offices: 1525 State St., Santa Barbara 93101, 805-899-3578; and 778 Osos St., San Luis Obispo 93401, 805-541-0170.

Rep. F. James Sensenbrenner, Jr. (R), Representative from Wisconsin, District 9

DC Office: 2332 Rayburn House Office Building, Washington, DC 20515, 202-225-5101; Fax: 202-225-3190.

District Offices: 120 Bishops Way, Brookfield 53005, 414-784-1111.

Rep. Jose E. Serrano (D), Representative from New York, District 16

DC Office: 2342 Rayburn House Office Building, Washington, DC 20515, 202-225-4361; Fax: 202-225-6001; e-mail: jserrano@hr.house.gov.

District Offices: 890 Grand Concourse, Bronx 10451, 718-538-5400.

―――――――

Rep. John Shadegg (R), Representative from Arizona, District 4

DC Office: 503 Cannon House Office Building, Washington, DC 20515, 202-225-3361; Fax: 202-225-3462.

District Offices: 1158 E. Missouri Ave., Phoenix 85014, 602-248-7779.

―――――――

Rep. E. Clay Shaw, Jr. (R), Representative from Florida, District 22

DC Office: 2267 Rayburn House Office Building, Washington, DC 20515, 202-225-3026; Fax: 202-225-8398.

District Offices: 1512 E. Broward Blvd., Ft. Lauderdale 33301, 305-522-1800.

―――――――

Rep. Christopher Shays (R), Representative from Connecticut, District 4

DC Office: 1502 Longworth House Office Building, Washington, DC 20515, 202-225-5541; Fax: 202-225-9629; e-mail: cshays@hr.house.gov.

District Offices: 10 Middle St., Bridgeport 06604, 203-579-5870; 888 Washington Blvd., Stamford 06901, 203-357-8277.

―――――――

Sen. Richard C. Shelby (R), Senator from Alabama

DC Office: 110 Hart Senate Office Building, Washington, DC 20510, 202-224-5744; Fax: 202-224-3416.

State Offices: 113 St. Joseph St., 438 U.S. Crthse., Mobile 36602, 334-694-4164; 1000 Glenn Hearn Blvd., Huntsville 35824, 205-772-0460; 1800 5th Ave., N., 321 Fed. Bldg., Birmingham 35203, 205-731-1384; 15 Lee St., 828 U.S. Crthse., Montgomery 36104, 334-223-7303; and 118 Greensboro Ave., Tuscaloosa 35401, 205-759-5047.

―――――――

Rep. E. G. (Bud) Shuster (R), Representative from Pennsylvania, District 9

DC Office: 2188 Rayburn House Office Building, Washington, DC 20515, 202-225-2431.

District Offices: RD 2, Box 711, Altoona 16601, 814-946-1653; and 179 E. Queen St., Chambersburg 17201, 717-264-8308; 1214 Oldtown Rd., Clearfield 16830, 814-765-9106.

―――――――

Sen. Paul Simon (D), Senator from Illinois

DC Office: 462 Dirksen Senate Office Building, Washington, DC 20510, 202-224-2152; Fax: 202-224-0868; e-mail: senator@simon.senate.gov.

State Offices: Kluczynski Bldg., 230 S. Dearborn, Chicago 60604, 312-353-4952; 3 W. Old Capital Plz., Springfield 62701, 217-492-4960; and 250 W. Cherry, Carbondale 62901, 618-457-3653.

―――――――

Sen. Alan K. Simpson (R), Senator from Wyoming

DC Office: 105 Dirksen Senate Office Building, Washington, DC 20510, 202-224-3424; Fax: 202-224-1315; e-mail: senator@simpson.senate.gov.

State Offices: P.O. Box 430, Cody 82414, 307-527-7121; Fed. Ctr., Casper 82601, 307-261-5172; Fed. Ctr., Cheyenne 82001, 307-772-2477; 2201 S. Douglas Hwy., P.O. Box 3155, Gillette 82716, 307-682-7091; 2020 Grand Ave., Laramie 82070, 307-745-5303; 2515 Foothills Blvd., Rock Springs 82901, 307-382-5097; and 1731 Sheridan Ave., Cody 82414, 307-527-7121.

Rep. Norman Sisisky (D), Representative from Virginia, District 4

DC Office: 2371 Rayburn House Office Building, Washington, DC 20515, 202-225-6365; Fax: 202-226-1170.

District Offices: Emporia Exec. Ctr., 425-H S. Main St., Emporia 23847, 804-634-5575; 43 Rives Rd., Petersburg 23805, 804-732-2544; and 309 County St., Portsmouth 23704, 804-393-2068.

Rep. David E. Skaggs (D), Representative from Colorado, District 2

DC Office: 1124 Longworth House Office Building, Washington, DC 20515, 202-225-2161; Fax: 202-225-7840; e-mail: skaggs@hr.house.gov.

District Offices: 9101 Harlan, Westminster 80030, 303-650-7886.

Rep. Joe Skeen (R), Representative from New Mexico, District 2

DC Office: 2367 Rayburn House Office Building, Washington, DC 20515, 202-225-2365; Fax: 202-225-9599.

District Offices: 1065 S. Main St., Las Cruces 88005, 505-527-1771; and 257 Fed. Bldg., Roswell 88201, 505-622-0055.

Rep. Ike Skelton (D), Representative from Missouri, District 4

DC Office: 2227 Rayburn House Office Building, Washington, DC 20515, 202-225-2876.

District Offices: 1616 Industrial Dr., Jefferson City 65109, 314-635-3499; 514-B N.W. 7 Hwy., Blue Springs 64014, 816-228-4242; 319 S. Lamine, Sedalia 65301, 816-826-2675; and 219 N. Adams St., Lebanon 65536, 417-532-7964.

Rep. Louise M. Slaughter (D), Representative from New York, District 28

DC Office: 2347 Rayburn House Office Building, Washington, DC 20515, 202-225-3615; Fax: 202-225-7822.

District Offices: 3120 Fed. Bldg., 100 State St., Rochester 14614, 716-232-4850.

Rep. Linda Smith (R), Representative from Washington, District 3

DC Office: 1217 Longworth House Office Building, Washington, DC 20515, 202-225-3536; Fax: 202-225-3478; e-mail: asklinda@hr.house.gov.

District Office : 1220 Main St., Vancouver 98660, 360-695-6292; and 719 Sleater-Kinney Rd., Lacey 98503, 360-923-9393.

Rep. Nick Smith (R), Representative from Michigan, District 7

DC Office: 1530 Longworth House Office Building, Washington, DC 20515, 202-225-6276; Fax: 202-225-6281; e-mail: mi107.smith@hr.house.gov.

District Offices: 121 S. Cochran Ave., Charlotte 48813, 517-543-0055; 209 E. Washington St., Jackson 49201, 517-783-4486; 4192 W. Maple St., Adrian 49221, 517-263-5012; and 81 S. 20th St., Battle Creek 29015, 616-965-9066.

_____

Rep. Christopher H. Smith (R), Representative from New Jersey, District 4

DC Office: 2370 Rayburn House Office Building, Washington, DC 20515, 202-225-3765; Fax: 202-225-7768.

District Offices: 1720 Greenwood, Trenton 08609, 609-890-2800; 427 High St., Burlington City 08016, 609-386-5534; and 100 Lacey Rd., Whiting 08759, 908-350-2300.

_____

Sen. Bob Smith (R), Senator from New Hampshire

DC Office: 332 Dirksen Senate Office Building, Washington, DC 20510, 202-224-2841; Fax: 202-224-1353; e-mail: opinion@smith.senate.gov.

State Offices: 50 Phillippe Cote St., Manchester 03101, 603-634-5000; 46 S. Main St., Concord 03301, 603-228-0453; and 1 Harbour Pl., Portsmouth 03801, 603-433-1667.

_____

Rep. Lamar S. Smith (R), Representative from Texas, District 21

DC Office: 2443 Rayburn House Office Building, Washington, DC 20515, 202-225-4236; Fax: 202-225-8628.

District Offices: 1st Federal Bldg., 1100 NE Loop 410, San Antonio 78209, 210-821-5024; 201 W. Wall St., Midland 79701, 915-687-5232; 1006 Junction Hwy., Kerrville 78028, 512-895-1414; 221 E. Main, Round Rock 78664, 512-218-4221; and 33 E. Twohig, San Angelo 76903, 915-653-3971.

_____

Sen. Olympia J. Snowe (R), Senator from Maine

DC Office: 495 Russell Senate Office Building, Washington, DC 20510, 202-224-5344; Fax: 202-224-1946.

State Offices: 2 Great Falls Plz., Auburn 04210, 207-786-2451; 68 Sewall St., Augusta 04330, 207-622-8292; 1 Cumberland Pl., Bangor 04401, 207-945-0432; 231 Main St., Biddeford 04005, 207-282-4144; 3 Canal Plz., Portland 04112, 207-874-0833; and 169 Academy St., Presque Isle 04769, 207-764-5124.

_____

Rep. Gerald B. H. Solomon (R), Representative from New York, District 22

DC Office: 2206 Rayburn House Office Building, Washington, DC 20515, 202-225-5614; Fax: 202-225-6234.

District Offices: Gaslight Sq., Saratoga Springs 12866, 518-587-9800; 337 Fairview Ave., Hudson 12534, 518-828-0181; and 21 Bay St., Glens Falls 12801, 518-792-3031.

_____

Rep. Mark Edward Souder (R), Representative from Indiana, District 4

DC Office: 508 Cannon House Office Building, Washington, DC 20515, 202-225-4436; Fax: 202-225-3479; e-mail: souder@hr.house.gov.

District Offices: 1300 S. Harrison St., Ft. Wayne 46802, 219-424-3041.

_____

Sen. Arlen Specter (R), Senator from Pennsylvania

DC Office: 530 Hart Senate Office Building, Washington, DC 20510, 202-224-4254; e-mail: senator_specter@specter.senate.gov.

State Offices: 600 Arch Street, Philadelphia 19106, 215-597-7200; Fed. Bldg., Liberty Ave. & Grant St., Pittsburgh 15222, 412-644-3400; 1159 Fed. Bldg., 6th & State Sts., Erie 16501, 814-453-3010; 1159 Fed. Bldg, Harrisburg 17101, 717-782-3951; Park Plaza, Scranton 18503, 717-346-2006; and P.O. Bldg., 5th & Hamilton Sts., Allentown 18101, 610-434-1444.

_____

Rep. Floyd D. Spence (R), Representative from South Carolina, District 2

DC Office: 2405 Rayburn House Office Building, Washington, DC 20515, 202-225-2452; Fax: 202-225-2455.

District Offices: 220 Stoneridge Dr., Columbia 29210, 803-254-5120; 1681 Chestnut St., P.O. Box 1609, NE Orangeburg 29115, 803-536-4641; 66 E. Railroad Ave., P.O. Box 550, Estill 29918, 803-625-3177; 807 Port Republic St., P.O. Box 1538, Beaufort 29901, 803-521-2530; 1 Town Center Ct., Hilton Head Island 29928, 803-842-7212.

_____

Rep. John M. Spratt, Jr. (D), Representative from South Carolina, District 5

DC Office: 1536 Longworth House Office Building, Washington, DC 20515, 202-225-5501; Fax: 202-225-0464; e-mail: spratt@hr.house.gov.

District Offices: 305 Fed. Bldg., Rock Hill 29731, 803-327-1114; 39 E. Calhoun St., Sumter 29150, 803-773-3362; and 88 Public Sq., Darlington 29532, 803-393-3998.

_____

Rep. Fortney H. (Pete) Stark (D), Representative from California, District 13

DC Office: 239 Cannon House Office Building, Washington, DC 20515, 202-225-5065; e-mail: petemail@hr.house.gov.

District Offices: 22320 Foothill Blvd., Hayward 94541, 510-247-1388.

_____

Rep. Clifford B. Stearns (R), Representative from Florida, District 6

DC Office: 2352 Rayburn House Office Building, Washington, DC 20515, 202-225-5744; Fax: 202-225-3973; e-mail: cstearns@hr.house.gov.

District Offices: 115 S.E. 25th Ave., Ocala 34471, 904-351-8777; 1726 Kingsley Ave., Orange Park 32073, 904-269-3203; and 111 S. 6th St., Leesburg 34748, 904-326-8285.

_____

Rep. Charles W. Stenholm (D), Representative from Texas, District 17

DC Office: 1211 Longworth House Office Building, Washington, DC 20515, 202-225-6605; Fax: 202-225-2234.

District Offices: 903 E. Hamilton St., Stamford 79553, 915-773-3623; 341 Pine St., Abilene 79604, 915-673-7221; and 33 E. Twohig Ave., San Angelo 76903, 915-655-7994.

_____

Sen. Ted Stevens (R), Senator from Alaska

DC Office: 522 Hart Senate Office Building, Washington, DC 20510, 202-224-3004; Fax: 202-224-2354.

State Offices: Fed. Bldg., Box 4, 101 12th Ave., Fairbanks 99701, 907-456-0261; 222 W. 7th Ave., Anchorage 99513, 907-271-5915; Fed. Bldg., Box 020149, Juneau 99802, 907-586-7400; 120 Trading Bay Rd., Kenai 99611, 907-283-5808; and 109 Main St., Ketchikan 99901, 907-225-6880.

————————

Rep. Steve Stockman (R), Representative from Texas, District 9

DC Office: 417 Cannon House Office Building, Washington, DC 20515, 202-225-6565; Fax: 202-225-1584.

District Offices: 2490 McFadin, Beaumont 77702, 409-838-0061; and 2102 Mechanic, Galveston 77550, 409-766-3608.

————————

Rep. Louis Stokes (D), Representative from Ohio, District 11

DC Office: 2365 Rayburn House Office Building, Washington, DC 20515, 202-225-7032; Fax: 202-225-1339.

District Offices: 3645 Warrensville Ctr. Rd., Shaker Heights 44122, 216-522-4900.

————————

Rep. Gerry E. Studds (D), Representative from Massachusetts, District 10

DC Office: 237 Cannon House Office Building, Washington, DC 20515, 202-225-3111; Fax: 202-225-2212.

District Offices: 1212 Hancock St., Quincy 02169, 617-770-3700; 146 Main St., Hyannis 02601, 508-771-0666; 166 Main St., Fed. Bldg., Brockton 02401, 508-584-6666; and 225 Water St., Plymouth 02360, 508-747-5500.

————————

Rep. Bob Stump (R), Representative from Arizona, District 3

DC Office: 211 Cannon House Office Building, Washington, DC 20515, 202-225-4576; Fax: 202-225-6328.

District Offices: 230 N. First Ave., Phoenix 85025, 602-379-6923.

————————

Rep. Bart Stupak (D), Representative from Michigan, District 1

DC Office: 317 Cannon House Office Building, Washington, DC 20515, 202-225-4735; Fax: 202-225-4744.

District Offices: 1120 E. Front St., Traverse City 49686, 616-929-4711; 111 E. Chisholm St., Alpena 49707, 517-356-0690; 1229 W. Washington St., Marquette 49855, 906-228-3700; 2501 14th Ave., Escanaba 49829, 906-786-4504; and 616 Sheldon Ave., Houghton 49931, 906-482-1371.

————————

Rep. Jim Talent (R), Representative from Missouri, District 2

DC Office: 1022 Longworth House Office Building, Washington, DC 20515, 202-225-2561; Fax: 202-225-2563; e-mail: talentmo@hr.house.gov.

District Offices: 555 N. New Balas, St. Louis 63141, 314-872-9561; and 820 S. Main St., St. Charles 63301, 314-949-6826.

————————

Rep. John Tanner (D), Representative from Tennessee, District 8

DC Office: 1127 Longworth House Office Building, Washington, DC 20515, 202-225-4714; Fax: 202-225-1765.

District Offices: 203 W. Church St., Union City 38261, 901-885-7070; Fed. Bldg., Jackson 38301, 901-423-4848; and 2836 Coleman Rd., Memphis 38128, 901-382-3220.

Rep. Randy Tate (R), Representative from Washington, District 9

DC Office: 1118 Longworth House Office Building, Washington, DC 20515, 202-225-8901; Fax: 202-225-3484; e-mail: rtate@hr.house.gov.

District Offices: 33305 1st Way, S., Federal Way 98003, 206-661-1459; and 10925 Canyon Rd., Puyallup 98373, 206-539-1322.

Rep. W. J. (Billy) Tauzin (R), Representative from Louisiana, District 3

DC Office: 2183 Rayburn House Office Building, Washington, DC 20515, 202-225-4031; Fax: 202-225-0563.

District Offices: 1041 Hale Boggs Bldg., 501 Magazine St., New Orleans 70130, 504-589-6366; 107 Fed. Bldg., Houma 700360, 504-876-3033; 210 E. Main St., New Iberia 70560, 318-367-8231; and 828 S. Irma Blvd., Gonzales 70737, 504-621-8490.

Rep. Gene Taylor (D), Representative from Mississippi, District 5

DC Office: 2447 Rayburn House Office Building, Washington, DC 20515, 202-225-5772; Fax: 202-225-7074.

District Offices: 2424 14th St., Gulfport 39501, 601-864-7670; 701 Main St., Hattiesburg 39401, 601-582-3246; and 706 Watts Ave., Pascagoula 39567, 601-762-1770.

Rep. Charles H. Taylor (R), Representative from North Carolina, District 11

DC Office: 231 Cannon House Office Building, Washington, DC 20515, 202-225-6401; Fax: 202-225-0519; e-mail: chtaylor@hr.house.gov.

District Offices: 22 S. Pack Sq., Asheville 28801, 704-251-1988; Cherokee Cnty. Cthse., 201 Peachtree St., Murphy 28906, 704-837-3249; and 200 S. Lafayette St., Shelby 28150, 704-484-6971.

Rep. Frank M. Tejeda (D), Representative from Texas, District 28

DC Office: 323 Cannon House Office Building, Washington, DC 20515, 202-225-1640; Fax: 202-225-1641.

District Offices: 1313 SE Military Dr., San Antonio 78214, 210-924-7383; and 202 E. St. Joseph St., San Diego 78384, 512-279-3907.

Sen. Craig Thomas (R), Senator from Wyoming

DC Office: 302 Hart Senate Office Building, Washington, DC 20510, 202-224-6441; Fax: 202-224-1724.

State Offices:2201 Fed. Bldg., Casper 82601, 307-261-5413; 2120 Capitol Ave., Cheyenne 82009, 307-772-2451; 2632 Foothills Blvd., Rock Springs 82901, 307-362-5012; and 325 W. Main St., Riverton 82501, 307-856-6642.

Rep. William M. Thomas (R), Representative from California, District 21

DC Office: 2208 Rayburn House Office Building, Washington, DC 20515, 202-225-2915; Fax: 202-225-2908.

District Offices: 4100 Truxtun Ave., Bakersfield 93309, 805-327-3611; and 319 W. Murray St., Visalia 93291, 209-627-6549.

Rep. Bennie G. Thompson (D), Representative from Mississippi, District 2

DC Office: 1408 Longworth House Office Building, Washington, DC 20515, 202-225-5876; Fax: 202-225-5898; e-mail: ms2nd@hr.house.gov.

District Offices: 137 Madison St., Bolton 39041, 601-859-5555.

Sen. Fred Thompson (R), Senator from Tennessee

DC Office: 523 Dirksen Senate Office Building, Washington, DC 20510, 202-224-4944; Fax: 202-228-3679.

State Office: 3322 West End Ave., Nashville 37230, 615-736-5129; 403 Fed. Bldg., 167 N. Main St., Memphis 38103, 901-544-4224; 315 Post Office Bldg., 501 Main St., Knoxville 37902, 615-545-4253; B-9 Fed. Bldg., 109 S. Highland St., Jackson 38301, 901-423-9344.

Rep. Mac Thornberry (R), Representative from Texas, District 13

DC Office: 1535 Longworth House Office Building, Washington, DC 20515, 202-225-3706; Fax: 202-225-3486.

District Offices: 724 S. Polk St., Amarillo 79101, 806-371-8844; and 811 6th St., Wichita Falls 76301, 817-767-0541.

Rep. Ray Thornton (D), Representative from Arkansas, District 2

DC Office: 1214 Longworth House Office Building, Washington, DC 20515, 202-225-2506; Fax: 202-225-9273.

District Offices: 1527 Fed. Bldg., 700 W. Capitol, Little Rock 72201, 501-324-5941.

Rep. Karen L. Thurman (D), Representative from Florida, District 5

DC Office: 130 Cannon House Office Building, Washington, DC 20515, 202-225-1002; Fax: 202-226-0329; e-mail: kthuman@hr.house.gov.

District Offices: 2224 Hwy. 44 W., Inverness 34453, 904-344-3044; 5700 SW 34th St., Gainesville 32608, 904-336-6614; and 5623 Rte. 19 S., New Port Richey 34652, 813-849-4496.

Sen. Strom Thurmond (R), Senator from South Carolina

DC Office: 217 Russell Senate Office Building, Washington, DC 20510, 202-224-5972; Fax: 202-224-1300.

State Offices: 1835 Assembly St., Columbia 29201, 803-765-5494; 334 Meeting St., Charleston 29493, 803-724-4282; 211 York St. NE, Aiken 29801, 803-649-2591; and 401 W. Evans St., Florence 29501, 803-662-8873.

———————

Rep. Todd Tiahrt (R), Representative from Kansas, District 4

DC Office: 1319 Longworth House Office Building, Washington, DC 20515, 202-225-6216; Fax: 202-225-3489.

District Offices: 155 N. Market, Wichita 67202, 316-262-8992; and 325 N. Penn, Independence 67301, 316-331-8056.

———————

Rep. Peter G. Torkildsen (R), Representative from Massachusetts, District 6

DC Office: 120 Cannon House Office Building, Washington, DC 20515, 202-225-8020; Fax: 202-225-8037; e-mail: torkma06@hr.house.gov.

District Offices: 70 Washington St., Salem 01970, 508-741-1600; 156 Broad St., Lynn 01901, 617-599-2424; 160 Main St., Haverhill 01830, 508-521-0111; and 61 Center St., Burlington 01803, 617-273-4900.

———————

Rep. Esteban E. Torres (D), Representative from California, District 34

DC Office: 2368 Rayburn House Office Building, Washington, DC 20515, 202-225-5256; Fax: 202-225-9711.

District Offices: 8819 Whittier Blvd., Pico Rivera 90660, 310-695-0702.

———————

Rep. Robert G. Torricelli (D), Representative from New Jersey, District 9

DC Office: 1026 Rayburn House Office Building, Washington, DC 20515, 202-225-5061; Fax: 202-225-0845.

District Offices: 25 Main St., Court Plz., Hackensack 07601, 201-646-1111.

———————

Rep. Edolphus Towns (D), Representative from New York, District 10

DC Office: 2232 Rayburn House Office Building, Washington, DC 20515, 202-225-5936; Fax: 202-225-1018.

District Offices: 545 Broadway, Brooklyn 11206, 718-387-8696.

———————

Rep. James A. Traficant, Jr. (D), Representative from Ohio, District 17

DC Office: 2446 Rayburn House Office Building, Washington, DC 20515, 202-225-5261; Fax: 202-225-3719.

District Offices: 125 Market St., Youngstown 44503, 216-743-1914; 5555 Youngstown-Warren Rd., Niles 44406, 216-652-5649; and 109 W. 3d St., E. Liverpool 43920, 216-385-5921.

———————

Rep. Walter R. Tucker, III (D), Representative from California, District 37

DC Office: 419 Cannon House Office Building, Washington, DC 20515, 202-225-7924; Fax: 202-225-7926; e-mail: tucker96@hr.house.gov.

District Offices: 145 E. Compton Blvd., Compton 90220, 310-884-9989.

———————

Rep. Fred Upton (R), Representative from Michigan, District 6

DC Office: 2333 Rayburn House Office Building, Washington, DC 20515, 202-225-3761; Fax: 202-225-4986.

District Offices: 421 Main St., St. Joseph 49085, 616-982-1986; and 535 S. Burdick St., Kalamazoo 49007, 616-385-0039.

———————

Rep. Nydia M. Velazquez (D), Representative from New York, District 12

DC Office: 132 Cannon House Office Building, Washington, DC 20515, 202-225-2361; Fax: 202-226-0327.

District Offices: 815 Broadway, Brooklyn 11206, 718-599-3658.

———————

Rep. Bruce F. Vento (DFL), Representative from Minnesota, District 4

DC Office: 2304 Rayburn House Office Building, Washington, DC 20515, 202-225-6631; Fax: 202-225-1968; e-mail: vento@hr.house.gov.

District Offices: 175 5th St. E., Box 100, St. Paul 55101, 612-224-4503.

———————

Rep. Peter J. Visclosky (D), Representative from Indiana, District 1

DC Office: 2464 Rayburn House Office Building, Washington, DC 20515, 202-225-2461; Fax: 202-225-2493.

District Offices: 215 W. 35th Ave., Gary 46408, 219-884-1177; City Hall, 6070 Central Ave., Portage 46368, 219-763-2904; and City Hall, 166 Lincolnway, Valparaiso 46383, 219-464-0315.

———————

Rep. Harold L. Volkmer (D), Representative from Missouri, District 9

DC Office: 2409 Rayburn House Office Building, Washington, DC 20515, 202-225-2956; Fax: 202-225-7834.

District Offices: 370 Fed. Bldg., Hannibal 63401, 314-221-1200.

———————

Rep. Barbara F. Vucanovich (R), Representative from Nevada, District 2

DC Office: 2202 Rayburn House Office Building, Washington, DC 20515, 202-225-6155; Fax: 202-225-2319.

District Offices: 300 Booth St., Reno 89509, 702-784-5003; 700 Idaho St., Elko 89801, 702-738-4064; and 6900 Westcliff St., Las Vegas 89128, 702-255-6470.

———————

Rep. Enid G. Waldholtz (R), Representative from Utah, District 2

DC Office: 515 Cannon House Office Building, Washington, DC 20515, 202-225-3011; Fax: 202-225-3491; e-mail: enidutah@hr.house.gov.

District Offices: 125 S. State St., Salt Lake City 84138, 801-524-4394.

———————

Rep. Robert S. Walker (R), Representative from Pennsylvania, District 16

DC Office: 2369 Rayburn House Office Building, Washington, DC 20515, 202-225-2411; Fax: 202-225-1116; e-mail: pa16@hr.house.gov.

District Offices: Lancaster Cnty. Crthse., 50 N. Duke St., Lancaster 17603, 717-393-0666; Exton Commons, Exton 19341, 215-363-8409.

_____

Rep. James T. Walsh (R), Representative from New York, District 25

DC Office: 1330 Longworth House Office Building, Washington, DC 20515, 202-225-3701; Fax: 202-225-4042.

District Offices: P.O. Box 7306, Syracuse 13261, 315-423-5657; and 1 Lincoln St., Auburn 13021, 315-255-0649.

_____

Rep. Zach Wamp (R), Representative from Tennessee, District 3

DC Office: 423 Cannon House Office Building, Washington, DC 20515, 202-225-3271; Fax: 202-225-3494.

District Offices: 6100 Eastgate Ctr., Chattanooga 37411, 615-894-7400; and 55 Jefferson Cir., Oak Ridge 37830, 615-483-3366.

_____

Rep. Mike Ward (D), Representative from Kentucky, District 3

DC Office: 1032 Longworth House Office Building, Washington, DC 20515, 202-225-5401; Fax: 202-225-3511; e-mail: mward2@hr.house.gov.

District Offices: 216 Fed. Bldg., 600 M.L.K. Jr. Pl., Louisville 40202, 502-582-5129.

_____

Sen. John W. Warner (R), Senator from Virginia

DC Office: 225 Russell Senate Office Building, Washington, DC 20510, 202-224-2023; Fax: 202-224-6295; e-mail: senator@warner.senate.gov.

State Offices: 600 E. Main St., Richmond 23219, 804-771-2579; 4900 World Trade Ctr., Norfolk 23510, 804-441-3079; 235 Fed. Bldg., 180 W. Main St., Abingdon 24210, 703-628-8158; and 1003 First Union Bank Bldg., 213 S. Jefferson St., Roanoke 24011, 703-857-2676.

_____

Rep. Maxine Waters (D), Representative from California, District 35

DC Office: 330 Cannon House Office Building, Washington, DC 20515, 202-225-2201; Fax: 202-225-7854.

District Offices: 10124 S. Broadway, Los Angeles 90003, 213-757-8900.

_____

Rep. Melvin L. Watt (D), Representative from North Carolina, District 12

DC Office: 1230 Longworth House Office Building, Washington, DC 20515, 202-225-1510; Fax: 202-225-1512; e-mail: melmail@hr.house.gov.

District Offices: 214 N. Church St., Charlotte 28202, 704-344-9950; 315 E. Chapel Hill, Durham 27702, 919-688-3004; 301 S. Greene St., Greensboro 27401, 919-375-9402.

_____

Rep. J. C. Watts, Jr. (R), Representative from Oklahoma, District 4

DC Office: 1713 Longworth House Office Building, Washington, DC 20515, 202-225-6165; Fax: 202-225-3512.

District Offices: 2420 Springer Dr., Norman 73069, 405-329-6500; and 601 S.W. D Ave., Lawton 73501, 405-357-2131.

_____

Rep. Henry A. Waxman (D), Representative from California, District 29

DC Office: 2408 Rayburn House Office Building, Washington, DC 20515, 202-225-3976; Fax: 202-225-4099.

District Offices: 8425 W. 3d St., Los Angeles 90048, 213-651-1040.

_____

Rep. David J. Weldon (R), Representative from Florida, District 15

DC Office: 216 Cannon House Office Building, Washington, DC 20515, 202-225-3671; Fax: 202-225-3516; e-mail: fla15@hr.house.gov.

District Offices: 2725 St. John St., P.O. Box 410007, Melbourne 32941, 407-632-1776.

_____

Rep. Curt Weldon (R), Representative from Pennsylvania, District 7

DC Office: 2452 Rayburn House Office Building, Washington, DC 20515, 202-225-2011; Fax: 202-225-8137; e-mail: curtpa7@hr.house.gov.

District Offices: 1554 Garrett Rd., Upper Darby 19082, 610-259-0700.

_____

Rep. Jerry Weller (R), Representative from Illinois, District 11

DC Office: 1710 Longworth House Office Building, Washington, DC 20515, 202-225-3635.

District Offices: 51 W. Jackson St., Joliet 60432, 815-740-2028; 3331 Chicago Rd., Steger 60475, 708-754-7552; and 628 Columbus St., Ottawa 61350, 815-433-0085.

_____

Sen. Paul D. Wellstone (DFL), Senator from Minnesota

DC Office: 717 Hart Senate Office Building, Washington, DC 20510, 202-224-5641; Fax: 202-224-8438; e-mail: senator@wellstone.senate.gov.

State Offices: 2550 University Ave., St. Paul 55114, 612-645-0323; 105 2nd Ave., S., Virginia 55792, 218-741-1074; and 417 Litchfield Ave., SW, Wilmar 56201, 612-231-0001.

_____

Rep. Rick White (R), Representative from Washington, District 1

DC Office: 116 Cannon House Office Building, Washington, DC 20515, 202-225-6311; Fax: 202-225-3524; e-mail: repwhite@hr.house.gov.

District Offices: 21905 64th Ave., Mountlake Terrace 98043, 206-640-0233.

_____

Rep. Edward Whitfield (R), Representative from Kentucky, District 1

DC Office: 1541 Longworth House Office Building, Washington, DC 20515, 202-225-3115; Fax: 202-225-3547; e-mail: edky01@hr.house.gov.

District Offices: 317 W. 9th St., Hopkinsville 42204, 502-885-0879; P.O. Box 717, Monroe Cnty. Courthouse, Tompkinsville 42617, 502-487-9509; 222 First St., Henderson 42420, 502-826-4180; and 100 Fountain Ave., Paducah 42001, 502-442-6901.

Rep. Roger F. Wicker (R), Representative from Mississippi, District 1

DC Office: 206 Cannon House Office Building, Washington, DC 20515, 202-225-4306; Fax: 202-225-3549; e-mail: rwicker@hr.house.gov.

District Offices: 500 W. Main St., Tupelo 38802, 601-844-5437; and 8625 Hwy. 51-N, Southaven 38671, 601-342-3942.

Rep. Pat Williams (D), Representative from Montana, District 1

DC Office: 2329 Rayburn House Office Building, Washington, DC 20515, 202-225-3211.

District Offices: 316 N. Park Ave., P.O. Box 1681, Helena 59624, 406-443-7878; 305 W. Mercury, Butte 59701, 406-723-4404; 302 W. Broadway, Missoula 59802, 406-549-5550; 2806 3rd Ave. N., Billings 59101, 406-256-1019; and 325 2nd Ave. N., Great Falls 59401, 406-771-1242.

Rep. Charles Wilson (D), Representative from Texas, District 2

DC Office: 2256 Rayburn House Office Building, Washington, DC 20515, 202-225-2401; Fax: 202-225-1764; e-mail: cwilson@hr.house.gov.

District Offices: 701 N. 1st St., Lufkin 75901, 409-637-1770.

Rep. Robert E. (Bob) Wise, Jr. (D), Representative from West Virginia, District 2

DC Office: 2434 Rayburn House Office Building, Washington, DC 20515, 202-225-2711; Fax: 202-225-7856.

District Offices: Elk Office Ctr., 4710 Chimney Dr., Charleston 25302, 304-342-7170; and 222 W. John St., Martinsburg 25401, 304-264-8810.

Rep. Frank R. Wolf (R), Representative from Virginia, District 10

DC Office: 241 Cannon House Office Building, Washington, DC 20515, 202-225-5136; Fax: 202-225-0437.

District Offices: 13873 Park Center Rd., Herndon 22075, 703-709-5800; and 110 N. Cameron St., Winchester 22601, 703-667-0990.

Rep. Lynn Woolsey (D), Representative from California, District 6

DC Office: 439 Cannon House Office Building, Washington, DC 20515, 202-225-5161; e-mail: woolsey@hr.house.gov.

District Offices: 1101 College Ave., Santa Rosa 95404, 707-542-7182; and 1050 Northgate Dr., San Rafael 94903, 415-507-9554.

Rep. Ron Wyden (D), Representative from Oregon, District 3

DC Office: 1111 Longworth House Office Building, Washington, DC 20515, 202-225-4811; Fax: 202-225-8941.

District Offices: 500 NE Multnomah, Portland 97232, 503-231-2300.

———————

Rep. Albert R. Wynn (D), Representative from Maryland, District 4

DC Office: 418 Cannon House Office Building, Washington, DC 20515, 202-225-8699; Fax: 202-225-8714.

District Offices: 9200 Basil Ct., Landover 20785, 301-773-4094; 6009 Oxon Hill Rd., Oxon Hill 20745, 301-839-5570; and 8061 Georgia Ave., Silver Spring 20910, 301-558-7328.

———————

Rep. Sidney R. Yates (D), Representative from Illinois, District 9

DC Office: 2109 Rayburn House Office Building, Washington, DC 20515, 202-225-2111; Fax: 202-225-3493.

District Offices: 230 S. Dearborn St., Chicago 60604, 312-353-4596; and 2100 Ridge Ave., Evanston, 60204, 708-328-2610.

———————

Rep. Don Young (R), Representative from Alaska, District 1

DC Office: 2331 Rayburn House Office Building, Washington, DC 20515, 202-225-5765; Fax: 202-225-0425.

District Offices: 222 W. 7th Ave., Anchorage 99513, 907-271-5978; 401 Fed. Bldg., Box 1247, Juneau 99802, 907-586-7400; Fed. Bldg., Box 10, 101 12th Ave., Fairbanks 99701, 907-456-0210; and 109 Main St., Ketchikan 99901, 907-225-6880.

———————

Rep. C. W. (Bill) Young (R), Representative from Florida, District 10

DC Office: 2407 Rayburn House Office Building, Washington, DC 20515, 202-225-5961; Fax: 202-225-9764.

District Offices: 627 Fed. Bldg., St. Petersburg 33701, 813-893-3191.

———————

Rep. William H. Zeliff, Jr. (R), Representative from New Hampshire, District 1

DC Office: 1210 Longworth House Office Building, Washington, DC 20515, 202-225-5456; Fax: 202-225-4370; e-mail: zeliff@hr.house.gov.

District Offices: 340 Commercial St., Manchester 03101, 603-669-6330; and 601 Spaulding Tnpk., Portsmouth 03801, 603-433-1601.

———————

Rep. Dick Zimmer (R), Representative from New Jersey, District 12

DC Office: 228 Cannon House Office Building, Washington, DC 20515, 202-225-5801; Fax: 202-225-9181; e-mail: dzimmer@hr.house.gov.

District Offices: 133 Franklin Corner Rd., Lawrenceville 08648, 609-895-1559; and 36 W. Main St., Freehold 07728, 908-303-9020.

———————

From: "Almanac of American Politics, 1996"

Bibliography

Aaron, Henry J., ed. (1981). *The Value Added Tax: Lessons from Europe*. Washington D.C.: Brookings Institution.

Aaron, Henry J. (1988a). "The Political Economy of a Value Added Tax in the United States," *Tax Notes*, **38**, 10, March 7, pp. 1111–1115.

Aaron, Henry J. (1988b). "The Value Added Tax: Sorting Through the Practical and Political Problems," *The Brookings Review*, **6**, Summer, pp. 1–16.

Aaron, Henry J., Harvey Galper, and Joseph A. Pechman, eds. (1988). *Uneasy Compromise: Problems of a Hybrid Income-Consumption Tax*. Washington D.C.: Brookings Institution.

Abbin, Byrle, Richard A. Gordon, and Diane L. Renfroe (1985). "International Implications of a Cash Flow Consumption Tax," *Tax Notes*, September 2, p. 1127.

Adams, Roy A., and Neil E. Harl. "The Flat Tax: Some Effects on Agriculture," *Tax Notes*, June 5, pp. 1377–1380.

Advisory Commission on Intergovernmental Relations (1983). *Changing Public Attitudes on Government and Taxes*. Washington D.C.

American Institute of Certified Public Accountants (AICPA) (1975). *Statement of Tax Policy 2: Value-Added Tax*.

American Institute of Certified Public Accountants (AICPA) (1990). *Design Issues in a Credit Method Value-Added Tax for the United States*.

Andrews, William D. (1972). "A Consumption Type or Cash Flow Personal Income Tax," *Harvard Law Review*, **87**, April, pp. 1113–1188.

Atkinson, Anthony B., and Joseph E. Stiglitz (1980). *Lectures in Public Economics*. New York: McGraw-Hill.

Auerbach, Alan J., and Laurence J. Kotlikoff (1987). *Dynamic Fiscal Policy*. New York: Cambridge University Press.

Ballard, Charles L., John K. Scholz, and John B. Shoven (1987). "The Value Added Tax: A General Equilibrium Look at its Efficiency and Incidence," in Martin Feldstein, ed., *The Effects of Taxation on Capital Accumulation*. Chicago: University of Chicago Press.

Barham, Vicky, S.N. Podar, and John Whalley (1987). "The Tax Treatment of Insurance Under a Consumption-Type Destination Basis VAT," *National Tax Journal*, **40**, June, pp. 171–182.

Bartlett, Bruce (1995). "Replacing Federal Taxes with a Sales Tax," *Tax Notes*, August 21, pp. 997–1003.

Bello, Judith H. (1991). Former General Counsel to the U.S. Trade Representative, *Factors Affecting U.S. International Competitiveness, Hearings Before the House Committee on Ways and Means*, 102d Cong., 1st Sess., p. 596.

Bernstein, Rachelle B., Andre P. Fogarasi, and Richard A. Gordon (1995). "Tax Reform 1995: Looking at Two Options," *Tax Notes*, July 17, pp. 327–333.

Boskin, Michael J. (1978). "Taxation, Saving, and the Rate of Interest," *Journal of Political Economy*, **86**, April, part 2, pp. 2–27.

Bradford, David (1980). "The Case for a Personal Consumption Tax," in Joseph A. Pechman, ed. *What Should be Taxed: Income or Expenditure?*, Washington D.C.: Brookings Institution.

Bradford, David (1986). *Untangling the Income Tax*. Cambridge, MA: Harvard University Press.

Bradford, David (1987). "On the Incidence of Consumption Taxes," in C. Walker and M. Bloomfield, eds., *The Consumption Tax: A Better Alternative?* New York: Ballinger, pp. 243–261.

Bradford, David (1988). "What Are Consumption Taxes and Who Pays Them?" *Tax Notes*, April 18, p. 383.

Brannon, Gerald M. (1986). "Does VAT Provide a Balance of Trade Advantage?" *Tax Notes*, March 31, p. 1387.

Brannon, Gerald M. (1988). "The Fairness of the Savings 'Loophole' in a Consumption Tax Depends on Having a Tax at Death," *Tax Notes*, March 14, p. 1253.

Brashares, Edith, Janet Furman Speyer, and George N. Carlson (1988). "Distributional Aspects of a Federal Value Added Tax," *National Tax Journal*, **41**, June, pp. 155–172.

Break, George (1985). "The Value Added Tax," *The Promise of Tax Reform*.

Browning, Edgar (1985). "Tax Incidence, Indirect Taxes, and Transfers," *National Tax Journal*, **38**, December, pp. 525–533.

Burke, Frank M. Jr. (1995). "Future Taxation of Petroleum Exploration and Development," *Tax Notes*, June 19, pp. 1655-1668.

Carlson, George N. (1980). *Value Added Tax, European Tax and Lessons for the United States*. Washington D.C.: U.S. Treasury Department, Office of Tax Analysis.

Carroll, Robert, Thomas S. Neubig, and Kathleen M. Nilcs (1995). "Impact of Structural Tax Reform on Nonprofit Organizations," *Tax Notes*, June 26, pp. 1785–1794.

Casanegra de Jantscher, Milka (1987). "Problems in Administering a Consumption Tax, in Charles E. Walker and Mark A. Bloomfield, eds., *The Consumption Tax: A Better Alternative?* Cambridge, MA: Ballinger.

Cnossen, Sijbren (1989). "The Value Added Tax: Questions and Answers," *Tax Notes*, **42**, 2, January 9, pp. 209–213.

Cnossen, Sijbren (1991). "Consumption Taxes and International Competitiveness: The OECD Experience," *Tax Notes*, September 2, p. 1211.

Cnossen, Sijbren (1995). "VAT Treatment of Immovable Property," *Tax Notes*, March 27, pp. 2017–2022.

Cohen, Sheldon S. (1995). "Taming the Tax Code," *Tax Notes*, September 19.

Congressional Budget Office (1992). *Effects of Adopting a Value Added Tax*. Washington, D.C., February.

Conrad, Robert F. (1990). "The VAT and Real Estate," in Malcolm Gillis, Carl S. Shoup, and Gerardo P. Sicat, eds., *Value Added Taxation in Developing Countries*. Washington D.C: World Bank.

Davies, James, France St-Hilaire, and John Whalley (1984). "Some Calculations of Lifetime Tax Incidence," *American Economic Review*, **74**, 3, September, pp. 633–649.

Due, John F. (1990). "Some Unresolved Issues in Design and Implementation of Value Added Taxes," *National Tax Journal*, **43**, 4, December, pp. 383–394.

Farnham, Alan (1987). "America's Leading Exporters," *Fortune*, July 20, p. 72.

Feldstein, Martin (1978). "The Welfare Cost of Capital Income Taxation," *Journal of Political Economy*, **86**, April, part 2, pp. 29–51.

Fullerton, Don, and Diane Lim Rogers (1993). *Who Bears the Lifetime Tax Burden?* Washington D.C.: Brookings Institution.

Fullerton, Don, John B. Shoven, and John Whalley (1983). "Replacing the U.S. Income Tax with a Progressive Consumption Tax," *Journal of Public Economics*, **20**, February, pp. 3–23.

Gann, Hal, and Roy Strowd (1995). "Deferred Tax Accounting for Tax Reform Proposals," *Tax Notes*, July 3, pp. 111–115.

Gibbons, Sam M. (1994). "Testimony Before the Commission on Entitlement and Tax Reform," October.

Gillis, Malcolm, Carl S. Shoup, and Gerardo P. Sicat, eds. (1990). *Value Added Taxation in Developing Countries*. Washington D.C: World Bank.

Godfrey, John (1995). "Armey, Shelby Introduce Latest Flat Tax Plan," *Tax Notes*, July 24, pp. 373–374.

Gordon, Fern, and Larry I. Good (1987). "The Canadian Government Develops a Business Transfer Tax," *Tax Notes*, March 23, p. 1221.

Graetz, Michael J. (1979). "Implementing a Progressive Consumption Tax," *Harvard Law Review*, **92**, 8, pp. 1575–1661.

Graetz, Michael J. (1995). "Current Flat Tax Proposals," *Tax Notes*, May 29, pp. 1256–1263.

Gravelle, Jane G. (1986). "International Tax Competition: Does it Make a Difference for Tax Policy?" *National Tax Journal*, **39**, September, pp. 375–379.

Gravelle, Jane G. (1988). "Assessing a Value Added Tax: Efficiency and Equity," *Tax Notes*, March 7, p. 1117.

Gravelle, Jane G. (1992). "New Tax Proposals: Flat, VAT, and Variations," *Congressional Research Service Report*, April 27, 1992.

Hall, Robert, and Alvin Rabushka (1983). *Low-Tax, Simple Tax, Flat Tax*. New York: McGraw-Hill.

Hall, Robert, and Alvin Rabushka (1985). *The Flat Tax*. Stanford: Hoover Institution Press.

Hall, Robert, and Alvin Rabushka (1995). *The Flat Tax, Tax Notes*—Special Supplement, August 4.

Henderson, Yolanda K. (1988). "Financial Intermediaries Under Value Added Taxation," *New England Economic Review*, July/August.

Hoven, Vernon. "Flat Tax as Seen by a Return Preparer," *Tax Notes*, August 7, pp. 747–755.

Kaldor, Nicholas (1955). *An Expenditure Tax*. London: Unwin University Books.

Kirchenheimer, Barbara (1995). "Nunn, Domenici Introduce 'USA' Tax to Replace Income Tax," *Tax Notes*, May 1, pp. 592–593.

Kirchenheimer, Barbara (1995). "Gephardt Introduces 10 Percent Tax for Most, Four Brackets for Others," *Tax Notes*, July 10, pp. 135–136.

Kotlikoff, Larry (1988). "The Case for the Value Added Tax," *Tax Notes*, April 11, pp. 239-244.

Kuttner, Robert (1987). "The Liberal Case for a Value Added Tax," in C. Walker and M. Bloomfield, eds., *The Consumption Tax: A Better Alternative*, Cambridge, MA: Ballinger, pp. 337–346.

Massa, Cliff, III, and David G. Raboy (1989). "The Canadian Value Added Tax: Does Anybody Care?" *Tax Notes*, October 23, p. 447.

McLure, Charles E., Jr. (1979). ""Tax Restructuring Act of 1979: Time for an American Value Added Tax?" *Public Policy*, **28**, 3, p. 306.

McLure, Charles E., Jr. (1987). *The Value Added Tax: Key to Deficit Reduction?* Washington: American Enterprise Institute for Public Policy Research.

McLure, Charles E. Jr. (1988). "State and Local Implications of a Federal Value Added Tax," *Tax Notes*, March 28, p. 1517.

Menchik, Paul, and Martin David (1982). "The Incidence of a Lifetime Consumption Tax," *National Tax Journal*, **35**, June, pp. 189–203.

Merrill, Peter R., and Harold Adrion (1995). "Treatment of Financial Services Under Consumption-Based Tax Systems," *Tax Notes*, September 19, pp. 1496–1500.

Merrill, Peter R., Ken Wertz, and Shveteank Shah (1995). "Corporate Tax Liability Under the USA and Flat Taxes," *Tax Notes*, August 7, pp. 741–745.

Metcalf, Gilbert E. (1995). "Value Added Taxation: A Tax Whose Time Has Come?" *Journal of Economic Perspectives*, **9**, 1, Winter, pp. 121–140.

Militzer, Ken (1990). "VAT: Evidence from the OECD," *Tax Notes*, April 9, p. 207.

Neubig, Thomas S., and Harold L. Adrion (1993). "Value Added Taxes and Other Consumption Taxes: Issues for Insurance Companies," *Tax Notes*, November 22, pp. 1001–1010.

Pechman, Joseph A., ed. (1980). *What Should Be Taxed: Income or Expenditure?* Washington, D.C.: Brookings Institution.

Poterba, James (1990). "Lifetime Incidence and the Distributional Burden of Excise Taxes," *American Economic Review*, **79**, May.

Phillips, Kevin P. (1987). "A Political Strategy for a Consumption Tax," in C. Walker and M. Bloomfield, eds., *A Consumption Tax: A Better Alternative*. Cambridge, MA: Ballinger, pp. 347–352.

Pollack, Sheldon (1995). "The Flat Tax: A Dissenting View," *Tax Notes*, May 29, pp. 1253–1256.

Raboy, David G. (1990). "The Trade Implications of VAT with Floating Exchange Rates," *Tax Notes*, May 14, p. 857.

Schenk, Alan (1989a). "Japanese Consumption Tax: The Japanese Brand VAT," *Tax Notes*, March 27, p. 1625.

Schenk, Allan (1989b). "Policy Issues in the Design of a Value Added Tax: Some Recent Developments in OECD Countries," *Tax Notes International*, July 1.

Schenk, Allan, and Oliver Oldman (1991). "Analysis of Tax Treatment of Financial Services Under a Consumption-Style VAT: A Report of the American Bar Association Section of Taxation on Value Added Tax," *Tax Lawyer*, **44**, 1, pp. 181–187.

Sheppard, Lee A. (1995a). "The Consumption Tax: Tax Protectionism," *Tax Notes*, July 3, pp. 13–15.

Sheppard, Lee A. (1995b). "The Consumption Tax: Borrowing as a Tax Shelter," *Tax Notes*, July 19, pp. 138–141.

Sheppard, Lee A. (1995c). "The Consumption Tax: Generational Equity," *Tax Notes*, July 24, pp. 383–386.

Slemrod, Joel (1992). "Do Taxes Matter?: Lessons from the 1980s," *American Economic Review*, **82**, pp. 250–256.

Slemrod, Joel (1995). "The Simplification Potential of Alternatives to the Income Tax," *Tax Notes*, February 27, pp. 1331–1338.

Starret, David A. (1988). "Effects of Taxes on Saving," in Henry J. Aaron, Harvey Galper, and Joseph A. Pechman, eds., *Uneasy Compromise: Problems of a Hybrid Income-Consumption Tax*. Washington: Brookings Institution.

Steuerle, Gene (1995a). "The Future of the Earned Income Tax Credit," *Tax Notes*, June 25, pp. 1818–1819.

Steuerle, Gene (1995b). "Can Flat Taxes Be Progressive?" *Tax Notes*, August 14, pp. 887–888.

Stockfish, J.A. (1985). "Value Added Taxes and the Size of Government: Some Evidence," *National Tax Journal*, **38**, December, p. 549.

Summers, Lawrence H. (1981). "Capital Taxation and Accumulation in a Life-Cycle Growth Model," *American Economic Review*, **71**, September.

Summers, Lawrence H. (1988). "Comment" (on paper by Starrett), in Henry J. Aaron, Harvey Galper, and Joseph A. Pechman, eds., *Uneasy Compromise: Problems of a Hybrid Income-Consumption Tax*. Washington: Brookings Institution.

Sunley, Emil (1988). "The Tax Challenge for the 1990s," *Tax Notes*, August 8, p. 621.

Sullivan, Martin A. (1995). "Computer Bytes to Sound Bites: JCT & Treasury Analyses of the Contract with America," *Tax Notes*, April 17, pp. 319–323.

Tait, Alan A. (1988). *Value Added Tax: International Practice and Problems*. Washington D.C.: International Monetary Fund.

Tanzi, Vito (1994). *Taxation in an Integrating World*. Washington, D.C.: Brookings Institution.

Tax Executives Institute (1992). *Value Added Taxes: A Comparative Analysis*. Washington D.C.: Tax Executives Institute.

Toder, Eric (1995). "Statement of Eric Toder, Deputy Assistant Secretary (Tax Analysis) Department of the Treasury, Before the Senate Budget Committee," U.S. Treasury Department, Office of Public Affairs, February 22. Also reprinted in *Tax Notes*, March 27, pp. 2003–2015.

Turnier, William J. (1984). "Designing an Efficient Value Added Tax," *Tax Law Review*, **39**, 2, Summer, pp. 435–472.

Turnier, William J. (1988). "VAT: Minimizing Administrative and Compliance Costs," *Tax Notes*, **38**, 11, March 14, pp. 1257–1268.

USA Tax System, Description and Explanation of the Unlimited Savings Allowance Income Tax System (1995). Report prepared by Ernest S. Christian and George J. Schutzer for Alliance USA, reprinted in *Tax Notes—Special Supplement*, March 10.

U.S. Congress, Joint Committee on Taxation (1991). *Factors Affecting the International Competitiveness of the United States* (JCS-7-91), June 14.

U.S. Congress, Joint Committee on Taxation (1993). *Methodology and Issues in Measuring Changes in the Distribution of Tax Burdens* (JCS-7-93), June 14.

U.S. Congress, Joint Committee on Taxation (1995a). *Description and Analysis of Tax Proposals Relating to Individual Saving* (JCS-3-95), February 8.

U.S. Congress, Joint Committee on Taxation (1995b). *Discussion of Issues Relating to "Flat" Tax Rate Proposals* (JCS-7-93), April 3.

U.S. Congress, Joint Committee on Taxation (1995c). *Description and Analysis of Proposals to Replace the Federal Income Tax* (JCS-18-95), June 5.

U.S. Department of Commerce, (1994). *Survey of Current Business*, July.

U.S. Department of the Treasury (1942). *Annual Report of the Secretary of the Treasury*.

U.S. Department of the Treasury (1977). *Blueprints for Basic Tax Reform*, January 17.

U.S. Department of the Treasury (1984). *Value Added Tax*, Vol. 3 of *Tax Reform* for *Fairness, Simplicity, and Economic Growth*, November.

U.S. Executive Office of the President (1995). *Analytical Perspectives, Budget of the United States Government, Fiscal Year 1996*. Washington D.C.: U.S. Government Printing Office.

U.S. General Accounting Office (1990). *State Tax Officials Have Concerns About a Federal Consumption Tax*. Washington, D.C.: March.

Vasquez, Thomas E. (1987). "Addressing Issues of the Regressivity of a Consumption Tax," in C. Walker and M. Bloomfield, eds., *The Consumption Tax: A Better Alternative?* Cambridge, MA: Ballinger pp. 311–328.

Von Furstenberg, George (1981). "Saving," in Henry J. Aaron and Joseph Pechman, eds., *How Taxes Affect Economic Behavior*. Washington, D.C.: Brookings Institution.

Walker, C. E., and Mark A. Bloomfield, eds. (1987). *The Consumption Tax: A Better Alternative?* Cambridge, MA: Ballinger.

Weber, Michael E. (1994). "Individual Income Tax returns, 1993: Early Tax Estimates," *Statistics of Income Bulletin*, Internal Revenue Service, Fall, Washington D.C.

Wetzler, James W. (1991). "The Value Added Tax: The Relevance of States' Sales Tax Experience," *Tax Notes*, August 5, p. 719.

Zodrow, George R. (1988). "A Direct Consumption Tax as an 'Add-on' Tax," *Tax Notes*, March 21, p. 1389.

Index